Who Put Blacks in That PLACE?

Who Put Blacks in That PLACE?

The Long, Sad History of the Democratic Party's Oppression of Black Americans...to This Day

Larry P. Horist

Published by

McHenry Press

www.McHenryPress.com

"Let's bring your book to life!"

Paperback ISBN: 978-1-964251-11-0

Cover design by Debbie Lewis

Printed in the United States of America

Dedication

To my dear friend George Blumel, a great patriot and wonderful human being, for his thousands of hours of labor in proofing, editing, and providing advice on the development of this book. It can be said with certainty that this book would never have been completed and published without his enormous support and assistance.

CONTENTS

SECTION 1: THE ERA OF THE GREAT HYPOCRISY (1930–1964)

SECTION 2: THE ERA OF CIVIL RIGHTS, *DE FACTO* RACISM AND URBAN UNREST (1963–PRESENT)

PREFACE

The Author's Road to Racial Understanding

Before entering the all-White Kelvyn Park High School, I was pretty much a typical kid. I graduated from the all-White St. Philomena Catholic School in a blue-collar neighborhood on the northwest side of Chicago.

I rarely saw a Black person, usually nothing more than passing on the street during a trip to downtown Chicago. All I knew in those early days was that Blacks and Whites did not seem to get along.

There was a lot of talk about the terrible things that would happen if a "nigger" family moved into my neighborhood. People were cautioned to avoid driving through Black neighborhoods, and most certainly not with your windows open and car doors unlocked.

I might have grown up with a wariness of Black people, but several events gave me a respect and even fondness for Black people—and set me on the road of civil rights activism.

The Candy Store

The only time I can recall actually using the n-word gratuitously was at the local candy counter when ordering those little licorice characters I loved. They were commonly called "nigger babies." At that age, about five or six, it was just a simple name to me without any social meaning. I can still recall begging my mother to purchase some for me. She scolded me both at the store and again when we got home. Because of her I was the only kid on my block who called them licorice babies.

The Jewel Food Store

One of my after-school jobs was to retrieve shopping carts from the snow-filled parking lot of the local Jewel food store. One dark snowy evening, I noticed a White woman on the far end of the parking lot struggling with three bags of groceries. I also observed a Black woman rushing toward her. I expected the worst. Instead, the Black woman helped hold two of the bags as the White woman dug around in her purse for the trunk key. After depositing the bags and slamming down the lid, I could see the thankful appreciation of the White woman. That Black woman's kindness had opened a new gateway of thinking about race relations. It was not all about hatred and animosity. I have often thought about that Black woman and how she would never know how she influenced my thinking and the course of my life.

DuSable High School

The Student Exchange Days was one way the school system tried to build better relationships between Blacks and Whites. The students from Chicago's segregated schools would be bussed to other schools to visit each other. In my case, approximately fifty students were bussed from my all-White Kelvyn Park High School to the all-Black DuSable High School.

Of that entire day, I have only one enduring memory. I was sitting in a classroom with a young Black girl to my right. I was smitten. I was actually shocked because I was smitten. She was trim, pretty, sexy in her tight Black skirt and flouncy White blouse. She had a killer smile. We exchanged a few words during the course of our forty-five-minute session, and then we both departed, never to be brought together again.

Believing at the time that it was sort of unnatural for Blacks and Whites to be attracted to each other, I felt a bit confused. I wished I could have gotten to know her. I would like to have gone out on a date, but I did not believe that was possible—and I resented that. My feelings did not seem natural according to the zeitgeist of the times. Either my feelings were wrong, or the cultural mores were wrong. I have learned it was the latter.

1828 North Kildare Avenue

I spent almost one-third of my life in a two-flat red brick building my grandfather built on North Kildare Avenue. My mother, dad, three much older brothers, and I shared the four-room apartment on the second floor—one bedroom for my parents and one for me and my three brothers.

Around my neighborhood, there was a lot of talk about blockbusting. That was when a Black family would move into a neighborhood and housing prices would drop as the Whites fled the neighborhood.

With two homes for sale on my block, the discussion of Blacks moving in was a topic of conversation among neighbors. We were exactly the type of neighborhood that could be targeted for blockbusting. We were lower middle class and not far from Division Street, the demarcation line that separated my White neighborhood from the segregated Black community.

One day, as my mother was making my dinner, she brought up the subject. She told me that if a Black family moved into the neighborhood, we may have to move away. I thought I understood her reasoning, but I was wrong.

She said that she was not brave enough to put up with the ugliness that would ensure. "It is not the fault of the colored people," she said. "It is the problem with our neighbors." She explained how the existence of a Black family would potentially create fear and anger in the neighborhood—maybe even violence. Her words surprised me. "I know it is not right, but I just don't have the courage or the heart to face all that," she said almost apologetically. While Whites blamed the Blacks, and Blacks blamed the Whites, I came to realize that both were the victims of the ruthless racist policies of city hall.

Al's Tap and Pizzeria

Al's was the local saloon for the blue-collar community, and a back-room pizza joint for the underage. One of the regulars was the local Democrat precinct captain. He was a gregarious sixty-ish Irishman. Even though I had already become a Republican, we would often have friendly discussions. I think he saw me more as John's and Lorraine's kid than political competition.

On one occasion, I raised a subject that had been bewildering me. How did Mayor Daley get the majority of both Black and White votes when they seem at odds with each other?

Without a moment to ponder, the Democrat precinct captain responded in his distinct Irish brogue. "It very simple, me boy," he said. "I go around this neighborhood and tell the voters that we need to vote for Mayor Daley because he is keeping the niggers from moving north of Division Street and ruining our nice neighborhood."

He continued. "Now, there's a guy like me, a nigger guy, who tells the folks south of Division that they have to keep voting for Mayor Daley if they want to get into public housing and get their welfare checks—or if they need a favor from city hall. They get taken care of as long as they know their PLACE." *PLACE*, that word stuck with me.

In that one conversation, that blue collar Irish Democrat precinct captain taught me more how the system really worked than my high school civics teacher and my college political science professors combined. It was the first, but not by far the last time, that I heard of Blacks having their own peculiar PLACE in which they must remain.

Chicago Westside Ghetto

After college, I saw fighting racism as a component of my character. Charles Percy, who would become the US Republican senator from Illinois, had launched a civic group called Call for Action to investigate housing violations in the inner-city ghettoes. One of the reasons the Black ghettoes had become dangerously dilapidated housing was that city hall simply did not enforce building codes, especially not on politically connected slumlords.

That was when I become personally involved in the tragic results of institutional racisms.

I found numerous code violations when I made a couple of visits to a family in a Westside four-flat. During those visits, I engaged with the family's youngest son, a child of about four or five.

Most times, the major plumbing problems in the ghetto were leaks or no hot water. This one was different. There was a constant leak of hot water in the bathtub. On that final visit, I noted the problem on my report, which was turned over to the Housing Department, which would mostly ignore our findings.

About a week later, I heard from another volunteer that the little boy had somehow blocked the drain. He then either fell into the water or entered the tub to play. He died from the scalding. I left the office and sat in my car and cried.

To this day, it is difficult to recall that event without having to fight back tears. I see that child's smiling face as vividly today as I did more than fifty years ago. Suddenly I saw how racism actually kills—and not just the overt violence of the Ku Klux Klan in the Old South or gang wars on the streets of our cities—but quietly in the daily lives of the residents subjected to institutional *de facto* racism.

My Daughter

The previous events of my life opened me up to the adoption of a Black high school girl needing a home. We had hired her to babysit my very young son and daughter. It turned out she was living in an unsafe family situation. She was planning to quit school and strike out on her own. Instead, we made her part of our family for the next forty-eight years—and counting. It led to a lifelong series of racial experiences as the two cultures merged in one family. In every meaning, Yvette became my daughter and a sister to my kids. She and her late Marine son—who was killed in Afghanistan—proved that unconditional love and pain know no racial boundaries.

Conclusion

What is remarkable is that all these events are not remarkable—other than the fact that they shaped the person I am today. These experiences gave me an affection for Black people, and an outrage over racism. It motivated me to make civil right advocacy a part of my personal and business life. It is what ultimately led to this book.

The book is not meant as a condemnation of the millions of Democrat voters – but of an institutional racist system that keep Blacks in that PLACE of oppression and secondhand citizenship.

The Meaning of "PLACE"

At first glance, the title of this book may seem to be needlessly provocative. But it was selected to bring about a better understanding of how the concept of PLACE has defined the Black experience in America for generations.

It refers to the physical PLACE of segregation, with its strict barriers imposed by law, policy, intimidation, or violence. The PLACE was those segregated communities in the post-emancipation southland. It is those segregated and impoverished inner-city ghettoes that still characterize America's major cities.

PLACE was also the physical separation at the micro levels. It was that portion of a restaurant or bus to which Negroes were assigned. It was that side of the walkway, that public toilet and that portion of the park. It was those inferior schools.

PLACE was not always a physical area, however. It was an attitude, a demeanor. Expressing an unpopular view, looking into the eyes of a White lady or failing to show proper respect and deference to a White citizen were indications that the Negro did not know his or her PLACE. It was failure to comply with this PLACE that resulted in the brutal death of Emmett Till, and many others. Negroes who failed to know their PLACE were considered uppity.

Who Put Blacks in that PLACE? was written to push back on the Democratic Party's false narrative of historic civil rights advocacy. While many people are aware of the Democratic Party's defense of slavery and the hundred years of Jim Crow racism that oppressed Black Americans in Dixie, they are not as aware of the role of the powerful Democrat political machines in the major cities that have segregated and imposed institutional *de facto* racism on millions Black citizens in urban America.

No book has gone into such detail to reveal the full extent of the Democratic Party's role in in maintaining and managing institutional racism for political benefit to this day.

BACKGROUND

It is easier to fool people than to convince them
that they have been fooled. --Mark Twain

"For more than 200 years, our party has led the fight for civil rights ... "
From the website of the Democratic National Committee—2015

In the opening sentence of their website history (above), the Democratic National Committee presented a lie of audacious proportions. This long-advanced false narrative has perpetrated the myth of Democratic Party beneficence to Black Americans. *Who Put Blacks in that PLACE?* presents the true history of the Democratic Party's role in racial oppression. The long history of institutional racism, segregation, social oppression, and vigilante violence has been the characteristic of the Democratic Party in the Old South for a hundred years after the Civil War, and in the Democrat-controlled cities to this day.

More astounding is the fact that the Democratic Party made the same false claim of civil rights advocacy in virtually every platform since the 1800s—even as racial oppression and criminal violence were the common tools of Democrat governance.

In 1872, the Democratic Party platform preposterously claimed itself to be the protector of the rights of all citizens. It stated:

> We [the Democratic Party] recognize the equality of all men before the law and hold that it is the duty of the Government in its dealings with the people to mete out equal and exact justice to all, of whatever nativity, race, color or persuasion, religion or politics.

This type of language was part of virtually every Democrat platform since—even as the Party fought against civil rights legislation and imposed both *de jure* and *de facto* institutional racism on millions of Black Americans.

In this book, you will learn the true story of segregation and Black oppression in great detail.

Certainly, America has evolved into a much better PLACE for Blacks. The American people can no longer be characterized as inherently racist.

But the remnants of the Democratic Party's long history of institutional oppression of Black America is still evident in America's major cities.

To call America a racist nation is to ignore the fact that billions of times every day Black people and white people interact peacefully and in social harmony. We pass on the streets, do favors for each other, serve each other in stores, play on sport teams together, come to each other's aid, and work side by side or under each other's supervision. We risk our lives to save each other in times of danger. We fight side by side as brothers and sisters in the field of combat. We become friends, lovers, and partners.

Despite that reality, racism still exists, most notably in America's major segregated Democrat-controlled cities in which millions of Black citizens are confined to a PLACE of inferior status.

SECTION 1

THE ERA OF THE GREAT HYPOCRISY
(1930–1964)

"Who are you going to believe, me or your own eyes?"
—Chico Marx in *Duck Soup*

The Black Transition

By 1930, the Democratic Party maintained a tight political grip on power in the states of the old Confederacy. The *de jure* institutional racism that was imposed following the withdrawal of Union troops from Dixie under the infamous Compromise of 1877 was as powerful and heinous as ever. Democrats had taken full control of the South by violence and unconstitutional Jim Crow laws. It is no exaggeration to say that there were no legal or constitutional elections in those southern states for almost a century after the Compromise of 1877. In the North *de facto* intuitional racism was in in full flourish in the major cities.

The Great Depression of 1929 drove both White and Black voters to the Democratic Party. By 1930, the nation was on the cusp of the historic switch of Black voters from the Republican Party to the Democratic Party.

The switch was fraught with challenges for the historically racist Democratic Party. How to accommodate the powerful racist power structure dominating the Party and still retain the loyalty of the newly attracted Black voters.

Institutional *de jure* racism would continue to maintain Democrat White supremacy in the south but not in the northern cities where Blacks had access to the polling place.

To succeed in keeping Blacks in their PLACE with historic segregationist and racist policies while keeping the Black vote, the Democratic Party had to redefine civil rights. It was no longer the rights guaranteed by the Constitution, but a new faux right of generational welfare administered through an oppressive social segregation system similar to that imposed on southern Blacks.

The switch to the Democratic Party was not out of a rejection of the Republican Party in terms of civil rights. Republican support continued despite the Black vote. The crossover was largely due to the economic hardship of the Depression and the desperate need for welfare.

The Democratic Party had to convince Blacks to abandon the constitutional civil rights of Abraham Lincoln, Frederick Douglass, Booker T. Washington, Dr. Martin Luther King Jr., and the Republican Party in favor of generational dependency on an increasing range of welfare benefits associated with the Democratic Party.

In a very real sense, the Democratic Party created what became known as the economic plantation. Blacks would be kept in their PLACE——a PLACE where they would remain segregated and continue to suffer the oppressive deprivations of education, quality housing, jobs, healthcare, public safety, access to upward mobility, and equal justice.

The Negro Vote

The 1930 election was the first opportunity to see the effect of the Depression on Black voters. In all previous elections since the Civil War those, Blacks who were allowed to vote gave overwhelming support to the Republican Party——the party of their emancipation and the party continuing to fight for their civil rights against Democratic Party racism and oppression.

The complete shift in the Negro vote did not happen in 1930. It did not even happen in 1932, when Franklin Roosevelt was the Democrat candidate. He received only 20 percent of the Negro vote. It was not until the 1936 presidential election—seven years after the start of the Great Depression—that the shift was seen. By then Roosevelt got 70 percent of the that vote.

Republicans Start Losing the Negro Vote

Certainly, the Depression was the dominant factor, but there were other reasons for the switch in party loyalty, not the least of which was the political ineptitude of the Republican Party. Cowered by blame for the

Depression, the GOP could not muster the willpower to function as an opposition party. Many Republican leaders surrendered long-held conservative principles and succumbed to the big government progressive and racist policies of the Roosevelt administration—most notably moving Blacks from jobs onto welfare.

The Great Depression and the loss of the Negro vote devastated the dominant Republican Party and left the Congress very narrowly divided in 1930. Republicans lost fifty-two seats in the United States House of Representatives, giving them only a one-seat majority. However, special elections necessitated by the deaths of Republican members prior to the seating of the new Congress gave Democrats control by one seat.

In the United States Senate, Republicans held on by a one-seat majority for the next two years. Given the political climate of the time, the loss of the presidency and the House and the blame the GOP was receiving for the market crash, the Senate majority meant little in terms of political influence.

Becoming Democrats

Throughout the 1930s, Democrats feared the loss of the newly gained Negro vote. They had every reason to be concerned. The October 16, 1944, issue of *Life* magazine covered this issue.

> Since 1940, increased prosperity and a growing resentment toward the Democratic Party have been swinging the Negroes back to Republicanism. In recent congressional and state elections, a majority of Negroes voted for Republicans. In New York in 1942 they went for [Republican Thomas] Dewey for Governor.

The GOP held on to a reasonable percentage of Black votes through the 1950s—although no future Republican president would get more than 40 percent of the Black vote. In the 1964 presidential election the bottom fell out for the GOP. President Johnson carried 94 percent of the Black vote against Barry Goldwater, who had shattered the image if not the fact of the Republican Party's commitment to civil rights.

Resisting the Switch to the Democratic Party

Not all Black leaders were in favor of switching allegiance to the party of Negro oppression. John Lynch, a Black Republican who had served in Congress during and after Reconstruction spoke out against the switch in the early 1930s:

> The colored voters cannot help but feel that in voting the Democratic ticket in national elections they will be voting to give their endorsement and their approval to every wrong of which they are victims, every right of which they are deprived, and every injustice of which they suffer.

The Davis-Bacon Act of 1931

The Davis-Bacon Act was passed in the last year of the Hoover administration. It was an ill-conceived effort to keep wages from continuing to fall as the Depression deepened.

While the original Davis-Bacon Act was sponsored by Republicans in Congress, it was immediately embraced and transformed by Roosevelt as a means of maintaining White access to jobs. Following his election in 1932, Roosevelt and the new Democrat majority in Congress passed a series of amendments to the Act to make it a powerful tool for organized labor and a more prejudicial weapon against Black employment.

According to the *Congressional Quarterly Almanac:*

> The Davis-Bacon Act of 1931, as amended in 1935 and 1940, required contractors and their subcontractors working on federal construction contracts amounting to $2,000 or more to pay their workers not less than the prevailing wages paid in the same area on similar projects. Determinations as to local prevailing wages were made by the Secretary of Labor. By law or reference, Congress had gradually applied the requirements of the Davis-Bacon Act to a wide variety of federal-aid programs, involving construction of housing, highways

and medical and educational facilities, as well as direct federal construction contracts.

The Roosevelt amendments, creating a localized prevailing wage requirement, was strongly supported by southern Democrats because it would effectively drive Blacks out of the workforce, freeing up those jobs for desperate unemployed White workers.

In subsequent years, congressional Republicans made several attempts to repeal Davis-Bacon or to amend it to make it more racially neutral. These efforts were constantly thwarted by congressional Democrats and their allied unions.

In later years, Davis-Bacon was dubbed the "last Jim Crow law" for good reason. While it ostensibly applied to all workers, just as the poll tax applied to all voters, it was administered by the Roosevelt administration to give White workers virtually exclusive access to the better paying union jobs.

Prior to the Depression, Negroes comprised more than 20 percent of construction workers. After the enactment of Davis-Bacon, Blacks were virtually eliminated from all federally funded projects. While longstanding Democrat racist policies had prevented Negroes from access to employment in the Democratic southland—especially to better paying jobs—the Davis-Bacon Act spread that barrier across the country.

Denying jobs to Negroes, or replacing employed Negroes with White workers, was no backroom secret. Democrats clearly made their intentions known. In an article in *National Review,* journalist John Fund wrote that "During the brief 40-minute debate the House held on Davis-Bacon in 1931, the racial motivation behind it was palpable."

Missouri Democrat Congressman John Cochran said:

> I have received numerous complaints in recent months about southern contractors employing low-paid colored mechanics getting work and bringing the employees from the South.

Alabama Democrat Congressman Miles Allgood echoed Cochran's comments:

> This is a fact. That [a New York] contractor has cheap colored labor that he transports, and he puts them in cabins, and it is labor of that sort that is in competition with White labor throughout the country.

Democrat congressman William Upshaw, of Georgia, complained about a "superabundance of large aggregation of Negro labor." The then president of the American Federation of Labor (AFL), William Green, pinpointed "colored labor is being brought in to demoralize wage rates."

According to Charles W. Baird of the Cato Institute:

> Excluded from White unions, the only way Blacks could compete for construction jobs was to work for union-free contractors for market wages lower than union-scale wages. Those union-free contractors and their Black employees were effectively excluded from those projects by Davis-Bacon, which was racist in intent and effect.

Looking ahead, the Republican supported Civil Rights Act of 1964, which helped open unions to Black membership, took some of the bias out of Davis-Bacon, but it still maintained the union's exclusive access to most government contracts—essentially eliminating opportunities for Black contractors.

The Republican administrations of Richard Nixon and Ronald Reagan introduced rules that reduced union discrimination against Blacks. As late as 1977, the US Government Accounting Office called for the repeal of the Davis-Bacon Act, arguing that it served no good purpose and unnecessarily increased the cost of government construction projects. Regardless, it remains the law of the land as of this writing.

Republican Justices Favor Civil Rights

As the Hoover administration was coming to an end, Republican-appointed justices dominated the Supreme Court by a seven-to-two majority, with Hoover having nominated three. They were generally favorable to civil rights. The justice widely recognized as the most racist was Democrat Justice James McReynolds, appointed by Woodrow Wilson.

In 1932, on the last days of the Hoover administration, the United States Supreme Court struck down a Texas election law that barred Blacks from voting in Democrat primary elections under the theory that it was a private organization and was beyond the reach of the Constitution and the Supreme Court. In *Nixon v. Condon* the Republican-dominated Court declared that the Constitution applied to political party primaries. This was a huge victory for the civil rights of Blacks, especially in the Democrat-controlled southern states.

Had the court upheld the Texas law, virtually every southern Democrat state would have enacted similar laws and essentially prevent Negroes from having any voice in choosing Democrat candidates. It would have made it impossible for any Black person anywhere in the south to be elected to public office.

Hitler, Sanger, and the Eugenics Movement

Hitler was already a notable political figure by the early 1930s. Rising to Chancellor in 1933, Hitler was not without his supporters in the United States. Many citizens of German ancestry organized clubs in support of Hitler. Since Hitler's genocidal programs included Negroes as well as Jews, many progressive Democrats associated with the eugenics movement embraced by Hitler as a means of achieving racial purification. Among the more prominent admirers of the Fuhrer was Margaret Sanger and members of her American Birth Control League. Their genocidal approach to the Negro problem tracked closely to Hitler's pogrom against Jews and Blacks.

Among Sanger's closest colleagues was Leon Whitney, the founder of the American Eugenics Society. Sanger and Whitney both believed in forced sterilization to reduce or eliminate births of those they claimed to be inferior human stock—essentially Blacks. Whitney would go on to praise Hitler as "one of the greatest statesmen and social planners in the world." The Fuhrer's genocidal opinions were published in Sangers' *Birth Control Review*.

After America was brought into the war by the Japanese attack on Pearl Harbor in 1941, and Germany subsequently declared war on the United States, Sanger's Birth Control League had to disassociate and eradicate its history of Nazi collaboration. The League's name was changed to Planned Parenthood. It did not, however, change its policy of sterilizing Negro women and terminating Negro births to diminish that population.

The Election of 1932

The election of 1932 was the most transformative since Lincoln's election in 1860. It ended seventy-two years of Republican dominance of national and state elections. It reflected the dramatic shift in the Negro vote from the Republican Party to the Democratic Party. It was also the beginning of the longest and most autocratic presidency in American history.

Despite the Depression, Republicans gave their party nominations for president and vice president to incumbents Herbert Hoover and Charles Curtis. Democrats nominated New York's popular and charismatic governor Franklin Delano Roosevelt.

Despite his later reconstructed reputation, Roosevelt was never a proponent of equal rights for Negroes. He was a lifelong White supremacist. He had served as assistant secretary of the navy in the racist administration of President Wilson. In that capacity, he signed orders for the construction of segregated washrooms in the Old Executive Office Building adjacent to the White House which, at the time, housed the departments of state, war (now defense) and the navy. He also played a key role in the segregation of the navy as part of Wilson's overall directive to segregate the entire armed forces.

At the time of the 1932 Democrat convention, Roosevelt was short of the necessary votes to secure the nomination. To secure the additional necessary votes, he placed a racist southern Democrat on the ticket. For vice president, Roosevelt selected United States Speaker of the House John Nance Garner of Texas.

John Nance Garner

Garner was one of the nation's most ardent racists and uncompromising segregationists—a fact well known to Roosevelt. Garner began his political career in 1898 when elected to the Texas House of Representatives. He was an avid supporter of Jim Crow legislation. He voted in favor of the poll tax in 1901 as a means of blocking Blacks from voting. Garner helped set up the system that kept Blacks away from the polls and kept Texas safely in the authoritarian grip of the all-White Democratic Party.

As a congressman, Garner was considered a Wilson progressive, supporting virtually all the president's economic programs at the time, while eagerly embracing Wilson's racist views. Contrary to popular belief, Democrat progressivism was all about economics. The most prominent progressives were also the most notable racists and White supremacists of their time.

Garner would break with Roosevelt over some of the New Deal's more socialistic policies and over his running for a third term.

University of Rhode Island history professor Erik Loomis specifically addressed Democrat Garner in his online blog article titled "A Disaster Averted: John Nance Garner and the 1940 Presidential Election." Loomis wrote: "Garner hated one thing more than the New Deal: people of color."

The 1932 Political Platforms

Despite the switch in Black voting, the GOP stuck with its historic loyalty to civil rights. The Republican Platform declared:

> For seventy years the Republican Party has been the friend of the American Negro. Vindication of the rights of the Negro citizen to enjoy the full benefits of life, liberty and the pursuit of happiness is traditional in the Republican Party, and our party stands pledged to maintain equal opportunity and rights for Negro citizens. We do not propose to depart from that tradition nor to alter the spirit or letter of that pledge.

The Democrat Platform made no mention of civil rights and offered no programs to specifically address the plight of the Negro in terms of financial wellbeing, civil rights, jobs, or education.

The election of 1932 was a crushing defeat for the Republican Party, giving Democrats a lock on the federal government. In addition to the presidency, the Democrat's one-seat majority in the United States House of Representatives was expanded to a ninety-six-seat majority. The Democrats gained twelve seats in the United States Senate.

Franklin Delano Roosevelt (1933–1945)

In the depth of the Great Depression, Whites not only wanted a preference over all new jobs, but they also wanted jobs Blacks already held. Jobs once beneath the dignity of White workers were being sought out of desperation.

As FDR assumed office in 1933, racist Southern Democrats controlled many of the most powerful committees in Congress. They included Senate Majority Leader Joseph Taylor Robinson (D-AR), House Majority Leader Joseph Burns (D-TN), Chairman of the Senate Finance Committee Pat Harrison (D-MS), Chairman of the Senate Appropriations Committee Carter Glass (D-VA), Chairman of the Investigatory Senate Banking and Currency Committee Duncan Fletcher (D-FL) and Chairman of the Senate Committee on Agriculture and Forestry Cotton Ed Smith (D-SC).

Ignoring the evidence of Roosevelt's personal racist and White supremacist beliefs, some historians explain away his opposition to civil right as a pragmatic necessity. He needed to have the support of powerful congressional Democrats if he had any hope of passing his New Deal legislation—and that meant acceding to their racist demands.

That attempt to polish FDR's image ignores the reality of FDR's long-standing and manifest belief in White supremacy. In the twelve-plus years Roosevelt resided in the White House, the Democratic Party continued its tradition as the nation's leading vehicle of institutional racism.

FDR proposed no civil rights legislation in his twelve years in office and refused to support anti-lynching legislation repeatedly introduced by congressional Republicans. Roosevelt's New Deal programs were designed to provide financial assistance to Whites only and to bar Blacks from union jobs. Virtually every New Deal was designed to replace Black workers with White workers. (The New Deal programs are dealt with in greater detail later in this book).

Warm Springs for Whites Only

There was no better example of FDR's personal racism than the spa he frequented at Warm Springs, Georgia. Many believe he was merely a patron of the spa for medical reasons. He was more than that.

In 1926, Roosevelt purchased the small local mineral water spring resort. It was alleged that the waters were beneficial for polio victims. Roosevelt was diagnosed with poliomyelitis in 1921 at age thirty-nine. (Modern medical professionals believe it was a misdiagnosed case of Guillain–Barré syndrome.)

Under his ownership, Roosevelt expanded the spa to be a nationally famous health resort for the rich and famous. He created the Warm Springs Foundation as a tax-free charity to operate the spa. He served as president of the foundation, its most prominent member and the magnet for America's elite visiting the spa. They would welcome the opportunity to support Roosevelt's favorite private charity with personal visits and large financial contributions—and on occasion enjoy his company. He hosted foreign dignitaries there.

In encouraging donations and the use of the facilities, Roosevelt apparently made false claims about the healing effect the waters had on his body. The National Park Service website promoting the spa claimed that Roosevelt experienced at least a partial cure from bathing in the waters of Warm Springs:

> Roosevelt arrived at the resort on October 3, 1924 hoping to find
> a cure. The next day, he began swimming and immediately felt an
> improvement. For the first time in three years, he was able to move
> his right leg.

FDR's medical records indicated no such improvements in his condition or that of anyone else. *The American Journal of Public Health* featured an article in 2007 by Naomi Rogers entitled "Race and Politics of Polio." It stated:

> The president was also said to have deceived the American people
> about the effects of polio on his own body. According to a whisper-
> ing campaign, polio had left him addicted to drugs, so erratic that
> he required a strait jacket, and was incontinent, sexually impotent
> and helplessly crippled.

While the funds were claimed to create an endowment for the foundation, the funds were often redirected to other civic and political purposes, and allegedly to Roosevelt himself. One of the major fundraising events was the president's annual birthday celebration. Rogers writes:

> At first the funds were intended to create a permanent endowment for Warm Springs. But gradually the Birthday Ball organizers redirected the money to the local communities that had raised it. The significance of this philanthropic policy shift away from Warm Springs was not widely appreciated by the American public.

Roosevelt was the main attraction at his annual Birthday Ball. America's elite were solicited for contributions. This including more than $100,000 donated by prominent Black Americans—an incredible amount of money during the Depression.

What has been lost in most modern histories of Roosevelt is that his wholly owned and operated spa was for Whites only. He even rejected a suggestion for a segregated facility on the grounds for Negro patients.

In southern racist tradition, however, the low-paid work staff was approximately half Negro. They served as maids, janitors, and aides to lift patients in and out of baths. The White staff was housed in the main building or in nearby private cottages. Black workers lived in more distant and less luxurious dormitories—a tradition that goes back to slavery.

FDR's personal refusal to allow Black children to use the spa, and revelations of the use of donated funds, created a growing embarrassment on the verge of scandal. In 1941, with help of the National Foundation for Infantile Paralysis, known popularly as the March of Dimes, Tuskegee Institute opened a heath facility for Black polio victims. The Tuskegee facility was necessitated because of Roosevelt's personal decision to ban Black children from Warm Springs. With only thirty-six beds, the Tuskegee facility was woefully inadequate to the need. Prominent physician W. Montague Cobb would later describe the Tuskegee facility as a "Negro medical ghetto."

Roosevelt praised the Institute for its establishment of the special heath center for Black victims of polio, giving him the appearance of concern for the Negro population while taking the pressure off integrating his own facility.

Most civil rights organizations, including the NAACP and the National Urban League, were offended by Roosevelt's racist policies and made their feelings known to Mrs. Roosevelt. According to Naomi Rogers, Yale's professor of the history of medicine:

Reverend J. S. Bookens of the African Methodist Episcopal Zion Church in Mobile, Ala, tried to have his paralyzed 9-year-old son admitted to Warm Springs and was told "Negroes [are] never admitted to that institution." This case was widely discussed in the Black press and spurred Walter White, secretary of the National Association for the Advancement of Colored People, to remind Eleanor Roosevelt that segregation at Warm Springs was the reason his association refused to sponsor Birthday Ball fund raising.

The Urban League argued that a change in policy "would be heartily welcomed by ten million otherwise socially disinherited American citizens." Whether Eleanor Roosevelt raised the issue with her husband is unknown, but there was no change in the policy.

About the same time, the *Chicago Tribune* printed a letter that noted:

There is a place in Georgia named Warm Springs where the President has endowed, or partially maintains, a sanitarium for the treatment of infantile paralysis. I have no doubt that what the humblest, most ragged, and illiterate little white child in the land would be admitted there for treatment, but the most cultured, refined, and well clothed Negro child would be denied admittance simply because it was a Negro.

With public outrage mounting, the spa's chief surgeon issued a public explanation for Roosevelt's Whites-only policy. His explanation is as damning as the policy. He said:

"[Warm Springs] is not a general orthopedic hospital. It treats and studies nothing but Infantile Paralysis. It maintains no wards, separate clinics, or segregated rooms. Aid and pay patients share the same facilities. We cannot take colored people for this reason."

By 1937, Roosevelt and his fellow trustees were again faced with the issue of integrating Warm Springs. While there was almost universal reluctance to admit Negroes, the trustees recognized the growing public relations problem and the political fallout for Roosevelt. They decided against serving Black children but agreed to "associate" with an all-Black medical facility as a means of stemming growing criticism.

After extensive deliberations trustee James M. Hooper summed up the sentiment of his fellow board members in saying "our facilities do not lend themselves to the comfortable housing and treatment of resident-colored cases. We do not feel that we could make such patients comfortable both physically and psychologically."

A 1937 decision by Roosevelt and the trustees to drop the Tuskegee Institute and other Black medical groups as recipients for that year's Birthday Ball funds created a firestorm in the Black community.

The Chicago Defender ran an article under the headline "We Donated, But They Left Us Out." The Warm Springs leadership had decided that "the Negro should solve his problem . . . through local medical practitioners, because statistics show that it (polio) is most prevalent among White people." Though untrue, the racist medical community proffered the false argument that Negroes were not as afflicted by polio.

Warm Springs remained segregated throughout Roosevelt's lifetime. After his death at Warm Springs in 1945, Rogers further noted that:

> Warm Springs remained segregated for many years. By the end of the 1940s it had set up a few "emergency" beds for local Black patients, but there were no Black physicians, nurses, therapists, or administrators, and the Warm Springs movie theater had an indoor picket fence indicating where Black employees could sit in the worst seats, separate from the White patients.

For the nineteen years that Roosevelt owned the facility, and despite his civil rights rhetoric, the mounting criticism from Whites and Blacks across the nation, and with disregard for the health of Black children, Roosevelt maintained his racist policies at Warm Springs to the day he died there.

The Tuskegee Study

In 1932, the United States Public Health Service (PHS) launched one of the most infamous, dangerous, and racist medical research projects in American history. Known as the Tuskegee Experiment, the study was designed to determine the long-term effects of untreated syphilis on Negro men.

The operative word in the name of the study is *untreated*. Quite simply, doctors in Alabama would monitor the progress of syphilis in the test subject without making any effort to treat or mitigate the disease. It was a practice that continued long after the discovery of penicillin as a cure for syphilis.

The study was commenced by Dr. Taliaferro Clark, a senior research director for the PHS. With a shortage of funds due to the Depression, Clark engaged in deceptive practices to recruit subjects, who were mostly uneducated sharecroppers. They were enticed into the program under the fraudulent claim that they would be receiving free treatment for an unspecified blood disease. Patients were told that the painful spinal taps were actually a curative treatment for the unspecified disease.

It was no coincidence that the program was launched under a racist administration in Washington and administered by officials of a southern Democrat state at the height of the era of segregation and racial terrorism, and that the subjects were all Black.

Defending his unethical practices, Clark said: "These Negroes are very ignorant and easily influenced by things that would be of minor significance in a more intelligent group."

The subjects were supposed to be observed for six to eight months and then receive treatment. The treatment phase was never seriously implemented, and patients were allowed to suffer the ravages of the disease until they died.

Amazingly, the study continued for forty years, even after national and international protocols and laws required patient consent for medical procedures—and almost thirty years after penicillin was commonly used as a cure for syphilis. Patients were not provided with penicillin and there were even reports that patients were intentionally infected with the disease as part of the program.

The program came to public attention when PHS whistleblower Peter Buxtun provided information to the *Washington Star* and the *New York Times* in the early 1970s. Upon learning of the program in 1972, President Nixon ordered it to be shut down immediately.

John R. Heller Jr., who was assistant in charge of onsite operations for the Tuskegee Study remained a defender of the program. In praising the program, Heller gave a response eerily reminiscent of the defense of Nazi human medical experiments in a 1964 oral interview with the National Institutes of

Health: "For the most part, doctors and civil servants simply did their jobs. Some merely followed orders, others worked for the glory of science." He later bragged: "We learned many, many things about the treatment of syphilis, and I saw syphilis in all of its stages, early and late."

He did not seem troubled by the fact that he could observe "late" stages because he denied the subjects treatment that would have cured them and saved their lives.

Heller would go on to be the director of the Public Health Services Division of Venereal Diseases, the director of the National Cancer Institute and president of the Sloan-Kettering Cancer Center.

The New "Civil Right"

One of the least appreciated transformational changes produced by Roosevelt and Depression-era Democrats was the cynical redefining of civil rights. From the Emancipation Proclamation to the beginning of the New Deal, civil rights had been largely defined by constitutional rights—those rights that were being denied to Negroes by Democrats in the former slave states and the major cities. These included the right to vote, to assemble, to speak freely, to equal justice, to access to education and jobs and, in many cases, to life itself. These rights represented the battle line between the Democratic Party's policies of institutional racism and Black oppression and the Republican Party's policies of personal freedom and equal opportunity for Blacks.

The new strategy evolved out of the economic desperation of the Depression. Within a generation, civil rights advocacy shifted from constitutional freedoms to a "right" to sustenance-level generational welfare. As the New Deal was driving Blacks out of jobs, the compensation was bare sustenance-level government welfare. This seeming beneficence was actually meant to keep Negroes in their PLACE.

The Chicago Democrat Machine played a leading role perfecting the popular model of *de facto* racist governance based on generational welfare dependency. By the time Roosevelt took office, Chicago had the second largest Black community in America—second only to New York City's Harlem.

Segregation and racism were not new to American urban centers, but Chicago developed the system to such an extent that the Windy City would later be credibly described as the most racist and segregated city in America. The role of Chicago in developing and implementing the Democratic Party's strategy of oppressing Negroes while maintaining their voting allegiance cannot be overstated.

The Chicago Machine and William Dawson

It was in Chicago that the Latin term *de facto* was first routinely applied as a modifier in describing a special form of institutional racism. *De facto* racism has been more enduring because it is not as obvious as the *de jure* segregation of the solid Democrat south. It is not as easily addressed by the courts.

The Chicago Democrats did not invent the votes-for-benefits concept. That was already the modus operandi of New York's Tammany Hall since the eighteenth century. The difference was that the Tammany organization, and its imitators, used privately sourced rewards in return for votes, such things as food, coal and, of course, money. It also might include jobs, obtaining building permits or "fixing" traffic citations. The Chicago model shifted the "bribes" to taxpayer financed benefits.

The strategy to control the vote through welfare did not occur organically by cultural evolution. It was a scheme perfected and implemented by the Chicago Democrat Machine. It was largely the cynical genius of a man named William Dawson.

Dawson began his political career as a Black Republican in 1930, just as Blacks were switching over to the Democratic Party. He was elected alderman from Chicago's Second Ward in 1932—a ward with a large Black population.

At the time, the White Democrat Committeeman of the Second Ward was Joseph Tittinger. Following the Democrat's older strategy, Tittinger doled out jobs and favors to the Ward's White minority—basically ignoring or discouraging the Negro vote. The Black community, however, was gaining in numbers and influence, and they demanded that Chicago Mayor Ed Kelly remove Tittinger for a Black ward boss. Which he did.

In Tittinger's place Kelly persuaded Republican Dawson to switch parties in return for controlling patronage in the Second Ward. As the new ward boss, Dawson developed an ingenious means to control the Negro vote in the all-Black segregated communities. He literally abandoned the fight for constitutionally grounded civil rights for a new faux "civil right"—access and dependency on welfare.

While Negroes gave Roosevelt overwhelming support in 1932, that loyalty seemed to be weakening in the late 1930s. As late as 1939, the allegiance of the Black vote to the Democratic Party was still fragile, and the Republican Party was gaining as a competitive political force. The majority of Blacks remained registered as Republicans until 1948.

The Black Submachine

Dawson's influence grew beyond the Second Ward. He became the go-to man for Chicago's entire Black population. He was the boss of what some called "the submachine." At Chicago's PBS affiliate WTTW, the article "DuSable to Obama" states:

> Dawson proved adept at organizing the increasing number of black Democrats on the South Side and soon consolidated his political power. He effectively used patronage and precinct workers to develop a strong voting bloc that generally gave local, state, and national Democratic candidates impressive majority votes. Dawson would eventually control as many as five wards, forming the city's first black political machine.

Based on his rhetoric more than his actions, Dawson became a hero to the Black community. Like the house slave of the early Nineteenth Century, however, Dawson's loyalty was to the White Democrat bosses in City Hall.

According to Christopher Manning in his 2009 book, *William L. Dawson and the Limits of Black Electoral Leadership*:

> Dawson was also leader of the African American 'sub-machine' within the Cook County Democratic Organization. In the predominantly African American wards, Dawson was able to act as

his own political boss, handing out patronage and punishing rivals just as leaders of the larger machine, such as Richard J. Daley, did. However, Dawson's machine had to continually support the regular machine in order to retain its own clout.

He chose to work on city politics from this stance, rather than to conduct open civil rights challenges, and did not support the work of Dr. Martin Luther King, Jr. in Chicago in the 1960s.

By 1957, Black leaders, such as Martin Luther King, were pushing back against both *de jure* racism in the south and the *de facto* racism in the major cities. With more aggressive civil rights activism on the rise, *The Chicago Defender,* a Black publication, said that Dawson as a civil rights leader was "non-committal, evasive, and seldom takes an outspoken stand on anything."

The Dawson Strategy Goes National

Dawson's welfare-for-votes scheme was so effective in recruiting and retaining Blacks for the Democratic Party in Chicago that he attracted national attention, including the eye of the president. FDR saw the value in the Dawson welfare-for-votes strategy.

Dawson was elected to Congress and was named assistant chairman of the Democratic National Committee. His specific responsibility at the DNC was to spread the welfare-for-votes concept to Black voters in other cities.

Black leaders like Dawson became part of the established Democrat political machine. In New York City's Harlem, congressmen William Clayton Powell took on the Dawson role under Big Jim Pemberton. The importance of Dawson, Pemberton and Powell to the Democratic Party was chronicled in a major feature article in *Life* magazine in 1944.

Democrats and Lynching

Since Democrats seized virtually absolute power in the southern states, their paramilitary terrorist organizations, such as the Ku Klux Klan, the Knights of the White Camelia, and the White Citizens' Councils, flourished. One of their primary means of intimidation was public lynchings.

Lynching became iconic after Democrats seized control of the South, and the practice was in full force in the 1930s. There was the beginning of a backlash, however. Americans became more outraged. This led to efforts by Republicans in Congress to make lynching as a federal crime and a violation of constitutional civil rights.

The rising call for action placed Roosevelt in a quandary. His lip service public stance was in favor of civil rights, but he politically sided with the powerful southern Democrat bloc in Congress based on their power and his own White supremacist views.

By 1934, the lynching of Negroes in the South reached the level of a national scandal. Still, Roosevelt and the Democratic Party refused to take any action.

The Lynching of Claude Neal

Even as the anti-lynching bill was being defeated in Congress, a horrific lynching in Florida grabbed national headlines. Though advertised as a lynching, the death of Claude Neal was a prolonged series of horrific tortures before his already mutilated and dead body was hung from a tree limb.

In 1934 Claude Neal was a suspect in the murder of a nineteen-year-old White girl. He was employed by her father. Neal was arrested in a neighboring state, but rather than being extradited by official means, he was kidnapped by a vigilante mob and brought back to Jackson County. Instead of being turned over to the authorities, the mob issued public invitations to Neal's lynching. There would be no trial.

According to an online research paper by the student resource service GaleGroup.com:

Local newspapers and a radio station, announcing that a "Negro" would be "mutilated and set afire," provided details concerning the place and time of the anticipated event. That afternoon, quite unexpectedly, news of the scheduled lynching was picked up and distributed nationally by the Associated Press. The response of the NAACP and many other concerned people to this news moved Florida governor David Sholtz to offer the Jackson County sheriff the assistance of the state's national guard. The offer was refused. The mob forced Neal to eat his penis, stabbed him with a knife repeatedly in his sides and stomach, and cut off several of his fingers and toes. After suffering such torture for almost two hours, Neal died before the hundreds of people who had gathered in a carnival-like atmosphere could see him lynched. Disappointed and enraged, the crowd—including many families—resumed the mutilation of the body before burning and hanging it from a nearby tree.

Neal's lynching was not an outlier. It is merely an example of the thousands of similar cases under Democrat one-party rule in Dixie.

New Pressure for Anti-Lynching Legislation

The murder and mutilation of Neal set off a national firestorm of protest. Two Democrat senators joined Republicans in introducing an anti-lynching bill.

The Costigan-Wagner Bill was reintroduced and endorsed by several governors, religious leaders, and university presidents. The Senate Judiciary Committee voted in favor of passage. This time forty-three senators and 123 members of the House endorsed the bill.

The NAACP carried out a national public relations campaign and personally lobbied Roosevelt and his attorney general Homer Cummings. Both refused to support the bill. Roosevelt called for an early vote on the measure, which limited debate and assured defeat.

The Senate Democrats immediately organized a filibuster which ended any further consideration of the bill. The filibuster was led by South Carolina Democrat senator Ellison Smith. Senate Democrats were able to defeat the measure after a seven-week verbal marathon. The determination of the southern Democrats was evident in the comments by North Carolina Democrat senator Josiah Bailey: "This is a cause worth dying for. It is a battle worth fighting if it takes until Congress begins its next session in January 1936. .... We'll speak day and night if necessary."

Yet another anti-lynching bill was introduced in 1937, it was expeditiously defeated by yet another southern Democrat-led filibuster. And again, Roosevelt signaled his objection by refusing to endorse it.

Union Racism

From its very inception, the trade union movement in America had been plagued with racism. With more Whites seeking employment due to the Great Depression, unions became even more racially exclusive.

Organized labor played an important part in formulating New Deal policies. Union leaders were allies of the Democratic Party and staunch supporters of President Roosevelt and his policies. Apart from some small Black or localized unions, organized labor was a Whites-only institution. Union leaders worked closely with Roosevelt to ensure that federal economic recovery programs maintained a White supremacy bias.

In an online article for the Capital Research Center entitled the "Untold, Racist Origins of 'Progressive' Labor Law" author Horace Cooper, senior fellow with the National Center for Public Policy Research and chairman of the Project 21, the leading voice of black conservatives, wrote: "Most people would be surprised to learn that this harm to Blacks has historically not been an unintended consequence of these pro-union policies, *but the intended result*" (emphasis added).

Cooper said that federal labor laws were intentionally crafted to "saddle Black men with extra burdens and limitations in order to (as racists often put it) protect White jobs. The idea of restricting Blacks' access to 'White jobs' was planted early in the twentieth century; took root in the 1920s; and blossomed during President Roosevelt's New Deal—a 'deal' created in significant part by an Alabama Klansman."

Cooper's comment about "an Alabama Klansman" is a reference to Democrat senator and future Supreme Court justice Hugo Black. (More about him later in this book).

While all White unionized labor received the praise of White Democrat politicians, Black labor was denigrated with such terms as "itinerant," "unskilled," "cheap," "bootleg labor" or simply "colored workers"—which all implied negative work habits. Democrat politicians made it clear that the labor movement was not for Blacks.

NAACP Opposes All-White Unions

As early as 1935, well into Roosevelt's first term and with Democrats in control of the US House and Senate, the NAACP responded to Whites-only unionism. At a congressional hearing, Walter Francis White, the chairman of the organization's legislative committee, stated:

> Organized labor is hostile to colored people. Practically every labor organization in the country denies Negroes the right of membership therein. Those which admit colored people restrict their employment to the least desirable work, and, because of the race or color of the darker members of the union, deny them the right to the skilled and, in some instances, the semiskilled positions, regardless of their training, skill, or experience.

The racial prejudice bred by Democrat politicians and Democrat union leaders had a secondary negative impact on Black employment. A NAACP legislative committee report noted:

> When a factory or job is unionized, the members of the union refuse to work with the colored workers because they do not belong to the union and refuse to admit the Negroes to the union because of their color.

Because union laborers often refused to work alongside Negroes even in non-union workplaces, Black workers were often denied access to even unskilled employment that was not subject to unionization.

Democrats Hand Over Harlem to Mafia

Harlem emerged as the iconic Negro ghetto in the 1930s. By the time of Prohibition, more than 250,000 Blacks were segregated into that small, crowded section of New York City. Scores of Blacks returning from "the war to end all wars" anticipated greater freedom and respect for their service to the nation. Instead, they found the Democrat political machines in the South and in the cities to be more racist and more intolerant than ever—a trend that continues to a lesser or less obvious degree well into the twenty-first century.

The Mafia and the Democratic Party

There has been a deep political partnership between the Mafia and the Democratic political machines that ruled over the urban centers. In fact, the mob could not operate without a level of political and legal protection provided by mayors, alderman, prosecutors and police commissioners.

The Mafia has always been notoriously racist. Often, the confrontation between the Mafia and the Black community would come in fights over control of gambling and vice, with the Mafia usually having the advantage of cooperation from city hall.

The Numbers Racket

Before it was taken over by the government and called the lottery, the numbers racket was a thriving, albeit illegal, enterprise in the ghettos. It was one of the few successful, Black-controlled enterprises. The numbers racket was considered small potatoes until the Depression hit. Eager to enhance revenues, the Italian Mafia muscled in with the support of Tammany Hall Democrats.

Stephanie St. Clair

The dominant numbers operation in Harlem was run by a Black woman, Stephanie St. Clair. Her chief competition was Casper Holstein.

James J. Hines, Tammany Hall's Democrat boss of Manhattan, was an ally of mobster Dutch Schultz, who, in turn, worked for Lucky Luciano. Together, they conspired to take over the Harlem-run numbers racket. Recruited for the job were such Murder, Inc. characters as Owney Madden, Meyer Lansky, and Bugsy Siegel. They unleashed a wave of terror and violence in Harlem under the approving eyes of Tammany Hall and the Democrats in city hall. More than forty people working for St. Clair were murdered.

Harlem's Black community was defenseless. Thanks to Mafia friends in Tammany Hall, the police protection that St. Clair and Holstein had once secured for themselves with bribes was no longer available. In fact, police became part of the takeover operation.

The 1920s and 30s were marked by brutal waves of violence. Crime writer Walter A. Bell, in his book *Black Gangs of Harlem: 1920–1939* wrote:

> Harlem's numbers operators were not prepared for an extended turf war, or the ruthlessness and violence inflicted by the mob. Many of them were badly beaten and some were even murdered by the mob's musclemen. It has been estimated that more than 40 murders and six kidnappings came on the heels of this turf war. Harlem's Black numbers runners began to disappear off the streets and its policy bankers began to mysteriously retire.

The Holstein Kidnapping

Casper Holstein was one of the wealthiest Blacks in Harlem thanks to his income from the numbers racket. He resisted the mob takeover and on September 23, 1928, was kidnapped by mob enforcers with a demand of $50,000. It has never been proven, but it is believed that the ransom was paid. Holstein was released soon after the kidnapping.

Despite the kidnapping, Holstein continued his numbers racket. Though he had always enjoyed police protection in the past, this time Holstein was arrested and jailed in what most believed was done on behalf of the mob, whose ties to Tammany Hall were stronger than Holstein's. While he languished in jail, the mob took over his business and sent Holstein into forced retirement.

Bumpy Johnson

In an operating method that was seen in the days of slavery, the mob employed Black crony enforcers to handle the White boss' business in Harlem. One of the more colorful guys was Ellsworth Raymond "Bumpy" Johnson. Originally part of St. Clair's operation, Bumpy saw the writing on the wall.

Despite his lack of schooling, Bumpy was an incessant reader and writer of poetry. Some of his works were published during the period known as the Harlem Renaissance. But mostly, he was a ruthless criminal.

Of Bumpy Johnson, Bell writes:

> Bumpy Johnson was filled with anger toward whites and the Jim Crow system they had established. He was determined to take advantage of every opportunity offered him. (Bumpy is quoted as saying), 'Sure I'm a thief and a pimp and a hood. What would you have me do? Go down to Grand Central Station and carry bags for dimes, or go back to Africa and take my pants off and run around in the jungle? Lucky Luciano can live at the Waldorf but it don't matter how much money I got, I can't walk in there and get me a room. Every time I look in the mirror I see the same black face. I ain't no Paul Robeson and I ain't no Angelo Herndon. I'm just an awful lot of black. All I got to do is stay black and die. White people ain't left us nothing but the underworld. They made hoods and thieves outta every nigger that's got guts'."

After Luciano had Shultz murdered, he made Bumpy the principal mob enforcer and banker in Harlem. Bumpy had become the "house nigger" for the Italian mob and their White Democrat friends in Tammany Hall. This was not the last time the mob and Democrat city officials conspired to take money-producing enterprises from Blacks in Harlem.

The Cotton Club

Among the most famous nightclubs in Harlem was the Cotton Club. Originally, it was called Club Deluxe and was owned by Jack Johnson, the Black world heavyweight boxing champion. Johnson was muscled out of ownership by mobster Owney Madden and his Democrat pals in "the Hall." Madden renamed it the Cotton Club. Although the Club featured many of the top Black entertainers of the day—including such famous names as Ella Fitzgerald, Billie Holiday, Duke Ellington, Nat King Cole, Lena Horne, Cab Calloway, and Ethel Waters—it was only open to White customers after the mob took over.

The mob in other cities followed the New York example of owning or controlling entertainment venues in the ghetto that offered Black entertainment to White-only audiences. There were notable exceptions in which Blacks retained ownership. It speaks again to the diametrically opposing roles of the Republican and Democratic parties.

Georgia State University Professor Paul Lombardo refers to these entertainment venues in his writing on Black organized crime" "The leading clubs in which famous black ragtime jazz musicians played were owned and/or managed by Black Republican Party organizers, who used the music to attract the attention of potential Black voters."

Mob Racism Expands

New York was not alone in the racist relationship between the Democrats in city hall and the local mob families. The 1930s mob was not exclusively Italian. It had both Jewish and Greek members, but they were all anti-Black. In the history of organized crime, there is no evidence of any Black person ever becoming a "made man"—although Black crime mobs arose, and Blacks were used as enforcers.

According to Rufus Shatzberg and Robert Kelly in *African American Organized Crime- A Social History:*

> Throughout the early period of white gang development, African Americans were not visible in the structure of any significant organized criminal process. Indeed, African American criminals who entered the twentieth century had no documented history of a leadership role or any significant active affiliation with any organized crime group.

Black mob enforcers like Bumpy Johnson would get a relatively small cut of the criminal proceeds. It was, however, a significant amount of money in the impoverished ghetto.

Fiorello La Guardia and Republican Mayors

In 1932, the people of New York elected Republican mayor Fiorello LaGuardia. He was only the fourth Republican mayor in New York history.

La Guardia had campaigned against both the corruption and racism of city hall under the control of the Democrats. His disdain for the intolerance against Blacks and immigrants stemmed from his own family experience as the son of an Italian immigrant. They suffered many of the same prejudices in jobs, housing, and general social acceptance as Blacks. The only difference was prejudice against Euroopean immigrant and refugee groups would subside as the population was assimilated into the greater American culture. Negroes were institutionally blocked from assimilation and pathways of opportunity by racist policies and violent enforcers.

As was the case with the few Republicans who would intermittently serve as mayors of major cities, La Guardia governed over a powerful Democratic Party substructure in terms of the city council, other city elected officials and the vast bureaucracy. Although backed by the national Republican Party with a strong civil rights platform, Republican mayors were limited in their ability to push civil rights. But they could do something.

Among La Guardia's notable appointments were Jane Bolin and Samuel Battle. Bolin was the first Black to receive a law degree from Yale University. LaGuardia appointed her to the Domestic Relations Court, where she served for forty years. Battle had been the first Black police officer in New York City. Battle became the first Black lieutenant in 1935. LaGuardia appointed him as the first Black parole commissioner in 1941.

The Midterm Election of 1934

After two years in office, Roosevelt's popularity was at a peak. In the 1934 midterm election, Democrats gained nine seats in the Senate, giving them a supermajority, and another nine seats in the House. The Republicans lost fourteen seats due to a gain of several seats by the Progressive Party, which had no seats in the previous Congress.

In the 1934 Democrat election wave, Chicago's Black Republican congressman, Oscar De Priest, was defeated by Democrat Arthur W. Mitchell.

Mitchell became the first ever Black Democrat to sit in the Congress—seventy years after the Civil War. This was after more than forty Black Republicans had served in the United States House and Senate. It would take another fifty-seven years (1993) for Democrats to elect a Black US Senator—twenty-six years after Republicans sent Edward Brooke of Massachusetts to the Senate in 1967 as the first Black senator since Reconstruction Carol Moseley Braun.

Roosevelt Snubs Black Olympians

The 1936 Olympic Games in Munich, Germany proved to be a great embarrassment for Adolph Hitler and his belief in Aryan superiority. No one upset the Fuehrer more than Black American track star Jesse Owens, who was the all-star of the event with four gold medals. He won gold in the 100-meter, 200-meter, and 400-meter relays and the long jump. Back home, Owens was the subject of ticker tape parades in Cleveland and New York. He was a national hero.

The events in Munich also revealed Roosevelt's deep-seeded White supremacist views. In celebration of the team's Olympic victories, Roosevelt invited the American team to the White House for official recognition. The invitation, however, was only extended to the White athletes. The Roosevelt White House was no PLACE for Blacks.

Refuting a claim that Hitler had snubbed Owens, the gold medalist responded, "Hitler didn't snub me. It was our president who snubbed me. The president didn't even send me a telegram." In 1936, Owens campaigned for Republican presidential candidate Alf Landon.

Roosevelt and his successor, Democrat Harry Truman, never officially recognized Owens' achievements. Owens finally received presidential recognition when Republican President Dwight Eisenhower invited him to the White House in 1955 and named him as Ambassador of Sports.

The Election of 1936

With the Great Depression unabated and the blame resting squarely at the feet of the Republican Party, the Democrats were in their strongest position since the Civil War. The re-nomination of Franklin Roosevelt was a foregone conclusion. For vice president, Roosevelt again tapped the racist Texan John Nance Garner.

The Republicans nominated Kansas governor Alf Landon. In a campaign speech Landon clearly saw the problem of presidential programs that would enslave people to government dependency:

> The President spoke truly when he boasted... 'We have built up new instruments of public power.' He spoke truly when he said these instruments could provide 'shackles for the liberties of the people... and... enslavement for the public.' These powers were granted with the understanding that they were only temporary. But after the powers had been obtained, and after the emergency was clearly over, we were told that another emergency would be created if the power was given up. In other words, the concentration of power in the hands of the President was not a question of temporary emergency. It was a question of permanent national policy. In my opinion the emergency of 1933 was a mere excuse. . . . The price of economic planning is the loss of economic freedom. And economic freedom and personal liberty go hand in hand.

The bulk of the Republican Party Platform dealt with the two most critical issues of the day—the economic recovery and the concerns over Roosevelt's alleged abuses of power. It did not, however, overlook the Party's longstanding support of Negro rights. The Republicans were critical of the racist policies of the Roosevelt administration that were working against Black employment. The platform stated:

We condemn the present New Deal policies which would regiment and ultimately eliminate the colored citizen from the country's productive life and make him solely a ward of the federal government.

Despite its policies in the south and the big cities, the Democratic Party Platform made a general statement of "equal rights to all and special privileges to none." Nowhere in the document, however, did it specifically address the unique needs of Black Americans.

Roosevelt Wins a Second Term

As anticipated, with overwhelming support from Negro voters, Roosevelt was reelected in a landslide victory. He won more than 60 percent of the popular vote and carried every state except Vermont and Maine.

Roosevelt garnered 71 percent of the Black vote in 1936 but the alliance between Blacks and the Democratic Party was still fragile. Despite the vote in the presidential elections, most Blacks were still registered as Republicans. This would be the case throughout Roosevelt's three-plus terms in office. It was not until the Truman election of 1948 that the majority of Black voters registered as Democrats.

Roosevelt's Black Cabinet, 1936

The Democratic Party's strategy in dealing with Negroes in the North, who were eligible to vote, required taking on an appearance of civil rights advocacy. This meant lip service support for Black aspirations, symbolic gestures, and liaison without actual empowerment.

In addressing all three of those objectives, Roosevelt created the Federal Council of Negro Affairs. It became more commonly known as the president's Black Cabinet. It was the result of increasing pressure on FDR to appoint Negroes to high public offices—positions with real powers. That was not something Roosevelt was willing to do. Instead, he created a powerless "advisory" board. It was said that they consulted more with Mrs. Roosevelt than the president.

The members included Blacks serving in lower ranking bureaucratic offices and some prominent civil rights leaders and activists. Among the more prominent members were:

Mary McLeod Bethune: Born in South Carolina during Reconstruction, her parents were former slaves. Her devotion was to Negro education, and she founded a school for young Black girls in Daytona, Florida, which was later merged with a Black boy's school and became known as Bethune-Cookman University.

Bethune was among the most prominent female civil rights leaders and was a staunch Republican prior to the Depression. In 1928, Bethune was invited to attend the Child Welfare Conference, and two years later, Republican president Hoover appointed her to the White House Conference on Child Health. Thanks to her close friendship with Mrs. Roosevelt, Bethune had more access to the White House than any American Negro, but it did not translate into accomplishments. Her recommendations were largely ignored by the president.

Dr. Ambrose Caliver: A graduate of Columbia University with a degree in education, he was the first Black person to earn a PhD in education. Republican president Hoover had appointed Caliver as a senior specialist in the education of Negroes in the Office of Education. Roosevelt kept Caliver in the same position and made him a member of the Black Cabinet. Like the other members, Caliver had no record of accomplishment with the Roosevelt administration in terms of policy.

William H. Hastie: William Hastie was an attorney with the Department of the Interior. He would later be appointed to the federal courts. In 1962, during the Kennedy administration, Hastie was a leading candidate for the seat on the United States Supreme Court, which was being vacated by Justice Charles Whittaker. Facing strong opposition from James Eastland, the racist Democrat chairman of the Senate Judiciary Committee, Kennedy rejected the idea of a Hastie nomination.

On January 18, 1943, Hastie resigned because Roosevelt refused to end racial segregation in the military. Hastie also charged that Negro soldiers were suffering from inadequate training and prejudicial assignments between Whites and Blacks.

Lawrence A. Oxley: He spent his career focused on Black employment and welfare. In 1925 he served as the director of the newly created Division of Work Among Negroes, which was part of the North Carolina State Board of Health. Writing about Oxley in *African American Leaadership*, author N. Yolanda Burwell wrote that he was "one of the most influential state welfare leaders of his time." Ironically, Oxley was a promoter of the Democrat's welfare-for-Blacks strategy.

Robert C. Weaver: He was the Black Cabinet member who would achieve the greatest political success. He was one of the best educated men in Washington with three degrees from Harvard. At the age of twenty-six, he was an aide to Harold Ickes, secretary of the interior. President Kennedy appointed Weaver as administrator of the Housing and Home Finance Agency. It was widely believed that Kennedy would appoint Weaver as the first Black Cabinet member for a newly created Department of Housing and Urban Development. That became another unkept promise by Kennedy, reinforcing his reputation among many Black leaders for civil rights advocacy on the campaign trail as all talk but no action when in office.

Following Kennedy's assassination, President Johnson would follow up on the establishment of the Department of Housing and Urban Development. He appointed Weaver as the first HUD secretary and as the first Black to serve in the official cabinet.

Members of Roosevelt's Black Cabinet were impressive in terms of their individual leadership, but they had virtually no influence over the president's racist New Deal policies.

Roosevelt's Supreme Court Appointments

Indicative of Roosevelt's racism was his accommodation to southern segregationist Democrats when making appointments to the Supreme Court. During his long tenure, Roosevelt placed eight justices on the Court. It was clear from these appointments that Roosevelt did not consider racist anti-civil rights views as a barrier—not even membership in the Ku Klux Klan.

Two members stand out for their active devotion to White supremacy and endorsement of segregation and institutional oppression of Negroes. They are Hugo Black and James Byrnes.

Justice Hugo Black and the KKK

In 1937, in his first opportunity to appoint a justice to the Supreme Court, FDR nominated Alabama Democrat senator Hugo Black. While modern political pop culture has cast Black as an enlightened progressive jurist, he, like many progressives of that era, was far from a civil rights advocate. He was an outspoken White supremacist and racist.

At the time of his appointment, Black was a proud and active member of the Robert E. Lee chapter of the Ku Klux Klan—a fact well known to Roosevelt. Black's nomination was opposed by numerous Negro groups, including the Black members of the National Medical Association. Their resolution stated that Black's appointment was "noxious to the entire country as well as the Black race."

As an attorney, Black built his public reputation as a defender of Klan members accused of murdering Negroes. He would pack juries with fellow Klansmen and use secret Klan hand signals to connect with jurors.

His all-White juries would routinely convict Black defendants. The same juries would acquit White defendants no matter the volume of evidence. In one case, they acquitted E. R. Stephenson, against whom the evidence clearly showed that he was guilty of murdering a Catholic priest, Father James E. Coyle, who aggressively promoted integration.

In his 1926 campaign for United States Senate, Black took his campaign to every Klavern in Alabama, preaching against both Negroes and Catholics. His finance chairman was the exalted cyclops of the Lee Klan.

Upon winning his nomination, Black referred to Klan support in his speech: "I realize that I was elected by men who believe in the principles that I have sought to advocate, and which are the principles of this organization [the KKK]."

While in the Senate, the future Supreme Court Justice joined his southern Democrat colleagues in consistently opposing Republican anti-lynching bills. In 1935, Black launched a filibuster that led to the defeat of the Costigan-Wagner anti-lynching bill.

Upon defeat of the anti-lynching bill, the *Pittsburgh Post-Gazette* reported how Black had grinned and shook hands with his fellow Democrats in their joyful victory in protecting racial lynching from federal justice.

On the Supreme Court, Black was part of a racist majority that consistently limited the scope of the civil rights acts. He supported Roosevelt's clearly unconstitutional incarceration of Japanese Americans in concentration camps. He wrote a dissenting opinion in a case that reversed the conviction of Black freedom riders. He complained that rulings supporting the right of Blacks to assemble and protest as nothing more than giving special benefit to Negroes. "Unfortunately, there are some who think that Negroes should have special privileges under the law," he said.

As a Supreme Court Justice, Black was among the majority of Democrat justices who decided the contested Georgia gubernatorial election in favor of Democrat racist Lester Maddox over Republican Howard Calloway in 1966.

Despite this extensive provable history of hard-core racism and devotion to the KKK, Black is ironically a heroic figure within the Democratic Party

Justice James F. Byrnes

In 1941, FDR nominated another close presidential confidant and staunch segregationist to the Supreme Court, Democrat senator James F. Byrnes of South Carolina. He resigned from the Court after only fifteen months to head FDR's Office of Economic Stabilization. He later went on to be governor of South Carolina on a platform of preserving segregation—and especially stopping schools from being integrated.

Byrnes was a close friend of South Carolina Democrat powerhouse "Pitchfork" Ben Tillman, whose political rise to power was based on his reputation for murdering several Black United States militiamen—a fact Tillman often openly bragged about on the campaign trail.

After joining Congress in 1910, Byrnes quickly became a close ally of one of America's most racist presidents, Woodrow Wilson. Like Roosevelt, Wilson was a leading opponent of anti-lynching legislation. He, along with Hugo Black, was instrumental in blocking both the Costigan-Wagner anti-lynching bill in 1935 and the Gavagan bill in 1937. He justified his opposition with the old Democrat claim that lynchings were needed "to hold in check the Negro in the south." Byrnes advanced the Democrat racist canard that "rape is responsible, directly or indirectly, for most of the lynching in America."

As Democrat governor of South Carolina (1951–1955), Byrnes was an aggressive foe of the United States Supreme Court's *Brown v. Board of Education* decision.

FDR's other nominations to the high court, which include Stanley Reed, Felix Frankfurter, Robert Jackson, and William O. Douglas, were more nuanced, but generally opposed to civil rights. The remaining two, Frank Murphy and Wiley Rutledge, established a positive record on civil rights, albeit not perfect. They were not enough to swing the Court away from its racist positions on civil rights as established by FDR.

Due to the makeup of the Roosevelt Court, there were virtually no decisions favorable to Negro rights. That would be the case until Republican president Dwight Eisenhower appointed Earl Warren as chief justice, replacing the outrageously racist chief justice Fred Vinson appointed by President Truman.

Poll Tax Declared Constitutional

In the 1937 *Breedlove v. Suttles* decision, the FDR Supreme Court declared that the poll tax, used primarily by southern Democrats to prevent Negroes from voting, was constitutional. This would be the case for twenty-seven years until the enactment of the Twenty-Fourth Amendment, which banned it in federal elections. It remained an issue in state elections for another year, when it was universally outlawed by the Republican authored and introduced Voting Rights Act of 1965.

Roosevelt initially spoke out in favor of abolishing the poll tax, but he dropped his support in the face of pressure from the southern Democrats in Congress. In 1939, Republicans led a bipartisan effort to abolish the poll tax in federal elections and a bill to abolish it was introduced. When southern Democrats attempted to kill the bill in committee, a discharge petition was passed to force the bill to a floor vote. It was passed 254 to 84, with strong opposition from southern Democrats.

With congressional sentiment running in favor of abolishing the poll tax, the southern Democrats in the Senate, joined by a few northern colleagues, once again used the filibuster to block the legislation. Poll taxes would continue to be used by racist southern Democrats to keep Blacks away from the polling booths for another twenty-five years despite periodic Republican attempts to outlaw it.

Southern Democrats wrapped the poll tax around the Constitution, but the real reason for its existence was made clear by Mississippi's rabid racist Democrat Senator Theodore Bilbo, who said:

> If the poll tax bill passes, the next step will be an effort to remove the registration qualification, the educational qualification of Negroes. If that is done, we will have no way of preventing the Negroes from voting.

Bilbo's comment reflects the Democrats effort to keep Negroes from voting and integrating. It was the consistent Democrat effort to keep Negroes in a PLACE of inferior status.

The Election of 1940

Heading into the election of 1940, the nation was focused on three major issues—the Depression, the prospect of entering the war in Europe and the controversy over a third term.

After eight years of Roosevelt's New Deal policies, the nation still had not recovered from the Depression. After more than eleven years since the stock market crashed in 1929, unemployment remained high, with Whites at more than 10 percent and Black unemployment more than double that of Whites. The New Deal was clearly not working for Black Americans because it was not intended to work for them. The economy would not recover until the start of war in Europe when massive purchases of military equipment and armaments by the French and British revitalized American industry.

Breaking George Washington's two-term tradition was controversial. Many Democrats opposed FDR's decision. Vice President Garner broke with Roosevelt over the issue, and he was replaced by former secretary of agriculture Henry Wallace.

Wallace was not the civil rights advocate as he was later portrayed in later years. He was a socialist progressive and a globalist. Wallace was a staunch advocate of the New Deal, which he surely knew was an amalgam of racist policies designed to transfer jobs from Blacks to desperate White workers. He was an outspoken advocate for organized labor, which played a major role in blocking Blacks from jobs, especially government contract work. The progressive movement of the era was largely racist in terms of Negro rights.

The Republicans reached outside the political structure and selected a little-known New York lawyer and businessman named Wendell Willkie. He had been a Democrat and was a delegate at the 1932 Democrat convention that nominated Roosevelt. He became a critic of Roosevelt's New Deal policies and switched to the GOP.

With the war looming and the president's unprecedented grip on power, FDR won a landslide victory over Willkie.

Segregated Armed Services

In 1936, Roosevelt had garnered more than 70 percent of the Black vote. With that in mind, he could not pursue overtly segregationist policies. He could, however, pay lip service to the plight of Black Americans without taking any action to bring about equality and justice. Nowhere is that more apparent than in the American armed forces.

Since the Revolutionary War, Blacks have taken up arms in the defense of this nation. They served with bravery and distinction, often accomplishing more than their White counterparts. Despite their service, Negroes were segregated within the ranks of the military by President Wilson, relegating them to a PLACE of inferior status as they served and when they returned home.

At the onset of the war, the NAACP called for an end of discrimination and segregation in the military. On June 8, 1941, NAACP executive secretary Walter White met with Roosevelt to convey the group's demands. The president listened but executed no change in policy. The American armed services would remain segregated.

White then joined with A. Philip Randolph and Bayard Rustin in proposing a massive march on Washington to protest the segregation of the military and the denial of jobs to Negroes in the developing post-Depression economy. Randolph was president of the Brotherhood of Sleeping Car Porters, one of the few Black unions. Rustin was a multi-movement civil rights activist, most notably associated with the Congress of Racial Equality (CORE). It was anticipated that more than 100,000 Black citizens would join the march.

Discrimination against the one and a half million Black servicemen (13 percent of the armed services) was obvious, and job discrimination by government contractors was not subtle. This is how the president of North American Aviation Company publicly expressed his corporate policy:

> While we are in complete sympathy with the Negro, it is against company policy to employ them as aircraft workers or mechanics . . . regardless of their training. . . . There will be some jobs as janitors for Negroes.

As momentum for the march grew, Roosevelt could no longer ignore the prospect of thousands of Blacks coming to the nation's capital to protest his racist policies. In return for having the march called off, FDR agreed to issue an executive order to end discrimination in hiring in the defense industry.

FDR did not acquiesce to the demand to desegregate the military but issued Executive Order 8802 to ostensibly end employment discrimination by government contractors. It was more of an empty symbolic gesture and largely meaningless.

According to the National Archives "Milestone Documents":

> Executive Order 8802 established the 'Committee on Fair Employment Practice.' More commonly known as the Fair Employment Practice Committee (FEPC), it has been disregarded by most historians as a powerless and ineffectual agency, especially in the South.

In a 2021 online commentary in *ThoughtCo* historian Robert Longley wrote:

> As the first official act of the federal government intended to advance equal opportunity in employment, EO 8802 was expected to immediately open the defense industry to minority job seekers. In practice, however, it had little effect.

Roosevelt achieved his objective. White abandoned the proposed march.

Executive Order 8802 was more of a window dressing than a serious effort to provide jobs to Black workers. Since virtually all government contracts were union jobs, and the unions refused to enroll Blacks, EO 8802 did not open up jobs for Black workers. The enforcement provisions were ignored without consequence. Black leaders were also disappointed that FDR refused to consider integrating the military.

Asian Racism

It is worthy of note that Roosevelt's White supremacist views extended beyond Black Americans to Asians and Native Americans. At the onset of World War II, he ordered the rounding up of Japanese men, women, and children to be confined at remote regions that can only be defined as concentration camps. This was even done to Japanese who were citizens of the United States. It was illegal, immoral, and a gross violation of the US Constitution.

In the 1944 decision, *Korematsu v. the United States,* Roosevelt's racist Supreme Court determined that his executive order imprisoning Japanese citizens was constitutional. The majority opinion for the clearly racist and unconstitutional action by FDR was written by two of the most prominent Democrat jurists on the Supreme Court, Roosevelt's Ku Klux Klan appointee Hugo Black and the so-called progressive icon Felix Frankfurter.

Roosevelt's White supremacy was evident when German and Italian citizens expressed concern over their fate in view of the Japanese round up. Though the United States was at war with both Germany and Italy at the time, Roosevelt assured them that, "no collective evacuation of German and Italian aliens is contemplated at this time." The reason was obvious.

Roosevelt's overall belief in White supremacy was reflected in his writings in 1925. He wrote:

> Californians have properly objected on the sound basic grounds
> that Japanese immigrants are not capable of assimilation into the
> American population... Anyone who has traveled in the Far East

knows that the mingling of Asiatic blood with European and American blood produces, in nine cases out of ten, the most unfortunate results.

Roosevelt's Southern Racist Legislation

Roosevelt's racism was in line with the predominant view among Democrats leaders. The Democratic Party of the era was dominated by racists and White supremacists. There was virtually no major opposition to the Jim Crow culture in the south or the *de facto* segregation in the Democrat cities in the North. The only voices calling for the end of Black oppression were from the Black leaders and the Republican Party, and they were routinely ignored.

According to Loyola University Professor Juan Perea: "Southern Democrats in Congress were unified in their desire to uphold segregation and to resist any threats to the Jim Crow South. They voted as a bloc to uphold the racist values of their region."

Back to Africa Movement in Black and White

The Depression again made strange bedfellows between Black nationalists and White segregationists, an unlikely pairing that was previously seen following the Civil War. Both favored the return of Negroes to Africa.

Chicagoan Mittie Maude Lena Gordon formed the Peace Movement of Ethiopia (PME) in 1932. Her group joined with others to provide petitions with more than 2 million signatures to Congress in support of an amendment introduced by racist Democrat senator Theodore Bilbo from Mississippi. He was one of the most outspoken racists in the Senate. His amendment to the Federal Work Relief Bill would have had the federal government deport more than 12 million Blacks to Liberia.

Bilbo has been described as a strident racist who believed in the inferiority of Jews and Blacks. He was a member of the Ku Klux Klan. He was unapologetic, saying, "No man can leave the Klan. He takes an oath not to do that. Once a Ku Klux, always a Ku Klux."

In 1928, Bilbo spread the rumor that Hoover had danced with a "negress." He unconvincingly denied having anything to do with a pamphlet incorporating a doctored photo of Hoover and a Black woman dancing.

Despite the large Black population in Washington, DC, Democrats chose Bilbo to chair the District of Columbia Oversight Committee. His duty was to keep Negroes in their PLACE by keeping them segregated to areas away from the central government district in order to keep them from intermingling with the White elite.

In response to an anti-lynching bill being debated in the Senate, Bilbo said while filibustering:

> If you succeed in the passage of this bill, you will open the floodgates of hell in the South. Raping, mobbing, lynching, race riots, and crime will be increased a thousand-fold; and upon your garments and the garments of those who are responsible for the passage of the measure will be the blood of the raped and outraged daughters of Dixie, as well as the blood of the perpetrators of these crimes that the red-blooded Anglo-Saxon White Southern men will not tolerate.

Roosevelt rarely spoke out against the racism of the Democrat-controlled Congress. It has been argued that Roosevelt did not want any legislation on his desk that would provoke the southern Democrat bloc in Congress—even a federal law against lynching.

Constitutional Rights No Longer Mattered

With the economic shift came a fundamental social shift. The value of personal freedom diminished and was replaced by the new paradigm of dependency. Public policy and taxation began the shift from local government to the central government in Washington.

Pandering to the natural anxieties, fears, and suffering of the American public, Roosevelt persuaded the nation that economic recovery could only come from the federal government—and that *he* was their savior and guardian.

Republican Inroads in the South

Though many credit the later "southern strategy" of Richard Nixon for bringing the southern states into the GOP column. In reality, it was part of a much longer trend that began under Roosevelt and continued into the 1990s when the GOP started gaining a majority in the southern congressional delegations for the first time.

In the mid-1930s, the solid Democrat South was truly solidly Democrat. The segregationist policies and racial violence were exclusively the consequences of Democratic Party governance. However, Republicans were making the first miniscule inroads in the southern congressional delegations, as described by Kevin D. Williamson in the *National Review*:

> Republicans would pick up 81 House seats in the 1938 election, with West Virginia's all-Democrat delegation ceasing to be so with the election of its first Republican. Kentucky elected a Republican House member in 1934, as did Missouri, while Tennessee's first Republican House member, elected in 1918, was joined by another in 1932. Throughout the 1940s and 1950s, the Republican Party, though marginal, began to take hold in the South — but not very quickly: Dixie would not send its first Republican to the Senate until 1961, with Texas's election of John Tower.

The early inroads, however, motivated the Democratic Party under FDR and Truman to accelerate the use of government welfare to lock in the Negro vote.

White German Prisoners

Roosevelt would occasionally talk about the desegregation of the military with Negro leaders, but he showed no interest in taking action to end racial prejudice in the military. It was not just a matter of maintaining separate combat units. Nowhere was the treatment of Negro soldiers more shocking and undeserved than in the military installations housing German POWs on American soil.

There were more than 300,000 captured Germans incarcerated in the United States—a large percentage in southern facilities where Jim Crow ruled supreme. In almost every way and every PLACE, the White German prisoners were treated better than the Black American soldiers.

German prisoners were under minimal security. They could leave camps unescorted, dine in local restaurants, and go to movies. One soldier wrote home:

> All in all, our life here is very orderly. We sleep in beds which have white covers, and we eat with knives and forks. Up till now, we were treated excellently. . . . When I was taken prisoner, I visualized a life of horror, but it is quite different.

German POWs had many of the privileges of southern Whites. They could use "Whites only" bathrooms and other facilities. They could sit in the Whites section of a bus or at the Whites-only counter.

This was in contrast to the view of Negro soldiers. Their lives were governed more by the cultural customs maintained by the local Democrat establishment. Negro captain Charles Thomas, in a letter to his family, recalled being terribly hungry at his Texas base.

> The station was doing a rush business with white civilians and German prisoners of war. There sat the so-called enemy comfortably seated, laughing, talking and making frines (*sic*), with the waitresses at the beck and call. If I had tried to enter that dining room the every (*sic*) –present MPs would have busted my skull, a citizen-soldier of the United States. My morale, if I had any left, dipped well below zero. Nothing infurieated (*sic*) me as much as

seeing those German prisoner of war receiving the warm hospitality of Texas.

The abuse of Negro soldiers extended to entertainment. Singer Lena Horne was booked for two concerts at Camp Robinson in Alabama. The first concert was for White soldiers only. The second was for Negro soldiers and German prisoners of war. The Germans were given the seats closest to the stage, with the Black soldiers being confined to less desirable seats in the Negro Section.

Seeing the audience as she appeared on stage, Horne exclaimed "Screw this!" and refused to perform. In all future military bookings, she would perform only before all Black audiences.

Negroes Need Not Apply

German POWs would take jobs as farm hands, loggers, or in commercial businesses. They would be picked up and returned to the military base by their employers—often after a social evening. They were invited to dine in restaurants or in homes where Blacks were unwelcome. Ironically, the POWs would often be taking jobs from local Blacks.

Where Negroes were employed, they would work alongside the White German POWs but were entitled to none of the social benefits or privileges. As one Alabama farmer put it, the availability of White German workers had "rather a good effect on some of our sorry Negro labor by tending to keep them on the job better." He might as easily have said, "keep the in their PLACE."

Despite the racial prejudice, German prisoners said that the American Negroes treated them with respect and actually saw the POWs more like "fellow prisoners," both being subjected to limited freedom.

The Riots of 1943

Almost eighty years after Negro Americans were declared to be free citizens, the reality of Democrat oppression in the South was matched by *de facto* racism in the cities in the North. Anger and frustration resulted in hundreds of racial incidents—occasionally resulting in full-blown riots. The war years were not an exception as 1943 saw major riots in New York, Beaumont, Texas, and Detroit. Among the most common triggers for Black unrest were police shootings in the North and false accusations of rape in the South.

Whatever triggered race riots, the real cause was longstanding racist housing, employment, criminal justice, and educational policies that prevailed under Democrat one-party regimes in both southern states and the northern cities.

The Harlem riot began with the shooting of a Black man, setting off protests. A false rumor spread that the man had been killed and the protest became a full-scale riot. Rioting, vandalism and looting continued for two days, leaving six people dead and hundreds arrested.

In Beaumont, Texas, after several Black men were taken into custody for allegedly raping a White woman—although she was unable to identify any of those arrested—White workers at the defense plant descended on the Black community, burning more than one hundred homes. In the five-day riot, two people were killed and more than 250 arrested. No one was ever charged with the murders.

Three days of rioting in Detroit only ended with the deployment of six thousand federal troops. Thirty-four people were killed and more than four hundred were wounded. The majority killed or injured by police or the military were Black. Millions of dollars of property in the Black community was destroyed or damaged.

Political Machine Bossism

The infamous E. H. Crump of Shelby County (Memphis), Tennessee is one of the lesser-known Democrat bosses despite that fact that he was one of the earliest and most powerful of the modern machine bosses. A *Time* magazine cover story in 1946 declared Crump to be "the most absolute political boss in the United States." It was the beginning of an era of big city bosses.

Crump ruled over the city of Memphis and the state of Tennessee for more than fifty years. He personally decided who would be mayor from 1910, when he decided that he should hold the office, until his death in 1954.

Crump was a diehard southern Democrat racist and segregationist—so much so that in 1948 he supported Strom Thurmond and the Dixiecrats against President Truman. In 1947, Crump refused to allow the Freedom Train organized by CORE to stop in Memphis because it carried copies of the Constitution and the Declaration of Independence. He did not want the people, especially Negroes, to read those documents.

Crump was unlike most southern racist bosses. He operated more in the style of northern Democrat machine mayors. Rather than use intimidation or violence against voter registration, Crump encouraged Black voting as long as he controlled the outcome. Crump pioneered an Election Day technique that became standard operating procedure for Democrat machine bosses in other parts of the country—and especially perfected by Chicago's infamous Daley machine. Crump would hold back the vote count in Shelby County until the rest of the state totals were recorded. He could then determine how many votes he needed to "produce" to carry the state for his favorite candidates. Even voters who failed to show up at the polling place would often find their vote had been tallied in favor of Crump's candidates.

Crump's legacy in Memphis was to leave a city highly segregated with a racist culture he promoted at every turn. Ironically, but perhaps not surprisingly, it turned out to be the place where Martin Luther King Jr. would be assassinated.

The Election of 1944

By 1944, Roosevelt was a gravely ill man. Still, he could campaign just enough to conceal his failing health. The press was compliant in keeping his condition from the American people. Only insiders knew a critical fact—that FDR would not survive the first year of his fourth term. Despite his declining health, he was very popular. The nomination of Roosevelt was a foregone conclusion. The main issue of the 1944 Democrat National Convention was the selection of a vice-presidential candidate. Party leaders, recognizing the fact that Roosevelt would not survive much longer, were looking for a president-in-waiting. Many Democrat powerhouses wanted the New Deal to die with Roosevelt, but Vice President Henry Wallace, as a socialist supportive of FDR's signature legislation, was too far to the left for the American voters.

The replacement choice came down to the irascible Supreme Court Justice William O. Douglas, who was campaigning hard for the nomination, and the affable Harry Truman. The selection of Truman, even with his past KKK membership and his ties to Tom Pendergast—the first big city boss of Kansas City, Missouri—represented a return of the Democratic Party's tradition of having a deep south southerner on the ticket. At the time of his selection, the southern Democrats had every reason to believe that Truman would be a defender of segregation. As a senator, he generally voted with the racist southern bloc, including supporting the filibuster that killed the 1937 anti-lynching bill.

Thomas Dewey emerged as the GOP candidate. He had built his national reputation as an ardent crime fighter as New York City's district attorney. After an unsuccessful run for governor in 1938, he was elected governor in 1942 and reappeared as a Republican presidential candidate in 1948.

An article in the *Journal of American Studies* entitled "Never Argue with the Gallup Poll" by Simon Topping referred to Dewey's record on civil rights as "arguably the best in the nation."

As governor, Dewey proposed and passed the first state law in the nation that specifically outlawed racial discrimination in hiring. He undertook a program of slum clearance and provided public housing for thirty thousand displaced and needy families.

For vice president, Dewey and the Republicans selected Ohio governor John Bricker. After losing as Dewey's running mate in 1944, Bricker went on to the United States Senate where he supported Eisenhower's civil rights proposals.

The Platforms

Under the heading "Racial and Religious Intolerance," The 1944 Republican Platform was very specific in its opposition to the racist policies practiced by the Democratic Party, as well as an undercurrent of anti-Catholicism. It stated:

> We unreservedly condemn the injection into American life of appeals to racial or religious prejudice.

> We pledge an immediate Congressional inquiry to ascertain the extent to which mistreatment, segregation and discrimination against Negroes who are in our armed forces are impairing morale and efficiency, and the adoption of corrective legislation.

> We pledge the establishment by Federal legislation of a permanent Fair Employment Practice Commission.

The GOP platform took aim at the Poll Tax: "The payment of any poll tax should not be a condition of voting in Federal elections and we favor immediate submission of a Constitutional amendment for its abolition." And again, Republicans called for anti-lynching legislation: "We favor legislation against lynching and pledge our sincere efforts in behalf of its early enactment."

The 1944 Democrat Platform hypocritically called for equal voting rights while Democrat political leaders in the south were imposing poll taxes, literacy tests and conducting violent intimidation, including lynching, as a means to thwart Negro voting:

> We believe that racial and religious minorities have the right to live, develop and vote equally with all citizens and share the rights that are guaranteed by our Constitution. Congress should exert its full constitutional powers to protect those rights.

The NAACP responded to the Democrat Platform by saying the reference to civil rights was "a misnomer. It is … a splinter. The Democratic mountain labored and brought forth a mouse of evasion."

To the extent civil rights played a role in the 1944 election, there was a stark contrast between the pro-civil rights position of the Republican Party and the almost unanimous opposition to civil rights by Democrats.

Dewey made a respectable showing with 46 percent of the vote to Roosevelt's 54 percent of the popular vote. In the Electoral College, however, Roosevelt crushed Dewey by 432 to 99.

As expected, on April 12, 1945, just eighty-two days into his fourth term, FDR passed away at the Whites-only spa he owned in Warm Springs, Georgia.

The Roosevelt Civil Rights Legacy

Though the debate rages about the effectiveness of Roosevelt's New Deal policies in bringing America out of the Great Depression, the record is clear that economic recovery never benefited the Negro community—and was never designed to do so. Despite his promises, Roosevelt never integrated the armed forces. His appointments of Blacks were largely symbolic and into positions that had little real influence.

Statistics well establish that Negroes faired much more poorly from the Roosevelt policies than did White America. What is less understood is that it was not an unanticipated outcome but a matter of intent. Between his racist New Deal programs and his strategy of generational welfare dependency, Roosevelt did more to block Black access to integration and upward mobility than any post-Civil War president.

The New (Raw) Deal for Negroes

Despite Roosevelt's later popularity among Black Americans, most civil rights leaders of the New Deal era opposed Roosevelt's programs. Civil rights advocate and author William Pickens stated that "the New Deal's legislative innovations for relief and recovery … either provided little or no assistance for Negroes or worked to their disadvantage."

The online Equal Justice Initiative, which highlights the major events affecting minorities since colonial times, says this about the New Deal:

> Throughout the 1930s, white Southern Democrats secured amendments excluding the majority of blacks from the benefits and protections of New Deal legislation that built the central pillars of the modern middle class. The Southern congressmen struck agricultural and domestic workers from the law establishing Social Security, barring over 60 percent of the black workforce overall, 85 percent of black women, and almost 75 percent of the Southern black workforce from receiving Social Security benefits. This included retirement benefits, welfare, and unemployment payments.

> The Southern Democrats, capitalizing on their control of leadership positions in Congress and their effective veto power over almost any legislation, similarly barred farm workers and domestic workers from the protections of laws creating modern labor unions, and setting minimum wage and maximum hours. The Southern legislators secured provisions requiring local administration of the GI Bill, small business loans, home mortgage assistance, educational grants, and nearly all forms of federal financial aid that built our modern middle class and the assets that can be passed from generation to generation. Southern Democrats also prevented Congress from including any anti-discrimination language in social welfare programs, such as hospital construction grants, school lunches, and community health services. As explained by Representative James Mark Wilcox from Florida, "You cannot put the Negro and the White man on the same basis and get away with it.

> As a result of this concerted effort by White Southern politicians, the unprecedented comprehensive government program represented by the New Deal disproportionately benefitted Whites and largely excluded Black people. The impact of this racially motivated, discriminatory legislating continues to profoundly impact the nation today. According to the Pew Research Center, White households possess roughly 20 times as much wealth as Black households, and

more than a third of Black people have zero or negative wealth, compared to just 15 percent of Whites.

The Equal Justice Initiative report focuses on White southern Democrats, but it fails to reflect the complicity of Roosevelt and the national Democratic Party. For the American Negro community, the New Deal was not a policy of beneficence, but might be better called a New Deal in hypocrisy.

While Roosevelt's programs, with their alphabet soup acronyms, are highly praised by latter-day liberals and most modern-day Black leaders, the true history has been largely trumped by political propaganda that has infected academia, media, publishing, and entertainment.

In a 2003 Cato Institute article entitled "How FDR's New Deal Harmed Millions of poor People," author by Jim Powell wrote:

> The price of Southern Democratic support for New Deal reforms was the exclusion of blacks from federal benefits and protections. Only in this way could Southern Democrats both support the reforms, which benefitted white industrial employees principally, without threatening the political economy of the racist South."

While southern Blacks were denied the right to vote, access to jobs and the financial benefit of various New Deal programs, those in the North were being put on general welfare dependency as the alternative to constitutional civil rights, integration, and upward mobility.

Using government money for votes was evident in the advice of the Indiana Democrat V. G. Coplen, who advised FDR's campaign manager, James Farley, to "use these projects to make votes for the Democratic Party."

The online *Digital History* provided a summarized history of Roosevelt's key New Deal programs:

> Most New Deal programs discriminated against blacks. The NRA, for example, not only offered whites the first crack at jobs, but authorized separate and lower pay scales for blacks. The Federal Housing Authority (FHA) refused to guarantee mortgages for blacks who tried to buy in white neighborhoods, and the CCC maintained segregated camps. Furthermore, the Social Security Act excluded those job categories blacks traditionally filled.

The best way to understand the racism embedded in Roosevelt's New Deal programs is to look at specific programs in greater detail.

National Recovery Act of1933

The National Industrial Recovery Act (NIRA) was to be Roosevelt's keystone legislation, establishing a broad range of powers for the government to control and manipulate the economy and market forces. The author of the NIRA was attorney Donald Richberg, one of Roosevelt's closest economic advisors. As general counsel and executive director of the National Recovery Administration, Richberg also drafted a number of Roosevelt's White-advantage recovery programs, including the Railway Labor Act and the Taft Hartley Act. He would later become one of the leaders of the so-called Massive Resistance Movement which fought against school integration in Virginia and elsewhere in the Democrat-controlled southern states. He authored the legislation in Virginia that was designed to thwart federal efforts to desegregate schools.

Apart from its underlying racism, the NIRA created more problems than it solved. Its all-out support of unions had an underlying racist outcome since most unions barred Negroes.

The Supreme Court struck down the NIRA to the universal praise of Black leaders and such organizations as the NAACP, which had strongly opposed the Act as prejudicial to Blacks. It was replaced by the National Recovery Act (NRA).

The National Recovery Act was seen as the enforcement vehicle for the old NIRA. Like the NIRA, the NRA came under severe attack from Black leaders and Republican opponents.

The NRA was vehemently opposed by the NAACP, and William Pickens was the first to call it the Negro Removal Act. He said:

> One of the first effects of the NRA programs to raise wages is to oust many Negroes from employment altogether. Minimum wage rates imposed by the NRA were generally higher than Negro workers were receiving, and employers preferred replacing previously cheap black labor with whites.

And in 2002 Ken Kersch, political science professor at Boston College, wrote:

> The National Recovery Administration, or 'NRA,' a lynchpin of Franklin Roosevelt's First Hundred Days, did not fare well in the African American press. Negro Removal Act, Negroes Ruined Again, and Negroes Robbed Again, were only a few of the epithets launched at what many blacks took to be a poisoned spoonful of alphabet soup.

Public Works of 1933

The Federal Emergency Administration of Public Works (later renamed the Public Works Administration (PWA) was created in 1933 to undertake large-scale public construction projects, including highways, bridges, airports, dams, hospitals, schools, and even warships. It also played a role in creating public housing that was a major feature in maintaining segregated communities—essentially keeping Negroes in their PLACE. The program constructed approximately thirty thousand units in five years.

Facing increasing criticism from the civil rights community, the Roosevelt administration agreed to support quotas for hiring Black workers in projects financed by PWA. The program got bogged down by resistance to Black hiring from unions and local Democrat politicians but in the end the quotas were added to the program. Even with the quotas there was a problem.

Congressional Republicans sought anti-discrimination policies in hiring workers under the Public Works Program, but unions and congressional Democrats successfully thwarted those efforts. Rather than have the federal government hire and pay the workers directly, those decisions were left up to contractors, unions, and the local governments. It was no secret, even to Roosevelt, that such an arrangement would have a dramatic negative effect on Negro employment, especially in the South and big cities.

Though Blacks were hired for the PWA projects despite undermining practices at the local levels, the number was relatively nominal compared to the need. The program continued to favor White employment and the promised quotas were never reached.

This disparity in jobs for Blacks would be seen in one of the most important public works projects, the Hoover Dam. This technological marvel constructed in 1931–35 employed some twenty-two thousand workers—fewer than thirty of them were Black.

Works Progress Administration of 1935

The Works Progress Administration (WPA) differed from the Public Works Administration in that it dealt with smaller projects more suitable for semi-skilled or unskilled workers—potentially disproportionately beneficial to Black workers. Over the course of its eight-year existence, the program employed millions of mostly unskilled workers.

The focus on the unskilled worker gave the WPA a greater potential in addressing the extraordinarily high levels of Black unemployment. As in other New Deal job programs, however, the WPA was subjected to fierce debate between those who wanted to broaden the scope of coverage and those interested in narrowing the coverage—essentially making the WPA a White worker program. The percentage of Black employment in WPA projects ranged around five percent.

Civilian Conservation Corps of 1933

The purpose of the Civilian Conservation Corps (CCC) was to provide public works project employment for unmarried men between the ages of eighteen and twenty-three. The age was later extended to twenty-eight-year-old men. It operated from 1933 to 1942 when the war brought the country out of the Great Depression. More than 3 million young men participated in the program. Work camps were set up near major projects and workers were given room, board and clothing and $30 wage per month. They were required to send $25 of that salary home to their families.

Though CCC provided some Blacks with employment, their numbers were comparatively low, and those who did participate were discriminated against from the onset. The entire program was largely segregated, with

Black workers assigned to their own projects and housed in 143 segregated camps where they were overseen by White supervisors.

In 1935, Roosevelt's CCC director, Robert Fechner, confirmed that there was a "complete segregation of colored and White enrollees." Picking up the popular theme of Democrat racists, he said that "segregation is not discrimination."

Segregation policy did prevent Blacks from working on the more desirable CCC projects. Even where they performed similar jobs, Blacks often received lower pay even though that was illegal.

Agricultural Adjustment Act of 1933

The online website *Digital History* provides a summarized history of Roosevelt's key New Deal programs. In addressing the Agricultural Adjustment Act, it reports:

> The story in agriculture was particularly grim. Since 40 percent of all black workers made their living as sharecroppers and tenant farmers, the Agricultural Adjustment Administration (AAA) acreage reduction hit blacks hard. White landlords could make more money by leaving land untilled than by putting land back into production. As a result, the AAA's policies forced more than 100,000 blacks off the land in 1933 and 1934."

The Agricultural Adjustment Act (AAA) was passed in 1933. It was designed to pay farmers to cut production as a means of increasing commodity prices. The specific programs were to be administered by the state governments. Even though Black farmers were technically eligible for financial assistance through AAA, virtually all the money flowed to White plantation owners.

According to Section 7 of the act, sharecroppers and tenant farmers were to be directly paid compensation for the land they set aside. Congressional Democrats objected, demanding that payment be administered through the racist state governments. Without any change in the law, Roosevelt's secretary of agriculture and future vice president Henry Wallace simply reinterpreted the meaning of Section 7 to comply with Democrat demands—essentially cutting off virtually all funds for Black sharecroppers and tenant farmers.

Without any financial support, and with their produce blocked from the market at the local level by the Democrat establishment, Black farmers were driven off the land and into the food lines. In many cases, White plantation owners would acquire the land of Black farmers for a nominal price, and they would receive the compensation for the very same land for which compensation was denied to the Negro farmer.

In addition, many descendants of the nineteenth century slaves were minimally engaged as low-income sharecroppers in the twentieth century—some working on the very farms and plantations on which their ancestors worked as slaves.

In one example, AAA provided more than $250,000 to cotton farmers in South Carolina. Since there was only a limited market for the cotton, the owners simply reduced the number of fields worked. As a result, fifteen thousand acres of cotton were taken out of production and hundreds of Black sharecroppers lost their jobs. This was repeated across the Democrat southland.

According to the New Jersey State Library's African American history curriculum, unit 11 on the Great Depression:

> The Agricultural Assistance Agency's crop subsidy program … actually led to the displacement of about 192,000 black sharecroppers because, contrary to the program's rules, they failed to receive any portion of the federal funds given white planters for reducing cotton production.

The impact on the unemployed sharecroppers was not limited to loss of income. Since the AAA did serve to increase the cost of farm products, the unemployed Blacks faced the reality of paying higher prices for food at a time when they had no income.

Tennessee Valley Authority Act of 1933

The Tennessee Valley Authority was created in 1933 as a public sector corporation created by federal charter. It was to serve a number of purposes including flood control, provide electrical energy for the region, and serve as a stimulus for economic development. The project represented the racial prejudices of the Roosevelt administration in two ways: loss of land and access to jobs.

The project flooded almost 750,000 acres and forced some fifteen thousand people off their land, including a great number of farmers. White farmers were compensated for their losses. Tenant farmers, who were mostly Black, received no compensation for the loss of their livelihood.

The TVA created thousands of jobs, but very few for Blacks and then only the lowest paid most menial tasks. According to an August 7, 2017, History Channel documentary "The workers were categorized by the usual racial and gender lines of the day. TVA hired a few African Americans for janitorial or other low-level positions."

TVA was unionized from its inception. What many saw as a break-through for American workers was another barrier to Black employment. There was no willingness by the unions to voluntarily open up membership to Negroes and no desire by Roosevelt and the Democrats to force them to do so.

Federal Housing Administration Act of 1934

The housing sector collapsed in 1929 along with the stock market and the banks. People were unable to keep up mortgages, so the banks wound up with the houses. With so many houses on the market, prices collapsed, reducing the value of the real estate assets held by the banks.

The Federal Housing Administration (FHA) was created to regulate interest rates on mortgages and the general terms. The initial underwriting standards developed in 1930 discriminated against minority home shoppers. Up to 1959, Blacks received barely two percent of the federally insured home loans—essentially eliminating qualified Black home buyers from access to mortgages.

As the program grew for White Americans, the result was a significant decline in the value of properties in segregated Black communities. Democrat policies in the major cities and in Washington were essentially creating worsening slum conditions in the Black ghettoes. The barrier to home ownership for Blacks was exacerbated by racist redlining policies imposed by local urban Democrat political machines.

Redlining

The prejudice against granting minority loans became official policy at the national level. FHA established guidelines in 1935 that resulted in redlining, driving mortgage investors away from minority areas.

According to the Roosevelt Research Institute's online blog:

> It (the Roosevelt administration) did not bring to an end the tremendous injustices that African Americans had to suffer on a day-to-day basis, and some of its activities, such as the work of the Federal Housing Administration, served to build rather than break down the walls of segregation that separated black from white in Jim Crow America.

That last phrase directly speaks to the goal of the Democratic Party that has long been concealed behind the false narrative of civil rights advocacy—the fact that Democrat New Deal policies had actually enforced institutional *de facto* segregation in the major cities and were designed to keep Negroes in their PLACE.

National Labor Relations Act of 1935

In 1935, key provisions of the unconstitutional National Industrial Recovery Act were incorporated in the National Labor Relations Act (NLRA), also known as the Wagner Act. The NAACP and the National Urban League were joined by virtually all major civil rights organizations in lobbying against it, but to no avail. The president and his southern Democrat friends in Congress prevailed.

The Wagner (NLRA) Act put the federal thumb on the scale in favor of the predominantly Democrat-controlled all-White labor unions. It established the pro-labor National Labor Relations Board to arbitrate disputes and oversee union representation elections.

Who Put Blacks in that PLACE?

Since unions were segregated, with most all-White unions representing higher paid skilled workers, Black groups opposed the provisions of the Wagner Act as prejudicial and harmful to the welfare of African Americans.

The minimum wage provision of the Wagner Act was intentionally designed by congressional Democrats to remove Blacks from jobs which would then be available to unemployed White workers. The act literally took jobs away from Blacks in large numbers.

According to Jim Powell, a senior fellow at the Cato Institute:

> The minimum wage regulations (of the Wagner Act) made it illegal for employers to hire people who weren't worth the minimum because they lacked skills. As a result, some 500,000 blacks, particularly in the South, were estimated to have lost their jobs.

Blacks were not officially barred from employment, but the Wagner Act essentially created a White-only union monopoly. The original draft of the Wagner Act had contained a civil rights provision that would have banned discrimination. The American Federation of Labor, a strong ally of the Democratic Party, lobbied against the provision and congressional Democrats were more than willing to remove it.

The fact that mandatory union membership would all but eliminate Black access to government jobs did not go unnoticed. Such civil rights leaders as Booker T. Washington, Marcus Garvey, and W. E. B. DuBois strongly protested, but their voices fell on deaf ears in the White House and on Capitol Hill.

As originally drafted, the Wagner Act would have covered all workers. The majority Democrats in the Senate, led by the southern bloc, returned the bill to the Education and Labor Committee chaired by Maryland Democrat Vincent Palmisano. The bill was amended to remove farm hands and domestic workers from coverage—essentially removing job categories with high numbers of Black workers.

New York Republican congressman Vito Marcantonio protested, saying that the amended bill would fail to address the worst working conditions in the country. He argued that it would allow the continuation of a plantation system that had Blacks working in "virtual slavery." It was in keeping with Democrat efforts to keep Blacks in their PLACE.

In his Capital Research Center article "The Untold Racist Origins of Progressive Labor Laws," Horace Cooper said that in removing the predominantly Black farm workers, the congressional Democrats had acted "to preserve the racially subordinate role of the black worker." Cooper concluded:

> It is a strange kind of social reform indeed that flatly and purposefully excludes those for whom the reform would purportedly be the most helpful. . . . In the 1920s and '30s, black tradesmen were generally barred from joining most labor unions, which meant that any mandated union wage was effectively a white man's wage and, at the time, would not be paid to an itinerant, non-unionized black construction crew.

Blacks were in the no-win position of being ineligible for higher paying jobs and then blamed for undercutting White workers by taking jobs at lower pay.

Fair Labor Standards Act of 1938

Ku Klux Klan member and Democrat senator Hugo Black is credited with being the father of the Fair Labor Standards Act (FLSA). He proposed the law first in 1932 and was an associate justice of the Supreme Court when it was passed in 1938. In concert with the major Democrat trade unions, Black crafted noble sounding legislation that was actually intended to, and did, depress Black employment. This bias against Negros in the FLSA and other New Deal programs was in no small measure due to the racial prejudices of Hugo Black. As a close friend and staunch ally of Roosevelt, his influence over New Deal programs was considerable and extensive.

Among the notable purposes of the FLSA was to establish the forty-hour work week and time-and-a-half overtime requirement for designated jobs. It also prohibited most children under eighteen from performing dangerous work. While the provisions were significant in their requirements, the act covered less than 750,000 workers—and barely covered Black workers at all. It also did not address Black unemployment which was running at catastrophic levels throughout Roosevelt's twelve-plus years in office.

Major provisions of the act were rendered meaningless when wartime inflation[1] raised wage levels above the legally required levels set forth in the law. During the next seventy-five years the act was updated to respond to changes in the workplace.

The Fallacy of the Minimum Wage

One of the evergreen policies of the far-left progressives since Roosevelt has been devotion to the minimum wage. It has always been sold as a means of improving the income of the lowest paid workers. It is claimed to be a benefit to low-income Black workers today even though it was originally enacted as a racist policy to remove Negroes from the workforce during the Depression and to suppress their wage scales. Whether one believes that was the intention or an unanticipated outcome, it is beyond refutation that it served to deny Blacks access to jobs during the Roosevelt administration.

Again, in Horace Cooper's article "The Untold, Racist Origins of 'Progressive' Labor Law," he wrote:

> Most Americans take for granted that the minimum wage and the 40-hour work week came about as a result of an effort in the early 20th Century to improve the lives of working Americans. Not true. In fact, these measures were rooted in the racism of the era and were part of an effort to benefit white workers at the expense of black tradesmen. The policies helped create persistent high unemployment among blacks—and shed light on the real motivations of so-called Progressives.

Many suggest that rather than helping the nation get out of the Great Depression, the minimum wage actually deepened and prolonged it—especially for Negro Americans. The increase in the minimum wage made it economically more difficult for business to hire people. While the increase in the minimum wage is beneficial for a short time for those who got it, it has a negative impact on those who lose jobs, are not hired in the first place, or are replaced by technology that becomes more affordable. As with the Davis-Bacon Act, the FLSA made Blacks less

1

employable by creating wage minimums that favored White hiring and White union workers.

According to University of Iowa law professor Marc Linder, the federal minimum wage established by the FLSA was intended to preserve "the social and racial plantation system in the south—a system resting on the subjugation of Blacks."

The FLSA gave further evidence of Roosevelt's racial hypocrisy. Cooper writes that Roosevelt expressed his concern for the "ill-nourished, ill-clad and ill-housed" farm workers. Yet, his FLSA legislation exempted them from coverage.

Hugo Black attempted to conceal his racist intent by claiming the exemptions applied only to "businesses of a purely local type which serve a particular local community." In fact, Black was protecting the large agricultural combines where Black labor worked for the meagerest of wages and under the most deplorable of conditions.

New Jersey Republican congressman Fred Hartley spoke forcefully against Black's contention. He said:

> We are told that this measure will raise the wages and lower the working hours of the exploited workers of America. If that is the case, then why is it that the poorest paid labor of all … has been omitted from the bill?

The New Deal Fails Black America

Despite the political mythology and false racial narratives advanced by the Democratic Party, Roosevelt's New Deal was not beneficial to Negro Americans in any way. As with Woodrow Wilson, the New Deal represented another example of progressive racism and hypocrisy—only this time the Democrats added welfare dependency as an alternative "civil right."

In his biography of civil rights leader William Pickens, historian Sheldon Avery said that Pickens had concluded that

> most of the New Deal's legislative innovations for relief and recovery, including the National Industrial Recovery Act (NIRA), the

> National Recovery Act (NRA), the Agricultural Adjustment Act
> (AAA), the Civilian Conservation Corps (CCC), the Tennessee
> Valley Authority (TVA), and the Public Works Administration
> (PWA), either provided little or no assistance for Negroes or worked
> to their disadvantage.

Roosevelt and the Democrats had woven the threads of racism into virtually all the major New Deal programs. These threads created institutional racial prejudices that have influenced public policy into the twenty-first century—especially in the major cities ruled over by Democrat political machines.

Roosevelt's Impact on Black Employment

Many in the Black community view Roosevelt with idolatry. They believe that he brought them out of the Great Depression—an erroneous impression that has been handed down from generation to generation.

Before the Great Depression, the Black unemployment rate was actually lower than the White rate at less than four percent—although Blacks disproportionately held jobs at the lower end of the wage scale. By 1932, as the Great Depression took hold, the White unemployment rate jumped to 25 percent, while the Black rate soared to approximately 50 percent. This disproportionate rise in the rate of Black unemployment was more the result of Roosevelt's New Deal laws discriminating against Negro employment than the Depression, itself.

Prior to the Depression, Blacks performed jobs that were below the dignity of White workers. Once the Depression hit, unemployed White workers were eager to take any job to be had. The Roosevelt New Deal policy was designed and implemented to displace Black workers with White workers.

In the late 1930s, as American industry began to produce arms and military supplies for the French and British war machines and in anticipation of a possible American entrance into the War, the unemployment rate dropped to approximately 20 percent—still a depression level rate. The Black rate, however, more than doubled the national average. This pattern of excessively high unemployment rates among Blacks in segregated cities has continued to this day. Based on unemployment figures over the decades, it is fairly argued that Black Americans confined to segregated ghettoes have not yet fully recovered from the Great Depression.

Roosevelt's False Narrative Endures

The Democratic Party is able to maintain the false narrative of civil rights advocacy despite the fact that the truth is in plain view. In 2002, the progressive Public Broadcasting System (PBS) produced a series entitled *The Rise and Fall of Jim Crow*. It highlighted the almost 100 years of southern segregation , prejudice and violence against Negro Americans.

A PBS online article about the program noted that more than two-thirds of the two million Black farmers had lost their income and hundreds of thousands of sharecroppers were forced to abandon their homes and fields during the Great Depression. It went on to say:

> Even 'Negro jobs' – jobs traditionally held by blacks, such as bus-boys, elevator operators, garbage men, porters, maids and cooks – were sought by desperate unemployed whites. In Atlanta, Georgia, a Klan-like group called the Black Shirts paraded carrying signs that read, 'No jobs for niggers until every white man has a job.' In other cities, people shouted "Niggers back to the cotton fields. City jobs are for white men."'

As is too often the case, the PBS left the false Democrat narrative unchallenged by failing to specify those responsible. It left the general impression that these were simply the results of hard economic times and a general White racist culture. In fact, these were the results of intentional racist policies implemented by the so-called progressive Democratic Party and their all-White trade union allies.

Final Word on Roosevelt

Roosevelt has three legacies. He is often revered as the man who brought America out of the Great Depression, uplifted the lives of Negro

Who Put Blacks in that PLACE?

Americans, and won World War II. Then there is the true legacy of a racist president whose economic policies prolonged the Depression, further oppressed Black Americans, and left the final act in winning the war to his successor, Harry Truman.

Eisenhower Begins Military Desegregation

Though President Harry Truman is often given credit for desegregating the armed services, he did not blaze the trail. Republican General Eisenhower had called for desegregation of the military and had actually done so. Using his power as Supreme Commander, Eisenhower integrated some combat units during World War II—four years before Truman's executive order, as reported in National Geographic:

> One major breakthrough came during the Battle of the Bulge, in late 1944, says Ambrose. General Dwight D. Eisenhower, faced with Hitler's advancing army on the Western Front, temporarily desegregated the army, calling for urgent assistance on the front lines. More than 2,000 black soldiers volunteered to fight.
>
> Similarly, demands in Italy called the Tuskegee Airmen to action. In 1944, they began flying alongside white pilots in the European theatre, successfully running bombing missions and becoming the only U.S. unit to sink a German destroyer.
>
> African American women also fought to serve in the war effort as nurses. Despite early protests that black nurses treating white soldiers would not be appropriate, the War Department **relented**, and the first group of African American nurses in the Army Nurse Corps arrived in England in 1944."

The word *relented* is emphasized because it clearly shows that Eisenhower's integration of Black and White service personnel was not received with enthusiasm by Democrats in Washington.

Harry Truman (1945–1953)

Harry S. Truman followed FDR's lead in promoting the strategy of political hypocrisy with respect to civil rights, as have so many succeeding Democrat presidents, governors, mayors, and lesser Democrat officeholders. He projected a public posture as an advocate of civil rights, but fully embraced welfare dependency model as the new civil rights. Many of his actions were more symbolic than substantive and often the result of political pressure from Republicans and Black civil rights groups. His most notable achievement was the desegregation of the armed services and the executive branch of the government in Washington, DC. The ascension of Missourian Harry Truman to the presidency upon the death of FDR once again put a southerner with a racist record in the Oval Office.

Truman started in business as a partner in a haberdashery shop. While it was only a short-lived career, that small-time merchant image became part of the Truman lore. Like Wilson, Truman, spent his formative years in a severely racist and segregated society. His hometown of Independence was a hot bed of racial strife. Blacks were commonly referred to as "niggers" or "coons"—and that was in the politest circles. Women would sometimes be differentiated from men and called a "negress." To their face, male Blacks of any age were called "boy" to emphasize White superiority. Children were called "pickaninnies," a onetime word of endearment that evolved to be a pejorative.

This influence was seen in 1913 when Truman was a twenty-nine-year-old aspiring politician. He said:

> I think one man is just as good as another so long as he's not a nigger or a Chinaman. Uncle Will says that the Lord made a white from dust, a black from mud, then He threw up what was left and it came down a Chinaman.

His rough language also applied to other non-Christian and/or non-WASP ethnic groups. In casual conversation, he would commonly refer to Jews as "kikes," Italians as "wops," and Asians as "chinks."

Truman Joins the Klan

In 1924 Truman paid ten dollars to become a member of the Ku Klux Klan. His membership was affirmed by many of his old friends in those early years. The Klan was very powerful in Jackson County, and Truman had political ambitions. He once ran for judge against two opponents who were both Klan members and lost. He joined the Klan to even the playing field. However, Truman's membership was short lived, and unlike his fellow progressive Woodrow Wilson, Truman did not bring loyalty to the Klan into the presidency.

The Pendergast Machine

Truman believed his political career would be better served by hooking up with the infamous Kansas City Pendergast Machine—run and named after "Boss" Tom Pendergast.

Truman initially gave up his Ku Klux Klan membership not because of its racial bigotry against Blacks, but because of its anti-Catholic prejudice. One of the conditions for support from the Irish Catholic Pendergast Machine was not belonging to any anti-Catholic organizations, especially the Klan. Truman's loyalty to the Klan and his later rejection of the Klan were the result of political opportunism rather than dedication to principle. The switch from Klan to Pendergast was not dramatic in terms of race issues since the Pendergast Machine was as racist as the Klan.

Tom Pendergast was pugnacious and belligerent. Negroes were routinely assaulted for not knowing their PLACE—which could have meant as little as just being Black in public. To what extent Truman was part of Boss Tom's street gangs is subject to historic debate. However, with Boss Tom, you had to go along to get along, and Truman was a favorite of Boss Tom.

Truman worked hard as a Pendergast operative and was rewarded with a judgeship in 1922 and then was elevated to presiding judge. In 1934, Pendergast tapped Truman to run for the United States Senate.

Tom Pendergast's machine shared the common Democrat machine characteristic of corruption—especially in terms of vote fraud. A Kansas City

Public Library online history of Harry Truman entitled "His Own Man" described the Pendergast machine:

> In 1936, the machine, led by Tom Pendergast, stuffed so many ballot boxes for Democratic candidates that more votes were tallied than the entire registered population of Kansas City. Cheating at the polls, appointing allies to city jobs, and using city resources for illegal income was nothing short of routine for political bosses of the era, but Pendergast had so far evaded detection by anyone in a position to stop him.

The association with Pendergast, who Truman never denounced, dogged him throughout his career—especially as he rose in the ranks of the Senate. The relationship caused Roosevelt to pass over Truman as his vice president in his earlier presidential elections. A dying Roosevelt relented only after Truman won reelection, the Pendergast machine had essentially gone out of business, and Boss Tom was on his way to federal prison for tax evasion.

Regardless, Truman heaped unbridled praise on the corrupt Pendergast, saying:

> He was an able clear thinker and understood political situations and how to handle them better than any man I have ever known. His word was better than the contracts of most men and he never forgot his verbal commitments.

Truman could not have risen to the ranks of political prominence in Missouri without embracing the state's racist culture. University of Iowa historian Colin Gordon described the two natures of Missouri as a border state in his book *Mapping Decline: St. Louis and the Fate of the American City.*

As a border state, Gordon said Missouri had "a tradition of anti-black racism and white supremacism more typical of a former slave state." At the same time, he saw Missouri's urban segregation and social ills as "more characteristic of Northern States." Whether intentional or not, Gordon identified the two paradigms of Democratic Party racism—*de jure* and *de facto*.

The New Truman

Like Roosevelt, Truman understood that the Democratic Party on the national level could not support overtly racial policies and have any hope of maintaining the Negro vote or the party's dominance on the national stage. By this time, the national Democratic Party was being pressured into a more pro-civil rights position by both Republicans and allied civil rights groups. The challenge was to pay lip service to civil rights at the national level without confronting the party's powerful racist leadership in the south and the major cities.

In 1947, as Truman approached his reelection, he gave a speech to the NAACP on the steps of the Lincoln Memorial. Truman said:

> It is my deep conviction that we have reached a turning point in our country's efforts to guarantee freedom and equality to all our citizens. Recent events in the United States and abroad have made us realize that it is more important today than ever before to ensure that all Americans enjoy these rights. When I say all Americans—I mean all Americans.

Truman's embrace of civil rights rhetoric came at a time that Blacks were becoming an increasingly more significant voting bloc—and prior to 1948, most Black voters were still registered Republicans. Truman desperately needed an overwhelming Black vote to have any hope of reelection in 1948.

Truman Civil Rights Bills

In 1946, 1947, and 1948, Truman sent civil rights bills to the Democrat-controlled Congress where they were anticipated to be met with certain rejection. Truman did not use the powers of his office to pressure for passage. The legislation, however, gave Truman bragging rights as a civil rights advocate without changing anything for Blacks suffering under his party's oppression in the South and in the cities. This strategy was later used by John Kennedy in his presidential campaigns.

The one area where Blacks were gaining some popular support was in opposition to the brutal violence suffered at the hands of the Dixie Democrat regimes. In 1946, Truman issued Executive Order 9808 establishing the President's Committee on Civil Rights (PCCR), which was to examine violence against Negro Americans within the United States. It made a number of sweeping recommendations to eliminate racial segregation and such racist policies as the poll tax. Truman never pushed the recommendations and in the six years of his presidency that followed Executive Order 9808 virtually none of the recommendations were implemented.

After almost eight years in office, Truman essentially left Negro Americans in the same PLACE they were when he took office.

Truman's Armed Forces Desegregation Order

Approaching the 1948 presidential election, Truman was in trouble—especially with Black Americans. Further complicating the situation was the fact that the Republican Party had made desegregation of the armed forces a plank in the party's 1948 platform which the Democratic Party had refused to do.

In response, Truman took a much stronger civil rights position in his campaign. He officially reversed two of Wilson's most discriminatory actions—the segregation of the armed forces and the executive branch of the federal government.

According to an article on the Library of Congress website entitled "NAACP - A century in the fight for freedom," the decisive pressure to integrate the armed forces also came from the NAACP, which threatened street demonstrations throughout the country.

On July 21, just months before the general election, Truman opened federal employment to Blacks with Executive Order 9980, and on July 26, he issued Executive Order 9981, which ordered the desegregation of the United States armed services. In so doing, Truman undertook two actions that were promised by Roosevelt but never delivered despite his twelve-plus years in the Oval Office. It was also an action that Truman did not take during his first three years as president.

Truman got the response he wanted. The Black newspaper, the *Chicago Defender,* carried a bold banner headline: "PRESIDENT TRUMAN WIPES OUT SEGREGATION IN THE ARMED FORCES."

The facts did not live up to the headline. Once reelected, Truman did virtually nothing to enforce his own order. It was not until 1954 that the last segregated military units were finally abolished by order of secretary of defense Charles Wilson, serving under Republican President Eisenhower. In just more than one year in office, Eisenhower ended segregation in the military—an accomplishment that Truman failed to achieve in almost eight years in office, and the four years following his own executive order.

Truman Allows Racism to Rule in the South

Under Truman, Democrat institutional racism was allowed to go as unchallenged as ever. Segregation remained. Negroes were still deprived the vote in the South. Unemployment remained high. The Ku Klux Klan and other paramilitary wings of the Democratic Party continued their murderous violence. Lynching remained a common practice. Jim Crow reigned supreme.

The Isaac Woodard Case

Sergeant Isaac Woodard (sometimes misspelled as Woodward in the historic record), a decorated Black military veteran, was honorably discharged from the US Army on February 12, 1946. Hours after his discharge he was traveling from Camp Gordon, in Georgia, to his home in North Carolina. At a rest stop enroute Woodard got into an argument with the bus driver about waiting for him to use the restroom. The driver begrudgingly agreed to wait.

At the next stop, in Batesburg, the driver called the local police. Woodard was removed from the bus by Sheriff Linwood Shull and some deputies. Rather than taking him to the jail, Shull and his crew took Woodard to a nearby alley, where they commenced brutally beating him—battering his eyes with nightsticks. They then arrested him for disorderly conduct and invented a false charge of drinking beer on the bus. It was clear from later testimony that nothing other than the "pit stop" had provoked the driver's decision to have Woodard taken into custody.

While in jail, Shull continued his beating of Woodard, and often pounded the nightstick into the sergeant's eyes. Woodard never saw the morning sunrise, or any sunrise again. He was blinded by Shull's merciless beatings.

Beaten and blinded, Woodard was hauled before a local judge and found guilty and fined $50. He requested medical help, and he waited more than two days in the jail before a doctor was provided. He was then sent to a hospital in South Carolina, where he received poor quality treatment typically given to Black patients.

His family reported him missing. Once found in the South Carolina hospital, he was transferred to a military hospital in South Carolina, where it was determined that his eyes had been ruptured and gouged beyond repair.

The Woodard case might have been lost in history among the millions of acts of criminal violence against Blacks had it not been for the publicity it drew.

The National Association for the Advancement of Colored People (NAACP) took up the cause. They first attempted to get action from the South Carolina's Democrat government but to no avail. Their initial approaches to the Truman administration also went unheeded.

The NAACP did succeed in getting the attention of one prominent personality with a growing national reputation, Orson Welles. The actor/radio commentator took up the cause and crusaded to bring justice to Woodard in four broadcasts. He called for criminal charges against Shull and his deputies. He blasted the Democrat officials in South Carolina for their inaction. In a 1988 retrospective exhibit on Welles, the Museum of Broadcasting gave credit to the actor for raising the issue to national prominence in July of 1946—five months after the attack on Woodard. The exhibit noted that: "The NAACP felt that these broadcasts did more than anything else to prompt the Justice Department to act on the case."

The ensuing public attention prompted by Welles had songwriters and singers doing ballads about the Woodard beating—including Woody Guthrie's "The Blinding of Isaac Woodard." Public outrage was on the rise with calls for Truman to take action.

It seems clear that neither the Truman Justice Department nor the president himself were moved by the event, but the publicity garnered by Welles created a public outcry that the White House could no longer ignore. Seven months after the attack on Woodard, Truman responded to the NAACP's request for a meeting with the group's executive secretary, Walter White. Following the meeting, Truman ordered his Justice Department to undertake an investigation.

The Justice Department was able to bring Sheriff Shull and his deputies into federal jurisdiction, arguing that the crime had been committed at a bus stop on federal property and that Woodard was in uniform at the time.

Truman's attorney general (AG) was Tom C. Clark. He was a southern Democrat born in Mississippi and raised in Texas during the peak of southern segregation and racism. Before becoming AG, Clark had been a key player in planning the forced transfer of Japanese Americans to internment camps. Despite that background, Clark has been praised by some as a staunch proponent of civil rights. As AG, he led cases against housing discrimination and participated in Truman's civil rights committee. That zeal was not evident in the Woodard case, however. According to *The Rebellious Life of Mrs. Rosa Parks* by Jeanne Theoharis:

> By all accounts, the trial was a travesty. The local U.S. Attorney charged with handling the case failed to interview anyone except the bus driver, a decision that [Presiding Judge Julius] Waring, a civil rights proponent, believed was a gross dereliction of duty. Waring later wrote of being disgusted at the way the case was handled at the local level, commenting, "I was shocked by the hypocrisy of my government...in submitting that disgraceful case."

In describing Clark, *Life* magazine, may have revealed why the prosecution of Woodard's attackers was so ineffective. It said, "He is a good prosecutor and good lawyer, but most of all he is a thorough politician."

Shull's attorney carried out the typical racist defense. He used racial slurs in describing Woodard and at one point said ruling against Shull should again have the South secede from the Union.

The outcome was predictable. Despite admitting to having beaten Woodard, the all-White jury found Shull and his deputies innocent. Upon announcing the verdict, the jury and White spectators burst out in applause.

The Election of 1948

Entering the campaign of 1948, the Democrats looked vulnerable. Truman was losing the confidence of Negro leaders. The National Democratic Convention ended with a major split on civil rights. Confidence in Truman's reelection potential was so low that there was a "dump Truman" effort that tried to lure General Eisenhower or Supreme Court Justice William O. Douglas into the race. The movement ebbed when both declined to run against Truman. Florida senator Claude Pepper made a last-minute bid but withdrew for lack of support.

Contrary to his rousing speech before the NAACP, Truman initially opposed proposals for civil rights planks in the Democrat Platform that were being offered by Wisconsin congressman Andrew Biemiller with the support of then Minneapolis mayor Hubert Humphrey. Truman tried to prevent the planks from being introduced out of fear of splitting the Democratic Party in the general election. In fact, they did. Facing the certainty of the inclusion of the planks into the platform, Truman ultimately gave his tacit endorsement so as not to further alienate Black voters.

Having succeeded to the presidency upon the death of Roosevelt, Truman served for three plus years without a vice president. For his reelection, he followed longstanding Democrat tradition by choosing a southerner, Senate minority leader Alben W. Barkley from Kentucky.

Barkley was a major figure in Paducah, the seat of government for McCracken County, Kentucky—a community with one-party rule and a history of violent institutional racism.

During his rise to prominence, Barkley belonged to several fraternal organizations, including the all-White Woodman of the World (WOW), which did not admit Blacks until 1977; the all-White Benevolent and Protective Order of Elks (BPOE), which resisted Black membership until 1976 and then introduced the "blackball" system to continue to prevent Blacks from joining; and the all-White Independent Order of Odd Fellows (IOOF), which did not end the ban on Black membership until 1971.

Barkley was also a member of the Improved Order of Redmen (IOOR). It was one of a number of Native American–themed socio-political organizations that sprang up around the time of the Revolutionary War. One of the branches became the infamous Tammany Hall in New York City. The group to which Barkley belonged was founded in 1886. Despite its Native American theme, the organization's constitution restricted membership to "a free White male of good character and standing."

Throughout the South, these fraternal groups shared membership and viewpoints with the more violent terrorist organizations such as the Ku Klux Klan.

As a state representative, Barkley had been a staunch supporter of Woodrow Wilson's racist domestic policies. He supported Wilson's racist son-in-law, William McAdoo, for the Democrat nomination to succeed Wilson in both 1920 and 1924. Later in the United States Senate, Barkley supported Franklin Roosevelt's racist New Deal policies. Loyalty to FDR and the Democrat's southern bloc resulted in Barkley being elected as the Senate majority leader in 1937.

The Republicans

As the election season approached, there was a grassroots movement within the Democratic Party to draft General Eisenhower. Despite polls suggesting he would easily win the election, he declined to run. With Eisenhower out, the leading candidates were New York governor Thomas Dewey and Ohio senator Robert Taft. Dewey had a strong lead on the first ballot, increased his margin on the second, and secured the nomination on the third. Dewey had a strong civil rights record. As governor, he enacted the first state-level civil rights legislation in the nation.

As a running mate, Dewey selected California governor Earl Warren, who would later become Eisenhower's pick for chief justice of the Supreme Court and the major force behind the *Brown v. Board of Education* decision that ended *de jure* school segregation in the South.

The Dixiecrats

As the 1948 presidential election approached, Senator Strom Thurmond took up the racist views of his southern Democrat colleagues. When Humphrey's civil rights planks were adopted by the Democrat convention, thirty-five southern delegates, already angered over Truman's executive order integrating the military, walked out of the convention. Led by Thurmond, they later met in Birmingham, Alabama, to form the States' Rights Democratic Party (which became commonly known as the Dixiecrats) and nominated Thurmond as their presidential candidate. The campaign slogan was Segregation Forever!

During the 1948 election, Thurmond used states' rights as the stalking horse for segregationists, but that did not mean he avoided the subject more directly. On the campaign trail, Thurmond said: "all the laws of Washington and all the bayonets of the Army cannot force the Negro into our homes, into our schools, our churches and our places of recreation and amusement." Thurmond clearly differentiated his "place" from the Negroes' PLACE.

The vice president nominee was Field J. Wright, Democratic governor of Mississippi. He was a man of his times. As governor, he made his position very clear on segregation with this warning to the Negro population:

> If any of you have become so deluded as to want to enter our White schools, patronize our hotels and cafes, enjoy social equality with the Whites, then true kindness and sympathy requires me to advise you to make your homes in some other state.

The Platforms

In the preamble of the 1948 Republican platform, the GOP expresses its historic devotion of equal rights:

> Constant and effective insistence on the personal dignity of the individual, and his right to complete justice without regard to race, creed or color, is a fundamental American principle.

Recognizing the continuing practice of lynching in the southern Democrat states, the GOP platform addresses it specifically:

> Lynching or any other form of mob violence anywhere is a disgrace to any civilized state, and we favor the prompt enactment of legislation to end this infamy.

The platform specifically singled out the egregious poll tax used by southern Democrat government to suppress Black voting:

> One of the basic principles of this Republic is the equality of all individuals in their right to life, liberty, and the pursuit of happiness. This principle is enunciated in the Declaration of Independence and embodied in the Constitution of the United States; it was vindicated on the field of battle and became the cornerstone of this Republic. This right of equal opportunity to work and to advance in life should never be limited in any individual because of race, religion, color, or country of origin. We favor the enactment and just enforcement of such Federal legislation as may be necessary to maintain this right at all times in every part of this Republic.

> We favor the abolition of the poll tax as a requisite to voting.

Recognizing Truman's failure to enforce his own executive order, the platform called for the end of Democrat president Woodrow Wilson's segregation of the armed forces:

> We are opposed to the idea of racial segregation in the armed services of the United States.

The preamble of the Democrat platform of 1948 made no mention of civil rights—but it did give support to the Democrats' welfare-for-votes scheme.

Under housing, it called for public house programs to address the slum conditions of America. The Democrats favored brick-and-mortar housing construction that would keep Blacks confined to their segregated PLACE in the urban ghettoes.

The Democrat platform was rife with platitudes founded on audacious hypocrisy:

> We again state our belief that racial and religious minorities must have the right to live, the right to work, the right to vote, the full and equal protection of the laws, on a basis of equality with all citizens as guaranteed by the Constitution.

The States Rights Democratic (Dixiecrat) Party platform focused solely on segregation and the party's opposition to civil rights. There was no mention of economic policy, social programs, or foreign affairs. It expressed its opposition to both the Republican and Democratic platforms. It was not vague on its support of racial segregation:

> We stand for the segregation of the races and the racial integrity of each race; the constitutional right to choose one's associates; to accept private employment without governmental interference, and to earn one's living in any lawful way. We oppose the elimination of segregation, the repeal of miscegenation statutes, the control of private employment by Federal bureaucrats called for by the misnamed civil rights program. We favor home-rule, local self-government and a minimum interference with individual rights.
>
> We oppose and condemn the action of the Democratic Convention in sponsoring a civil rights program calling for the elimination of segregation, social equality by Federal fiat, regulations of private employment practices, voting, and local law enforcement.

Election Results—1948

There was little chance of Thurmond winning the presidency, but there was deep concern within the Democratic Party that he could throw the election to Dewey. Though the popular vote was very close—causing the *Chicago Tribune* to publish the erroneous headline "Dewey defeats Truman"—Truman won overwhelmingly in the Electoral College.

Thurmond carried four southern states with 39 electoral votes, including one vote from a faithless elector in Tennessee. Even if these had been added to Dewey's 189, the New York governor would have fallen far short of Truman's 303 electoral votes.

Simon Topping, in his essay "Never argue with the Gallup Poll: Thomas Dewey, Civil Rights and the Election of 1948" lays the blame for Dewey's defeat to his failure to promote his civil rights record. He wrote:

> Truman, like much of the historiography, credited his victory to the farm vote, and this was undoubtedly an important factor, but

it is clear that without the votes of African Americans Truman could not have won. This piece will examine why Dewey lost, surveying his record on civil rights as governor (arguably the best in the nation) and his abject failure to convert, indeed, to even attempt to convert, this record into African American votes in 1948. This failure is made more curious by the fact that he was constantly being warned by African American Republicans and his closest confidante about the pivotal nature of the African American vote. Yet Dewey, a notoriously lethargic campaigner, would ignore their admonishments.

While the racist Dixiecrats split from the presidential ticket in the 1948 election, it is important to remember that they remained as a major power and influence within the Democratic Party. Having failed to become a serious political force on their own, the thousands of Democrats, officeholders and voters who broke away in 1948 returned to the party after the election.

The Mid-Twentieth Century Transition

The reelection of Truman proved to be a turning point in the politics of American racism. The civil rights movement was on the march. Issues that had been ignored or swept under the rug emerged as the front-burner issues of the next generation. Progress would be made and thwarted at the same time. There was a new dynamic, a new paradigm, in the issues of race. Institutional racism would be challenged, but not yet totally defeated.

Even with Blacks voting for the Democratic Party in increasing numbers in the 1930s and 1940s—and the national party projecting an image of racial tolerance and civil rights advocacy—institutional racism proved to be pernicious, requiring the Democratic Party to enter a level of political hypocrisy unlike any period since the days of Reconstruction and southern Redemption.

With the support of the national Democratic Party, a new generation of powerful racist leaders arose, leading up to the volatile civil rights confrontations of the1950s and 1960s. The policies and actions of this new class of racist leaders in the Democratic Party would exert undue negative influence on the civil rights movement into the twenty-first century.

There arose a cadre of segregationist southern Democrats in the United States Senate and House of Representatives who would become infamous as the battle for civil rights took center stage in the mid-1950s. With virtually automatic reelection victories, and the arcane and anachronistic congressional seniority system, racist Democrats were able control of the most powerful congressional committees. They, along with their gubernatorial counterparts in the segregated states, became a vanguard of opposition to civil rights legislation and enforcement. In every sense, this bloc of southern segregationist senators and governors controlled the Congress and to a large extent the national Democratic Party.

Though there were sincere pro-civil rights voices within the Democratic Party, the party itself was either overtly racist or acquiescent to the powerful racist bloc. Martin Luther King had the latter group in mind when he wrote in his book *Stride Toward Freedom*: "He who passively accepts evil is as much involved in it as he who helps to perpetrate it."

Civil Rights Gain Momentum in the 1950s

True civil rights advocates, such as Hubert Humphrey and Walter Mondale, were totally marginalized within the national Democratic Party. The momentum for civil rights legislation would come from the Republican Party, and it began in the 1950s with the election of Dwight David Eisenhower.

From the Compromise of 1877 to the election of Eisenhower in 1952, it could be argued that there was a great stalemate in the battle over civil rights. The South was still totally under the unconstitutional *de jure* racism of segregation and Jim Crow laws imposed by the ruling Democratic Party. The violent paramilitary arms of the Democratic Party were still a scourge to the freedom and safety of Negroes who failed to know their PLACE. In the North, the great urban centers remained governed by Democrat one-party political machines and *de facto* segregation and racism was as effective in oppressing Blacks as the *de jure* policies in the South.

As the twentieth century reached its midpoint, the mood of the nation began to change. A new class of civil rights activists rose, led by the charismatic Martin Luther King. The election of Eisenhower, the first Republican president in twenty years, gave the Republican Party increased power in pursuing its historic civil rights platform more aggressively. The power of the Democrat's racist southern bloc began to diminish.

Regional Council of Negro Leadership

Theodore Roosevelt Mason Howard was a surgeon and civil right activist. Like his namesake, he was a Republican and great admirer of Booker T. Washington. He believed that civil rights could best be achieved by a combination of protests and Negro successes in assimilating through education and ambition. He was a strong advocate of minority enterprise.

Throughout his life, he was a founder or participant in numerous civil rights organizations. In 1951, while living in Mississippi, he founded the Regional Council of Negro Leadership and called for a boycott of all gas stations that did not provide any bathroom facilities for Blacks. He distributed thousands of signs and bumper stickers saying, "Don't Buy Gas Where You Cannot Use the Restroom." Later, in 1955, he mounted a campaign against the White Citizens' Council when the racist group worked to deny credit to anyone, White or Black, supporting integration of Negro rights.

One of Howard's most important roles in civil rights advocacy was mentoring, befriending, encouraging, and supporting young civil rights activists—many of whom gained much greater recognition than Howard. His rallies would attract the biggest names in the civil rights movement, including such notables as US Supreme Court justice Thurgood Marshall, congressman Charles Diggs, Roy Wilkins of the NAACP, voting rights activist Fannie Lou Hamer, gospel singer Mahalia Jackson, and many more.

When fourteen-year-old Emmett Till was murdered in Mississippi in 1955, and local Democrat law enforcement officials showed little interest in finding the killers, Howard hired a private agency to investigate the case and protect potential witnesses. His involvement in the case made him a target of the Democrat violent hate groups, causing him to sleep with a Thompson submachine gun (Tommy gun) at his side.

Howard later moved to Chicago where he pursued both civil rights and a successful professional career. He became head of the (Black) National Medical Association and medical director of S. B. Fuller, a household products company owned by Samuel B. Fuller, one of the nation's wealthiest Black entrepreneurs. Like Howard, Fuller was also a dedicated Republican.

Howard was a founder of the Chicago League of Negro Voters, an organization designed to confront the racist Democrat political machine of Mayor Richard J. Daley. In 1958, Howard ran for Congress against the Democrats principle Black crony, congressman William Dawson—the leading architects of the scheme to replace constitutional civil rights for generational welfare dependency. His candidacy had little chance against the well-oiled and corrupt Democrat machine. Despite favorable publicity and the support of leading Black independents, the machine delivered 72 percent of the vote to Dawson—by hook or by crook.

Howard passed away in 1976.

The Election of 1952

The Great War was over but President Truman's bungled "containment policy" brought America into Korea as a "police action" that has never officially ended to this day. The economy was improving. Democrats retained their iron grip on the South and on most large cities—and the party's policies of segregation *de jure* and *de facto* were in full force. The former, however, was in its dying days. The election of 1952 was a turning point. Though eligible for reelection, Truman chose not to run.

As their standard bearer in 1952, the Democratic Party selected Illinois governor Adlai Stevenson, the grandson of Vice President Adlai Stevenson, who served in the second term of Grover Cleveland.

According to John Frederick Martin, author of *Civil Rights and the Crisis of Liberalism: The Democratic Party, 1945-1976*, Stevenson was favored over other Democrat contenders because of his more moderate views on civil rights, especially those of his chief rival Tennessee senator Estes Kefauver. Kefauver was not among the most rabid segregationists. He was described as lukewarm on civil rights at the time. He would later vote in favor of Eisenhower's 1957 and 1960 civil rights measures, although he consistently opposed full desegregation.

With the southern segregationist Democrats still a major power in the national party, they had enough influence to always have a southern segregationist on the national ticket. Stevenson chose Democrat segregationist senator from Alabama, John Sparkman, as his running mate. Sparkman was a dyed-in-the-wool southern gentleman who was devoted to the South, as was evident in his thesis on the 1894 campaign for governor of Alabama. The paper glorified former Confederate colonel William C. Oates.

Sparkman was one of 101 of southern Democrat congressional leaders who would later sign the Southern Manifesto, a challenge to the 1954 Supreme Court decision ordering racial integration of schools.

He voted "nay" on both the Eisenhower Civil Rights Act of 1957 and 1960 and was rewarded with the vice presidential nomination, which signaled the Democratic Party's continued tolerance of Black segregation and oppression in the south.

Republicans nominated "Ike" Eisenhower. Ike was arguably the most popular public figure in America. As the World War II commander of the Allied Army, he brought victory and peace to the world. He was virtually the preemptive candidate for the presidency. He was heavily courted by both parties, with Truman making a personal plea for Eisenhower to join the Democratic Party. Instead, he opted to accept the Republican nomination.

As a military man, Eisenhower had little record on civil rights other than his campaign statements. His one specific action took place near the end of World War II. As Supreme Commander, Eisenhower took the initial steps to integrate the military.

For vice president, Eisenhower selected California congressman Richard M. Nixon. Though Nixon gained his greatest fame in Congress as a Communist fighter, he had a strong record on civil rights—having supported virtually all civil rights legislation that came before Congress in his tenure. It was a record that won him the admiration and personal friendship of Martin Luther King.

The Platforms

The 1952 Republican platform contained a direct criticism of the Democratic Party's violation of civil rights. It charged that the Democrats had "arrogantly deprived our citizens of precious liberties by seizing powers never granted."

And in another section, it stated:

> We deplore the duplicity and insincerity of the Party in power in racial and religious matters. Although they have been in office as a Majority Party for many years, they have not kept nor do they intend to keep their promises.

In view of the large Black population of the nation's capital, the GOP support of voting rights was considered a civil rights issue. "We favor self-government and national suffrage for the residents of the Nation's Capital," the Republican platform stated.

Ignoring the plight under the prejudicial and violent Democratic Party policies against Black Americans in the south and the major cities, the Democrat platform continued to present itself as the party of human rights. At a time when schools in the South and in the major cities were strictly segregated, the education plank of the platform ignored that reality. It stated that "every American child, irrespective of color, national origin, economic status or place of residence should have every educational opportunity to develop his potentialities." But not in the same schools.

Perhaps the most audacious claim was the Civil Rights plank stated:

> The Democratic Party is committed to support and advance the individual rights and liberties of all Americans.

> Our country is founded on the proposition that all men are created equal. This means that all citizens are equal before the law and should enjoy equal political rights. They should have equal opportunities for education, for economic advancement, and for decent living conditions.

> We will continue our efforts to eradicate discrimination based on race, religion or national origin.

While the platform called for many positive future civil rights actions, it was no small irony that this same Democratic Party would function in the 1950s as the greatest opponent of and impediment to civil rights progress. Even in the regions where it enjoyed autonomous power, the Democratic Party continued to carry out some of the most outrageous and horrific activities in an attempt to maintain White superiority and racial segregation and oppression.

In terms of civil rights, the Democratic Party Platform of 1952 was nothing more than a continuation of the false narrative that began in the late 1800s. It was a case study in hypocrisy.

Election Results, 1952

The presidential campaign of 1952 ended twenty years of Democrat occupancy of the Oval Office. Credited with America's victory in World War II, and with a charismatic personality punctuated by his iconic smile, Eisenhower was handily elected as the thirty-fourth President of the United States. Both his slogans, "I Like Ike" and "It's Time for a Change," resonated with a public ready for peace and prosperity, and voters gave Eisenhower a landslide victory over Governor Stevenson and Senator Sparkman.

Ironically, the end of the Democratic Party control of the White House came in the first year that the nation went without a racial lynching since 1881.

Advocates of the later Nixon southern strategy theory fail to note the significance of the 1952 election, when a Republican candidate carried southern states for the first time since Hoover. Republican Dwight Eisenhower carried Florida, Texas, Tennessee, and Virginia. Of the nineteen presidential elections since 1880, this was only the fourth time a Republican presidential candidate carried any of the states in the solid Democrat South. This was the precursor to the eventual collapse of the Democratic Party's iron-fisted rule over the states of the old Confederacy.

Dwight David Eisenhower (1953–1961)

While progressive historians often cite the 1964 Civil Rights Act as the seminal moment that launched the modern civil rights movement, they ignore the dramatic role of Eisenhower and the Republican Party almost a decade earlier. It is irrefutable that the true modern civil rights movement was launched by Eisenhower.

Eisenhower was arguably the most pro-active civil rights president since Ulysses S. Grant. It was Eisenhower who dealt segregation its first fatal blows with his appointment of Earl Warren to the Supreme Court. Eisenhower advocated and signed the first civil rights legislation since Reconstruction. He backed his commitment by being the first president to send federal troops into southern states to enforce the Constitution and federal law since post-Civil War Reconstruction.

Nelson Rockefeller

While still only president-elect, Eisenhower had named New York Republican businessman and civil rights leader Nelson Rockefeller as chairman of an advisory committee on government organizations. Eisenhower implemented all thirteen of Rockefeller's proposals for reorganizing the federal government. Most notably, his work led to the creation of the Department of Health, Education and Welfare (HEW). One of the primary purposes of HEW was to address the plight of Negro Americans trapped in urban poverty since the Great Depression.

According to Richard Norton Smith in his book *On His Own Terms: A Life of Nelson Rockefeller*:

> Rockefeller achieved virtual total prohibition of discrimination in housing and places of public accommodation. He ... increased by nearly 50% the number of African Americans and Hispanics holding state jobs. ... He outlawed "blockbusting" as a means of artificially depressing housing values and banned discrimination in the sale of all forms of insurance. He established he first state human

rights commission in the nation and appointed Eleanor Roosevelt as its first chairman.

Department of Health, Education and Welfare

The concept of a cabinet-level department dedicated to education and welfare was first proposed by Republican president Warren G. Harding in 1923. It was taken up and enacted by Eisenhower early in his first term as part of his Reorganization Plan No. 1 of 1953. Under the law in those times, Eisenhower had the power to create the cabinet department without the action of Congress—although Congress could pass a resolution vetoing such action. The law was later changed to prevent presidents from creating such agencies and the Supreme Court declared the congressional veto to be unconstitutional. To head the new Department of Health, Education and Welfare (HEW), Eisenhower appointed Oveta Culp Hobby, the commanding officer of the Women's Army Corps.

Health, education, and welfare were, in many ways, key elements of the struggle for civil rights. HEW included the critically important Office for Civil Rights (OCR). Black civil rights leaders were virtually unanimous in their praise of Eisenhower's action.

Poverty and Oppression Move North

The Eisenhower years have generally been described as a time of peace and prosperity. This was certainly true of the nation as a whole. Poverty rates dropped, except among Black Americans languishing in the Democrat-controlled segregated South and the big cities in which the iconic Democrat political machines were exerting one-party rule. Poverty rates increased in the major metropolitan areas as southern Blacks moved to the northern cities in pursuit of better conditions and greater job opportunities. Instead, they were moving from one Democratic Party segregated stronghold to another—moving from *de jure* segregation to *de facto*. The PLACE for Negroes in the big, twentieth century, northern cities was only marginally better than the Old South. Perhaps the most significant improvement for the Black community was the reduction, although not the elimination, of vigilante violence.

Brown v. Board of Education, 1954

There can be no doubt that the most important Supreme Court civil rights case of the twentieth century was *Brown v. Board of Education of Topeka Kansas*. In *Brown*, the Supreme Court was again considering the doctrine of "separate but equal" that was established in 1898 in *Plessy v. Ferguson*.

Why the case dealt with Topeka, Kansas, has to do with the cleverness of the Supreme Court. They were facing similar cases in other states, including South Carolina, Delaware, and Virginia. The court combined all the cases and chose to lead off with the Kansas case to avoid making the decision appear to be simply a North-South issue.

Chief Justice Fred Vinson

In early debate, it seemed clear that at least four of the nine justices were leaning toward overturning the highly prejudicial *Plessy* decision. The main problem was Chief Justice Fred Vinson. Vinson was a racist and a supporter of the *Plessy* decision. Like all chief justices, he had enormous influence and power over the outcome of cases.

Vinson was also one of President Truman's closest friends. Truman initially appointed Vinson to be secretary of the treasury. When Truman decided not to seek another term as president, he tried unsuccessfully to convince Vinson to run. Truman most certainly was aware of Vinson's views on race and segregation when he appointed him chief justice.

In subsequent decisions, Vinson consistently supported the principle of "separate but equal" and the decision in *Plessy v. Ferguson*.

When *Brown v. Board of Education* was heard by the Supreme Court, Vinson used his influence as chief justice to have four of the justices question the wisdom of overturning *Plessy*. Vinson would likely have prevailed is keeping *Plessy* as the law of the land, but he died during deliberations. Had he lived longer there would have been no Earl Warren and no *Brown v. The School Board* decision for the foreseeable future.

In his SCOTUS Blog, California law professor Carlton Larson wrote:

> There's a pretty strong consensus that Chief Justice Fred Vinson was the worst Chief Justice of the twentieth century. The conventional view goes something like this: Vinson was a bumbling, incompetent political hack, an intellectual lightweight with minimal understanding of complex legal issues, a card-playing crony of Harry Truman who continued to advise Truman even after taking his seat on the Court, a reactionary with horrific instincts in key civil liberties cases, and, worst of all, a major obstacle to unanimity in Brown v. Board of Education. By this account, the best thing Vinson ever did was to die of a heart attack at precisely the right moment—in the middle of the Brown proceedings in 1953, thus allowing his successor, Chief Justice Earl Warren, to author a unanimous opinion invalidating racial segregation in public schools.

Earl Warren

Vinson's death gave President Eisenhower the opportunity to appoint a new chief justice. He chose Republican Earl Warren, the governor of California.

Warren did not reveal his views on *Brown v. Board of Education* during his confirmation hearings. He argued that it would be inappropriate to influence a case before sitting in judgment. While there was some validity to that argument, Warren was as much concerned at getting his nomination past the powerful southern Democrat senators who might have scuttled him if he came across as a civil rights advocate. Once on the Court, Warren made his views very clear.

Warren would lead the Court in a number of decisions that directly or indirectly affected the civil rights of African Americans. He did so, not always from technical legal arguments, but from his general sense that segregation was simply wrong.

Warren spent his first days on the Court meeting with each of the justices to persuade them to produce a unanimous decision to overturn *Plessy v. Ferguson.* He felt it was important for the Court to be clear so as not to have dissenting opinions to provide an opportunity for southern Democrats to seek a reversal in the future.

He succeeded in effectively using his power as chief justice to make history in a unanimous nine vote decision to begin the process of ending racial segregation in the Democrat southland.

Senator Kennedy

As a senator, John F. Kennedy continued his tradition of opposition to civil rights legislation. He said he supported *Brown v. Board of Education* but to most historians, his backing was not out of deep moral conviction. Rather than expressing all-out support for the principle involved, Kennedy accepted the decision by often saying it was now the "law of the land" and he was "obliged" to obey it. While many northern legislators were pressuring Washington to act, as the Supreme Court directed, "with all deliberate speed," Kennedy remained vague on implementation. In the book *John F. Kennedy: An Unfinished Life,* author Robert Dallek claimed Kennedy's devotion to civil rights always seemed "more political than moral."

Dwight Eisenhower

With *Brown v. Board of Education,* Eisenhower had the power to act definitively on civil rights. Among his first actions as president was ordering the District of Columbia schools to be integrated. It also paved the way for his 1957 and 1960 civil rights acts.

Southern Democrats Resist Desegregation

The Democrat response to *Brown v. Board of Education* was swift. A phalanx of southern Democrats—led by Virginia Senator Harry Byrd Sr.—united in opposition and pledged themselves to using every means possible, legal and otherwise, to defend their racist policies.

While *Brown v. Board of Education* was heralded as the end of school segregation, it was only the beginning of the end. It resulted in yet another round of civil disobediences, court challenges, dubious political tactics, and outright defiance by Democrat officials in the South—and the maintenance of *de facto* segregation in the northern cities.

The Stanley Plan of Virginia

As soon as the *Brown v. Board of Education* decision was handed down by the Supreme Court, Byrd launched a campaign to preserve segregated schools in his home state of Virginia. This initial effort was known as the Stanley Plan, named after the segregationist governor of Virginia.

Thomas Stanley was one of the most loyal members of Byrd's political machine. The Stanly Plan was a legislative package with five major provisions. Public schools would not be allowed to integrate. Any school district that chose to integrate would lose all state funding. Any school that integrated could be summarily closed by the governor. Finally, it repealed laws that allowed school districts to be sued.

Byrd was more than a United States senator. A onetime member of the Ku Klux Klan, Byrd was the boss of Virginia Democrat politics for most of his lifetime. In a 1965 obituary, *Time* magazine noted that "While decrying federal 'paternalism,' Byrd ruled his own domain with a feudalistic hand."

With the senior Byrd in the United States senate and Harry Byrd, Jr. in the state legislature, the father and son team coordinated a campaign to preserve segregated schools in their home state of Virginia. The tactics and strategies they developed became the game plan throughout the segregated Democrat states of the South for the next ten years.

The Southern Manifesto and Massive Resistance Movement

As a supplement to the Stanley Plan, Byrd senior drafted a harsh response to the Supreme Court's decision entitled the "Declaration of Constitutional Principles." It became more popularly known as the Southern Manifesto. It stated:

> The unwarranted decision of the Supreme Court in the public school cases is now bearing the fruit always produced when men substitute naked power for established law.

> The Founding Fathers gave us a Constitution of checks and balances because they realized the inescapable lesson of history that no man or group of men can be safely entrusted with unlimited power. They framed this Constitution with its provisions for change by amendment in order to secure the fundamentals of government against the dangers of temporary popular passion or the personal predilections of public officeholders.

> We regard the decision of the Supreme Court in the school cases as clear abuse of judicial power. It climaxes a trend in the Federal judiciary undertaking to legislate, in derogation of the authority of Congress, and to encroach upon the reserved rights of the states and the people.

> The original Constitutional does not mention education. Neither does the Fourteenth Amendment nor any other amendment. The debates preceding the submission of the Fourteenth Amendment clearly show that there was no intent that it should affect the systems of education maintained by the states.

> The very Congress which proposed the amendment subsequently provided for segregated schools in the District of Columbia.

When the amendment was adopted in 1868, there were thirty-seven states of the Union. Every one of the twenty-six states that had any substantial racial differences among its people either approved the operation of segregated schools already in existence or subsequently established such schools by action of the same law-making body which considered the Fourteenth Amendment.

As admitted by the Supreme Court in the public school case (Brown v. Board of Education), the doctrine of separate but equal schools "apparently originated in Roberts v. City of Boston (1849), upholding school segregation against attack as being violative of a state constitutional guarantee of equality." This constitutional doctrine began in the North-not in the South-and it was followed not only in Massachusetts but in Connecticut, New York, Illinois, Indiana, Michigan, Minnesota, New Jersey, Ohio, Pennsylvania and other northern states until they, exercising their rights as states through the constitutional processes of local self-government, changed their school systems.

In the case of Plessy v. Ferguson in 1896 the Supreme Court expressly declared that under the Fourteenth Amendment no person was denied any of his rights if the states provided separate but equal public facilities. This decision has been followed in many other cases. It is notable that the Supreme Court, speaking through Chief Justice Taft, a former President of the United States, unanimously declared in 1927 in Lum v. Rice that the "separate but equal" principle is " within the discretion of the state in regulating its public schools and does not conflict with the Fourteenth Amendment."

This interpretation, restated time and again, became a part of the life of the people of many of the states and confirmed their habits, customs, traditions and way of life. It is founded on elemental humanity and common sense, for parents should not be deprived by Government of the right to direct the lives and education of their own children.

Though there has been no constitutional amendment or act of Congress changing this established legal principle almost a century old, the Supreme Court of the United States, with no legal basis for such action, undertook to exercise their naked judicial power and substituted their personal political and social ideas for the established law of the land.

This unwarranted exercise of power by the court, contrary to the Constitution, is creating chaos and confusion in the states principally affected. It is destroying the amicable relations between the white and Negro races that have been created through ninety years of patient effort by the good people of both races. It has planted hatred and suspicion where there has been heretofore friendship and understanding.

Without regard to the consent of the governed, outside agitators are threatening immediate and revolutionary changes in our public school systems. If done, this is certain to destroy the system of public education in some of the states.

With the gravest concern for the explosive and dangerous condition created by this decision and inflamed by outside meddlers.

We reaffirm our reliance on the Constitution as the fundamental law of the land.

We decry the Supreme Court's encroachments on rights reserved to the states and to the people, contrary to established law and to the Constitution.

We commend the motives of those states which have declared the intention to resist forced integration by any lawful means.

We appeal to the states and people who are not directly affected by these decisions to consider the constitutional principles involved against the time when they too, on issues vital to them, may be the victims of judicial encroachment.

Even though we constitute a minority in the present congress, we have full faith that a majority of the American people believe in the dual system of government which has enabled us to achieve our greatness and will in time demand that the reserved rights of the states and of the people be made secure against judicial usurpation.

We pledge ourselves to use all lawful means to bring about a reversal of this decision which is contrary to the Constitution and to prevent the use of force in its implementation.

In this trying period, as we all seek to right this wrong, we appeal to our people not to be provoked by the agitators and troublemakers invading our states and to scrupulously refrain from disorder and lawless acts.

The manifesto was signed by nineteen members of the United States Senate. To implement the manifesto Byrd mobilized his southern Democrat colleagues in a movement of "massive resistance." Signatories to the manifesto in the United States Senate were all Democrats from southern states. They included some of the most infamous names of racial intolerance. Those senators signing the manifesto (by state) were:

John Sparkman (D) and Lister Hill (D) of Alabama
J. W. Fulbright (D) and John L. McClellan (D) of Arkansas
George A. Smathers (D) and Spessard L. Holland (D) of Florida
Walter F. George (D) and Richard B. Russell (D) of Georgia
Allen J. Ellender (D) and Russell B. Long (D) of Louisiana
John Stennis (D) and James O. Eastland (D) of Mississippi
 Sam J. Ervin Jr. (D) and W. Kerr Scott (D) of North Carolina
Strom Thurmond (D) and Olin D. Johnston (D) of South Carolina
Price Daniel (D) of Texas
Harry F. Byrd (D) and A. Willis Robertson (D) of Virginia

Of the nine southern segregated states, only one United States Senator, Ralph Yarbrough of Texas, did not sign the manifesto. The signers represented the hard-core cabal of Democrat racists in Congress, but it was by no means a complete list of legislators accepting segregation and inequality. Like their congressional colleagues in the Senate, southern House Democrats lined up to sign the manifesto, including some of the chamber's most prominent and powerful members. Altogether, there were seventy-seven signers in the House from eleven southern states.

The Massive Resistance

As a follow-up to his Southern Manifesto, Byrd set out to organize uniform resistance to *Brown v. Board of Education* throughout the Democrat southland. In announcing his plan, Byrd said, "If we can organize the Southern States for massive resistance to [*Brown v. The Board of Education*, I think that in time the rest of the country will realize that racial integration is not going to be accepted in the South."

The Massive Resistance Movement was being rolled out just as the 1956 presidential election season was commencing. It would create the greatest civil rights challenges and opportunities for the White House. Far from being intimidated by Byrd's plan, Eisenhower and the congressional Republicans were prepared to push back—and they did with legislation and federal troops.

Democrats' Racist Establishment

In terms of civil rights implementation, the Democratic Party was controlled by a cabal of racist governors in the south, and racist Democrat political machines in the North that rose to prominence in the 1930s and 1940s. The list includes some of the most infamous personalities associated with racial prejudice. Their negative influence in thwarting civil rights progress extended into the 1970s and, in some cases, beyond. They are the election officials that shaped the Democratic Party in the mid-twentieth century and made it the nation's most enduring and successful promoter of White supremacy and institutional racism.

Those highlighted here are merely a small sampling of the most infamous among the thousands of government officials, vigilantes, and community supporters who made up the Democratic Party's racist hierarchy and infrastructure. It would take more pages than this book could contain just to list the names of the local, state, and national racist Democrat officeholders since the mid-1950s.

The Senate's Racist Caucus

In addition to Harry Byrd Sr. and Jr., the United States Senate had a powerful group of segregationist members. Due to their actions and influence, a few deserve a deeper look at their careers.

Robert C. Byrd of West Virginia

Robert C. Byrd of West Virginia served fifty-seven years in Congress (from 1953 to 1959 as a representative and from 1959 to 2010 as a senator). At the time of his death, he was the longest serving member of the Senate in American history. He out-survived and out-served all of his old southern racist Democrat colleagues.

Byrd was a member of the Ku Klux Klan—the last known Klan member to serve in Congress. He was not only a member of the Klan but founded his own chapter in Crab Orchard, West Virginia, in the early 1940s. He served as Kleagle and Exalted Cyclops.

In his later years, Byrd often downplayed his role in the Klan, understating his years of participation. In early campaigns, Byrd claimed to have joined in 1942 and quit in 1943, with no further involvement in the Klan. He said:

> After about a year, I became disinterested, quit paying my dues, and
> dropped my membership in the organization. During the nine years
> that have followed, I have never been interested in the Klan.

He was lying when he expressed his disinterest in the Klan. As late as 1946, he wrote to the Imperial Wizard that "The Klan is needed today as never before, and I am anxious to see its rebirth here in West Virginia." With the help of the Klan, Byrd ran the most powerful politic machine in the state, which was based on the KKK's violent opposition to Black voting rights.

When campaigning in his first bid for the West Virginia United States Senate seat in 1958, Byrd gave speeches in defense of the KKK, saying that many of the terrible acts attributed to the Klan were done by others. Byrd followed the racist tradition of calling political enemies "niggers" even if they were White.

Byrd Can't Stop Loving the Klan

Over the years, Byrd described the Klan in the most benign manner, as a group of upstanding businessmen. He incredulously denied that the Klan was ever racist, anti-Jew, or anti-Catholic.

He ignored a history of lynchings despite the fact that the Tuskegee University archives documented more than twenty-eight Negro lynchings in West Virginia from the late 1880s to the early 1900s—despite the state's low Black population. Before his involvement in the Klan, Byrd would most certainly have known of two documented lynchings that occurred in West Virginia in 1931. These horrific acts did not dissuade Byrd from organizing a local chapter of the KKK, and spending years praising the organization.

According to Eric Pianin, writing for the *Washington Post* in 2005, "By the time Byrd began organizing for the Klan ... the organization had largely morphed into a money-making fraternal organization that was virulently anti-Black, anti-Catholic and anti-Semitic."

In Byrd's attempt to explain his involvement with the Klan in his autobiography, *Child of the Appalachian Coalfields,* he inadvertently demonstrated just how deeply the terrorist Klan had penetrated the Democratic Party's political, civic, and social structure. He wrote:

> In those days, as I was told, many of the upstanding people in the communities belonged to the Klan. Doctors, lawyers, clergymen, judges, businesspeople, and laborers—including women—were members of

the organization. Many of the 'best' people were members—even senators and other high officials. It was with such background impressions, therefore, that I sought to become a member of the KKK.

Byrd Opposes Integrating the Armed Forces

Just prior to launching his political career, Byrd expressed his anger and dismay with Truman's plan to integrate the armed services. In a 1945 letter to the Senate's most outspoken and outrageous racist at the time, Democrat Theodore Bilbo of Mississippi, Byrd wrote that "Rather I should die a thousand times, and see old Glory trampled in the dirt never to rise again, than to see this beloved land of ours become degraded by race mongrels, a throwback to the blackest specimen from the wilds."

In his last years in the Senate, Byrd explained away his long history of animosity toward Negros by saying it was due to "that southern atmosphere in which I grew up, with all of its prejudices and its feelings." Interestingly, he blamed his racism on that "southern atmosphere" that was the product of his own Democratic Party's policies.

Opposition to the 1964 Civil Rights Act

Despite his refurbished image, Byrd revealed some of that "southern atmosphere" in a 2001 television interview when he said:

> There are white niggers. I've seen a lot of white niggers in my time, if you want to use that word. We just need to work together to make our country a better country, and I'd just as soon quit talking about it so much.

Proving again that racial prejudice is no obstacle to advancement in the Democratic Party, Byrd was honored by his Democrat Senate colleagues by twice electing him Senate Majority Leader. Upon his death in 2010, Democrats lauded him as one of America's greatest senators, referring to him as "the conscience of the Senate."

Then Secretary of State Hillary Clinton was effusive in her eulogy of Byrd, completely disregarding his racist past. She called him her "friend and mentor" and described him as "a man surpassing eloquence and nobility." She went on to say: "He was not only [the Senate's] longest serving member. He was its heart, its soul, and its historian."

James Eastland of Mississippi

James Eastland was appointed to the Senate after the death of Senator Pat Harrison. He served from 1943 to 1978. Eastland was vehemently pro-segregation and a firm believer in the inferiority of Negroes. In stating his support for segregation on the floor of the Senate, he said:

> The Southern institution of racial segregation or racial separation was the correct, self-evident truth which arose from the chaos and confusion of the Reconstruction period. Separation promotes racial harmony. It permits each race to follow its own pursuits, and its own civilization. Segregation is not discrimination… Mr. President, it is the law of nature, it is the law of God, that every race has both the right and the duty to perpetuate itself. All free men have the right to associate exclusively with members of their own race, free from governmental interference, if they so desire.

Like many southern politicians, Eastland put a soft romantic spin on segregation. He denied the harsh conditions and the violence, and the existence of the Ku Klux Klan in Mississippi. When three civil rights volunteers—James Chaney, Andrew Goodman, and Michael Schwerner—disappeared, Eastland refused to acknowledge the obvious. Rather, he called their disappearance a hoax.

In a private conversation with President Johnson, Eastland responded to the president's concern.

Johnson: "Jim, we've got three kids missing down there. What can I do about it?"

Eastland: "Well, I don't know. I don't believe there's … I don't believe there's three missing."

Johnson: "We've got their parents down here."

Eastland: "I believe it's a publicity stunt."

The three civil rights activists were later found brutally murdered. In response to the *Brown v. Board of Education* decision, Eastland said:

> On May 17, 1954, the Constitution of the United States was destroyed because of the Supreme Court's decision. You are not obliged to obey the decisions of any court which are plainly fraudulent sociological considerations.

Recognizing Eastland's penchant for blaming many problems on Black criminality and integration, Johnson once said: "Jim Eastland could be standing right in the middle of the worst Mississippi flood ever known, and he'd say the niggers caused it."

In 1956, and despite his staunch racist opinions, Senate Democrats named Eastland to the powerful Judiciary Committee, which would handle virtually all civil rights legislation. As chairman of the Senate Judiciary Committee, Eastland could block civil rights legislation from getting a floor vote.

He joined other southern Democrat senators in attempting to head off the confirmation of Thurgood Marshall as the first Black to serve on the Supreme Court. They failed. He had hoped to kill the 1964 Civil Rights Act in committee, and if that failed, defeat it by filibuster. Because of the overwhelming support of Republican senators led by Minority Leader Senator Everett Dirksen, of Illinois, the filibuster was ended, and the bill enacted into law.

Allen J. Ellender of Louisiana

Allen J. Ellender, who served in the Senate from 1937 to 1972, was among the signers of the Southern Manifesto and was considered as among the more zealous segregationist senators. He maintained his opposition throughout his life, voting against the Civil Rights Act introduced in the Senate.

Like so many hard-core racist Democrats, Ellender had no problem winning the respect and patronage of his colleagues. Just before he died during his 1972 reelection campaign, he was elected to the post of president pro temp of the Senate by his fellow Democrats.

Sam Ervin Jr. of North Carolina

Senator Sam Ervin, Jr. was a stereotypical southern lawyer who liked to spin humorous yarns. Though by all standards a highly professional lawyer, he self-effacingly characterized himself as a simple country boy. Because of his scholarly approach, Ervin served the southern Democrats as their constitutional advisor. He was an eloquent defender of the Democrats policy of segregation and Jim Crow voting requirements.

The Broadus Miller Case

In 1927, while serving as counsel for Burke County, North Carolina, a Black man named Broadus Miller was being sought for allegedly killing a White teenage girl. A manhunt was formed by sheriff deputies and included a volunteer citizen posse.

During the search for Broadus, White public ire was aroused by prominent newspaper woman Beatrice Cobb, who published a succession of articles demonizing Broadus. He was finally found in a wooded area near the village of Linville Falls. Rather than being arrested, he was gunned down in cold blood by a member of the posse.

Ervin defended the killer by invoking a law that allowed any private citizen to summarily kill anyone deemed to be an outlaw. Following the murder, Broadus' body was returned to Burke County and publicly displayed in front of the courthouse—an act of public humiliation that was often inflicted on Negroes in the Old South.

Ervin won the case and subsequently served on the North Carolina judiciary, rising to associate justice of the state's supreme court. From there, he was appointed to the US Senate seat of Clyde Hoey, who had died. Hoey would gain some notoriety for opposing annexing of Hawaii as a state because there were too few White people.

Ervin used his legal skills to assist in the drafting of the Southern Manifesto and was a key promoter of the Massive Resistance Movement against school desegregation. In many ways, he gave the racist actions of the southern Democrats an aura of intellectual credibility and constitutional legitimacy. He believed that segregation was a matter of states' rights and that the equal justice clause of the Constitution applied only to White people.

Ervin came to public attention during the impeachment hearings of President Nixon.

J. William Fulbright of Arkansas

J. William Fulbright, who served in the Senate from 1945 to 1974, was another example of how the national leaders of the Democratic Party saw no hypocrisy in praising and promoting the most racist public officials within their ranks. Fulbright was among those signing the Southern Manifesto and a staunch foe of civil rights. Yet, he is among the more honored and respected Democrats in America—praised by his party, fawning historians, and the public press.

His name was attached to the legislation he introduced, which created one of the most famous student exchange programs in the nation. A Fulbright Scholarship is one of the most coveted prizes in academia, which is ironic in that academia tends to judge harshly those with racist pasts.

In 1995, President Bill Clinton, who interned with Fulbright, offered unabashed praise of his fellow Arkansan in a eulogy:

> We come to celebrate and give thanks for the remarkable life of J. William Fulbright, a life that changed our country and our world forever and for the better. . . . In the work he did, the words he spoke and the life he lived, Bill Fulbright stood against the twentieth century's most destructive forces and fought to advance its brightest hopes.

It is not clear what Clinton meant by standing up to "the twentieth century's most destructive forces" in view of Fulbright's standing up *for* segregation, Jim Crow and Black oppression. It is hard to argue that those were not among the leading destructive forces in America. Fulbright was not standing against destructive forces when he participated in the filibuster of the 1964 Civil Rights Bill.

Fulbright was both a mentor and father figure to Bill Clinton and a highly respected statesman in the eyes of Hillary Clinton—so much so that she associated her own exchange program with the racist Senator.

According to the Fulbright U.S. Student Program's website:

> The Bureau of Educational and Cultural Affairs (ECA) of the U.S. Department of State inaugurated the J. William Fulbright – Hillary Rodham Clinton Fellowship in academic year 2012-13. Initially titled the Fulbright Public Policy Fellowship, the award was renamed to honour former Secretary of State Hillary Rodham Clinton for her dedication to public service and role in the program's creation.

Fulbright is another example of the Democratic Party's tradition of sanitizing the reputations of some of its most infamous members.

Russell B. Long of Louisiana

Russell B. Long, another signer of the Southern Manifesto and supporter of Massive Resistance to school desegregation, was a member of the powerful Long dynasty in Louisiana. Smathers served in the Senate from 1948 to 1987. Both his father and mother had preceded him in the US Senate. His father was the flamboyant populist Louisiana governor and senator who was assassinated shortly after announcing his plan to run for president.

Long despised the Warren Court and referred to its majority who generally sided with criminal and civil rights plaintiffs as the "dirty five." He accused the Court of provoking hostilities between Whites and Blacks and undertook efforts to limit Supreme Court justices to twelve-year terms.

His racist positions did not bother Democrat leadership. Just a year after Russell voted against the 1964 Civil Rights Act, his fellow Democrats elected him assistant majority leader. He was also chairman of the powerful Finance Committee.

Even as he was honored with praise and position by his fellow Democrats, he retained his racist views. When President Johnson signed the 1964 Civil Rights Act, Russell joined senators Herman Talmadge and Richard Russell (no relation), both of Georgia, and others in boycotting the 1964 Democrat National Convention in protest.

Long retired from the Senate in 1987 after serving for thirty-nine years. His presence in the Senate through most of the 1980s is another example that refutes the narrative that President Nixon engineered a GOP takeover of the South with a racist southern strategy in 1968. The diminishing racist voters in the South still had their champions in the likes of Russell Long years after Nixon left office.

John L. McClellan of Arkansas

John L. McClellan, who served in the Senate from 1943 to 1977, was a signer of the Southern Manifesto and supporter of the Massive Resistance. He also voted against the Republican anti-lynching legislation and vehemently opposed President Eisenhower's use of federal troops to integrate Central High School in Little Rock.

He opposed the use of force by the federal government to enforce integration, saying "I believe it to be without authority of law. I am very apprehensive that such action may precipitate more trouble than it will prevent."

Encyclopedia.com reported that McClellan broke with President Truman over the civil rights language in the Democrats' 1948 platform:

> By the time of the 1948 elections, however, McClellan had become so disenchanted with the liberal program of the Harry S. Truman administration and by the civil rights plank of the Democratic Party that he declared himself an Independent Democrat and handily won reelection to the Senate.

Richard Russell of Georgia

Like so many hard-core racists, Senator Richard Russell of Georgia was an honored and respected Democrat leader. He served in the Senate from 1933 to 1971. His service in "the world's most deliberative body" did not end with his being voted out of office by the rise of more tolerant voters in Georgia, but by his death.

Not only were Russell's racist views tolerated by the greater Democratic Party, but he also became the president pro tempore of the Senate. After his passing, one of the three Senate office buildings was named in his honor. The two other Senate office buildings were named after civil rights advocates, Democrat senator Phil Hart of Michigan and Republican senator Everett Dirksen of Illinois.

Russell was one of the primary authors of the Southern Manifesto, calling for massive resistance to the *Brown v. Board of Education* desegregation decision. Progressive Michael Tomasky, writing in *The Daily Beast* in 2016, said this of Russell:

> He opposed every piece of civil rights legislation that came his way. In fact, he had participated in his first anti-civil rights filibuster the year before [the] 1936 election, when he helped block an anti-lynching law. He helped block another anti-lynching law in 1938.

In one campaign, Russell expressed his White supremacy views to the people of Georgia in the boldest of terms. He said:

> As one who was born and reared in the atmosphere of the Old South, with six generations of my forebears now resting beneath Southern soil, I am willing to go as far and make as great a sacrifice to preserve and ensure White supremacy in the social, economic, and political life of our state as any man who lives within her borders.

Though he would later soften his language, his actions in the Senate continued to express his segregationist, White supremacist views.

In his article "Why Does the Senate Honor a White Supremacist? It's Time to Ditch Richard Russell for Bob Dole," Tomasky concluded:

> It's no longer forgivable … that one of only three Senate office buildings has to bear his name. … Sorry, a racist who spent 30 years making sure Black children went to inferior schools and Black adults couldn't vote doesn't deserve to be in their [Senators Hart's and Dirksen's] company. The Senate must change the name.

In a spirit of bipartisanship, Tomasky suggest that the building be renamed after either Minnesota Democrat senator Hubert Humphrey or Republican senator Robert Dole—both courageous advocates of civil rights. The main difference was that Doles' vote in favor of civil rights legislation was consistent with the Republicans in Congress, while Humphrey had caused the Dixiecrat exodus in 1948 and had to work against Democrat filibusters and minimal support from his own party.

In addition to the Senate office building, Russell was honored with a postage stamp in 1981. His name is on the federal building in Atlanta, as well as on numerous streets, airports, university halls and schools throughout the state. His statue is on the Capitol grounds in Atlanta.

George Smathers of Florida

In 1950, George Smathers was urged by President Truman to run in the Florida Democrat primary against incumbent senator Claude Pepper, a moderate southern Democrat who had led an effort to dump Truman as the presidential nominee in 1948. Smathers served in the Senate from 1951 to 1969.

It was alleged that Smathers appealed to the uneducated backwater residents using benign words but making them sound bad. *Time* magazine reported in the 1950 article "FLORIDA: Anything Goes" this quote of Smathers':

> Are you aware that Claude Pepper is known all over Washington as a shameless extrovert? Not only that, but this man is reliably reported to practice nepotism with his sister-in-law, he has a brother who is a known homo sapien, and he has a sister who was once a thespian in wicked New York. Worst of all, it is an established fact that Mr. Pepper, before his marriage, habitually practiced celibacy.

Whether the reports were apocryphal or not, Smathers offered the enormous sum of $10,000 to anyone who could produce any proof that he had made such statements. No one ever claimed the bounty, but the legend has endured.

In terms of civil rights, however, Smathers was a typical southern segregationist Democrat. He lambasted the Supreme Court for the *Brown v. Board of Education* decision and opposed the appointment of Thurgood Marshall as the first Black justice of the Court. He signed the Southern Manifesto and participated in the Massive Resistance movement to block school desegregation.

Associated Press's 2007 obituary of the ninety-three-year-old Democrat claimed that "Early in his career he was considered a moderate, but by the time he left office in 1969, he had a tarnished legacy as an opponent of civil rights."

John Sparkman of Alabama

John Sparkman, who served in the Senate from 1946 to 1979, grew up in rural Alabama during a time of raging racism. His father was a tenant farmer and deputy sheriff. As in most of Alabama in those days, sheriffs and their deputies were among the most feared enforcers of the southern Democrats' apartheid policies. He signed the Southern Manifesto and supported the Massive Resistance Movement.

Despite his long racist history, Sparkman was chosen by Democrat presidential candidate Adlai Stevenson to be his running mate in 1952. However, signing the Southern Manifesto was a step too far. Stevenson dropped Sparkman as his running mate in his second presidential campaign in 1956, replacing him with US Senator Estes Kefauver of Tennessee, a southerner who had not signed the Southern Manifesto.

Sparkman summed his view on segregation and voting rights in his attack on the Civil Rights Commission. He said:

> The Civil Rights Commission should never have been brought into existence. It has been the most prejudiced in its viewpoint and has fomented trouble and racial disturbance since its inception. It should be abolished, not extended.

Senator John Stennis of Mississippi

John Stennis was a United States Senator from Mississippi from 1947 to 1989. He succeeded Theodore G. Bilbo, previously noted as one of the most outrageous racists in post-Civil War history.

Stennis was part of the southern Democrat bloc that thwarted civil rights legislation in the 1940s to the mid-1960s. Like his Dixie Democrat colleagues, Stennis voted against all the major civil rights legislation and against the bill creating the Martin Luther King national holiday. He signed the Southern Manifesto and embraced the Massive Resistance following the *Brown v. Board of Education* decision by the Supreme Court.

Early in his law career, Stennis prosecuted three Black sharecroppers who were beaten and tortured into confessing to a murder that they did not commit. The conviction was overturned by the United States Supreme Court in *Brown v. Mississippi,* which banned confessions gained through torture. The transcript of the trail clearly demonstrated that Stennis was aware of the torture.

In the 2007 *The Atlantic* article "The White Supremacist Caucus," Matthew Yglesias wrote: "Having gained a reputation in the 1930s as the kind of guy who didn't mind torturing confessions out of Black defendants, Stennis was a natural to succeed Bilbo in the Senate."

Although one of the Senate's most racist members, the Democrats elevated him to the prestigious position of president pro tempore in his final years in office. He was only one of two members of Congress to have a Navy ship named in their honor. Among his Democrat Senate colleagues Stennis was known ironically as Mr. Integrity.

Stennis continued to be nominated and reelected by the Democratic voters of Mississippi for twenty years after the 1964 Civil Rights Act. His hold on the racist vote tends to refute the claim that southern GOP victories were based on the votes of the diehard segregationists. He retired in 1989 and was the last Democrat to serve Mississippi in the United States Senate.

James Strom Thurmond of South Carolina

Strom Thurmond was the oldest person ever to serve in Congress, retiring shortly after his one hundredth birthday. He served in the Senate from 1956 to 2003. He was the longest serving member of the Senate, until fellow southern Democrat, Harry Byrd, surpassed Thurmond's forty-eight-year run.

Thurmond was a highly decorated war hero. He joined the service in 1942 and landed in Normandy by glider at the age of forty-two.

Among the powerful southern segregationists, the story of Strom Thurmond is the most complex and convoluted. While some elements of Thurmond's career fit with his southern Democrat colleagues, other things did not.

As governor of South Carolina, from 1947 to 1951, Thurmond was considered a racial moderate and a bit of a reformer. While he supported segregation, he truly believed that it should be as equal as possible. He did not believe that Blacks were inferior and did not have a youthful history of violence against Blacks as was so common among many Democrats who assumed high office in the South. He spoke out against violence and was never a member or a supporter of the Ku Klux Klan. As governor, he supported a range of equal rights for Blacks, and provided funding for Black schools.

Thurmond hired more Black staff workers than many of his northern liberal Democrat counterparts. He promoted Blacks to positions of power in government. He supported the bill in support of the Martin Luther King national holiday.

While such actions suggest that Thurmond was not the worst of the southern Democrats, he was still a segregationist. He ran for president on a racist platform. He claimed, and the record shows, that Thurmond, like several other long-time segregationists, gave up his most extreme prejudicial feelings and rhetoric in later life.

The Willie Earle Case

Thurmond's relatively moderate racial credentials among southern Democrats were reinforced when he pressured local authorities to arrest those responsible for the lynching of Willie Earle, who was believed to be the last passenger picked up by cab driver Thomas Brown.

Brown was found mortally wounded next to his cab. Before justice could be served, a group of mostly cab drivers forced the jailer at gun point to hand over Earle, which he did without protest. Earle was beaten, lynched, and shot in the head.

Under pressure from Thurmond, thirty-one men were put on trial. While most admitted complicity in the lynching, they blamed each other for the actual murder. As was the tradition in the South, the all-White jury found them all not guilty. Though the perpetrators were never punished, the American Civil Liberties Union (ACLU) and the NAACP both expressed their gratitude to Thurmond for his extraordinary efforts in pursuing the case.

The Ellie Mae Washington-Williams Story

Not since slave owner Thomas Jefferson has there been so much controversy over an interracial relationship between a White political aristocrat and a Black domestic.

It was only after his death at the age of one hundred that it was publicly revealed that this one-time staunch segregationist had a prolonged romantic relationship with a Black domestic in the Thurmond household. He was twenty-two and she was sixteen when the relationship commenced. It resulted in the birth of a baby girl, Essie Mae Washington-Williams.

Though the liaison and offspring were kept secret, Thurmond maintained a lifelong relationship with his mistress and his daughter. He provided financial support, including paying for the daughter's college education. They would occasionally meet in his office or at other locations. Although they never dined together in public, Thurmond never denied his fatherhood. Her name is included along with Thurmond's other children on the senator's memorial in Columbia, the South Carolina state capital.

In her book, *Dear Senator: A Memoir by the Daughter of Strom Thurmond,* Washington-Williams said that she loved her father. "He was very good to us," she wrote. She did not consider him to be a racist despite his feeling about segregation.

Upon hearing of the early death of Washington-Williams' mother at the age of thirty-eight, the daughter said, "tears filled his [Thurmond's] eyes." She quotes Thurmond as saying, "My God, what a terrible thing. I truly cared for that woman."

It is difficult to imagine the old racist Thurmond joining the pro-civil rights Republican Party as he did in 1964. Ironically, as a Republican, Thurmond was vilified by Democrat leaders even as they named buildings and streets, and erected statues, honoring the likes of Talmadge, Russell, Tillman, and Stennis.

Democrat Racist Governors of the 1960s

Eugene Talmadge of Georgia

For more than half a century, the Talmadge family dominated Georgia politics. Starting in 1932, Eugene Talmadge was elected to four terms as governor, but only served three since he died prior to his inauguration to the fourth term. Even by southern Democrat standards, Talmadge was an extreme and violent White supremacist.

"It's fair to say," said University of Georgia history professor Robert Pratt, "he's one of the most virulently racist governors the state has ever had," as reported in the 2007 NBC News article "Ex-governor investigated in 1946 lynchings."

When the dean of the University Georgia, Walter Cocking, proposed the admission of Black students, Talmadge called for his removal. When the board of regents declined, the governor replaced members of the board and Cocking was removed. The university was stripped of its accreditation because of Talmadge's interference.

The Incident at Moore's Ford Bridge

While most southern Democrat leaders were circumspect regarding their support for KKK-style terrorism and lynching, Talmadge was much more open. Like Woodrow Wilson, Talmadge publicly expressed his support of the Klan.

One of the most glaring examples of his direct support of violence against Negroes had to do with the lynching of two married couples—Roger and Dorothy Malcom and George and Mae Murray Dorsey—at Moore's Ford Bridge in Monroe, Georgia during the 1946 gubernatorial campaign. Dorothy Malcom was seven months pregnant at the time.

Roger Malcom had been accused of stabbing a White farmer during a fight. There were rumors that George Dorsey, a United States Army veteran, was romantically involved with a White woman. Though not illegal, it was tantamount to a death sentence by the KKK and other Democrat terrorist groups.

A White farmer, Loy Harrison, paid $600 to bail Malcom out of the county jail. He was driving both couples back home when a group of White citizens surrounded the car and removed the Black occupants. They were strung up to a tree and then shot to death. Harrison told the FBI agent sent in to investigate the murders that he could not identify any of the perpetrators even though they were not masked. The Black citizens were equally silent out of fear of retribution, with one of them telling the FBI that they were all warned not to talk.

FBI agents were immediately suspicious that Talmadge had played an indirect role in the murders. He was in a very tough race and needed the support of the White voters of Monroe. In examining the case, Professor Pratt said: "I'm not surprised ... historians over the years have concluded the violently racist tone of his [Talmadge's] 1946 campaign may have been indirectly responsible for the violence that came at Moore's Ford."

Talmadge's role was much more active than his campaign rhetoric. Per the FBI, Talmadge personally met with George Hester, the brother of the famer who had been stabbed. According to an unidentified witness, Talmadge had offered immunity to anyone involve in "taking care of" the Negroes. No charges were ever brought against any of the fifty-five suspects identified by the FBI, including a number of state employees known to the governor.

The possibility of Tallmadge's involvement was never in the official FBI report, but it was brought to FBI Director J. Edgar Hoover's attention in a letter indicating that the information "may be of some future interest."

In his final run for governor in 1946, Eugene Talmadge was reelected on a totally racist campaign. His main issue was opposition to the United States Supreme Court's *Smith v. Allwright* decision, which ruled the all-White Democrat primary elections were unconstitutional.

Talmadge was mortally ill even before the election. Anticipating that he may not survive to the inauguration day, his people noted that in the event of his death, the state legislature would select the governor from the second and third place candidates. Since Talmadge was running unopposed, they surreptitiously conducted a write-in campaign for his son Herman. The strategy did not work, but Herman was elected later, in a 1948 special election.

Like Richard Russell, Eugene Talmadge is honored with a statue on the Georgia state capitol grounds, and his name is on a key bridge over the

Savannah River. Efforts to have his name removed from the bridge have been unsuccessful, so far.

Herman Talmadge of Georgia

Having been elected governor in the special election of 1948, Democrat Herman Talmadge—son of Eugene—was reelected to a full term in 1950. Barred from seeking a third time, Talmadge ran and was elected to the United States Senate in 1956. In that campaign, Talmadge elevated his racism to religious belief when he said: ''God advocates segregation.''

Talmadge had signed the Southern Manifesto and was part of the Massive Resistance Movement against school desegregation. Of school desegregation, Talmadge said: "There aren't enough troops in the whole United States to make the White people of this state send their children to school with colored children."

In its 2002 obituary, *The New York Times* described Herman Talmadge as "an old-fashioned Southern populist who built schools as governor of Georgia and then called for stopping desegregation by closing them."

The obituary also alluded to the real reason the Republicans rose in the south. Not because the GOP assumed the racist vote. The *Times* obituary accurately reported that the old racist Democrat Tallmadge "lost his bid for a fifth term in the Senate in 1980 when he could not keep up with changes in the Georgia electorate"

The *Times* further noted that Talmadge's Republican successor, Matt Mattingly, "enjoyed strong support from Black voters."

Despite his racist views, fellow Georgia Democrat senator Zell Miller proclaimed Talmadge to be "Georgia's greatest governor of the twentieth century."

Racist Democrat senators were not exclusively the problem. Equally determined to keep Blacks in their PLACE were a collection of Democrat governors. In many ways, they were more influential in implementing racist polices—politically and socially—than the racist senators.

It was the governors who had the greatest implementation powers over institutional racism in law enforcement, voting, school segregation, and the social life of Black citizens. It was the governors in the south and mayors in many northern cities, who used the authoritarian power of one-party rule to create and maintain segregation and oppression of Black Americans.

Virtually every Democrat governor of a former Confederate state from 1865 to the mid-1900s was openly racist. Not only did they fight Congress and the courts in matters of civil rights, but they presided over a reign of terror that denied Black citizens their basic constitutional and civil rights and oversaw the operations of such para-military terrorist organizations as the Ku Klux Klan, the Knights of the White Camellia, the Red Shirts, and the White Citizens' Councils, to name a few. Democrat governors were culpable in the thousands of Black Americans who were summarily murdered, making lynching one of the iconic cultural practices of the times in the South.

George and Lurleen Wallace of Alabama

George Wallace was governor for three terms (1963–67, 1971–79 & 1983–87). Wallace was perhaps the most well know of the modern Democrat racist governors in the 1960s. He is infamous for his attempt to block the integration of the University of Alabama in 1963 by standing in the doorway. He ran four times for president on a racist platform, saying "segregation now, segregation tomorrow, segregation forever." He opposed the Civil Rights Act of 1964 and the Voting Rights Act of 1965 and supported violence against civil rights activists. After his first term, he was succeeded in office by his wife, Lurleen, who carried on the Wallace racist traditions in Alabama. George would go on to two more non-consecutive terms. In his final years, he expressed regret for his segregationist policies.

Lester (Axe Handle) Maddox of Georgia

Lester Maddox gained initial fame and his nick name as a brutal racist who chased Blacks away from his restaurant with an axe handle. As governor he supported segregation and opposed the mixing of races in any circumstances. Maddox wanted to keep Blacks in their PLACE. He brought back the Confederate battle flag as an honored symbol of Black oppression.

Ross Barnett of Mississippi

Ross Barnett was a violent racist who defied federal court orders to admit James Meredith to the University of Mississippi. In blocking Meredith, Barnett incited riots in which two people died. He opposed interracial sport teams playing in Mississippi.

Orval Faubus of Arkansas

Orval Faubus was most infamous for his use of the Arkansas National Guard to prevent nice Black youngsters from enrolling in Little Rock Central High School. Republican president Dwight Eisenhower deployed federal troops to intervene. He was so intent on preventing school integration that he closed all the public schools in Little Rock for an entire school year.

Racist Mayors Beyond the South

Keeping Negroes in their PLACE was not just a goal of Democrats in the southern states of the old Confederacy. Democrat political machines in the North and West developed a *de facto* form of institutional racism that oppressed Black citizens in similar fashion to their southern political colleagues.

This was largely in response to the Great Migration of newly freed slaves who moved away from southern racism, believing they would find freedom in the major cities that were not part of the Confederate states. While virtually all Democrat mayors of America's largest cities relied on institutional *de facto* racism to maintain political control, a few stand out for their extreme and overt racist policies.

Richard J. and Richard M. Daley of Chicago

Perhaps the most infamous racist mayor in America was Chicago's Richard J. Daley. He began his career as head of a social club that attacked Blacks who did not know their PLACE. Some historians claim that Daley was the person of interest in the murder of a young Black man. He was never charged. Daley perfected and presided over what had been called the most racist political machine in America.

Daley embraced the construction of high-rise public housing, but it was not to provide better housing for those trapped in the segregated inner-city. It was to prevent Blacks from moving beyond the boundaries of the strictly segregated neighborhoods. His son Richard M. Daley reinforced segregation by constructing physical barriers, such as cul-de-sacs, viaducts, and walls to limit Black movement throughout the city. A main street, Archer Avenue, was cut off to limit mobility in the northside ghetto.

Sam Yorty of Los Angeles

Sam Yorty governed with racist policies. He opposed federal funding of anti-poverty programs and refused funds designated for urban renewal in the Black community. He denounced Martin Luther King as a communist sympathizer. Yorty endorsed the brutal racist tactics of police chief William Parker, who referred to the Black participants in the Watts riots as behaving like "monkeys in a zoo." Yorty vetoed a fair housing ordinance that would have made discrimination illegal. He opposed school busing and integration.

Frank Rizzo of Philadelphia

As Philadelphia police commissioner Frank Rizzo had a reputation for abusing Black citizens and arrestees and was accused of creating a culture of police misconduct against Black people. He routinely harassed Black citizens and encouraged humiliating public strip-searches.

As mayor, he made no secret of his disdain for the Black population.

He imposed legal and financial burdens on the segregated Black community by cutting social services. He opposed the construction of public housing. Rizzo routinely referred to Blacks as niggers. He was defeated in a racially charged campaign in which he told voters to vote White. Rizzo attempted to make a comeback by switching to the Republican Party, but he failed. Rizzo's statue was finally removed from in front of the Municipal Services Building in 2020 by Mayor Jim Kenney, who said, "the statue is a deplorable monument to racism, bigotry, and police brutality for members of the Black community, the LGBTQ community, and many others. The treatment of these communities under Mr. Rizzo's leadership was among the worst periods in Philadelphia's history."

The aforementioned Democrat racist senators, governors, and mayors are only a small sampling of the most infamous of the class. There will be examples of their specific racist policies later in this book.

Democratic Party Leadership

Throughout the second half of the twentieth century, the national leadership of the Democratic Party acquiesced to the powerful political leaders in the South and the major cities. Even into the twenty-first century, institutional *de facto* racism was ignored or denied under the totally false narrative of civil rights advocacy. This hypocrisy would allow institutional racism to flourish in the major cities—arguably the last vestiges of the Democratic Party's long oppression of Black Americans.

However, even the national Democrat leaders could not avoid the groundswell of public pressure for action against their Party's denial of equal rights for America's Black citizens, The pressure would reach critical mass in the mid-1900s.

The Eisenhower administration proposed and supported civil rights legislation. It also appointed Blacks to high positions. Among Eisenhower's black appointments was James Wilkins as assistant secretary of labor. When Labor Secretary James Mitchell was unable to attend a Cabinet meeting, Wilkins participated. It was the first time a black person had ever participated in a formal cabinet meeting in the White House. The Democratic

Party, however, was profoundly racist across the nation. It was in opposition to civil rights legislation in the South and ambivalent in the North. In 1954, Senator John F. Kennedy spoke to the NAACP. He did not lay out any plans he had or would propose to advance civil rights. Rather than issuing a call for action, he declared the passage of civil rights legislation to be unlikely.

According to Nick Bryant in *The Bystander,* Kennedy merely reported that there were "very dim prospects of any suitable civil rights legislation being passed by this Congress." He conveniently omitted the fact that it was his own Democratic Party that presented the major barrier, and that his own record in Congress was generally supportive of his southern segregationist colleagues.

In winning control of the United States Senate in 1954, with southern Democrats holding many of the most power positions and with Lyndon Johnson as the Senate Majority Leader, civil rights legislation faced major legislative obstacles.

John Kennedy's opposition to civil rights legislation was again evident in his opposition to the so-called Powell Amendment. The Amendment was introduced in 1956 by black Democrat New York Congressman Adam Clayton Powell, who represented Harlem. It would have denied federal school construction funds to states with segregated schools. Kennedy joined with the southern Democrats in their successful effort to block the amendment in the Senate.

The White Citizens' Councils

Following *Brown v. Board of Education* in 1954, violent opponents of racial integration began to organize in the South, often with the participation and encouragement of top Democrat officeholders. Among the more successful organizations was the White Citizens' Council (WCC). It was founded as an alternative to the increasing unpopularity of the more violent Democrat terrorist groups, such as the KKK.

The WCC developed chapters throughout the South. Unlike the Ku Klux Klan, the WCC did not meet in secret or wear concealing robes. They did, however, take up much of the Klan's racist views and propensity for promoting if not committing violence. In his 1995 book *I've Got the*

Light of Freedom, author and historian Charles M. Payne described the councils as "pursuing the agenda of the Klan with the demeanor of the Rotary Club."

The WCC publicly eschewed violence as a tactic. Rather, they used the social and business communities to intimidate or "punish" Blacks and civil rights supporters. Their methods included boycotting businesses, refusing personal or business loans, evicting people from rental residences, and getting people fired from their jobs. Local papers would publish the names and addresses of people who signed civil rights petitions or joined civil rights groups such as the NAACP. The provocation of violence, however, was the result of their targeting citizens and groups.

According to Payne, the WCC's professed non-violence was more in theory than reality. He wrote: "Despite the official disclaimers, violence often followed in the wake of Council intimidation campaigns."

Violence was not always an indirect outcome of council events. During the 1955 Montgomery bus boycott, Democrat US Senator James Eastland addressed a large WCC meeting at which a flyer was distributed to the audience. Mocking the Declaration of Independence, it read:

> When in the course of human events, it becomes necessary to abolish the Negro race, proper methods should be used. Among these are guns, bows and arrows, sling shots and knives. We hold these truths to be self-evident that all Whites are created equal with certain rights; among these are life, liberty and the pursuit of dead niggers.

Mississippi Fights Back

In response to *Brown v. Board of Education,* the Mississippi legislature created the Mississippi State Sovereignty Commission. In his 1994 book entitled *Local People: The Struggle for Civil Rights in Mississippi,* John Dittmer described the commission as a "secret police force that owed its primary allegiance to the White Citizens' Council." The purpose of the Commission was to gather intelligence using spies planted within civil rights groups and to use intimidation and disruptive tactics to thwart progress by those groups.

One of the more concise explanations of post-*Brown v. Board of Education* era in Mississippi was written by Charles Bolton for the Center for Oral History and Cultural Heritage at the University of Southern Mississippi. Bolton wrote:

> In 1954, when the U.S. Supreme Court declared segregated schools unconstitutional in the *Brown v. Board of Education* decision, the gap between white and black education created by fifty years of support for white (only) education was exceedingly wide. While the *Brown* decision meant that the dual school system in Mississippi was now illegal, white Mississippians made clear that no attempts to abandon the dual school system would be tolerated. When groups of black Mississippians in Natchez, Vicksburg, Yazoo City, Clarksdale, and Jackson pressed for adherence to the decision in 1955, they were stopped swiftly, decisively, and repeatedly. And for a decade after *Brown*, white Mississippians resorted to private and state-sanctioned economic and, sometimes, physical intimidation to block black attempts to desegregate Mississippi schools. While squashing any efforts by black Mississippians to assert their new legal rights, the state of Mississippi also proposed, as an alternative to desegregated schools, a massive equalization program to improve black schools.

> Lawsuits by black parents in Biloxi, Jackson, and Leake County, who were supported in their efforts by the NAACP's Legal Defense Fund, finally led to the first court-ordered school desegregation in the state in the fall of 1964. In the following year, because of the passage of the 1964 Civil Rights Act and the 1965 Elementary and Secondary Education Act, most Mississippi school districts reluctantly adopted freedom-of-choice desegregation plans, which essentially provided that any student could choose to go to any school in a district. Freedom-of-choice desegregation, however, only offered five years of token desegregation and the preservation of largely segregated schools. The problem was that in the 1960s, most black Mississippians really did not have freedom of choice. Between 1964

and 1969, black parents who chose white schools for their children were subjected to numerous forms of intimidation: some were pressured or fired by their employers; some lost their housing; some lost their credit at the local bank; and others received threatening phone calls, had crosses burned on their lawns, or were victims of physical intimidation. In 1968, largely because of the continuing resistance of white Southerners to school desegregation, the Supreme Court ruled in *Green v. County School Board* that freedom of choice was ineffective and no longer an acceptable method of desegregation. In October 1969, the Supreme Court essentially said enough is enough, and in a landmark decision involving thirty Mississippi school districts, Alexander v. Holmes, the court ordered the immediate termination of dual school systems and the establishment of unitary ones. Thus, many Mississippi school districts had to begin the complete integration of their school systems in mid-year, during January and February of 1970.

It took sixteen years after *Brown v. Board of Education* for the Mississippi schools to begin a serious program of integration, and during those sixteen years of official resistance, the Democratic Party held control of the state and its municipal governments.

"M" is for Mississippi and Murder

A rash of racial murders in Mississippi motivated the NAACP to highlight them in a pamphlet entitled "M is for Mississippi and Murder." It is no coincidence that among the most strident Democrat racist governments in America, Mississippi would have the highest Black murder rate. Among the many political and social reasons for this dubious distinction, the most important may be the failure to investigate, prosecute, or convict Whites in the murder of Blacks. While it was common among southern Democrat sheriffs, prosecutors, and judges to use prosecutorial discretion to not put Whites on trial, Mississippi stood out in its contempt for the lives of Negroes.

Since the Civil War, more than five hundred Negroes had been given "southern justice" in Mississippi by vigilante groups, private citizens, or one of the Democratic Party's paramilitary organizations, such as the White Knights or the KKK. Many of the victims were lynched, but many more were murdered in a variety of other gruesome manners.

The ambivalence to these horrific murders permeated the Democratic Party all the way up to the White House, where President Franklin Roosevelt and the Democrats in Congress had consistently opposed Republican-supported anti-lynching legislation.

Lynching became less popular in the South after the new electronic media of television broadcast the horrors of southern vigilante justice across the nation. Prior to the expansion of television into millions of American homes, the Democrat terrorist groups were satisfied with publicizing their brutality through local media as a means of intimidation. The growing national revulsion to lynching led future southern Democrat terrorists to rely more on the three Bs—bombs, bullets, and beatings.

Civil Rights Martyrs

George W. Lee

George W. Lee was a successful businessman and a Baptist Preacher in Belzoni, Mississippi—a town referred to as "Bloody Belzoni" because of its history of racial violence. He was also the first Negro to successfully register to vote in Humphreys County. The White Democrat leadership was particularly opposed to Black voting rights since Negroes were a majority of the population. To maintain White racist power, Democrats had to prevent Negro registration at all costs.

Lee was a leader in the Regional Counsel of Negro Leadership. He was joined in his registration efforts by his friend Gus Courts of the NAACP.

As Lee and Courts became more successful at registering Black voters, they were subjected to threats from the White Citizens' Council. Because of the threats, Lee was offered protection by the local Democrat leadership, but only if he ceased all voter registration activities. He refused. Courts also refused when the local bank demanded that he turn over all the NAACP's financial records or leave town.

On May 7, 1955, Lee was shot in the head while in his car. The NAACP sent Medgar Evans, who would himself become a victim of "southern justice," to investigate the death. Democrat sheriff Ike Shelton said that Lee had died in a car crash and that metal particles found in his body were from auto shrapnel. He refused to order an autopsy. An examination by two Black physicians, however, established that Lee died from gunshot wounds to his head and that his car was apparently stopped by a shot into the right rear tire.

The FBI compiled evidence against Peck Ray and Joe David Watson who were members of the White Citizens' Council. Despite the evidence the local Democrat prosecutor refused to file charges or present the case to a grand jury.

The issue was brought to Democrat governor Hugh L. White, who refused requests to investigate the murder. White was a devoted segregationist. He was among those who believed that segregation could be maintained by making some improvements in the Black school systems, especially where inequities were obvious, such as teacher pay. His plan was rejected by Black civil rights leaders who wanted integration and by Democrat politicians who refused to spend more money on "nigger schools."

Lee's wife ordered the casket to remain open so the world could see the condition of her beloved husband. This would inspire a similar decision by the mother of Emmett Till, who was murdered in 1955. Many consider Lee to be the first martyr of the modern civil rights movement.

Courts continued his civil rights activities despite threats from the Citizens' Council. On November 25, he was shot and wounded while working in his store. Witnesses provided the sheriff with descriptions and the license number of the car from which the shots were fired. The sheriff made no effort to find the shooter.

As many predicted, and the Democrat leaders feared, the ability of Blacks to vote in Belzoni and the greater Humphreys County brought dramatic changes to the region. Belzoni eventually elected a Black mayor, Wardell Walton, who was succeeded by a female Black mayor, Lenora Holmes Sutton. Remembering the dark days of Democratic rule, the Blacks of Humphreys County played a major role in the election of Republicans in Mississippi. In 2014, more than 80 percent of the predominantly Black citizens of Humphreys County voted for Republican senator Thad Cochran.

Reflecting on the Cochran victory, Mayor Walton, upon the polls closing, said:

> I'm sure that George Lee would be smiling at the impact that black voters have had in trying to determine the next senator for the state of Mississippi, 50 years after the Freedom Summer, and the passage of the civil rights bill.

He added that "Cochran has been very responsive to the community, to the constituency and the state regardless of race."

Lamar Smith

Lamar Smith was a local farmer and veteran of World War I. He was a member of the Regional Counsel of Negro Leadership in Brookhaven, Mississippi. At 10 o'clock in the morning of August 13, 1955, Smith was in front of the Brookhaven courthouse helping Black voters to register and fill out absentee ballots. The use of an absentee ballot was a means for southern Negroes to avoid intimidation or violence at the polling locations.

In broad daylight, and in front of several witnesses, Smith was shot to death. Among the witnesses was Sheriff Robert E. Case, who had seen the bloodied murderer flee the scene but made no attempt to apprehend him. Later in the day, three men were arrested, but no charges were ever brought.

Emmett Till

One of the most sensational murders occurred in Money, Mississippi, on August 28, 1955, when fourteen-year-old Chicagoan Emmett Till was kidnapped, tortured, mutilated and lynched while visiting relatives in Mississippi. The impact of the event on the American public was heightened when Till's mother ordered the casket to remain open to show the nation the horrific suffering her son had endured.

Despite overwhelming evidence, an all-White jury acquitted the murderers, Roy Bryant and J. W. Milam. Protected against a second trial by the double jeopardy provision of the United States Constitution, they later were paid for their public confessions by *Look* magazine. They expressed no remorse for what they did.

Reminiscent of Democrat Governor Barnett's statement suggesting that Negroes live in Mississippi because they prefer the state's segregationist policies, the Citizens' Council blamed the NAACP for Till's death. The Council claimed that segregation was the best means of protecting Negroes. In response, the NAACP's Roy Wilkins damned the culture of Mississippi under Democratic Party leadership by saying that "there is in the entire state no restraining influence of decency, not in the state capital, among the daily newspapers, the local clergy, nor any segment of the so-called better citizens." Fortunately, other civil rights activist avoided "southern justice."

Rosa Parks Leads the Way

On December 1, 1955, a rather shy seamstress took a seat in the front "Whites only" section of a bus in Montgomery, Alabama. Her arrest for this moment of protest against the Democrat establishment of Montgomery was one of the seminal events in civil rights history. This was an intentional effort to broaden the fight against segregation and to create a test case for a legal challenge.

Following the arrest of Rosa Parks on December 1, 1955, a group of Black civil rights activists lead by Reverend Ralph Abernathy organized a boycott of the Montgomery bus system. Among those who volunteered to assist the effort was a twenty-six-year-old Black minister who had only recently arrived in the community, Martin Luther King.

The boycott was so successful that the group decided to extend the boycott and founded the Montgomery Improvement Association. According to Parks, Dr. King was chosen to lead the group because "he was relatively new to the community and so did not have any enemies."

Since the group did not wish to rile the worst instincts of Montgomery's Democrat leadership, it decided to take a softer approach. They would not push for school integration despite the recent *Brown v. Board of Education* ruling of the Supreme Court.

Republican Martin Luther King Jr.

Two years after the Rosa Parks incident, Dr. King founded the Southern Christian Leadership Council (SCLC) as his civil rights platform. He was joined by other Black Republicans, including his closest associate, Ralph Abernathy. This should come as no surprise since Dr. King recognized that it was the Democratic Party that had passed and enforced the Jim Crow laws and the Democratic Party that was literally sponsoring the terrorist tactics against innocent Black citizens. He would later travel north to Chicago and Cleveland to confront the racist Democrat political machines there.

Unlike his successors, Jesse Jackson and Al Sharpton, who were partisan activist Democrats and promoters of the false civil rights of welfare dependency, Dr. King subordinated his partisan views to the greater civil rights campaign. However, he did lean to the Republican Party throughout most of his life. This was confirmed by members of his family, including his niece Alveda King. Dr. King's one notable exception was Republican presidential candidate Barry Goldwater, who had voted against the 1964 Civil Rights Act. Dr. King openly campaigned against Goldwater but returned to the Republican Party to support his close friend Richard Nixon in 1968.

The Chicago Machine

By the mid-1960s, the racist political machine of Mayor Richard J. Daley was coming into full boom. In many ways, the Windy City was the state-of-the-art example of Democratic Party urban political machine governance and institutional *de facto* racism.

While the Chicago Democrat machine had its roots in the early 1930s, a distinction can be made between the old machine and the new machine. That transition was due to the rise of Richard J. Daley—a man who became known simply as Da Boss. In 1955, after one term as city clerk, Daley was tapped by the boys in the back room to head the machine.

This should come as no surprise since in the 1930s Chicago was the incubator of urban *de facto* racism in which generational welfare dependency replaced basic constitutional civil rights for the millions of Black citizens,

Daley presided over arguably the most racist city administration in America and became embroiled in some of the most controversial and violent civil rights events of the twentieth century. The pernicious racism of Chicago under Daley and the Democrat machine led Martin Luther King to select the Windy City for his first major civil rights campaign outside of the South.

Daley was raised in the all-White and predominantly Irish neighborhood of Bridgeport—one of the most dangerous sections of the city for Blacks. The Hamburg Athletic Club was a significant reason for that, and Daley was its leader. Graffiti on the edge of the neighborhood warned Blacks to stay away, with such messages as "Bridgeport Nigger Beaters" followed by a phone number.

Daley's election as mayor began the new era of racism in Chicago—racism much subtler than the brutal *de jure* segregation in the old Democrat southland, and even less obvious than the harsh *de facto* segregationist policies of the old machine and its so-called Democrat social clubs as violent street enforcers. It was a racism fully embracing the hypocrisy of the false narrative of welfare as civil rights that was started in Chicago by William Dawson—the machine's political overseer for the city's segregated ghettoes.

Chicago is arguably the most Democrat major city in America. It has not had a Republican mayor since 1931. That is the longest run of Democrat mayors of any major city except for Atlanta, Georgia, which has not had a Republican mayor since the end of Reconstruction in 1879.

The endemic racism of the Democrat machine was the very reason that Martin Luther King selected Chicago when he decided to bring his civil rights crusade north for the first time. Dr. King had made speaking tours and supported voter drives in other northern cities, such as Cleveland, but never a full crusade. Whether in the South or the North, Dr. King was always pushing back against the racism of administrations dominated by Democrats.

According to the *Encyclopedia of Chicago:*

> Chicago politics is a national cliché, evoking images of a one-party system, dominated by a boss-controlled Democratic political machine whose crafty politicians dangle patronage before competing ethnic and racial groups in return for votes.

The *Encyclopedia* alludes to the beginning of the false civil rights narrative of generational welfare:

> The New Deal of the 1930s and the Great Society of the 1960s gave the Democratic Party access to new funds and programs for housing, slum clearance, urban renewal, and education, through which to dispense patronage and maintain control of the city.

The *Encyclopedia* further rebuts the myth perpetrated by Daley and the machine that they had little responsibility for the poor quality of education in the predominantly Black schools:

> Although the mayor appointed the Board of Education, the school system was independent of the municipal government and its funding kept separate from the municipal budget. This structure meant that the mayor's office could simultaneously exert influence on the schools and disavow any political responsibility for managing or funding the system.

The *Encyclopedia* left no uncertainty over the city's use of *de facto* racism and segregation to keep the Black community in an isolated PLACE of lower status—and the use of Black cronies to support the system:

> Mayor Daley and the Democrats also controlled Chicago politics by exploiting growing racial and class antagonisms. From the 1940s, growing African American and Hispanic populations competed for jobs, housing, and schools. Middle-class Whites fled to the suburbs and the Democrats retained the support of ethnic, working-class Whites by allowing *de facto* social and economic segregation in neighborhoods, housing, jobs, and schools.

It would be totally appropriate and accurate to amend the last sentence to add, "well into the twenty-first century."

Democrats use the formal services and welfare of government as bribes to maintain loyalty. For Black leaders, this could take the form of lucrative contracts, public office, or jobs for family members. For the average voters, such bribes might include a patronage job, "fixing" a speeding ticket, fraudulent welfare benefits, or the old standby, a bit of cash in exchange for a vote. It was euphemistically called "street money" by the politicians.

Ironically, Black voters are so habitually inclined to vote the Democrat ticket, that the Black precinct captains often kept much of the street money for themselves. That makes no difference to the folks in city hall as long as the precinct comes in with a 90-plus percent Democrat vote. In some cases, the vote has exceeded 100 percent of those who requested ballots. Such corruption is iconic of the Democrat urban machines—and is widely known and accepted as the normal course of business by the general public.

Just as political corruption goes unabated in Chicago, the Windy City's reputation for institutional racism is as pernicious, prevalent, and pervasive as ever. According to a 2016 article by the Illinois Policy Institute by Mike Adams:

> Chicago remains one of the most segregated cities in America, according to new studies by the Chicago Urban League and researchers at American University. But the city's segregation is not just the legacy of a racist past: Chicago-area governments continue to actively pursue policies that were originally intended to prevent racial integration.

The article went on to say:

> A quarter of Chicago's neighborhoods have both a majority-Black population and a poverty level of over 40%. Moreover, approximately 80% of Blacks live in "isolated" neighborhoods where they have little contact with people of other races. This arrangement did not occur by accident. Historically, Chicago and its suburban municipalities explicitly pursued racial segregation through a collection of policies known as exclusionary zoning. Although lawmakers no longer use racial justifications for segregationist policies, many of those same policies remain, prolonging and exacerbating racial and class segregation.

As journalist Ta-Nehisi Coates' 2014 story in *The Atlantic* on reparations outlined "Chicago has a particularly sordid history when it comes to race and housing. The city's policies and their consequences have contributed to deep levels of residential segregation."

Chicago's segregation and racism, and that of most major cities, is widely established by experience, common knowledge, and extensive research. The false narrative of Democrat civil rights advocacy deflects placing the appropriate blame for racist policies on the governing class—the Democratic Party. Masking those responsible makes it almost impossible to effectively address the issue of institutional *de facto* racism in a productive way.

If there was any racial policy to which the Chicago Democrat machine was most dedicated, it was segregation —keeping Blacks in their PLACE. In a report entitled "Residential Segregation and Neighborhood Conditions in U.S. Metropolitan Areas" Douglas S. Massey showed how Chicago became America's most segregated big city. Using a Black isolation index to indicate segregation, the analysis showed Chicago with a Black isolation of 10 percent in 1900—about average for most big cities. By 1930, with the impact of the Great Migration of Blacks moving north, Chicago had an astounding 70 percent isolation index—far ahead of every other major city studied. It was 31 percentage points above the national average. Other cities with above average isolation indexes included Cleveland (51%), St. Louis (47%) and Cincinnati (45%)—all cities that would experience racial unrest and rioting under Democrat rule.

In the early 1940s, Chicago segregation was designated to keep Blacks in their PLACE. Douglas Park, Grand Boulevard, and Washington Park were known as the Black Belt. This was noted in a 2013 NBC article by Edward McCelland entitled "White Flight, By the Numbers." McCelland stated, "What's most striking about Chicago's pattern of racial distribution is the almost total absence of whites in black neighborhoods."

The two primary means for maintaining segregation boundaries were red lining and school districting.

Post Massive Resistance

While northern cities were perfecting their unique form of *de facto* racism, the South was in a growing cross-conflict between the old guard segregationist and a new constituency of more moderate voters.

Brown v. Board of Education did not bring swift sweeping integration to southern schools. Democrat resistance, however, was doomed to failure eventually, even though it took almost twenty-five years after the *Brown* decision. The key element in advancing school integration was breaking the Democratic Party's one-party control of the southern states. Ironically, by the 1980s southern schools were generally more integrated than their counterparts in the major Democrat cities in the North.

The Civil Rights Project at Harvard University, as reported in an article in *West Virginia History* in 2008, stated that by the late 1980s, the South had "witnessed the greatest increase in racial integration" and could "boast the highest level of school integration in the nation." It is more than coincidence that there exists a correlation between the eventual integration of southern schools and the rise of the Republican Party throughout the region—a success that contrasts with the persistent segregation in the urban centers under long-time Democrat governance.

Even as Republicans gradually took the reins of government in the 1970s, 1980s, and beyond, pockets of old-style southern Democrat racism would continue under Democrat municipal leadership in many smaller towns and cities. Places like Cumming, Georgia, and Cleveland, Mississippi, would continue racist policies into the twenty-first century (detailed later in this book).

The Confederate Battle Flag

As Eisenhower and Republicans were unleashing a new wave of civil rights legislation and executive actions from the federal level, Democrat governors in the South rose in opposition. As the symbol of their defiance, Democrat administrations in Dixie began to display the Confederate battle flag in places of honor. In addition to flying the banner atop state capitol buildings next to the American flag, it was added to state seals, license plates, and official stationery. Democrat governors chose to resurrect the iconic battle flag as opposed to the Confederate "national" flag to express a war of hostility to integration.

In 1956, Georgia's Democrat governor Marvin Griffin, a vociferous advocate of segregation, and Georgia's Democrat legislature changed the design of the state flag to incorporate the now familiar Confederate battle banner. This led other racist Democrat governors and legislators to incorporate the battle flag as a state icon. It soon appeared on homes and businesses throughout the South.

This was not only an act of defiance against Eisenhower and the Republican Party, but further intimidated the Black residents of Georgia. In many ways, it gave an appearance of official sanction to the increasingly violent resistance. The Confederate battle flag would remain imbedded in the Georgia standard until removed in 2003 under the Republican administration of Governor George E. "Sonny" Perdue.

Governor Griffin and the Sugar Bowl

Governor Griffin's racist policies spilled over into sports and had an ironic impact on future Republican president Gerald R. Ford, who, at the time, was a senior member of the University of Michigan football team. In 1934, the Georgia Tech Yellow Jackets refused to play Michigan unless the team's Black player, Willis Ward, would not appear on the field. The team protested. Despite the opinion of the Michigan team members, Michigan students, and alumni, school officials acquiesced.

Ward was Ford's best friend and roommate at the time. To protest the decision, Ford announced that he would not play in the game. This would have been a further blow to the team since Ford was a star player. Ford relented only when Ward insisted he play for the benefit of the team.

Though Ford's protest did not get Ward on the field for the game, it was said that a very angry Ford "hard tackled" those chiding Michigan for having a "nigger" as a fellow team member.

In 1956, the same year that Georgia had the Confederate battle flag again flying over the state capitol, the Pittsburgh Panthers were to play the Georgia Tech Yellow Jackets in the Sugar Bowl. There was a problem for Griffin. The Pittsburgh team included halfback Bobby "Rosy" Grier.

To keep Grier from playing, Griffin wrote to the school's Board of Regents and requested that no Georgia teams be involved in sporting events where Blacks were players, or even Blacks were spectators. Because of pressure from civil rights groups and fans of both teams, the game was played with Grier participating. The Sugar Bowl color racial ban was broken.

Georgia Tech won a 7 to 0 victory over Pittsburgh, the result of a controversial first quarter interference call against Grier by a hometown referee. Post-game films of the play proved the obvious, that it was a bad call—and likely racially motivated.

In stark contrast, during the California governorship of Republican Goodwin Knight, the 1956 Rose Bowl between Michigan State and UCLA was played between two integrated teams without any controversy.

In 1966, Griffin would come out of private life to campaign for Lester "Axe Handle" Maddox. And in 1968, Griffin was Democrat governor George Wallace's vice-presidential running mate on the American Independent Party until he was replaced by Air Force general Curtis LeMay.

The Election of 1956

The election of 1956 was little more than a referendum on Eisenhower's first term. Though he and Nixon were reported not to be the most compatible teammates, Eisenhower stayed with Nixon as his vice president.

Stevenson was again nominated by the Democrats. However, he chose to replace Sparkman on the ticket with yet another southern segregationist, senator Estes Kefauver of Tennessee. This was an odd selection since Kefauver was considered to be too much of a southern racist for the presidential nomination in 1952. Still, his selection by the convention reaffirmed the power of the segregationist faction of the Democratic Party. Kefauver, however, did not secure the nomination without a fight.

There was an effort to secure the vice-presidential nomination for Massachusetts senator John Kennedy. In an ironic turnabout in political polarization, Kennedy, the northern senator with a consistent anti-civil rights record was up against Estes Kefauver, who was considered a southern moderate racist even though he frequently expressed his uncompromised opposition to school integration.

Kennedy's stand in opposition to civil rights legislation in Congress gained him the support of many southern segregationist Democrat leaders.

Who Put Blacks in that PLACE?

They were wary of Kefauver, but in the final analysis, it was Kefauver who prevailed.

The Platforms

The Republican Party platform's call for proper education for "every child" was especially pointed in view of the poor quality of minority education in the segregated schools under Democrat operation in both the North and the South. In 1956, the Republican Party "determined to press all such actions that will help ensure that every child has the educational opportunity to advance to his own greatest capacity."

The section on Civil Rights was long and detailed with regard to both accomplishments and goals:

> The Republican Party points to an impressive record of accomplishment in the field of civil rights and commits itself anew to advancing the rights of all our people regardless of race, creed, color or national origin.
>
> In the area of exclusive Federal jurisdiction, more progress has been made in this field under the present Republican Administration than in any similar period in the last 80 years.

The accomplishments of Eisenhower's first terms included:

- Appointing record numbers of Blacks to high government positions.
- Ending segregation in the military.
- Ending the segregation of the District of Columbia, including government offices, public facilities, schools, theaters, restaurants, and playgrounds.
- Elimination of discrimination in all federal employment.
- Elimination of discrimination by government contractors.
- Ended segregation in veteran hospitals.

The GOP platform placed emphasis on school integration in the South, drawing a stark distinction between it and the Democratic Party:

> The Republican Party accepts the decision of the U.S. Supreme Court that racial discrimination in publicly supported schools must be progressively eliminated. We concur in the conclusion of the Supreme Court that its decision directing school desegregation should be accomplished with "all deliberate speed" locally through Federal District Courts. The implementation order of the Supreme Court recognizes the complex and acutely emotional problems created by its decision in certain sections of our country where racial patterns have been developed in accordance with prior and long-standing decisions of the same tribunal.

In 1956, the Democratic Party platform ignored the reality of its oppressive policies in the southern segregated states and in the northern cities and put forth a platform completely detached from reality. It was a narrative filled with outrageous falsehoods:

> The Democratic Party is committed to support and advance the individual rights and liberties of all Americans. Our country is founded on the proposition that all men are created equal. This means that all citizens are equal before the law and should enjoy all political rights. They should have equal opportunities for education, for economic advancement, and for decent living conditions.

The Democrat platform promised to "eradicate discrimination based on race, religion or national origin." The party promised to "continue its efforts to eliminate illegal discriminations of all kinds, in relation to (1) full rights to vote, (2) full rights to engage in gainful occupations, (3) full rights to enjoy security of the person, and (4) full fights to education in all publicly supported institutions."

As this plank of the Democrat's platform was being approved, Democrat leaders in Congress, in the major cities, and in the South were engage in the Massive Resistance Movement to deny Black citizens all four of those articulated rights.

The Black Vote

In the 1950s, there were some indications of a shift in Black voting away from the Democrats. The issuance of the Southern Manifesto and the election of Mississippi segregationist Democrat James Eastland as chairman of the powerful Senate Judiciary Committee were especially offensive to the civil rights community.

NAACP executive secretary Roy Wilkins argued that the Democrat opposition to civil rights was enough to have Blacks support Eisenhower. Wilkins said, "with Eastland on your necks and with every southern politician yelling that we won't get our rights until doomsday, we cannot be any worse off than we are."

Civil rights leaders, such as James Farmer and Roy Ennis, were already in the Republican camp.

Eisenhower Reelected

Eisenhower and Nixon sailed to an easy second term victory carrying the nation, except for the solid Democrat South. In fact, the state-by-state election map looks very similar to 1952. There was, however, the hint of growing Republican influence in Dixie. The only change in the map was the addition of Kentucky and West Virginia to the GOP column.

It is arguable that Eisenhower would have carried more southern states had it not been for the barriers Democrats erected to Black voting. Across the nation, Eisenhower won an impressive 42 percent of the Black vote. The was the highest percentage since the Great Depression.

Civil Rights Act of 1957

Popular Democrat mythology places the emergence of the contemporary civil rights movement with the Civil Rights Act of 1964, and erroneously credits the Democratic Party with being the prime mover. The first Civil

Right Act since Reconstruction was in 1957, during the administration of Republican President Eisenhower.

Eisenhower's Civil Rights bill had several important key provisions:

- It created the Federal Civil Rights Commission with the power to hold hearings and subpoena witnesses.
- It added additional protection of voting rights by empowering the Commission to "investigate allegations of citizens 'in writing, under oath or affirmation,' that they were denied the right to vote based on color, race, religion, or national origin." And to "study and gather information on legal developments constituting a denial of the equal protection of the laws."
- It appointed a special assistant attorney general in the Justice Department to handle civil rights issues.
- It eliminated the requirement that federal juries be deemed "competent" in the opinion of local authorities. In southern Democrat states, it was usually determined that only Whites were competent to serve on juries.
- It allowed for civil rights cases to be tried by federal judges instead of local juries. Southern Democrats were outraged by what was known as Title III, the provision that empowered the United States attorney general to enforce all civil rights laws, including school integration and voting rights.

The Role of Lyndon Johnson

At the time of the 1957 Civil Rights Bill, Lyndon Johnson had an unbroken record of opposition to all civil rights legislation. In 1950, when Republican senator William Langer led another attempt to pass a law banning lynching and eliminating the poll tax, Johnson voted with his fellow Democrats to table the bill—essentially killing it. As Senate majority leader, Johnson organized the opposition to Eisenhower's 1957 civil rights legislation.

On May 14, 1957, Virginia's racist Democrat senator Harry F. Byrd entered into the Congressional Record a speech he had given earlier to the Hampton Roads Maritime Association expressing his strong opposition to the Republican civil rights bill. He expressed exceptional opposition to the provision that would have empowered the United States attorney general to enter cases on behalf of Negroes who had been denied their constitutional rights. He said:

> One of these bills is especially offensive and I shall submit my discussion to that one. It would establish in Washington a special bureau which would send its agents into the South and originate suits against southerners.

He further begged the question:

> What have we done to deserve this treatment? We have fought for constitutional democracy. We have fought for it in 1860. We have fought to the last ditch with the most conspicuous bravery in human history. Finally, in defeat by sheer numbers, we won everlasting world esteem.
>
> We took our defeat with fortitude as we went through the terrible days of reconstruction.

Byrd went on to support an alternative bill sponsored by two fellow southern segregationists, Strom Thurmond of South Carolina and James Eastland of Mississippi, which would maintain the practice of all-White juries.

Byrd complained that Eisenhower's proposal would achieve its goals in that it "would give to the government, for the first time, the authority necessary for effectual enforcement of federally guaranteed civil rights." He quoted the prescient observation of a federal judge, who said that "the integration problem will never be resolved in Virginia until we have a different political leadership."

Byrd was correct, but not in the way he envisioned. The integration problem in Virginia, and across the nation, was resolved with Republican ascendency in the South.

For the first time, Johnson and his southern segregationist colleagues faced the fact that Eisenhower and the congressional GOP had the votes to pass civil rights legislation. Johnson did the only thing he could do and that was to have it watered down by assigning it to a committee headed by

Eastland, arguably one of the most strident racists in Congress. After gutting the bill, Johnson wanted it both ways.

In *The Presidency of Lyndon B. Johnson* author Vaughn Davis Bornet writes:

> Johnson sought recognition from civil rights advocates for passing the bill, while also receiving recognition from the mostly southern anti-civil rights Democrats for reducing it so much as to kill it.

The final bill was a great disappointment to Martin Luther King and most other civil rights leaders, although Dr. King reluctantly urged Eisenhower to sign it.

Kennedy Sides with Segregationists

John F. Kennedy served in the Senate throughout the Eisenhower administration. In his first race for Congress, Kennedy developed a pattern of campaigning that was replicated in all his future elections. It was based on the racial hypocrisy that characterized the Democratic Party since Blacks switched away from the Republican Party.

With a large Black population in his congressional district, Kennedy paid lip service to civil rights and the need to address the institutional inequities that afflicted the Black community. In the office, he would do nothing to address the problems. In fact, he generally voted with the southern Democrat bloc on civil rights issues.

Much to the disappointment of Massachusetts civil rights leaders, Kennedy did not propose or support any civil rights legislation during his tenure in the House and only voted for one civil rights bill in the Senate after he joined Johnson and southern Democrats in watering it down.

Kennedy joined with the southern Democrats, voting to have the 1957 civil rights bill assigned to Eastland's Judiciary Committee. It was generally assumed that Eastland would be able to use his power to kill the bill in committee. While it was not possible to stop the bill due to Eisenhower's and the Republican Party's overwhelming support, Johnson and Eastland were able to strip the critically important Title III from the bill, with Kennedy voting with the southern Democrats in removing the key enforcement provision.

Johnson and the southern Democrats then led a fight to have the jury competency language (Title IV) changed to enable the continuation of all-White juries. Kennedy again voted with the segregationists. However, the amendment to gut Title IV was defeated, and the jury provision remained in the final version of the bill.

Democrat opposition was intense, and many expected the bill to be defeated by filibuster, a standard and generally successful tactic of the southern Democrats. In an effort to stop passage, Senate majority leader Johnson had South Carolina's Democrat senator Strom Thurmond take to the floor and commence what would become the longest one-man filibuster in American history—some 24 hours and 18 minutes.

The efforts by congressional Democrats to water down Eisenhower's civil rights legislation was successful. According to the 1997 book *The Civil Rights Act of 1964: The Passage of the Law That Ended Racial Segregation* by Colorado College Professor Robert D. Loevy:

> The Democratic Senate Majority Leader Lyndon Baines Johnson of Texas realized that the bill and its journey through Congress could tear apart his party, whose southern bloc was opposed to civil rights, while northern members were more favorable toward them. Southern senators occupied chairs of numerous important committees because of their long seniority. Johnson sent the bill to the Judiciary Committee led by Senator James Eastland of Mississippi, who proceeded to drastically alter the bill. He deleted the public accommodations section, which would have outlawed racial discrimination in hotels, restaurants, theaters, and other places open to the public. He also removed the section that would have authorized the Attorney General to file suits to desegregate public schools.

Congressman Howard Smith

In the House, Democrat representative Howard Smith of Virginia chaired the all-important Rules Committee, which controlled the flow of legislation. Smith was a dyed-in-the-wool segregationist. Many years later,

Georgia's Black Congressman and civil rights icon John Lewis would demand that Smith's portrait, which hung in the Rules Committee hearing room, be removed. In describing the Democrat congressman, Lewis said:

> It is an affront to all of us ... [Smith is] perhaps best remembered for his obstruction in passing this country's civil rights laws. A man who in his own words never accepted the colored race as a race of people who had equal intelligence and education and social attainments as the White people of the South.

It is noteworthy that a man of Smith's opinions was not only one of many similar-minded Democrats in Congress at the time, but that he and so many other racist Democrats were given such powerful leadership positions by the party in general. In fact, Smith would again play a key role in blocking congressional action on the 1964 civil rights bill.

Johnson's Pseudo Support

If Johnson had his way, the 1957 Civil Right bill would have had the same doomed fate of earlier attempts. Ever the political pragmatist, he concluded that the only alternative to a strong civil rights bill was a weak one. He also may have been considering his future in a changing America.

In a 2014 opinion piece political consultant and author Roger Stone wrote:

> It was only in 1957 when Lyndon Johnson was pointedly told by *Washington Post* publisher Phil Graham and aide Jim Rowe that he, LBJ, had better pass some sort of civil rights bill if he was going to have even a shot at being acceptable to northern liberals as the Democratic nominee for president in 1960, something that LBJ had been lusting after for decades.

Johnson's final bill had removed Justice Department oversight and left violation of civil rights up to local all-White juries, leading former First Lady Eleanor Roosevelt to call the bill a "toothless fakery."

With strong opposition from both northern and southern Democrats, even the watered-down Eisenhower civil rights bill was in jeopardy in the Senate. The vote was tied. Vice President Nixon officially presided over the

Senate with the power to vote to break a tie. He did so, and the Republican 1957 Civil Rights Act—weakened as it was by congressional Democrats—passed Congress and was sent to Eisenhower for his signature.

Dr. King's Letter to Vice President Richard Nixon

Because the bill had been watered down by Johnson, Kennedy and the southern Democrats, some civil rights leaders proposed that the bill not be passed nor signed by the president. In August of 1957, however, Dr. King wrote to Vice President Nixon encouraging passage of the bill:

Mr. Richard Nixon, Vice-president
The United States of America
Washington, D.C.
Dear Mr. Nixon:

> For several weeks I have been intending to write you, but an extremely busy schedule has stood in my way. First, I want to express my sincere appreciation to you for so graciously receiving me and my colleague Rev. Abernathy in your office during the month of June. I will long remember the rich fellowship which we shared together and the fruitful discussion that we had.

> Since our meeting together many significant things have happened in the life of our nation, particularly in the realm of civil rights. Just this morning our local paper revealed that the compromised Civil Rights Bill was finally passed by the Senate. After considering all angles I have come to the conclusion that the present bill is far better than no bill at all. This limited bill still provides district judges with power to maintain order and to insist upon compliance with their orders.

> This could be a powerful incentive in changes in behavior and attitude. I realize that many sincere leaders, both Negro and white, feel that no bill is better than the present bill, and that since we have

waited this long for civil rights legislation, we can afford to wait an additional year to get stronger legislation in this area.

While I sympathize with this point of view, I feel that civil rights legislation is urgent now, and the present limited bill will go a long way to insure it. So it is my hope that the President will not veto the bill.

It is also my firm conviction that the full effect of the Civil Rights Bill will depend in large degree upon the program of a sustained mass movement on the part of Negroes. History has demonstrated that inadequate legislation supported by mass action can accomplish more than adequate legislation which remains unenforced for the lack of a determined mass movement. This is why I am initiating in the south a crusade for citizenship in which we will seek to get at least two million Negroes registered in the south for the 1960 elections. With the enthusiasm that we hope to kindle and the aid of the Civil Rights Bill this should not be difficult.

Let me say before closing how deeply grateful all people of goodwill are to you for your assiduous labor and dauntless courage in seeking to make the Civil Rights Bill a reality. This has impressed people all across the country, both Negro and white. This is certainly an expression of your devotion to the highest mandates of the moral law. It is also an expression of your political wisdom. More and more the Negro vote is becoming a decisive factor in national politics.

The Negro vote is the balance of power in so many important big states that one almost has to have the Negro vote to win a presidential election.

Again, let me thank you for your hospitality and generosity. You have my prayers and best wishes for the great work that you are doing in making our democracy a living reality. With persons like you occupying such important positions in our nation I am sure that we will soon emerge from the bleak and desolate midnight of man's inhumanity to man to the bright and glittering daybreak of freedom and justice for all men.

Please extend my best regards to Mrs. Nixon and our other friends around the White House.

Very sincerely yours,

Martin Luther King, Jr., Minister

P.S. At your earliest convenience I hope you will see your way clear to speak to the President concerning the conference that we discussed. It was a real pleasure talking with you by telephone the other day.

The tone of the letter clearly demonstrates Dr. King's friendship and the close working relationship between the Republican Eisenhower administration and America's leading civil rights leader.

Dr. King maintained a working friendship with Nixon and made no secret of the fact that he voted for Nixon in 1960. This is understandable when you consider that in all his crusades, South and North, Dr. King was protesting exclusively against Democratic Party racism—from the Edmund Pettus Bridge in Selma to the streets of Chicago. Unlike later civil rights activists, such as Jesse Jackson and Al Sharpton, Dr. King preferred to keep his crusades away from his personal partisan leanings and focused on basic civil rights defined by the Constitution and federal law. Jackson and Sharpton aligned themselves as political partisans and advocates of the Democratic Party that created the oppression of entitlement and generational dependency.

Despite strong opposition from Democrats, and the reservations of some civil rights supporters, the weakened bill was passed by Congress—the first civil rights law since the 1875 Civil Rights Act enacted under Republican president Ulysses S. Grant and a Republican Congress. It was an unprecedented achievement by the Eisenhower administration and congressional Republicans. The 1957 Civil Rights Bill represented the first time that any

Democrat in Congress had ever voted in support of a major civil rights bill in American history.

All forty-three Senate Republicans voted in favor of the 1957 act, while Democrats were split, twenty-nine in favor and eighteen opposed, with three Democrats ducking the issue by not voting at all. A notable Senate vote against the 1957 Civil Rights Bill was future president John Kennedy.

The House vote had Republicans favoring the bill by 167 to 19. House Democrats could barely muster a majority with 118 in favor and 107 opposed. On September 9, 1957, Eisenhower signed the Civil Rights Act into law.

The passage of the Civil Rights Act of 1957 was a milestone. It was the beginning of the end of the Democratic Party's ability to use Congress and the filibuster as a firewall against civil rights progress. This confined the Democrat's effort to preserve institutional segregation and racism primarily to a state-based resistance movement.

Little Rock School Intervention

Just two weeks after the passage of the 1957 Civil Rights Act, a major confrontation over school integration took place in Little Rock, Arkansas.

Following the Supreme Court's ruling in *Brown v. Board of Education*, some southern school districts decided they had no choice but to adhere to the Court decision—Little Rock, Arkansas, was one of them. The plan called for the initial enrollment of Blacks in the Little Rock Central High School in the fall of 1957. The NAACP selected nine outstanding Black students, who became known as the Little Rock Nine, to be the first to enroll. What had been anticipated as a reasonably smooth transition became the issue of the day across America.

Democrat governor Orville Faubus called out the Arkansas National Guard to block admission of the Little Rock Nine. In an effort to stave off violence, Eisenhower had summoned Faubus to the White House and strongly urged him to obey the Supreme Court. Faubus returned to Little Rock and withdrew the National Guard. This resulted in violent street protests incited by local Democrat officials and their White supremacist terrorist affiliates.

The Black students were allowed to enter Little Rock High but had to be removed from the campus after only three hours when riots broke out outside the school. One of the Little Rock Nine, Elizabeth Eckford, later described her feelings as the students were taken from the school:

> They moved closer and closer. ... Somebody started yelling. ... I tried to see a friendly face somewhere in the crowd—someone who maybe could help. I looked into the face of an old woman, and it seemed a kind face, but when I looked at her again, she spat on me.

In response to the violence, Eisenhower signed Executive Order 10730, authorizing the use of military force to enforce the law and protect the students. He sent the 101st Airborne to Little Rock. He also took federal control over the Arkansas National Guard so that they would no longer be under the command of Governor Faubus. Federal troops remained in Little Rock for the remainder of the school year.

This was a momentous moment in civil rights history, and one that is largely ignored in contemporary civil rights narratives. It represented the first time that federal troops had entered a Democrat segregated state to protect the constitutional rights of Black Americans since federal soldiers were removed as part of the tragic Compromise of 1877.

Dr. King Praises Eisenhower

Eisenhower announced his decision to send in federal troops on a September 24 radio broadcast to the nation. The day after the announcement, Martin Luther King sent the president a letter praising his action.

The president

The White House

> I wish to express my sincere support for the stand you have taken to restore law and order in little rock, Arkansas. In the long run, justice finally must spring from a new moral climate. Yet spiritual forces cannot emerge in a situation of mob violence.

You should know that the overwhelming majority of southerners, Negro, and White stand firmly behind your resolute action. The pen of history will record that even the small and confused minority that oppose integration with violence will live to see that your action has been of great benefit to our nation and to the Christian traditions of fair play and brotherhood.

Martin Luther King jr. President
Southern Christian Leadership Conference.

If Dr. King and the Republicans were willing to enforce civil rights, the old Dixie Democrats remained as determined to oppose them in every way possible. As an ardent White supremacist and staunch defender of segregation, Faubus was not about to yield to the Constitution, the Supreme Court, the President of the United States, the Congress, or the federal military. Almost a year later, Eisenhower invited Martin Luther King and several other civil rights leaders to the White house for a meeting on June 23, 1958. This was the first time that Dr. King had been invited to the Oval Office. They agreed on the need for another civil rights law to re-establish some of the provisions removed from the 1957 bill by Johnson and the Democrat majority in the Senate.

The Lost Year

Little Rock Central High School was integrated for only one year. In 1958, Faubus followed Virginia's Democrat senator Harry Byrd's call for massive resistance and closed all Little Rock's public schools to avoid integration. His action required a referendum of the people of Little Rock. Faubus promised that once the referendum was passed, the state would lease the buildings to private schools under a segregated system. With the governor and the Democratic leadership behind the effort, the referendum passed handily.

When Faubus was blocked by federal courts from creating his segregated private schools, he closed the public schools in Little Rock in what became known as "the lost year" of education. This brought the wrath of the

White citizens of Little Rock down on the Black community—especially the NAACP leadership and the Black students who they blamed for causing the civil unrest and closing their public schools. In 1959, the Supreme Court struck down Faubus' action as illegal and unconstitutional.

In an effort to set aside the requirements of *Brown V. Board of Education*, the southern Democrats resurrected an old strategy—nullification. While the claim that a state could nullify acts of Congress was largely settled by the Supreme Court in the late 1800s, the Dixiecrats made a long shot attempt to resurrect the issue, claiming that the states could essentially nullify federal laws or Supreme Court rulings if they had a materially negative effect on the state.

The Little Rock school board had begun to comply with the high court's ruling with a desegregation plan but backed off under pressure from Faubus and the legislature. The school board, guided by Faubus, then filed a case in the United States District Court to nullify the Supreme Court decision by suspending the plan to desegregate the Little Rock public schools on the basis that it was disruptive to the peace of the community and would potentially cause violence. They called for the re-establishment of a segregated system.

In support of the action, the Democrat-controlled Arkansas state legislature amended the state constitution so that students did not have to attend integrated public schools—a state constitutional provision that nullified *Brown V. Board of Education* in the minds of Arkansas' Democrat leaders.

The local district federal court ruled in favor of the Little Rock request. It was later overturned by a federal court of appeals, which declared that the "intolerable and chaotic situation" predicted by Faubus was due solely to the actions of the Democrat political leadership. What became known as *Cooper v. Aaron* went before the Supreme Court.

The Supreme Court yet again held that state courts and state legislatures had no authority to nullify the rulings of the highest court in the land. It also denied that even a local federal court had such power. It stated that federal laws "can neither be nullified openly and directly by state legislators or state executive or judicial officers nor nullified indirectly by them through evasive schemes for segregation."

Despite *Brown v. Board of Education,* the Civil Rights Act of 1957 and the use of federal troops to enforce school integration laws, more than 90 percent of southern Black children remained in inferior segregated schools. The Democrat administrations in the segregated states had shown themselves to be resilient, tenacious, clever, and determined in the use of evasive schemes to preserve segregation. Their efforts to maintain White supremacy and segregated schools, and the associated violent oppression of Negroes, would not end until the latter half of the twentieth century as the old racist Democrat leadership lost their grip on America's southland.

Urban Democrat Racism

Even as the southern Democrat bloc was mounting its massive resistance campaign against integration, the party's urban leaders were refining *de facto* racism in the major cities. Perhaps the most important factor in keeping Blacks impoverished, segregated, and dependent on the great urban political machines is the lack of quality education. Without a decent education, young Black men and women are denied basic academic skills that can pave the way to college educations or career-potential employment.

With so many years of governance over the American ghettoes and so many examples of the ways and means to good education, it is impossible to believe that the quality of inner-city minority schools is an unanticipated outcome. Maintenance of a ghettoized dependent population is so beneficial to the political power and financial strength of the Democratic Party that it is reasonable to see poor schools as a racist scheme. Even *de facto* segregation is institutional in that it is the product of government policy. It is noteworthy that the difference in the quality of education and condition of the schools in cities with segregated minorities occurs even though both the White students and the Black students are part of the same school system with the same leadership and the same funding.

The Harlem 9

Five years after *Brown v. Board of Education* Black students in Harlem, New York, were still attending inferior segregated schools. It had been more than sixty years since any new school building was constructed to serve the

Black community. The existing schools were dilapidated. The teaching staff was of the poorest quality. These were all the result of longstanding racist city hall policies.

In 1956, Black civil rights activist Mae Mallory was fed up with the public school education being provided to the Black children of Harlem. She founded Harlem 9 as a protest movement. They challenged the *de facto* segregation policies of New York's still powerful Tammany Hall and the Democrat administration of mayor Robert F. Wagner by attempting to have their children transferred to higher quality White school. They filed lawsuits against both the city administration and the administration of so-called progressive Democrat governor W. Averell Harriman. The NAACP joined in support of the lawsuits.

Little was being gained through the Democrat-controlled courts, so in 1958, Malloy and the Harlem 9 called for a Black boycott. More than ten thousand school families participated. The Wagner administration retaliated against the parents by trying to prosecute them for negligence for not sending their children to schools. The attempt failed.

In 1960, the Harlem 9 won their lawsuit and hundreds of Black students were allowed to transfer their children to integrated schools. There was a downside. The longstanding racist and *de facto* segregation policies of city hall had created a racist culture in the White population. Whites began to take their children out of the integrated schools or not enroll them in the first place. Schools in New York and other major cities were being abandoned by what was termed "White flight."

With growing Black populations, the initially integrated schools were being treated like the old ghetto schools. Maintenance was cut, teacher performance dropped, and the quality of education became inferior. They eventually took on the characteristics of many of the other ghetto schools. Eventually, New York schools would be more segregated in the twenty-first century than they were in the 1960s.

Civil Rights Act of 1960

The Civil Rights Act of 1960 was intended to restore some of the provisions stripped out of the 1957 bill by the Democrats under the leadership of majority leader Lyndon Johnson and Judiciary chairman James Eastland. Johnson's pragmatic political view was obvious in his explanation to his southern Democrat colleagues.

> These Negroes, they're getting pretty uppity these days, and that's a problem for us, since they've got something now they never had before: the political pull to back up their uppityness. Now we've got to do something about this—we've got to give them a little something, just enough to quiet them down, not enough to make a difference.

While Senator Strom Thurmond still holds the record for the longest individual filibuster for his effort to defeat the Republican Civil Rights Act of 1957, it is not the longest filibuster in Senate history. Johnson realized that to defeat civil rights legislation, he would have to engineer a filibuster longer than one individual could sustain. That occurred in 1960, when he changed the rules and introduced a relay Democrat filibuster against the Civil Rights Act in which eighteen southern segregationist senators took turns speaking in opposition. Johnson also allowed an unprecedented fifteen-minute break at one point. Together, the segregationists held the Senate floor for 125 hours and 31 minutes, not including the break.

With the Republican administration in full support of the 1960 Civil Rights Act, Johnson recognized that the filibuster in and of itself was no longer a reliable weapon against such legislation.

Rather than face the prospect of a cloture vote that would cut off the filibuster and set a precedent, he used it as a bargaining chip. Johnson used the filibuster to gain concessions to render the bill ineffective by removing the enforcement provisions and then passing the weakened bill. Both Johnson and Kennedy voted for the relatively toothless bill.

Eisenhower Appoints Civil Rights Judges

In his book about the early civil rights era, *An Easy Burden,* Martin Luther King protégé Andrew Young wrote that it was Republican appointed judges that played a major role in defeating segregation and institutional racism in the South. Young specifically noted that "the southern segregationists were all Democrats." He further stated that the strongest judges on civil rights were appointed by Eisenhower, concluding that "these judges are among the many unsung heroes of the civil rights movement." Young would go on to be mayor of Atlanta, Georgia, and ambassador to the United Nations—positions he would not likely have attained without the civil rights record of Eisenhower and the Republican Party. Ironically, he gained his political successes as a Democrat.

In his 1965 book, *Waging Peace*, Eisenhower praised Nixon's work in the area of civil rights. He wrote that "Since 1953, our Vice President had served as chairman of a committee which sought to eliminate discrimination on the basis of race or color in the employment practices of government con-tractors." Ike noted that Nixon "had been a troubleshooter in politics and in civil rights, and he had a special talent for understanding and summing up the views of others."

Eisenhower Legacy

Eisenhower left office as one of the more popular presidents in American history, and with one of the best civil rights records since post-Civil War Reconstruction. His eight years in the Oval Office was often referred to as a time of peace and prosperity. His popularity was worldwide. Upon leaving office, Eisenhower traveled to the major nations of the world, where he was enthusi-astically greeted by world leaders and throngs of millions of cheering citizens.

In terms of civil rights, Eisenhower's legacy was the passage of the first two civil rights bills since the Republican laws and constitutional amend-ments of the Reconstruction era. Weakened as they were by the Democrats in Congress, they represented an important step forward. They had broken through the Democrats' civil rights block that had prevailed for more than ninety years and set the stage for the civil rights legislation of the 1960s.

Eisenhower's appointments of Earl Warren to the Supreme Court led to a unanimous vote in *Brown v. Board of Education*. The Eisenhower administration was the first since Republican president Grant to send federal troops into Dixie to enforce federal civil rights laws and Supreme Court decisions.

Eisenhower put the power of the Oval Office behind a constitutional amendment to allow Washington residents to vote in presidential elections. The Twenty-Third Amendment was passed out of Congress in 1960 and formally ratified by the states in 1961.

The Election of 1960

Given the reputation of Eisenhower as the hero of World War II, his ending the fighting in Korea, his personal popularity, and the fact that he governed over a time of economic growth and prosperity, the Republicans should have been positioned to win the 1960 presidential election. They were also poised to regain the loyalty of Black America as the party of civil rights.

Republicans chose Vice President Nixon as the party's standard bearer. He selected former Massachusetts senator Henry Cabot Lodge Jr., who at the time was serving as ambassador to the United Nations.

The Lodge political dynasty had a long family history as staunch abolitionists going back to colonial days. It is claimed that Lodge had cost the ticket southern votes, when he suggested that Ralph Bunche, a Black American, would be an ideal choice for a cabinet position.

Progressive Democrats despised Nixon over his defeat of congresswoman and liberal icon Helen Gahagan Douglas, who made a bid for the United States Senate in 1950 when incumbent Senator Sheridan Downey withdrew in favor of *Los Angeles Daily News* owner Manchester Boddy. Because of her far leftist leaning, Boddy dubbed her the "Pink Lady—down to her underwear." After defeating Boddy, Douglas faced Nixon with endorsements and financial support from fellow congressman John F. Kennedy. In a hard-fought battle, Douglas coined the term "Tricky Dick" to describe Nixon.

In terms of presidential aspirants, Democrats had a large field of serious candidates and a number of "favorite son" candidates, who ran in their state primaries to control the votes at the convention. Many, including former president Harry Truman, who supported Missouri senator Stuart Symington, thought Senator Kennedy to be too young and too inexperienced for the office of president.

Symington was hurt, however, by his refusal to address segregated audiences in the South. Both Kennedy and Johnson were more than willing to appear at segregated forums. Former Illinois governor Adlai Stevenson, the 1952 and 1956 Democrat standard bearer, had the support of Eleanor Roosevelt. No one could stop the Kennedy juggernaut, and he won the nomination on the first ballot.

Kennedy surprised many by selecting Lyndon Johnson for his vice-presidential running mate. It was a shrewd political move. Though Kennedy had voted in Congress with the southern segregationists on civil rights legislation, his pro-civil rights campaign rhetoric was discomforting to the powerful Democrat southern bloc. They wanted one of their own on the ticket as had been the case with past Democrat presidential tickets.

Those who see Lyndon Johnson as the president who signed the 1964 Civil Rights Act will fail to understand that Kennedy's selection of Johnson was largely due to his southern segregationist and racist record at the time. There was little evidence of Johnson's later pro-civil rights positions. The ticket needed a vice-presidential candidate who could assuage southern segregationist concerns. Johnson was the ideal person for that task.

Kennedy officially won a narrow victory, although many historians now believe that the victory was due to massive vote fraud in both Illinois and Texas. They argue that Chicago's Democrat machine under Richard J. Daley and the political machine of Lyndon Johnson in Texas had produced enough fraudulent votes to give Kennedy the Electoral College victory. Both the Johnson forces and the Chicago machine had already earned a well-established reputation for stealing elections. In producing the victory in Illinois, Mayor Daley and patriarch Joe Kennedy had engaged the services of Mafia kingpin Sam Giancana.

Washington Plantation Master

At the time of the 1960 presidential election, Washington, DC, was in transition. Although Eisenhower enabled DC citizens to vote for the president, the District, established by the Constitution, was still ruled over "in all matters" by Congress. While there has been a long history of proposals to give the residents of Washington some of the representative rights and powers of other American citizens, these efforts languished.

In the 1960s, the District was officially governed by a commission appointed by the president. But for all practical purposes, Washington was essentially governed by the chairman of the House District Committee. At the time, it was South Carolina's racist Democrat "Johnny Mac" McMillan.

At the dawn of the 1960s, Democrat congressional leaders would elect McMillan, a staunch segregationist who voted against every civil rights legislation that came before Congress, to rule over the Black citizens of the nation's capital. McMillan was also a signer of the Southern Manifesto and a leader in the Massive Resistance movement against school desegregation.

When Lyndon Johnson later appointed Walter Washington, a Black man, as the first mayor-commissioner, McMillan mockingly responded by sending the new mayor a truck load of watermelons, which the congressman described as letters from home.

The fact that the Democrats in Congress would repeatedly elect a southern racist to govern over a city with a large Black population illustrated the racial hypocrisy that permeated the Democratic Party.

In 1974, Republican president Richard Nixon ended Washington, DC's, provincial style government by signing home rule legislation that gave the predominantly Black voters of the District the right to elect their own government for the first time. Ironically, Walter Washington would become the first popularly elected mayor of the city of Washington.

John Fitzgerald Kennedy (1961–1963)

John Fitzgerald Kennedy came into office as the youngest elected president—slightly older than Teddy Roosevelt who ascended to the Oval Office upon the assassination of President McKinley.

Even though Eisenhower was among the most active presidential supporters of civil rights, and the Republican Party had a long and largely unblemished history in support of civil rights, Kennedy was key in setting the stage for what became the long unfounded Democratic Party narrative of Republican Party racism. With the support of a fawning press, pseudo historians and a friendly educational and publishing establishment, the false narrative became a widely held belief into the twenty-first century. The Democrat narrative became so accepted that it literally wiped out much of the public's awareness of the existential roles the Republican Party played in the fight for civil rights, especially the critical importance of the GOP in the 1957, 1960, 1964, and 1965 civil rights acts.

Despite his noble campaign promises, Kennedy did little in putting forward a pro-active civil rights agenda in his first three years. Kennedy's greatest civil rights achievements were reactive, most notably the deployment of federal troops to protect the Freedom Riders in 1961, and in that instance, he was pushed hard by his brother, attorney general Robert Kennedy. It was not until the lead-up to the 1964 campaign that Kennedy again talked about future legislative action on civil rights to correct some of the deficiencies in the 1957 and 1960 acts—deficiencies that he played a key role in creating.

Whether the motivation for civil rights activity was from the attorney general or the president, the common historical view of Kennedy places him in the vanguard of the civil rights movement. Kennedy's reputation as a civil rights activist rests largely on the legacy of the 1964 Civil Rights Act—a law that was left to be passed in memoriam by his successor Lyndon Johnson and congressional Republicans. Despite his reputation, Kennedy was not responsible for any civil rights legislation during his entire political career. Kennedy died without ever fully supporting a single piece of civil rights legislation in Congress or as president. Regardless, he received more than 70 percent of the Black vote.

According to the PBS series *The American Experience* history documentary:

> John Kennedy was elected president in 1960 partly because of his promise to secure equal rights for black Americans. Yet, once in office, he and his brother Robert, the attorney general, sought to avoid too great an involvement in the politically divisive struggle. Violent Southern conflict about black civil rights overtook the Kennedys, forcing them to intervene on the side of the integrationists. Still, President Kennedy resisted sending strong civil rights legislation to

Congress, unwilling to risk further alienating the powerful Southern conservatives blocking his domestic program.

In the above quote, this author believes it would have been more precise and accurate to have replaced the word *conservatives* with *Democrats*. Calling conservatives "racists" has been a longstanding misapplication of the term and part of the Democrat's false narrative of history. The southern Democrats were not philosophic conservatives—the fundamental requirement of which is devotion to the Constitution.

The popularity of the young charismatic president was as emotional as it was rational. Kennedy brought movie star glamour and the glitter of high society back to the White House.

Among Blacks, the devotion to the Kennedy family reached almost religious proportions. Photos of Dr. Martin Luther King Jr. flanked by Jack and Bobby Kennedy appeared next to images of Jesus in millions of Black homes. Black political activist K. Carl Smith captured the sentiment when in his book *Frederick Douglas Republicans,* he wrote:

> There is plenty of truth in the saying that a picture is worth a thousand words. As I looked back over my life, the Kennedy-King-Kennedy image led to my blind and total loyalty to the Democratic Party.

He further wrote:

> Similar to many blacks, through this image, I believed with all my heart that JFK and RFK were close members of my family. I was convinced they were supporters of Dr. King and champions of the Civil Rights Movement.

Smith would later give up his theological devotion to the Kennedy myth. Smith's study of history led him to convert to the Republican Party and begin a crusade on radio and television to educate the American public, Black and White, of the true legacy of the Democratic Party. He founded an advocacy group called the Frederick Douglass Republicans (with the ironic acronym FDR) to spread the Republican principles of the nineteenth-century abolitionist and personal friend of Abraham Lincoln.

Freedom Riders

The Congress of Racial Equality (CORE) was founded in 1942 by a biracial group headed by Republican civil rights activist James L. Farmer. CORE was dedicated to nonviolent protest and relied on grassroots leadership. He was often cited in the press as one of the big four civil rights leaders of his time.

Farmer's CORE worked with Dr. Martin Luther King Jr. and John Lewis, a member of the Student Nonviolent Coordinating Committee (SNCC) who rose to become a congressman from Georgia. The group organized the Freedom Riders that traveled through the South in 1961.

They organized a group of thirteen Freedom Riders—seven Blacks and six Whites—to ride a Greyhound bus from Washington to New Orleans, to arrive on May 17 to commemorate the seventh anniversary of the Supreme Court's *Brown v. Board of Education* decision. The first violent incident occurred on May 12 in Rock Hill, South Carolina. John Lewis, White Freedom Rider and Navy veteran Albert Bigelow, and another Black rider were viciously attacked as they attempted to enter a Whites-only waiting area. This was only the beginning of the violent reaction to the Freedom Riders.

According to the JFK Library website, there were mass arrests in North Carolina and Mississippi. Though the "crimes" were considered relatively minor, even by southern standards, those arrested in Mississippi were subjected to strip searches, public humiliation, and brutality at the hands of vengeful citizens by the local Democrat authorities.

At the direction of Mississippi's Democrat governor Ross Barnett, demonstrators were sent to Parchman Farm, the state's maximum-security prison. Beds were often removed from the cells, forcing the incarcerated to sleep on hard cement floors without blankets.

On May 14, 1961, an angry mob in Anniston, Alabama, followed the bus in their automobiles, and someone threw a bomb into the bus. The Freedom Riders escaped the bus as it burst into flames, only to be brutally beaten by members of the surrounding mob. Another Freedom Rider bus traveled to Birmingham, Alabama, and those riders were also beaten by an angry White mob. Birmingham public safety commissioner, Democrat Bull Connor, stated that although he knew the Freedom Riders were arriving and violence awaited them, he posted no police protection at the station because he said it was Mother's Day.

In response to the violence, attorney general Robert Kennedy was pressured by civil rights leaders to take action. If President Kennedy lacked enthusiasm for the civil rights battle, his brother Robert did not. He sent four hundred federal marshals into the southern states to protect the Freedom Riders and called on the Interstate Commerce Commission to order the desegregation of all interstate travel.

Farmer was in constant fear for his own life. He said, "Anyone who said he wasn't afraid during the civil rights movement was either a liar or without imagination. I think we were all scared. I was scared all the time. My hand didn't shake but inside I was shaking."

During one of his visits to Louisiana in 1963, Farmer was being tracked down by state troopers. Fearing southern justice, a local undertaker had Farmer play dead in the back of a hearse and drove the civil rights leader out of town.

In 1968, Farmer ran a losing campaign for Congress in New York as the Liberal Party candidate. He was endorsed in that campaign by the Republican Party. He had voted for Richard Nixon in both 1960 and 1968 and served in the Nixon administration as assistant secretary of the Department of Health, Education and Welfare (HEW), as it was known at the time.

Kennedy's Supreme Court Decision

Kennedy had his only opportunity to appoint a member of the United States Supreme Court when associate justice Charles Whittaker resigned due to ill health. The president was strongly urged to appoint federal appellate judge William Hastie as the first Black to serve on the Court. Kennedy rejected the recommendations, recognizing that he would face strong opposition from racist Senate Democrats, especially Judiciary chairman James Eastland of Mississippi. With Eastland in charge of the hearings, confirmation of Hastie would have been extremely unlikely. Instead, Kennedy appointed Byron White, a deputy attorney general in the Robert Kennedy

Justice Department who was placed in charge of protecting civil rights. He had been given the task to negotiate with fellow Democrat and then Alabama governor John Patterson. To whatever extent White actually negotiated with Patterson, it appears to have had no significant effect.

John Patterson

John Patterson was typical of southern Democrat governors of the period. As Alabama's attorney general, he used every technical legal device and outright defiance of federal law and court orders in thwarting the *Brown v. Board of Education* school desegregation ruling. At one point, he banned the NAACP from operating in the state.

In 1958, Patterson was the Ku Klux Klan's candidate for governor. As was so often the case, he was considered a member of the progressive wing of the Democratic Party because of his funding of public works projects, White education, and medical treatment facilities.

When Black students demonstrated for an end to discrimination at Alabama State University, Patterson ordered a mass expulsion. He was the protector and implementer of Alabama's Jim Crow laws.

Patterson continued to play a prominent role in Alabama politics. As late as 1984, and despite his staunch segregationist record, he was appointed to the Alabama Court of Criminal Appeals by fellow segregationist and then Democrat governor George Wallace.

Governor Ross Barnett

Mississippi's Democrat governor Ross Barnett is yet another example of the tolerance of the national Democratic Party leaders for outrageously racist governors within the Party. Barnett was among the most aggressive defenders of segregation. He was an active leader in the White supremacist Citizens' Council. Like many southern racists, Barnett, a onetime Baptist Sunday school teacher, claimed that segregation was God's plan. He said: "The good Lord was the original segregationist. He put the Black man in

Africa. He made us White because he wanted us White, and He intended that we should stay that way."

He even argued that Negros favored segregation. According to Barnett, the reason Mississippi had the highest percentage of Negroes of any state in America was because, "they love our way of life here, and that way is segregation."

Sit-Ins

In the early 1960s, the civil rights movement employed a tactic known as sit-ins in which groups of Blacks would take up seats in Whites only accommodations or would protest in public places by sitting on the ground. The catchy term led to such variations as "wade-ins" at segregated public swimming pools and church sponsored "pray-ins" at White churches.

The sit-in concept was said to have started in 1960 when a group of Blacks quietly took up seats at the dining counter of a Woolworth "dime store" in Greensboro, North Carolina, and requested service. It was a form of passive resistance. Rather than march and chant, protestors would just sit quietly.

Those participating were subjected to verbal threats and physical violence. Democrat public officials would deploy law enforcement to forcibly remove those occupying the seats reserved for Whites only. Within a year some fifteen hundred demonstrators were arrested, many being convicted of trespassing.

The sit-ins had their desired effect. Images of peaceful Black students being tormented, harassed, and even injured by angry White mobs, and set upon by heavily armed police, exposed the underbelly of institutional racism in the Democrat southland.

Bell v. Maryland

The issue of access to public amenities reached the United States Supreme Court when a group of Black students carried out a sit-in at Hooper's Restaurant in Baltimore, Maryland, in 1960. At the time, Baltimore was a typical southern Democrat segregated city. The new Democrat mayor, J. Harold Grady, had the group arrested for criminal trespassing. Grady had just succeeded twelve-year racist Democrat mayor Thomas L. J. D'Alesandro Jr.

Thomas J. D'Alesandro Jr., served as mayor of Baltimore from 1947 to 1959. He presided over a racist administration. He promoted the erection of Confederate monuments—and praised Confederate generals at dedication ceremonies. He was a supporter of Baltimore's segregated schools. As late as 1966, D'Alesandro Jr. supported George Mahoney, an outspoken segregationist for governor of Maryland. Mahoney was a key player in the Democrats' Massive Resistance movement against school integration.

Baltimore's White racist regimes would continue after Grady, when Thomas J. D'Alesandro III would take over his father's position in city hall. The D'Alesandro men were the father and brother of former house speaker Nancy Pelosi.

Given the White supremacist power structure in Maryland, the conviction of the students by the Baltimore Circuit Court was not surprising. Nor was the fact that the convictions were upheld on appeal by Maryland Court of Appeals. The convictions were vacated by the United States Supreme Court and the case was sent back to the lower court for reconsideration. The dissenting opinion upholding the convictions and the decision of the circuit and appellate courts was issued by Democrat justice Hugo Black— the former member of the Ku Klux Klan who was one of the architects of Franklin Roosevelt's racist New Deal programs—and who FDR appointed to the high court.

James Meredith and Ole Miss

In 1962, when a young Black Air Force veteran named James Meredith applied for admission to the all-White University of Mississippi, known commonly as Ole Miss, he was denied four times. In an effort to stop the registration, the Mississippi Institutions of Higher Learning named Governor Barnett the official school registrar.

Kennedy attempted to resolve the situation with calls to Barnett. When Barnett continued to refuse admission to Meredith, Kennedy found it necessary to again use federal law enforcement to compel compliance with federal law. He sent federal marshals to accompany Meredith in applying for admission for a fifth time.

On September 13 of that year, the Democrat governor went on radio to address the people of Mississippi in what he called "our greatest crisis since the War Between the States." It seemed more like a call for violence than a plea for peace. He said that "having long since failed in their efforts to conquer the indomitable spirit of the people of Mississippi and their unshakable will to preserve the sovereignty and majesty of our commonwealth, they [the federal government] now seek to break us physically with the power of force."

He called on the Democrat supporters of racial bigotry to rise up:

> The day of expediency is past. We must either submit to the unlawful dictates of the federal government or stand up like men and tell them no. The day of reckoning has been delayed as long as possible. It is now upon us. This is the day, and this is the hour. Knowing you as I do, there is no doubt in my mind what the overwhelming majority of loyal Mississippians will do. They will never submit to the moral degradation, to the shame and the ruin which have faced all others who have lacked the courage to defend their beliefs.

Barnett made no pretense of the reason for his call to arms. While he did not specifically call for individual violence, there could be no mistaking his meaning. He called on the Democrats in position of power and their supporters among the general public to engage in an insurrection:

> I have made my position in this matter crystal clear. I have said in every county in Mississippi that no school in our state will be integrated while I am your Governor. I shall do everything in my power to prevent integration in our schools. I assure you that the schools will not be closed if this can possibly be avoided, but they will not be integrated if I can prevent it. As your Governor and Chief Executive of the sovereign State of Mississippi, I now call on every public official and every private citizen of our great state to join me.

This radio address characterized the view of the Democratic Party leadership across the South.

Later in September of 1962, Barnett attended a football game between the Ole Miss Rebels and the Kentucky Wildcats. He was greeted by more than forty thousand fans waving Confederate battle flags. A huge Confederate flag was spread over the field at half time. While the audience was chanting, "We want Ross," Barnett walked out on the fifty-yard line and gave his famous sixteen-word speech: "I love Mississippi! I love her people! Our customs. I love and I respect our heritage."

The next day, the campus erupted in riots in opposition to integration, resulting in scores being injured and two people being killed. Kennedy then did what Eisenhower had done before him. He sent US soldiers to the scene and federalized the Mississippi National Guard to restore peace.

For defying federal authority, Barnett was fined $10,000 and sentenced to jail. A southern appeals court reversed the decision, ridiculously claiming Barnett had been in "substantial compliance with the orders of the court."

Barnett was so racially prejudice that he banned Mississippi State University from playing Loyola University in a National College Athletic Association (NCAA) matchup because the Chicago team was integrated. The Mississippi team refused to obey the edict and participated in the game to Barnett's great displeasure.

Barnett left office in 1964 but not before reaffirming his support for segregation and his opposition to any Republican influence in Mississippi.

In 1966, Robert Kennedy visited Old Miss. He took on Barnett directly, claiming that the then former governor had asked to have photographs taken of him that would show US troops pointing the guns at him as an indication of his courage and defiance. The students roared with laughter. After his speech, Kennedy received a standing ovation from more than five thousand students—a stark contrast from Barnett's appearance four years earlier.

Barnet was so outraged by the speech that he bitterly attacked Kennedy with the following statement:

> It becomes a man who never tried a lawsuit in his life, but who occupied the high position of United States attorney general and who was responsible for using 30,000 troops and spent approximately six million dollars to put one unqualified student in Ole Miss to return to the scene of this crime and discuss any phase of this infamous affair. . . . I say to you that Bobby Kennedy is a very sick and

dangerous American. We have lots of sick Americans in this country but most of them have a long beard. Bobby Kennedy is a hypocritical, left-wing beatnik without a beard who carelessly and recklessly distorts the facts.

For the first time in many years, the Republican Party nominated candidates for governor and lieutenant governor in Mississippi. Barnett called for Republicans to be driven out of Mississippi. He feared that Republicans would undermine the Democrat-enforced segregation and Jim Crow laws and be more aligned with the northern states. He said he was "fed up with these fence-riding, pussyfooting, snow-digging Yankee Republicans."

Bull Connor and Birmingham

In January of 1963, Democrat George Wallace was sworn in for the first of his three non-consecutive terms as governor of Alabama. In April of that year, Martin Luther King launched one of his more noted civil rights campaigns. It was the first time Dr. King had expanded his civil rights efforts beyond Georgia. It gained him wide criticism from both the White establishment and many of his colleagues in the civil rights movement.

Dr. King selected Birmingham because he considered it among the most segregated and oppressive cities in America. He formed an alliance with Reverend Fred Shuttlesworth of the Alabama Christian Movement for Human Rights and his own brother, the Reverend A. D. King, who lived in Ensley, Alabama. On March 24, there was a bombing of a Black residence that seriously injured two people.

The initial series of protests, which started on April 3, were relatively small and did not garner a lot of public attention nationally. Though peaceful, they resulted in the arrests of scores of participants. That changed.

Democrat public safety commissioner Eugene "Bull" Connor gained national fame for the brutal police response to peaceful demonstrations. He deployed increasingly violent tactics against unarmed marchers. The images of police using dogs, fire hoses, and batons to attack the unarmed demonstrators became the lead news story across the nation. Almost one thousand demonstrators were arrested, and the name Bull Connor was indelibly etched into the infamous history of institutional racism.

On April 11, 1963, Democrat city officials obtained a court order essentially barring Dr. King's coalition from any further demonstrations. On Good Friday, April 12, Dr. King was joined by Reverend Ralph Abernathy and Reverend Shuttlesworth in defying that court order. They were arrested. It was during this incarceration that Dr. King penned one of his most important communications.

Letter from Birmingham Jail

The letter was a very long statement of his beliefs and strategies, plus a defense of his approach to civil rights. It was addressed to his fellow clergy but intended for a broader audience. It was also a message to those in the civil rights movement who were criticizing Dr. King's expanding the movement beyond his base in Georgia and for moving beyond negotiation to confrontation.

It started out:

> My Dear Fellow Clergymen:
>
> While confined here in the Birmingham city jail, I came across your recent statement calling my present activities "unwise and untimely." Seldom do I pause to answer criticism of my work and ideas … But since I feel that you are men of genuine good will and that your criticisms are sincerely set forth, I want to try to answer your statement in what I hope will be patient and reasonable terms.

By way of explanation, Dr. King continued:

> I am cognizant of the interrelatedness of all communities and states. I cannot sit idly by in Atlanta and not be concerned about what happens in Birmingham. Injustice anywhere is a threat to justice everywhere. We are caught in an inescapable network of mutuality, tied in a single garment of destiny. Whatever affects one directly,

affects all indirectly. Never again can we afford to live with the narrow, provincial "outside agitator" idea. Anyone who lives inside the United States can never be considered an outsider anywhere within its bounds.

Dr. King made it clear why he selected Birmingham, a city within a state that he recognized as being under the control of the Democratic Party's most racist leadership, who he referred to as "the city fathers."

Its ugly record of brutality is widely known. Negroes have experienced grossly unjust treatment in the courts. There have been more unsolved bombings of Negro homes and churches in Birmingham than in any other city in the nation. These are the hard, brutal facts of the case. On the basis of these conditions, Negro leaders sought to negotiate with the city fathers. But the latter consistently refused to engage in good faith negotiation.

Many civil rights leaders argued to be more patient and to rely more on negotiations than confrontations. Dr. King addressed this specifically in his letter.

For years now I have heard the word "Wait!" It rings in the ear of every Negro with piercing familiarity. This "Wait" has almost always meant "Never." We must come to see, with one of our distinguished jurists, that "justice too long delayed is justice denied."

In another portion of the letter, Dr. King underscored his point with a moving passage describing Negro life in the South. He did not refer to the Democratic Party by name, but since it was in total control of the South and the proponents and implementers of segregation, the implication is obvious.

Perhaps it is easy for those who have never felt the stinging darts of segregation to say, "Wait." But when you have seen vicious mobs lynch your mothers and fathers at will and drown your sisters and brothers at whim; when you have seen hate filled policemen curse, kick and even kill your black brothers and sisters; when you see the vast majority of your twenty million Negro brothers smothering in an airtight cage of poverty in the midst of an affluent society; when you suddenly find your tongue twisted and your speech stammering

> as you seek to explain to your six year old daughter why she can't go to the public amusement park that has just been advertised on television, and see tears welling up in her eyes when she is told that Funtown is closed to colored children, and see ominous clouds of inferiority beginning to form in her little mental sky, and see her beginning to distort her personality by developing an unconscious bitterness toward white people; when you have to concoct an answer for a five year old son who is asking: "Daddy, why do white people treat colored people so mean?" When you take a cross county drive and find it necessary to sleep night after night in the uncomfortable corners of your automobile because no motel will accept you; when you are humiliated day in and day out by nagging signs reading 'white' and "colored"; when your first name becomes "nigger," your middle name becomes "boy" (however old you are) and your last name becomes "John," and your wife and mother are never given the respected title "Mrs." When you are harried by day and haunted by night by the fact that you are a Negro, living constantly at tiptoe stance, never quite knowing what to expect next, and are plagued with inner fears and outer resentments; when you are forever fighting a degenerating sense of "nobodiness"--then you will understand why we find it difficult to wait.

Dr. King closed his 6,918-word letter with a bit of jailhouse humor.

> Never before have I written so long a letter. I'm afraid it is much too long to take your precious time. I can assure you that it would have been much shorter if I had been writing from a comfortable desk, but what else can one do when he is alone in a narrow jail cell, other than write long letters, think long thoughts and pray long prayers?

The Children's March

In May of 1963, James Bevel and other leaders of the SCLC planned the Children's Crusade to draw greater attention to the plight of Black school children. The idea did not have universal approval from civil rights leaders. Malcolm X opposed the idea, saying that "Real men don't put their children on the firing line." Despite the concerns, the idea won wide support from the community and the students.

On May 2, thousands of school children left their school to march to the 16th Street Baptist Church—the headquarters of the Birmingham campaign. The response by public safety commissioner Bull O'Connor shocked the nation. The school children were chased by police dogs, beaten with clubs and cattle prods, and attacked with high power fire hoses that ripped at their clothing. They were arrested and more than fifteen hundred were confined to a cell block meant for six hundred prisoners. They were released then re-arrested and bussed to the county fairgrounds.

The violent scenes appeared on television and in newspapers across the nation causing an outburst of public outrage. Locally, the Birmingham business community demanded a restoration of peace and order. Their businesses were suffering.

On May 5, marchers descended on the jail where many children were still being held. When it became obvious that the protests in Birmingham could not be ended by vigilante violence, local business leaders agreed to meet with civil rights leaders to negotiate an end to the demonstrations.

On May 10, 1963, leaders of the civil rights movement and Sidney Smyer, representing the Birmingham business community announced the Birmingham Truce agreement. It called for the easing of some segregations policies, the release of incarcerated demonstrators and the creation of a committee on racial problems and employment as an ongoing vehicle for future negotiations of segregationist policies. Dr. King and his colleagues declared it a great victory for the movement.

However, the Democrat city administration strongly criticized the agreement, and Bull Connor expressly refused to adhere to the terms of the agreement. The next day, Governor Wallace ordered state troopers to withdraw from Birmingham, and Dr. King left town.

Random marches, sit-ins and demonstrations continued throughout April. In one event, a large group of children marched on the police department to protest police violence and abuse.

Following the police round-up, the members of the all-Democrat Birmingham Board of Education ordered the expulsion of 1,081 students who had been arrested for participating in demonstrations. A federal judge ruled the expulsions were illegal and ordered the students returned to school.

The KKK Comes to Birmingham

An investigator named Ben Allen received a tip from a source within the Ku Klux Klan that a bombing was being planned. He advised Wallace to keep the troops in Birmingham, but the governor refused.

Coincidentally, there was a rally of Klan leaders from throughout the South taking place in Bessemer, Alabama. Referring to the Birmingham Truce, imperial wizard Bobby Shelton urged the rejection of "any concessions or demands from any of the atheist so-called ministers of the nigger race or any other group here in Birmingham."

That evening, the Gaston Motel, where Dr. King had been staying, received a bomb threat. The motel was owned by A. G. Gaston, a Black businessman.

A. D. King's Home Bombed

Shortly after ten o'clock on the night of June 11, uniformed Birmingham police officers were seen by Roosevelt Tatum placing a package near the front door of the A. D. King residence. The younger King and his wife were sitting in the living room, and their five children were asleep in their bedrooms. The package exploded. As King was ushering his family out the rear door a second explosion when off. Tatum ran to the rear of the house and found Reverend King and his wife fleeing with their five children. After hearing what Tatum had seen, King placed a call to the Federal Bureau of Investigation. Speaking of the house, King later said, "Its brick and that's the only thing that saved us."

Gaston Motel Bombing

Little more than an hour later a bomb exploded outside of Room 30 at the Gaston Motel—the room where Martin Luther King had been staying. FBI informant Gary Rowe and subsequent investigations suggested that the bombings were the work of the Ku Klux Klan's known bomber, Bill Holt.

For the remainder of May, civil rights protests were greeted with various levels of brutal law enforcement from arrests to beatings. Several other locations also were bombed.

James Baldwin and the Robert Kennedy Meeting

In the spring of 1963, writer and activist James Baldwin was in the center of national attention due to a May 17 *Time* magazine cover story in which he wrote, "There is not another writer who expresses with such poignancy and abrasiveness the dark realities of the racial ferment in North and South." Even then, the "ferment in the North and South" was notably in jurisdictions governed by the Democratic Party.

Shortly thereafter, Baldwin sent a telegram to the attorney general blaming the violence that had occurred in Birmingham directly on Washington, including FBI director J. Edgar Hoover, Mississippi's racist senator James Eastland, and on President Kennedy himself for not using "the great prestige of his office as the moral forum."

In response, attorney general Bobby Kennedy invited Baldwin and a small number of celebrity activists, including Lena Horne, Harry Belafonte, Martin Luther King's attorney Clarence Benjamin Jones, writer Lorraine Hansberry, and Jerome Smith, to a private off-the-record meeting at the attorney general's Manhattan apartment. Smith was a young activist who had been among those beaten in Mississippi.

Jones indicated that the meeting dealt with a series of complaints against the Kennedy administration. He brought to the attorney general's attention the appointment of several federal judges who had "openly and avowedly, prior to their appointment, indicated their flagrant segregationist views."

Jones also questioned the "effectiveness" of White FBI agents assigned to civil rights cases.

Kennedy, growing increasingly testy, attempted to provide examples of how the Justice Department was supporting civil rights. At that point, young Smith broke down in tears and rebutted Kennedy. "I've seen you guys stand around and do nothing more than take notes while we're being beaten," he said.

Kennedy intentionally turned his back on Smith, which caused Hansberry to point to Smith and say: "You've got a great many very, very accomplished people in this room, Mr. Attorney General. But the only man who should be listened to is that man over there." After the conversation between Kennedy and Smith became more heated, Hansberry continued:

> Look, if you can't understand what this young man is saying, then we are without any hope at all because you and your brother are representatives of the best that a White America can offer; and if you are insensitive to this, then there's no alternative except our going in the streets ... and chaos.

The meeting ended with the delegation storming out of Kennedy's apartment. After the meeting, Kennedy ordered J. Edgar Hoover to increase surveillance of Baldwin and others in attendance. As a result, Baldwin, a homosexual, was deemed by the FBI to be a pervert and communist, and the State Department restricted his passport.

Kennedy Under Pressure to Act on Civil Rights

With the Democrat administrations in the South being as lawless as the party's paramilitary terrorist groups, the brutality against Negroes was reaching proportions not seen since the Democrats violent takeover of the South during the period referred to by the racist leaders as the Redemption in the late 1800s.

With the civil rights leadership condemning the White House for inaction and with the public increasingly outraged by the atrocities being perpetrated by the Democrat leaders in the South—and with the president's reelection in the balance—the Kennedy brothers were under pressure to take definitive action. For the first time, President Kennedy had to make good on his campaign rhetoric.

Under pressure from his brother, President Kennedy finally agreed to act. He ordered troops to be sent to an air force base near Birmingham, promising to do whatever was necessary to prevent future violence. It was the first time in American history that a Democrat president used federal forces to enforce civil rights—an action that Republican president Eisenhower had done less than a decade earlier and Republican president Grant had done almost a century earlier.

Public sentiment also convinced Kennedy to again propose civil rights legislation to Congress. He could no longer merely talk about the need for civil rights legislation. He needed to demonstrate action—at least enough to appease the civil rights leadership without causing schism with his party's hardcore segregationists in Congress. Despite his campaign rhetoric, civil rights leaders were wary. They had seen how his 1960 campaign promises evaporated after his election.

Beyond Birmingham, civil rights controversies were propping up all over the South.

Integrating the University of Alabama

Democrat Governor Wallace had pledged to stop Black students from enrolling in the University of Alabama. He had promised to personally "stand in the schoolhouse door" to block their application. On June 11, Wallace stood in front of the door of the university's Foster Auditorium to bar two Black applicants, Vivian Jones and James Hood, from entering. Their admission had been ordered by federal courts.

Standing in the doorway, Wallace was confronted by United States deputy attorney general Nicholas Katzenbach and general Henry Graham of the Alabama National Guard, which had been federalized by Kennedy.

Katzenbach ordered Wallace to step aside, but the governor refused and instead gave a speech on states' rights. Katzenbach called the president, who spoke with General Graham. The general then reluctantly spoke directly to

Wallace, saying, "Sir, it is my sad duty to ask you to step aside under the orders of the President of the United States."

After a few more words, Wallace stepped aside, and Jones and Hood were admitted.

That evening, Kennedy addressed the nation in as powerful a civil rights speech ever given by a Democrat President of the United States. In many ways, he picked up on the sentiments expressed in Dr. King's letter from Birmingham jail. He said:

> The heart of the question is whether all Americans are to be afforded equal rights and equal opportunities, whether we are going to treat our fellow Americans as we want to be treated. If an American, because his skin is dark, cannot eat lunch in a restaurant open to the public, if he cannot send his children to the best public school available, if he cannot vote for the public officials who represent him, if, in short, he cannot enjoy the full and free life which all of us want, then who among us would be content to have the color of his skin changed and stand in his PLACE? Who among us would be content with the counsels of patience and delay?

Kennedy used the speech to announce his intention to submit legislation to Congress to further guarantee the rights of Black Americans. He said:

> I am … asking the Congress to enact legislation giving all Americans the right to be served in facilities which are open to the public— hotels, restaurants, theaters, retail stores and similar establishments.

For the nine years since the Supreme Court ordered the end of segregated school systems, Democrat administrations in the South could maintain segregated schools, and *de facto* segregation still existed in most Democrat-controlled cities of the North. Although Kennedy did not call out those responsible by party affiliation, he did note the conditions in the solid Democrat southland:

> Too many Negro children entering segregated grade schools at the time of the Supreme Court's decision nine years ago will enter segregated high schools this fall, having suffered a loss which can never

be restored. The lack of an adequate education denied the Negro a chance to get a decent job.

The day after Kennedy's speech, the nation witnessed yet another example of racial violence under Democrat governance.

Medgar Evers and Justice Delayed

Medgar Evers was a military veteran and leader in the NAACP. He had moved to Mississippi with his wife and three children. From the start, he had become an activist for civil rights, eventually becoming the field secretary for the NAACP. He fought diligently against the Democrat power structure in Mississippi, mainly focusing on the intimidation activities of the Democrat's local enforcer organization, the White Citizens' Council.

On June 12, 1963, Evers was gunned down in the driveway of his home by Byron De La Beckwith, a member of two of the Democratic Party's paramilitary auxiliaries, the White Citizens' Council and the Ku Klux Klan.

Despite significant evidence and testimony, all-White juries in two successive trials failed to reach a verdict. There was a dramatic moment in the second trial. Former Democrat Governor Ross Barnett walked into the court room, interrupting the testimony of Myrlie Evers, wife of the slain civil rights leader, to greet the judge and jury and shake hands with De La Beckwith. While it is not likely his presence changed the anticipated outcome of the trial, it was seen as an endorsement for vigilante action. De La Beckwith walked out of court a free man.

Like many White supremacists in the South, De La Beckwith attempted to use his notoriety to gain public office, in this case the Democratic nomination for lieutenant governor in 1967. He was not successful.

By 1994, Mississippi was a much different place than under the rule of the old Democrat regimes. Kirk Fordice was Mississippi's first Republican governor since 1876 and only the third GOP governor in the state's history at that time. That was also the year the De La Beckwith case was re-opened at Fordice's direction based on investigative articles in the *Jackson Clarion Ledger*. Ironically De La Beckwith was prosecuted by the same district attorney office that had freed him under Democrat rule thirty years earlier. This time he was convicted of first-degree murder by an integrated jury and sentenced to life in prison.

"I Have a Dream"

In a time of deep despair among Blacks in the south and northern cities. Dr. Martin Luther King gave a measure of optimism and hope.

Just over two months after Medgar Evans was assassinated, King gave his most memorable and prophetic speech. It was on August 28, 1963. More than two hundred thousand people of all ethnic backgrounds and from all regions of the nation gathered on the Washington Mall to celebrate the one hundredth anniversary of the Emancipation Proclamation. On the steps of the Lincoln Memorial, with the massive statue of the revered Republican president over his shoulder, Dr. King delivered his famous "I Have a Dream" speech.

The speech stirred the nation. It provided even more popular support for the ending of the Democratic Party's racial tyranny that still gripped the South and many of the northern urban centers. It spurred Congress into action but put the executive branch on edge, including President Kennedy.

Much has been publicly revealed about J. Edgar Hoover's efforts to discredit King, but the role of President Kennedy and his brother is less known. Robert Kennedy often denied knowing of the FBI wiretaps on King and his associates. It was a preposterous denial. He had to authorize them—as he did after the meeting with Black leaders in his Manhattan apartment.

In responding to a question about how the Kennedys were targeting King, Yale University American history professor Beverly Gage, who had researched the subject, wrote:

> There was a lot of back-and-forth between the FBI and the Kennedy White House, and they were certainly sharing the fruits of what they found both before and after the wiretaps. So, it's quite clear at this point, though he denied it at certain points in his life, that Robert Kennedy did authorize the wiretaps on King and on his associates.

It's a little less clear that he knew about the bugging of the hotel rooms. But he certainly authorized the wiretaps. And the FBI was quite openly sharing a lot of this information with the White House, and the Kennedys really were responding to it.

Gage said that the Kennedys were "very cautious" regarding civil rights issues because they were "part of a Democratic Party that was very reliant on the votes of the solid South."

Despite the public denials, it is clear that President Kennedy and the attorney general had not only authorized the wiretaps but kept in close contact with Hoover over emerging details—and used those details for political advantage.

By May of 1963, President Kennedy was grappling with the growing pressure from civil rights leaders and, more importantly, the general public. During a privately recorded meeting on May 20, Kennedy said: "I think we ought to have some of these other meetings before we have it in the King group; otherwise, the meetings will look like they got me to do it."

In the same recording, Kennedy said meeting with King would look like "[Karl] Marx coming to the White House." He then laid out his plan. "I'd like to have at least some Southern governors or mayors or businessmen in first," he said. "And my program [the civil rights legislation] should have gone up to the Hill first."

The Election of 1964

As the nation moved into the 1964 election, and Kennedy had begun his reelection campaign, the president spoke eloquently about the need for civil rights legislation. Many civil rights leaders were not confident in Kennedy's commitment despite his rhetorical support of civil rights and the introduction of legislation. They were well aware of his lip service support of civil rights in previous campaigns—and his lack of action once in office.

They recalled his string of broken campaign promises and his votes in support of the segregationist position of his southern Democrat colleagues. Kennedy's lack of commitment for civil rights was even noted on the official Kennedy Presidential Library website history, which states:

> But Kennedy's narrow election victory and small working margin in Congress left him cautious. He was reluctant to lose southern support for legislation on many fronts by pushing too hard on civil rights legislation.

> President Kennedy may have been reluctant to push ahead with civil rights legislation, but millions of African Americans would not wait. Eventually, the administration was compelled to act.

There was a real question whether Kennedy would use the power of the White House to try to win passage of his promised civil rights legislation or would accede to the opposition by the powerful segregationist Democrats in Congress. It was widely believed that once in office Kennedy would introduce a bill and have it assigned to the Senate Judiciary Committee, headed by racist Democrat James Eastland. If Eastland did not kill or cripple the bill in committee, as had been the practice in the past, Senate Democrats would filibuster, and Kennedy would give up the fight. Up to that time, there had never been a successful cloture vote to end a filibuster on a piece of civil rights legislation.

The Kennedy Civil Rights Bill in Congress

As the Kennedy Library history noted, the president was more or less compelled to take action in view of the rising tide of public anger over the Democrat's racial atrocities taking place in the southern states. His own credibility and his reelection were on the line.

The bill Kennedy submitted was a much weaker piece of legislation than the civil rights act that would pass in 1964. It brought immediate criticism from many civil rights leaders. It did not address the very serious problem of police brutality under Democrat regimes—police brutality that was so evident on television screens across American. The Kennedy bill did not give the Justice Department the power to initiate lawsuits against blatant discrimination. The ban on discrimination in private accommodations—buses, restaurants, etc.—was considered too weak to have much of an impact.

The Kennedy bill was taken up by the House Judiciary Committee under the chairmanship of New York congressman Emmanuel Celler a pro-civil rights Democrat. With support of Republican committee members, the bill was amended to specifically ban segregation in all public venues, not just schools. It banned racial discrimination in hiring and strengthened the provision outlawing segregation in private businesses.

Most important, the Republicans in the Celler Committee added a provision that would enable the United States attorney general to file anti-discrimination lawsuits. This was similar to Title III, which Democrats, including Kennedy and Johnson, voted to strip from the 1957 and 1960 Republican civil rights acts. The civil rights community considered this an essential provision if the law was to have real meaning. Kennedy opposed it twice in the past and chose not to include it in his proposed legislation.

Scuttling the Civil Rights Bill

The bill was voted out of the Celler Committee in October. Instead of putting it up for a floor vote, Kennedy had it reassigned to the Rules Committee, which was headed by segregationist Democrat congressman Howard Smith, who was fairly described as an avid racist. As noted previously, congressman John Lewis had Smith's portrait removed from the committee conference room because of his outrageous racial bigotry.

This was the very political ploy the civil rights community had feared. Smith promised to keep the legislation locked up in his committee. He kept his promise, and the bill never came to a floor vote while Kennedy was president. It was the same ploy and the same committee Kennedy used in 1960.

Kennedy, who did little to fight for his civil rights legislation, most certainly had anticipated the outcome. For all practical purposes, the civil rights bill for which he is given so much credit was dead in committee with Kennedy acquiescence and likely intention. The proposed legislation would have likely died in committee had it not been for and the same committee Kennedy's fateful trip to Dallas.

The 16th Street Baptist Church Bombed

In September of 1963 a bomb composed of fifteen sticks of dynamite ripped through the 16th Street Baptist Church that had been the headquarters of Dr. King's Birmingham campaign. Four young girls died in the blast. Twenty-two others were injured.

The perpetrators were identified soon after the bombing, but justice would not come for many years. According to the FBI the bombing was the work of Thomas Blanton, the son of Edwin "Pops" Blanton, a well-known racist agitator; Herman Cash, an active KKK member; Robert Chambliss, another KKK member who was believed to have committed a number of previous bombings of Black residences; and Bobby Cherry, a member of the Klan and a Marine Corps–trained demolitions expert. Cherry also had a reputation for pistol whipping Blacks or using brass knuckles. He had previously used them on Reverend Fred Shuttlesworth.

Though known to authorities, the four were protected from prosecution by the racist legal system controlled by Democrat prosecutors. It was not until 1977 that Robert Chambliss was convicted. Blanton and Cash were not convicted of murder until 2001 and 2002 respectively. Cherry died in 1994 and was never brought to trial.

While the bombing intensified public outrage and increased the pressure on President Kennedy to take action, it had little impact on the president's civil rights legislation. That remained locked up in Smith's Committee in the House.

Kennedy Campaigns in Dallas

In November of 1963, Kennedy traveled to Dallas. There was a subtext of racial politics involved. The evolution for segregation to integration was one of the factors that split the party in the Lone Star State. Most of the entrenched old guard Democrats were devoted to the old segregationist traditions and willing to fight for them. There were, however, others who believed that the Democratic leadership was on the wrong side of history—and that stubborn adherence to segregation would provide Republicans an opportunity to make additional inroads in the South. They were not wrong.

With his proposal for a new Civil Rights Act already dead in Congress, Kennedy hoped to use whatever goodwill he could muster to keep the Democrats in this critical state united. Bringing Mrs. Kennedy was part of the goodwill strategy.

Paying Homage to the Segregationists

Kennedy wanted to reinforce political ties to his party's segregationist wing. With that in mind, Vice President Johnson arranged for Kennedy to be the main speaker at a dinner in Houston honoring fourteen-term congressman Albert Thomas, who entered Congress at the height of the Great Depression. He was generally described as a "typical southern Democrat," a euphemistic phrase suggesting he was a staunch segregationist.

In his speech, Kennedy avoided any mention of his civil rights legislation. Instead, he focused on pork barrel issues, especially Washington's investment in the Houston Space Center. More than three thousand of Houston's elite were in attendance.

Paying homage to Thomas did not fit well with Kennedy's campaign narrative as a promoter of civil rights. It was the kind of campaign event that led civil rights leaders to question Kennedy's sincerity. Even to this day, the JFK Library's detailed online history of Kennedy's fateful 1963 campaign visit to Texas does not mention the Thomas dinner.

Kennedy Assassinated

How Kennedy would have pursued civil rights became a matter of speculation on November 22, 1963, when he was assassinated in Dallas, Texas. Upon his assassination, the civil rights bill became part of his folk lore and legacy, which Lyndon Johnson took it up arguably as much out of political pragmatism than devotion to the cause.

The Kennedy administration policies reflected the pervasive hypocrisy of the Democratic Party in terms of civil rights. While the national leadership spoke forcefully in favor of civil rights and took actions when the hostility of segregation hit the national news, the greater Democratic Party and its legislative platform was mostly influenced by accommodation and acquiescence to the power of the segregationist faction. In many ways, this segregation power was akin to what was once known as slave power, describing the political power of the Democrat-controlled slave states in the mid-nineteenth century.

Ironically, the Kennedy assassination proved to be a turning point in the effort to pass meaningful civil rights legislation. What Kennedy was unwilling to do while alive, was done in his memory after he died.

SECTION 2

THE ERA OF CIVIL RIGHTS, *DE FACTO* RACISM AND URBAN UNREST (1963–PRESENT)

"Burn baby, burn!"
—Disc jockey Nathaniel "Magnificent" Montague,
during 1965 Watts race riots.

Introduction

Following the civil rights era of the 1960s, America entered yet another unique period of racism. It is hopefully the last bastion of institutional oppression of Black Americans, and the last attempt to keep millions of Black citizens in a PLACE of impoverished segregation and second-rate citizenship.

For more than a century, the *de facto* racism and segregation found largely in America's major cities has been widely documented and reported. It had co-existed with the more flagrant and more obvious *de jure* racism found in the states of the old Confederacy—which essentially ended in the civil rights era of the mid-twentieth century. Urban *de facto* institutional racism, however, has continued in Black communities in the major urban centers to this day.

The very term *de facto racism* entered the popular lexicon to explain a more subtle form of institutional racism that has plagued the nation's major Democrat-controlled cities for generations.

In many ways *de facto* racism has been more pernicious because the racism is carried out behind a façade of laws that seem to protect the civil rights and equality of Black Americans—and behind the false narrative of Democratic Party civil rights advocacy. Surprisingly, institutional *de facto* racism flourishes with the political support of many Black political leaders, whose power, profit, and prestige are dependent on the maintenance of the institutional racist system.

Conversely, the post 1964 era of institutional racism is characterized by several counter trends beneficial to Black Americans. The official end of the hundred years of Jim Crow *de jure* racism in the states of the old Confederacy, the Republican defeats of southern racist regimes in the south, the affirmative action programs of the Nixon administration and greater Black integration into all levels of American society.

The modern-day challenge is to eradicate the last vestige of *de facto* institutional racism from America's great urban centers, in which millions of Black citizens are still relegated to a PLACE of physical segregation and social oppression.

To understand the modern era of institutional *de facto* racism, one must understand one indisputable fact. The Democratic Party controls—and has controlled for many years—the major segregated cities in which millions of Black Americans live in poverty, deprived of education, jobs, quality housing, upward mobility, social interaction, safe streets, and maintained infrastructure. That is not an unavoidable circumstance, but rather the result of intentional polices that form the bases of *de facto* racism.

To understand the hold of the Democratic Party over the majority of Black Americans one only need look at the leaders in the cities with the largest Black population. The list below shows the which party holds the mayor's office and how long since a Republican has held the seat. The top ten Black population cities are:

City	Mayor Party (since)
New York, NY	D (2011)
Chicago, IL	D (1931)
Philadelphia, PA	D (1952)
Detroit, MI	D (1962)
Houston, TX	D (1939)
Memphis, TN	D (1991)
Baltimore, MD	D (1967)
Los Angeles, CA	D (2001)
Washington, DC	D (1961)
Dallas, TX	D (2011)

Other major cities with large Black populations in alphabetical order.

City	Mayor Party (since)
Atlanta	D (1879)
Boston	D (1930)
Newark	D (1953)
Philadelphia	D (1952)
Pittsburgh	D (1934)
San Francisco	D (1964)
St. Louis	D (1953)

The city council membership, other elected officials and major appointees in these cities reflect the same overwhelming dominance of the Democratic Party. The urban centers of America tend to be governed by one-party rule—and have been for generations.

It is noteworthy that the seventeen cities listed above account for the vast majority of the most frequent and most violent outbreaks of racial unrest since *Brown v. the Board of Education*—unrest ironically borne out of frustration over the oppression imposed by the very politicians the majority of Blacks elect to office at the urging of Black leaders who serve the interest of the racist political machines for their own personal power, privilege, prestige, and profit. If these cities can be described as economic and political plantations, then many of the Black elected officials are the "house Negroes."

As the era of official *de jure* segregation comes to an end in the solid Democrat southland, institutional *de facto* racism remains in play. In the South it is seen in the Massive Resistance movement against school integration. In the major cities, it is the continuation of the institutional *de facto* racism. Against that backdrop we have the new era of civil rights. Enter President Lyndon Baines Johnson.

Lyndon Johnson (1963–1965)

The public was in shock not only by the assassination of a president but from the jarring shift in leadership from the charisma and elegance of Camelot to the hard scrapple crudeness of rural Texas. It was as if the White

House took a leap back in time. Johnson was savvy enough to recognize the public perception. The Kennedy family and friends bitterly despised the man who took Kennedy's office and legacy. Johnson's major accomplishment would be the passage of the Kennedy Civil Rights Act—an accomplishment many leaders in the Black community doubted Kennedy himself would have achieved or even would try to achieve.

Prior to his ascendency to the presidency, Johnson was among the most ardent of White supremacists and pro-segregationists Democrats in America. In a speech in Austin, Texas in 1948 Johnson said:

> This civil rights program about which you have heard so much is a farce and a sham; an effort to set up a police state in the guise of liberty. I am opposed to that program. I fought it in the Congress. It is the province of the state to run its own elections. I am opposed to the anti-lynching bill because the federal government has no business enacting a law against one kind of murder than another... If a man can tell you who you must hire, he can tell you who not to employ. I have met this head on.

Johnson held those views until he became president, and he aligned with Senate Republicans, headed by Illinois' pro-civil rights Republican minority leader Everett McKinley Dirksen, to produce some of the most important civil rights legislation of the century. His alliance with the GOP was critical. Without it, the Dixiecrats would most certainly have been able to again use the filibuster to block any civil rights legislation impinging on southern segregationist policies for years to come.

Sophomoric Racism

Johnson personified the ignorant and deep-seeded sophomoric racism of his southern Democrat roots. It manifested often in his private discussions and even in strange ways.

He believed that Blacks were inordinately fearful of snakes. Johnson would place one in the trunk of his car. He would then tell a Black gas station attendant to check something in the trunk. Johnson delighted in seeing the guy jumping around in fear. On one such occasion, it is reported that Johnson narrowly escaped being beaten with a tire iron for his practical joke.

The N-word

It is likely that no twentieth century president so frequently and so indiscreetly used the word *nigger* in referring to Black Americans, even when addressing them directly. In writing for MSNBC Online, Adam Serwer said that "Johnson was practically a connoisseur of the n-word." Even when privately discussing the 1964 Civil Rights Act, he consistently referred to it disparagingly as the "nigger bill." Despite his later reputation as an advocate of civil rights, those who knew Johnson, even friends, have reported on his many expressions of racial intolerance.

In his memoir, *Capitol Hill in Black and White,* long time Johnson chauffer, Robert Parker, recalled Johnson asking if he would prefer to be addressed by Robert rather than boy or nigger. When Parker said he would prefer "Robert," Johnson shot back as if he had sprung a trap:

> As long as you are black, and you're gonna be black till the day you die, no one's gonna call you by your goddamn name. So, no matter what you are called, nigger, you just let it roll off your back like water, and you'll make it. Just pretend you're a goddamn piece of furniture.

Johnson was also a master of "code-switching" or subtly changing one's normal speech style to fit the audience. Johnson biographer, Robert Caro, wrote that Johnson would calibrate his language by switching between "nigra" and "negra" depending on the regional background of the audience.

Johnson was also a pragmatic man. When he could not defeat the Republican civil rights bills of 1957 and 1960, he used his power as Senate majority leader to water them down—essentially making them less enforceable. He told several of his southern colleagues that in the absence of a weak bill, the Republicans would pass very tough civil rights legislation.

Fannie Lou Hamer and the
Freedom Democratic Party

Fannie Lou Hamer was one of the examples of the hardship and danger imposed on Blacks in the Democrat southland. On August 23, 1962, civil rights activist James Bevel was in Ruleville, Mississippi, to give a sermon at a local church. In that sermon, he appealed to the Negro congregation to get registered to vote. In the pews was Fannie Lou Hamer. Inspired by the sermon, she decided to take up the challenge.

Hamer was well aware of the many consequences for a Black attempting to register Black voters. Harassment and intimidation were the least of the possibilities. Beatings and lynchings were not uncommon. Hamer once said:

> I guess if I'd had any sense, I'd have been a little scared — but what
> was the point of being scared? The only thing they could do was kill
> me, and it kinda seemed like they'd been trying to do that a little bit
> at a time since I could remember.

During a trip to Charleston, South Carolina, Hamer was arrested by the local police on false charges along with other members of her group. While in jail, they were repeatedly beaten by police. Police would also hold her down while White inmates were given Blackjacks to beat prisoners. It took Hamer months to recover from her wounds, but the physical and emotional scars stayed with her for the rest of her life.

Undaunted, Hamer went on to organize a series of "freedom" events in Mississippi. One of her volunteers was a Tuskegee University student named Sammy Younge. He was shot and killed by a gas station attendant for attempting to use the "Whites only" washroom. Younge did not know his PLACE.

Though a Republican, Hamer attempted to protest against the racist leadership of the Democratic Party from within. In early 1964, Hamer registered more than 60,000 Black voters in Mississippi—mostly from counties with large Negro populations where few, if any, were previously registered to vote.

The success of that effort led her to found the Freedom Democratic Party in the hope of bringing the civil and voting rights message into the Democrat National Convention. Her group was offered two token seats on the Democrat convention platform committee, but they were not allowed to have any official delegates seated on the main floor. According to a 2016 online article by Barbara Ransby in *Progress Magazine:* "They were the voice of principle, but they made their case outside the convention walls—on the Atlantic City boardwalk, singing, praying and protesting."

Democrat Policy of Eugenics Lives On

Hamer was also a victim of the southern Democrats' policy of racial genocide. While in a Mississippi hospital in 1961 for removal of a tumor, the doctor performed an unnecessary hysterectomy without Hamer's consent—denying her and her husband the possibility of having children. This was a common practice in southern hospitals and was a carryover of the 1930 eugenics movement launched by the racist founder of Planned Parenthood, Margaret Sanger. Hamer used her experience to bring public attention to the "Mississippi appendectomies," forced sterilizations and illegal abortions performed on Black women. She and her husband later raised two adopted children.

New York School Boycott

With Democrat political machines resisting the integration mandate of *Brown v. Board of Education*, Black activists began ramping up their protests against the longstanding *de facto* segregation in the urban centers. In New York, the effort was led by Bayard Rustin, a long time national civil rights leader and follower of Martin Luther King and Reverend Milton Galamison, chairman of the Citywide Committee for School Integration.

Besides being a civil rights activist, Rustin was at times a socialist or communist. He was a pacifist and a gay man promoting gay rights. His multiple causes limited his civil rights activities. Even within the movement, his pacifism and open gayness were criticized.

In an article in *Real Clear Politics* entitled "What Tributes to Bayard Rustin Leave out," Cathy Young wrote:

> Shamefully, he was forced out of the Southern Christian Leadership
> Coalition (which he had co-founded) in 1960 after black Harlem
> Congressman Adam Clayton Powell tried to get leverage over King
> by threatening to spread rumors that he and Rustin were in a sexual
> relationship.

The actions of Congressman Powell reflect how even Black machine politicians were part of the Democratic Party's *de facto* racism. Rather than undermine the civil rights movement with the distraction of his sexuality, Rustin often avoided public appearances—but he was a key behind-the-scenes strategist for virtually all major civil rights events.

Rustin had evolved into a neoconservative, a philosophy he came to believe better represented his lifelong commitment to civil rights. Like Booker T. Washington and Malcom X, Rustin would speak out against Democrat apostates in the faux civil rights movement.

Young, in her Real Clear Politics column, said:

> Labels aside, Bayard Rustin was a great American and a true hero.
> He had firsthand experience of oppression and prejudice; yet for
> him, human rights activism was never about solidarity with his own
> group but about freedom, justice and dignity for all.

Upon his death in 1987, President Reagan praised Rustin's lifetime commitment to civil rights. In 2013, Rustin was posthumously awarded the Presidential Medal of Freedom from President Obama.

Rustin and Galamison believed that a boycott of New York's segregated Black schools was necessary. They had hoped that the United Federation of Teachers (UFT) would endorse the walkout, but the teachers' union declined, saying that they would defend only teachers who participated. Despite the lack of union support, the walkout was a stunning success. More than 400,000 teachers and students stayed home—and many participated in peaceful public protests. It was billed as the largest civil rights demonstration in American history up to that point.

When Rustin and others announced plans for a second boycott, the teachers' unions, under pressure from the Democrat city administration, opposed the idea and withdrew their promise to even defend participating teachers.

Many civil rights leaders, such as Oliver Leeds of the Brooklyn chapter of the Congress of Racial Equality (CORE) and Al Vann, president of the Afro-American Teachers Association, saw the reversal of the UFT as the beginning of a larger opposition to civil rights by school unions. Leeds and Vann would cite the UFT's refusal to support the 1964 integration campaign as proof that an alliance between teachers' unions and the Black community was impossible.

As would be the case for the next fifty-plus years, the education lobby and unions became major supporters and funders of Democrat political machines in the major cities—essentially becoming an arm of the Democratic Party. Not only would they do nothing to improve education for Black students in the inner cities, but they would actively oppose beneficial programs that would threaten Democratic Party's political dominance, such as integration and school choice programs that would allow students to transfer out of failed ghetto schools.

In New York, the UFT offered what has become a standard approach to inner city education—wage demands in excess of inflation, increased benefits, shorter work time, more compensatory time, and smaller class size as a means of increasing the number of union dues–paying teachers. While these programs had a ring of beneficence, they were largely advanced to increase union membership and the resultant political contributions to the Democratic Party. Each child confined to even the worst schools represented money and political clout for the union and Democratic Party. Keeping children in a PLACE of inferior education was a key element in maintaining power and the flow of political contributions.

Seeing through the claims, Black community activists led by the African American Teachers Association (ATA), opposed the plan—seeing it as a means to maintain White control and therefore segregation of the urban school systems.

Since many of the best schoolteachers resisted teaching in Black schools, the ATA, whose members were part of the UFT, proposed transferring teachers on an involuntary basis. The UFT fought the idea. The union also fought against providing incentive pay to attract better teachers to the failing inner-city schools.

The UFT proposed a plan that would allow teachers to remove disruptive students and have them sent to "special" schools. The ATA argued that it would only accelerate racism and *de facto* segregation. When the UFT went out on strike to impose the disruptive student rule, most ATA members quit the UFT. When the ATA held a tribute to Malcolm X that presented Afrocentric music and dance, the UFT had the ATA members disciplined.

Ocean-Hill Brownsville and Local Control

With only 8 percent of teachers and 3 percent of administrators being Black, the ATA civil right leaders campaigned for community control. The New York Board of Education approved a plan that would experiment in community control for the Ocean Hill-Brownsville school district. The Ford Foundation provided a grant of $44,000 to finance the experiment. In many ways, it was similar to the later magnet and charter school concepts. And as in the latter case too, the school unions opposed the plan, calling it union busting.

One Man, One Vote

By the mid-1960s, the issue of voting rights was reaching a fever pitch. The civil rights movement took up a historic slogan that had been used around the world to push for colonial independence: "one man, one vote."

One of the issues that involved racism was the design of legislative districts. The influence of the Black vote could be diminished by either consolidating Blacks in one district to eliminate the election of more than one representative or by dividing of a Black community into several districts to prevent any Black candidate from winning a majority in any district. There was also a tendency to create legislative districts that diminished the power of urban centers with large minority populations to the advantage of the more rural and Whiter communities. It all depended on the situation. These are tactics widely used by Democrats in the urban centers to this day.

As might be expected, the issue came to the Supreme Court from a case of racial redistricting in Alabama. In *Reynolds v. Sims,* the Court ruled that all districts must be based on a relatively equal distribution of the population. In writing for the majority, Republican Chief Justice Earl Warren wrote: "Legislators represent people, not trees or acres. Legislators are elected by voters, not farms or cities or economic interests."

This decision increased the voting power of Black vote throughout America.

The Twenty-Fourth Amendment

In 1937, the United States Supreme Court, in a unanimous decision in *Breedlove v. Suttles*, had declared that generally applied voting requirements, such as the poll taxes, literacy tests, and the grandfather clauses, were technically constitutional. As a means of putting an end to such Jim Crow laws throughout the nation, it was determined that a constitutional amendment would be required. Such an amendment could apply only to federal elections—basically Congress and the presidency. The amendment was sent by Congress to the states in 1962 and subsequently ratified in January of 1964.

Twenty-two Senate Democrats voted against, or present, in opposition to the Amendment. Only one of the Senates' Republicans voted against the amendment. In the House, Republicans gave the amendment 90 percent support, while Democrats split with only 57 percent favoring the amendment. It was a bipartisan outcome, but the power and impact of the racist Democrat coalition was evident, even if in decline.

Civil Rights Bill of 1964

The ability to pass sweeping civil rights legislation in the 1960s was made possible by a confluence of several events. Both institutional racism and personal prejudices were receding. The last vestiges of America's institutional racism were found in two area—the Old South and the major cities. Both were largely the exclusive domain of the Democratic Party.

Television brought into every American living room the brutality of the Democrat regimes. Police were seen indiscriminately using water hoses, dogs, clubs, and guns on helpless Black demonstrators. Prior to television, the violent abuse at the hands of the Democrat terrorist organizations and local police were never so graphically seen by the public.

Johnson was feeling the same public pressure that forced his predecessor, President Kennedy, to take up symbolic, lip-service civil rights advocacy. Another major factor was the continuing pressure from Republican members of both the House and Senate, who overwhelmingly supported civil rights legislation and had passed the 1957 and 1960 Civil Rights Acts.

Despite Kennedy's lack of commitment to civil rights, people viewed the passage of the 1964 civil rights legislation as a tribute to the legacy of the slain president. Ironically, it was unlikely that any civil rights legislation would have been enacted had he lived.

Johnson Becomes an Advocate

For the first time in his life, Johnson saw significant political benefit in championing civil rights. His support of the Civil Rights Bill of 1964 and the Voting Rights Bill of 1965 is mired in controversy as to the true reasons for his conversion. What is clear, however, is that Johnson obviously did abandon his earlier disdain for civil rights legislation. He pushed and he pushed hard to win passage. Speculation regarding Johnson's switch from strident segregationist to dedicated civil rights activist centers on three theories.

One theory is that Johnson had a fundamental change of heart, that he had come to believe in the justification and necessity for civil rights legislation. It is a theory advanced by those whose goal seems to be to burnish Johnson's image for contemporary partisan advantage and the longer reach of history.

There is a more pragmatic theory—a variation of the first. It claims that Johnson was advised by several people, including Philip Graham, publisher of the *Washington Post*, that any hope of reelection to a second term would be derailed by opposition to civil rights.

There is a third more cynical theory: that Johnson recognized the need to keep Black voters in the Democrat party. This partisan pragmaticism was later seen in his Great Society and War on Poverty programs, which he is reported to have told a group of southern senators that his welfare legislation would "keep the niggers voting Democrat for 200 years."

The political pragmatism argument was advanced by Johnson historian Robert Caro in an interview for the Library of Congress online blog. Caro described Johnson as a man who

" when compassion and ambition finally are pointing in the same direction, then Lyndon Johnson becomes a force for racial justice."

Noting Johnson's change from opponent of civil rights to an advocate, President Obama later addressed Johnson's remarkable political metamorphous when he said: "During his first twenty years in Congress, he opposed every civil rights bill that came up for a vote, once calling the push for federal legislation a farce and a shame."

Whatever his motivation, Johnson ultimately used his position as president to win passage of the 1964 Civil Rights Bill in the only way possible, relying on the overwhelming support of congressional Republicans that had long pushed and successfully enacted the only civil rights legislation since post-Civil War Reconstruction.

Per the Kennedy Library official website:

> [Johnson] used his connections with southern White congressional leaders, and with the assistance of Robert Kennedy's Justice Department and the outpouring of emotion after the president's assassination, the Civil Rights Act was passed as a way to honor President Kennedy.

Although the library implies that Johnson used his connections to gain the support of southern White congressional leaders, it must be noted that his efforts were not entirely successful. Even with the power of the White House and a long reputation for getting what he wanted in Congress, Johnson could not win over nearly enough of his southern colleagues in the House and Senate to pass any legislation—and there was always the issue of the filibuster.

In his Election Realignment and the Outlook for the American Democracy, Arthur Paulson notes that   most of the opposition to the Civil

Rights bill came from southern Democrats. At the start of the debate on the bill that summer, *Jim Crow was still alive and living almost entirely within the Democratic Party*" (emphasis added). Paulson further noted that "on the congressional roll calls on the civil rights bill, the Republicans still looked like the party of Lincoln. In both houses, the Republican majorities for the bill were larger than the Democrat majorities."

Paulson pointed out that the Democrats were split, with southern Democrats driving the greatest opposition to the bill, but "the Republican majorities for civil rights in the summer of 1964 were overwhelming."

Of the ninety-three members of Congress in the southern Democrat delegation, only seven voted in favor of the 1964 Civil Rights Act. Four of the seven came from Texas, where Johnson could exert his strongest influence.

The 1964 Civil Rights Act was on its way to passage thanks to the critical support of the Republican leadership in Congress. As the JFK Library website notes, "the comprehensive civil rights bill cleared several hurdles in Congress and won the endorsement of House and Senate Republican leaders."

The Senate

While passing the bill with a bipartisan majority was fairly certain, thanks to the overwhelming Republican support, there was less certainty if there were the sufficient sixty-seven votes to bring cloture to the southern Democrats likely filibuster.

The ever-eloquent Senate Republican leader Everett Dirksen, of Illinois, was the first senator to rise and speak in favor of the bill, saying the law was needed: "if the unequivocal mandate of the Fifteenth Amendment . . . is to be enforced and made effective, and if the Declaration of Independence is to be made truly meaningful."

Democrats Attempt to Block the Bill

Despite their diminished influence, the southern segregationist Democrats continued their post-Civil War tradition of opposing all civil rights legislation.

If they could not defeat the bill in a floor vote, could not bury it in committee or block it with a filibuster, Senate Democrats made every effort to water it down through the amendment process. North Carolina Democrat Sam Ervin offered an amendment to remove a provision that would automatically trigger federal involvement in specific cases of discrimination in favor of arbitrary decisions by southern federal judges. With the proposed amendments failing, Democrats resorted to the filibuster.

On June 9, West Virginia's Democrat senator Robert Byrd took the floor to launch the Dixiecrats' filibuster. He spoke for more than fourteen hours before there was a call for a cloture vote to force an end to the filibuster.

Senator Dirksen rose to make the argument for cloture. The official United States Senate website described the Illinois senator's comments:

> Noting that the day marked the 100th anniversary of Abraham Lincoln's nomination to a second term, the Illinois Republican [Dirksen] proclaimed, in the words of Victor Hugo, "Stronger than all the armies is an idea whose time has come." He continued, "The time has come for equality of opportunity in sharing in government, in education, and in employment. It will not be stayed or denied. It is here!"

The cloture vote was essential to stopping the filibuster and win the passage of the Bill. When the final bill came up to a vote, Senate Republicans provided most of the votes in favor of ending the filibuster. Without the overwhelming support of the GOP, the cloture vote would have failed and the Civil Rights Act of 1964 would have been blocked from passage for another generation. This represented the first time that a Democrat filibuster of a civil rights bill was successfully ended by a cloture vote and most of the credit belonged to Senator Dirksen.

The reputation of Kennedy and the Democratic Party as proponents of civil rights is an ironic and false narrative. In many ways, the Civil Rights Act of 1964 did little more than restore powers and provisions that

Kennedy, Johnson, and the Democrats in Congress had removed from the Republican's 1957 and 1960 civil rights acts. The 1964 Act closed some of the loopholes that had enabled southern Democrats to avoid compliance—particularly those provisions that would have enabled the Justice Department to enforce the rights of Black citizens.

The Civil Rights Act of 1964 was officially enacted on July 2, 1964. *Time* magazine honored Senator Dirksen with its cover for his key role, saying "It is Dirksen's bill, bearing his handiwork more than anyone else's."

The Election of 1964

Following the assassination of President Kennedy, the Johnson team immediately went into campaign mode with less than one year to the general election and even less time to the primaries and Democratic Party convention.

The nation was reeling in the aftermath of the murder of a charismatic president. It was sinking deeper into the quagmire of the Vietnam War and the civil rights movement had become a front burner issue. Between the freedom fighters standing up to the Democrat leadership in the South and the violent anti-war terrorism in the major cities, the grounds of America were running with blood unlike any time since the Civil War.

The Republicans

The nomination of Barry Goldwater was a great victory for the conservative faction of the GOP, but it would prove to be a disaster for the image of the Republican Party. Goldwater's single vote against the 1964 Civil Rights Act enabled Democrats to dishonestly, but successfully, label the GOP as opposed to civil rights.

Ironically, Goldwater had been one of the champions of civil rights legislation in Congress. He voted in favor of the civil rights bills in 1957 and

1960. For his running mate, Goldwater picked a relatively obscure fourteen-year Republican Congressman William Miller, of New York, who was co-author of the 1957 and 1960 civil rights acts—facts that never reached public awareness at that time or since.

Goldwater voted no based on his belief that the act would violate the Constitution. Later in life, Goldwater stated that his vote against the Civil Rights bill was among the biggest political mistakes of his career. Regardless, the damage was done.

The Democrats

Johnson was practically assured to be the Democrat nominee. His only challenge came from Alabama's racist Democrat governor George Wallace. While Wallace did well in a few primaries, he did not win any electoral votes.

At the nominating convention, the Democrats had a bit of a kerfuffle over the Mississippi delegation. The officially seated delegation was all White and had been elected in a White-only Democrat primary used by southern Democrats to keep Blacks out of power. The seating was challenged by the Mississippi Freedom Democratic Party (MFDP) headed by Fannie Lou Hamer. Convention liberals were willing to split the delegation 50/50, but Johnson opposed the idea and supported the all-White delegation. To settle the issue, Johnson agreed to give two seats on the platform committee to the MFDP.

For his running mate, Johnson selected Minnesota senator Hubert Humphrey. Humphrey was one of the few leading Democrats who had a long unbroken record in support of civil rights. His efforts to force the issue at the 1948 Democratic convention led to the walkout by the Dixiecrats and nearly cost Truman his reelection. Humphrey was also the floor leader responsible for producing Democrat votes for the 1964 Civil Right Act. Though he could not persuade the southern segregationist coalition, he did produce enough to get the bill passed.

The Election Results

Johnson won in a landslide. He was transformed as a champion of civil rights despite his reputation as a diehard southern racist for most of his political career. It was no small irony that the Democrat candidate was perceived as the champion of civil rights legislation even though he had opposed it throughout his political career—and the Republican candidate who had faithfully supported civil rights legislation throughout his career was assumed to be the enemy of civil rights.

In little more than a year after ascending to the presidency upon the assassination of John Kennedy, Lyndon Johnson was sworn in as President of the United States on his own. His election in 1964, however, was again an indication of the power of the southern Democrat bloc. He joined Wilson, Truman, Carter, and Clinton as one the five twentieth century southern-reared Democrat presidents—the only exceptions being Franklin Roosevelt, Barack Obama, and Joe Biden.

Urban Unrest

The 1964 Civil Rights Act did not cool the anger and frustrations of those trapped in the segregated ghettoes. It did not solve all the issues—and it did not quell the southern Democrats' devotion to racial oppression—to keeping Black Americans in their PLACE.

Like all the past civil rights amendments and laws, actual implementation was thwarted by those supposedly empowered to enforce them. The Democrat-run cities would continue with systemic *de facto* racist policies for another sixty years and counting. They would continue to be the loci of racial unrest—marked by deadly protests and riots.

Addressing this period, the Olympia (Washington) School District offered this assessment of the riots of the 1960s as part of their social studies curriculum under the heading *The American RIOTS of the 1960's and 70's:*

> [M]ore riots occurred in broken-down ghetto, low-income (or, as
> some said, 'no-income') sections of major cities. A smaller L.A. riot,

a riot of approximately 3000 angry citizens in Harlem, N.Y., others in Milwaukee and Selma. Then, the two most destructive (in their toll on lives and property) took place in the summer of 1967 — the first in Newark and then, the worst of all, in Detroit. The citizens of these and other communities were angry at a government and a society that had continued to ignore their needs for far too long. Campaign promises never materialized; city, state, and federal governments seemed inept to those who felt 'locked' in the squalid depression of the ghettos. *For all the political rhetoric and government studies of these poverty-stricken city centers, the future seemed as if there would be simply more of the same.* (emphasis added)

The source of the problem was seen in the targets of the protests and riots. It was the Democrat political machines that controlled the city halls—the schools, the police, the restrictive housing policies.

King, the Nobel Prize and the FBI

Within days of Johnson's reelection, Martin Luther King was heading to Oslo, Norway, to receive the Nobel Peace Prize—at the time the youngest person to be so honored. On the eve of that event, Federal Bureau of Investigation director J. Edgar Hoover publicly described King as "the most notorious liar in the country." This was another chapter in the ongoing effort by both the Kennedy and Johnson administrations to discredit King by weaponizing the FBI.

According to Professor Gage:

Hoover and Lyndon Johnson were actually very good friends. They had been neighbors in the '40s. They lived on the same street. … They were both people who loved to kind of trade in secret information. So, you have this very odd situation in which Lyndon Johnson is simultaneously kind of publicly championing the Civil Rights Act, publicly championing a lot of civil rights activism in the middle of 1964, but in these much more private conversations they're making jokes about King, particularly about his extramarital affairs, which

> the FBI had really started finding out about in sort of '63, '64. This
> is the kind of gossip that certainly Lyndon Johnson ... and Hoover
> himself liked to share. *So, you have a real disconnect both on the part
> of the FBI, but also on the part of the White House, between what it is
> that they are saying publicly during these years and what it is that they're
> talking about in private.* (emphasis added)

As allegations of infidelity were spreading through the political grape-
vine, King received an unsigned letter from a supposed civil rights leader
distraught over King's alleged extramarital affairs—a letter that threatened
to expose the civil rights leader unless he took "drastic action." The letter,
accompanied by an allegedly incriminating audio tape, hinted at suicide as
King's only way out. "King," the letter stated, "there is only one thing left
for you to do. You know what it is. ... You are done. There is but one way
out for you. You better take it before your filthy, abnormal fraudulent self is
bared to the nation."

Later evidence established that the letter not only originated from the
FBI but was likely authored by Hoover's deputy director William Sullivan.

Civil Rights Reform and Welfare Dependency

Recognizing the advantage of being the party of minority dependency,
Johnson moved to expand the so-called entitlement programs as the War on
Poverty component of his signature Great Society theme. His motivation
was arguably more political than humanitarian. That is borne out by the
results over the years. The more than a trillion dollars spent on behalf of
segregated and impoverished Blacks have kept them voting Democrat, but in
terms of ending segregations and impoverishment, the War on Poverty funds
resulted in no discernible benefit.

Like all the civil rights legislation in the past, the 1960s acts did not
end the Democratic Party's pernicious devotion to institutional *de facto* racism and segregation in the major cities. The South would not dramatically
change on racial policies until Republican governors and legislatures made
inroads in Dixie in the 1970s and 1980s.

Education under Democrats

The centerpiece of Black oppression historically was the denial of education—a feature of racism that has continued unabated from the days of slavery well into the twenty-first century. Policing and jobs were major concerns in the Black ghettoes, but the number one issue of the 1960s was education.

Arguably the most heinous, immoral, and destructive denial of civil rights is in education. Depriving a person of education in the city-run public schools denies access to colleges and career level jobs. It prevents a person who might otherwise be a doctor, business leader, scientist, lawyer, or inventor from fulfilling their rightful ambitions and opportunities.

The racism of the urban school systems is evident in the test scores in which Black outcomes in reading comprehension, math, and all other disciplines are considerably lower than White scores. Racist city officials and legions of Democrat precinct workers spread the narrative that Negroes were naturally slow learners, lacked good parenting, and were essentially lazy by nature.

Racist school policies confined Blacks to a PLACE where abject poverty, anger and frustration could lead to crime—and where a lack of opportunity condemns them to the bare sustenance of generational welfare dependency.

Ever since *Brown v. the Board of Education* segregated schools have been the frontline in the racial battlefield. The Massive Resistance movement launched by Democrats in response to *Brown* decision was in full force in the mid-1960s.

Most public schools in Democrat run cities were strictly segregated as a matter of unofficial policy—and that continues to be true in the third decade of the twenty-first century. This was done by confining Blacks to certain neighborhoods and basing school district boundaries on racial housing boundaries.

School districts were designed to assure that Black schools and White schools would remain separate and unequal. It is no coincidence that the large urban public school systems are functionally reminiscent of those in the old segregated, solid Democrat southland. In the same school system, White students receive quality education, leading to college and careers, while Black students in the same school system were, and are, deprived of basic education, and condemned to low-level, unskilled jobs or no jobs at all.

Who Put Blacks in that PLACE?

Racial separation has been, and is, the means by which to misapply educational resources—ensuring quality education in White districts, even in poor White neighborhoods, while denying such support in Black districts.

Segregation of the Black community and the schools served two callous goals. It kept the community more controllable in terms of political information and the vote. Furthermore, poor quality education would restrict employment opportunities which shackled successive generations of impoverished minorities to neighborhood-based welfare dependency. This double fault has been going on for so long that it defies reason to believe it is accidental or unintended.

While the Massive Resistance to school desegregation was being carried out by Democrat regimes in the South, the municipal Democrats were waging the same battle against integration in the big cities.

By design and neglect, the mostly minority Chicago Public School System was often cited, and justifiably so, as the worst in the nation for Blacks. The poor quality of minority education in Chicago, and other major cities, cannot be explained by incompetence or accident. It is not an unanticipated outcome. It is the result of willful racist policies designed and implemented to maintain political power. Ghetto residents were persuaded to trade their votes for the seeming beneficence of the Democrat leadership—beneficence found in public housing, food stamps, rent subsidies, and other welfare programs. The benefits never included quality education and decent jobs.

Follow the Money

Each child imprisoned in the urban public schools represents money for the union and the Democrat machine. States provide thousands of dollars to the school systems for each child enrolled and in attendance. The more students, the more dues-paying teachers. The bulk of the money goes into very generous benefits and pensions paid to the very people who stand in the way of quality education. With billion-dollar pension funds to invest, the unions wield enormous political clout. A generous portion of these dues goes to the Democrat candidates and officeholders by way of union campaign contributions. The school unions are literally funding inferior education.

A recent analysis shows that all education unions give money almost exclusively to the Democratic Party. The Illinois Federation of Teachers generally gives 86 percent of its Political Action Committee money to the Democrat machine. For the Chicago Teachers Union that figure runs in excess of 96 percent in recent years. This flow of money depends on keeping as many children as possible warehoused in what is ironically said to be an education system.

Chicago Leads the Way in School Segregation

Under Boss Daley, Chicago was declared to be the most segregated city in America, with school districts drawn along the politically imposed racial borders and resulting in all White schools and all Black schools. The quality of education differed dramatically. While *Brown v. Board of Education* imposed some level of integration on the all-White schools in Dixie, it did nothing to integrate all Black schools in the Democrat cities, where school segregation was the result of racist districting. In terms of racial segregation in Chicago, it was business as usual.

According to the online *Encyclopedia of Chicago* "School desegregation became an issue in Chicago during the years following World War II, as the city's African American neighborhoods expanded and school officials adjusted boundary lines to assure that school districts remained as segregated as the housing market."

As in virtually all other Democrat cities, racist policies were used to create educational disadvantage for Black students. The *Encyclopedia of Chicago* further noted: "In black neighborhoods schools were overcrowded, with many on double shifts. Class sizes were smaller in white schools than in black ones."

In the early 1960s, Chicago school superintendent Benjamin Willis, hired by Mayor Daley, strongly opposed integration of the school system. Rather than integrate, he added mobile classrooms to ghetto schools to address the severe overcrowding. Again, from the *Encyclopedia of Chicago:*

School superintendent Benjamin Willis rejected calls for desegregation, and the portable classrooms added to black schools were derisively labeled "Willis Wagons." In 1963 massive demonstrations were staged by students and parents to protest Willis's policies. Public outcries intensified in the wake of commissioned reports recommending dramatic steps to redress educational inequality.

The Department of Health, Education and Welfare had been established by Republican President Eisenhower to address the educational issues that impacted most severely the poor and minority communities. The administration attempted to pressure Chicago to act against both segregation and the lower performance of Chicago's unequal separated schools. However, according to the *Encyclopedia of Chicago,* "Threats by the U.S. Department of Health, Education, and Welfare to withhold federal funds until a desegregation plan was developed were thwarted by Mayor Richard J. Daley's intervention."

Basically, Daley had used his great influence with the Democrat administration of Lyndon Johnson to get the federal government to back off—and they did.

When Willis' successor, James Redman, attempted to bus Black children into White schools to comply with court orders, the Democrat machine fought back. The *Encyclopedia* reports that "Hostile demonstrations greeted such efforts on the city's Northwest and Southwest Sides. Redmond and other school leaders found themselves hampered by board members and local [Democrat] politicians reluctant to anger whites opposed to integration."

Note that the efforts were again hampered by the Democrat power structure which saw itself as representing the views of the White citizens over the needs of the Black community.

The racial tension caused by the resistance to school integration by the political leaders created racial anxiety among the White public. Scare tactics were used by Democrat ward and precinct workers to paint a horrific picture of integration. They implied that schools and the neighborhoods would suffer from the slovenly and criminal Black students. Using the same fearmongering as their southern Democrat colleagues, the Democratic Party's ward and precinct organizations suggested that White girls would be subjected to unwelcomed advances of the worst kind by the morally challenged Black students.

This led Whites to abandon the public school's system for nearby private and parochial schools. "White flight" from the city to the suburbs also contributed to the exodus of White students from the public schools.

Eventually, the Chicago Public School System became largely a segregated minority system. Chicago schools evolved into largely segregated school populated almost exclusively by Black and Hispanic students. It was achieved by school districting based on racial segregation.

The Marva Collins Story

One of the more compelling rationales for allowing children to transfer out of the failing public schools is what happens when they do. They perform better.

Marva Collins demonstrated that a private institution could be used where public schools were failing. She originally spent fourteen years teaching in the Chicago Public School System but grew increasingly frustrated with what the Encyclopedia Britannica referred to as "apathy, neglect, and hostility toward inner-city students, most of whom were poor and black."

Collins had her own assessment of public education for Blacks. "The longer I taught in the public school system," she said, "the more I came to think that schools were concerned with everything but teaching. Teaching was the last priority."

Collins' efforts to improve education within the public school system were greeted with hostility, intimidation, and harassment from city hall.

In *Hindsight: The Wisdom and Breakthroughs of Remarkable People*, Guy Kawasaki wrote:

> Marva Collins, who taught Shakespeare and Plato to Black eighth graders in Chicago's inner city, was driven out of her public school. Her success doomed her because if one student breaks loose and floats to the top, that is a wonderful thing, and the dedication of Marva Collins can be warmly rewarded. But what if a third of her class breaks loose? Suddenly everyone in the city is looking at all these sludge classes and asking if it is just barely possible that they aren't sludge classes.

Kawasaki went on to observe that "No system can survive unless the myths of the system are honored and celebrated and worshipped."

Who Put Blacks in that PLACE?

Dissatisfied with the methods and outcome of the public school system, and the acrimony of the school and political hierarchy, Collins founded and operated Westside Prep based on classical education—a curriculum that many in the education lobby argued was "too challenging" for Black inner-city students. According to the Collins biography:

> Collins created her low-cost private school specifically for the purpose of teaching low-income black children whom Collins felt that the Chicago Public School System, had labeled as being learning disabled. Collins said she had the data to prove that students were teachable and were able to overcome obstacles of learning via her teaching methods, which she said eliminated behavioral issues and allowed students to flourish.

Collins believed that inner city kids could do well educationally if given the right learning environment—and she proved it with the very kids the public school system was failing. Her success, however, placed the Chicago Public School System in a bad light, and she was subjected to unrelenting harassment from city hall, including efforts to shut down her school.

The harassment was not just from the public school education community, but from the Democrat political leadership that ran the schools. Even after launching her school, she was harassed by government inspectors. Students were actually discouraged from attending Westside Prep by local Black politicians. She was accused of all sorts of illegal activities without any evidence.

The success of Westside Prep did, however, draw the attention of the news and entertainment industries. The Marva Collins story was a movie starring Cecily Tyson and Morgan Freeman. The promotion for the movie read:

> Cicely Tyson stars in this truth-based story about a dedicated school-teacher who transcends the limitations of a broken public school system by using her own money to open a prep school catering to the underserved youths of the inner city. Originally aired as a "Hallmark Hall of Fame" special, this inspirational biopic, narrated by Emmy Award-winning Edward Asner, also stars Academy Award winner Morgan Freeman and Roderick Wimberly.

Tyson also starred in a television production about Collins. Her success was highlighted in a documentary on CBS.

Republican president Ronald Reagan was so impressed with Collins' approach to education that she was on his short list for secretary of education. In 2004 Republican president George Bush awarded Collins the prestigious National Humanities Medal.

Her story is also an example of why school vouchers are so important to the segregated communities. City hall finally won out. Westside Prep closed in 2008 due to a lack of enrollment and funding. It is certainly arguable that this would not have happened if Chicago politicians and school unions had not fought against her school and the entire concept of school choice.

Despite the best efforts of those supporting civil rights and integration, America's schools continue to be governed by Democrat political machines, continue to be largely segregated, and continue to provide minorities with inferior education. The summary of the *Encyclopedia of Chicago* addressed this grim outcome:

> Despite the existence of a federally mandated office of desegregation compliance in the Chicago Public Schools, school desegregation has been quite limited in Chicago. Pockets of integration existed by the late 1990s; magnet schools on the city's North and Southwest Sides continued to attract many of the system's white students. But in vast areas of the city, children attended predominantly black or Hispanic schools. Despite some halfhearted efforts in the late 1960s and 1970s, Chicago never developed an exchange program between suburban and city schools, and suburban schools remained largely segregated as well.

Chicago is not unique in racist governance, but rather representative of the Democrat-controlled major urban centers throughout America. Comparisons between Chicago and such cities as New York, Baltimore, and Los Angeles are marked by some distinctions in the policies of institutional racism but without much difference for the segregated and impoverished Black communities.

New York School Segregation

The Democrat regimes in New York City traveled a policy route similar to Chicago, and virtually the same as all modern segregated school systems in the Democrat cities. In a 2014 article in the *New York Daily News*, writer Ben Chapman reported:

> Schools in New York suffer from the worst racial segregation of any U.S. state, and city schools also earn depressingly dismal marks for diversity, a damning report released Wednesday said.

> Many Black and Hispanic kids in New York attend schools with almost no white classmates, according to the paper from the Civil Rights Project at the University of California at Los Angeles.

The author of the report, Gary Orfield, wrote that "New York State has consistently been one of the most segregated states in the nation — no Southern state comes close to New York."

The *Daily News* article quoted Mona Davids, president of the New York City Parents Union, as saying: "Segregation is alive and well in New York City. Every child does not have access to an equal education. It's scary."

What is stunning about this assessment of the New York City racial divide is that it has had some of the most self-proclaimed progressive Democrat (and occasional progressive Republican) mayors in America.

Even as such Republican mayors as John Lindsay and Michael Bloomberg sat in the mayor's chair, the bulk of municipal power rested with the Democratic Party, which controlled most other elective offices and the bureaucracy. Both Lindsay and Bloomberg were more philosophically aligned with Democrat progressive and political policies—including institutional *de facto* racism. They both eventually switched to the Democratic Party to pursue higher office.

Los Angeles School Segregation

Back in 1961, a Black parent facing the long-standing history of school segregation in Los Angeles attempted to enroll her daughter in the nearby predominantly White South Gate High School. Her application was refused solely because the daughter was Black. She was told to enroll the daughter in the more distant predominantly Black Jordan High School.

A lawsuit was filed on behalf of the young student by the American Civil Liberties Union in 1963. The administration of Democrat mayor Sam Yorty and his school board vigorously fought the suit. Though the Yorty administration proposed several window dressing desegregation measures, the courts deemed them all insufficient. In 1965, after years of frustration, the ACLU expanded its legal action to include the entire Los Angeles school system.

In 1970, the judge in the case ruled that the Los Angeles Board of Education and the Los Angeles Unified School District had both violated the United States Constitution and the California Constitution and ordered that the city produce a serious desegregation plan. The subsequent plan submitted by the Democrat administration was again deemed unacceptable by the court.

In 1979, the California state legislature passed a constitutional amendment stating that local school boards were not obligated to exceed the provisions of the Fourteenth Amendment. This coupled with a lawsuit by an anti-busing group basically ended all official efforts to put an end to segregation in the Los Angeles schools.

In a 2014 blog article entitled "Fault Lines: Segregation in Los Angeles Schools," KCRW radio personality Jolie Myers writes: "Sixty years after *Brown vs. Board of Education* declared that segregation was unconstitutional, Los Angeles schools are as segregated as ever."

In addressing the characteristic of the unequal education for minority students, Myers lists deficiencies that can be found in virtually every segregated urban school system under Democrat governance. The deficiencies could have applied to the segregated and unequal school systems in the not-so-long-ago Democrat southland.

- Children who attend segregated schools are less likely to graduate high school.
- Kids in segregated schools don't perform as well on state tests.
- Children who attend segregated schools are more likely to be suspended from school.
- Kids in segregated schools have higher rates of absenteeism.

In summary, Myers challenges the status of Chicago and New York by claiming the dubious honor that "Los Angeles is one of the most segregated large cities in the country." In making such a claim, Myers underscores the Democratic Party's consistent policy of racial school segregation that goes back to 1877—again thwarting the Constitution, federal laws, and court orders. The Massive Resistance that southern Democrats launched in opposition to *Brown v. Board of Education* has continued to this day—only more as a dirty little secret than a publicized campaign. It is why Blacks continue to live in segregated areas with segregated schools.

Miami Retains Southern-Style School Segregation.

Between 1957 and 2009, Democrats have held the mayor's office in Miami for forty-six out of the fifty-two years—including the years of the greatest racial unrest. Miami has had a Republican mayor since 2009, but most of the other offices and the bureaucracy have remained in the control of Democrats.

As a southern state, Florida was part of the Democrats Massive Resistance to school desegregation. The state's two Democrat senators, Spessard Holland and George Smathers, were both signers of the Southern Manifesto.

In his 2010 book, *50 Years after Brown: Segregation in the Miami-Dade County Public Schools*, James R. Moore wrote:

> Fifty years after the *Brown v. Board of Education* decision outlawed *de jure* segregation in American schools, many school districts remain segregated. Despite numerous efforts aimed at desegregation, residential segregation—the primary barrier to significant school desegregation—remains entrenched throughout the United States. The Miami-Dade County Public Schools, the nation's fourth largest school system, provides an excellent example of a segregated metropolitan region that produced a segregated school system and defied numerous efforts at significant school desegregation.

Baltimore Re-Introduces Segregation

Like most cities in post-World War II America, Baltimore schools were generally segregated. The city has had an unbroken history of Democrat administrations since 1947, including the racist regimes of a father-and-son team, Thomas D'Alesandro, Jr. and Thomas D'Alesandro III—also the father and brother of former House Speaker Nancy Pelosi.

Initially, Baltimore responded positively to *Brown v. Board of Education* by allowing its city-wide schools to be integrated. Later, however, race-based school districting was introduced, resulting in the resegregation of the schools. Since the city's neighborhoods were largely segregated, it was not difficult to draw new district lines to create Black and White school districts.

In his book, *The Politics of School Desegregation* Robert L. Cain explains that "the Baltimore school system was accused of intentionally segregating schools through districting. Many civil rights leaders protested this and asked for reform in the system. The reform was slow and is still being sought after today."

In Baltimore, the common characteristic of pernicious urban school segregation and educational inferiority for Black students remains today as the result of an unbroken line Democratic Party governance.

"Johnny Mac" McMillan:
Washington Plantation Master

At the time of the 1960s riots, Washington, DC, was in transition. It was a unique metropolis created by the Constitution as a special district to be ruled over "in all matters" by the Congress. While there had been a long history of proposals to give the residents of Washington some of the representative rights and powers of other American citizens, these efforts languished.

This changed when Republican president Dwight Eisenhower put the power of the Oval Office behind a constitutional amendment to allow Washington residents to vote in presidential elections. The Twenty-Third Amendment was passed out of Congress in the last days of the Eisenhower administration and formally ratified by the states in 1961.

The District of Columbia was officially governed by a commission appointed by the president. For all practical purposes, Washington was governed by the chairman of the House District Committee.

In the 1960s, Democrat congressional leaders would ironically elect "Johnny Mac" McMillan, a staunch segregationist who voted against every civil rights legislation that came before Congress, to rule over the segregated Black citizens of the nation's capital. McMillan was also a signer of the Southern Manifesto, and he had no intention to integrate schools in the nation's capital.

When Lyndon Johnson later appointed Walter Washington, a Black man, as the first mayor-commissioner of the District, McMillan mockingly responded by sending the new mayor a truck load of watermelons, which the congressman described as letters from home.

The fact that the Democrats in Congress would repeatedly elect a southern racist to govern over a city with a large Black population illustrates the racial hypocrisy that has permeated the Democratic Party throughout its history.

In 1974, Republican president Richard Nixon ended Washington, DC's, provincial style government by signing home-rule legislation that gave the predominantly Black voters of the District the right to elect their own local government for the first time. Walter Washington would become the first popularly elected mayor of Washington, DC.

Selma—March 1965

Alongside education, voting rights have been a major issue since the end of the Civil War. In the period between 1957 and 1965 America experienced a sharp increase in violent and murderous intimidation by the Democratic Party's paramilitary groups and even official police departments in the South over the issue of voting rights. This violence appeared on the news across the nation and led the way to public demands for action.

In 1965, Selma, Alabama, became the focus of the voting rights movement. Under the authority of Democrat Sheriff Jim Clark, Blacks in Selma were prevented from registering and voting booths by administrative barriers, Jim Crow laws, intimidation, and violence. Clark was an imposing military looking figure who carried a signature cattle prod in addition to his gun and billy club. Clark created a Ku Klux Klan posse as a terrorist enforcer of racist policies

When the Student Nonviolent Coordinating Committee (SNCC) organized a voter registration effort, Clark and his forces violently attacked the group. Hundreds were beaten and more than three hundred students were arrested for holding a perfectly constitutional peaceful protest near the courthouse. His efforts were very successful. Less than three hundred of the city's potential fifteen thousand Black voters were registered.

Even with Johnson in the White House and Bobby Kennedy still attorney general, civil rights leaders were frustrated by the inaction of Washington in addressing civil rights violations and the growing violence. Frustrations ran high when Johnson let known his intention to indefinitely delay any action on the Voting Rights Bill that had been co-drafted and introduced by Illinois Republican senator Everett Dirksen.

With Democrat governor George Wallace refusing to allow the march, the organizers turned to the federal courts. On March 21, Republican Federal judge Frank Johnson overruled Wallace and allowed the march to proceed.

Per SNCC's executive secretary James Forman, there was a dual purpose in the Selma protest. He said:

> Our strategy, as usual, was to force the U.S. government to intervene in case there were arrests—and if they did not intervene, that inaction would once again prove the government was not on our side and thus intensify the development of a mass consciousness among blacks. Our slogan for this drive was "One Man, One Vote."

To draw attention to voter suppression, King and fellow Southern Christian Leadership Conference activist James Bevel began planning demonstrations in Alabama in January of 1965.

During a voting rights protest on February 18, a young, unarmed protester named Jimmie Lee Jackson was shot and killed by James Bonard Fowler, a Marion, Alabama police officer, while trying to protect his mother.

Writer and activist James Baldwin traveled to Selma. He witnessed sheriff deputies and state troopers attacking marchers with clubs and cattle prods. In a speech to a Black church congregation, Baldwin sarcastically laid the blame for the violence on "the good White people on the Hill," refer-ring to the Democrat-controlled Congress. Baldwin also specifically blamed President Johnson and the late President Kennedy for their years of inaction.

Since Johnson and Jack Kennedy had been able to strip out the key enforcement provisions from the 1957 and 1960 acts, the Justice Department was only able to instigate seventy-one lawsuits—which resulted in a modest increase in the number of southern Black voters.

Bloody Sunday

The incident that may have had the greatest impact on the passage of the Voting Rights Act of 1965 was the violence on what became known as Bloody Sunday. On March 7, 1965, Black protestors were brutally assaulted by police and the White citizens of Selma as they attempted to cross the Edmund Pettus Bridge spanning the Alabama River.

Martin Luther King had organized a peaceful march to go from Selma to the Alabama state capital in Montgomery to protest segregation and the denial of voting rights.

Democrat Governor George Wallace ordered state troopers to join with local law enforcement to stop the march at the bridge. As protestors began marching across the bridge, the law enforcement contingents and many local citizens went on a rampage of bloody violence against the marchers. Hundreds were injured, fifty seriously.

Though not at the moment of the bridge crossing, the Selma demon-strations turned deadly when a Unitarian minister, James Reeb, was fatally beaten in a late-night attack by a group of thugs who were said to have been either members or sympathizers of the Democrat's paramilitary terrorist groups, such as the Ku Klux Klan.

With national attention riveted on the violence in Selma, President Johnson was compelled to intervene. He sent federal troops to Selma, after which the marchers were able to travel the fifty miles to Montgomery under the protection of the military. The march was peaceful in terms of overt violence, but those participating were subjected to taunts and verbal attacks along the way.

The public reaction to the violence and pressure from congressional Republicans forced Johnson to reconsider his decision to "table" the Voting Rights Act. He now had to bring it to a vote.

Voting Rights Act of 1965

The need for the 1965 Act was the result of the Democratic Party's opposition and outright disobedience to constitutional amendments, federal laws and Supreme Court decisions designed to guarantee the voting rights of Black Americans.

The Voting Rights Act of 1965 was described as "An Act to Enforce the Fifteenth Amendment to the Constitution of the United States." Republicans enacted the Fifteenth Amendment in 1870 specifically to give Blacks their constitutional right to vote. It was reinforced by the Republican Enforcement Acts of the 1870s and the Civil Rights Acts of 1957, 1960, and 1964. None of those actions were sufficient to force compliance by the Democratic Party.

Southern Democrats continued to defy the law through illegal and unconstitutional actions, including Jim Crow laws, administrative improprieties and government sponsored terrorism—and without virtually any condemnation or interference from the national Democratic Party. It would not be an exaggeration to say that from the Compromise of 1877, which turned the Confederate states over to the Democratic Party, to the early 1970s there was never a constitutionally valid election held in any of the segregated southern states. For more than one hundred years a defiant Democratic Party used authoritarian rule to block Black Americans from their fundamental constitutional right to vote.

Even in the history of world nations, rarely have such fraudulent elections been conducted on such a grand scale and for such a long duration as what took place in what was commonly known as America's solid Democrat South. The rigging of elections so prevalent in Dixie can only be compared to the worst third-world authoritarian regimes.

Dirksen leads Voting Rights Fight

Republican Senate Minority Leader Dirksen played a central role in drafting the 1965 Voting Rights Act. He was aided in the drafting by Attorney General Nicholas Katzenbach. The GOP leader's role was so critical that SB 1564 was known informally as the "Dirksenbach bill." With the backing of Johnson and the overwhelming support of Republican senators, the voting rights bill was introduced by Dirksen in the Senate on March 17, 1965.

While Democrats controlled both the Senate and the House, Johnson recognized that there was still a powerful anti-integration and anti-voting rights caucus within his own party. He and Dirksen feared the southern Democrat bloc would use technical rules and the filibuster to kill the legislation.

This was of concern because the bill would be assigned to the Judiciary Committee, still headed by one of the Senate's most ardent segregationists, James Eastland of Mississippi. To prevent him from killing it in committee, the full senate, thanks to overwhelming GOP support, voted to force Eastland to bring the bill to the floor through a discharge petition.

After a few technical maneuvers by southern Democrats to either kill the bill or water it down, it came up for a vote. Republican Dirksen was the first to rise in support of the bill he drafted and introduced. "This legislation," he said, "is needed if the unequivocal mandate of the 15th Amendment is to be enforced and made effective, and if the Declaration of Independence is to be made truly meaningful."

The bill was subsequently passed by the Senate. As with the Civil Rights Act of 1964, the Republicans provided greater support than the Democrats. Looking at it another way, 26 percent of the Democrat senators opposed the bill while only four percent of the GOP voted in opposition.

The House

The future of the Voting Rights Bill was less certain in the House of Representatives, where southern Democrats chaired powerful committees. Upon introduction, HR 6400 was referred to the Judiciary Committee chaired by New York congressman Emanuel "Manny" Celler. It was quickly voted out of committee. Like the 1963 Kennedy legislation, the bill was then referred to the Rules Committee chaired by Virginia segregationist Democrat Howard Smith. Smith strongly opposed the bill, but unlike 1963 he was forced to release the bill to the full House for debate and a vote because of the overwhelming support of Republican legislators.

Republican congressman William McCulloch of Ohio introduced a separate bill that would have banned literacy tests but weakened other portions of HR 6400. Southern Democrats seized on the McCulloch bill as a means of defeating the stronger Dirksenbach bill. Support for the McCulloch bill virtually evaporated after Virginia Democrat congressman William Tuck, in an unusual display of candor, endorsed the alternative measure because the Dirksenbach bill would actually guarantee Negros the right to vote.

The House defeated the McCulloch bill and proceeded that same day to pass HR 6400 by a wide margin. While the vote between parties was closer, Republicans still provided a greater margin in the final vote.

The Voting Rights Act of 1965 was signed into law by Johnson on August 6, 1965. In the era of civil rights legislation, the party of Lincoln was true to its heritage—and sadly so was a powerful faction of the Democratic Party.

The Meaning of the Voting Rights Act

The Voting Rights Act of 1965 was different than all the civil rights legislation of the past in that it was carefully crafted to address specific problems in specific states. It did not apply to the nation as a whole, but only to those states with histories of racial discrimination. Without overtly saying so, it was an extremely partisan bill. In defining the egregious "conditions" to be rectified in "certain jurisdictions," the targets of the Voting Rights Act of 1965 were the states and lesser jurisdictions with long histories of racial discrimination in voting. These "certain jurisdictions" were all controlled exclusively by the Democratic Party—and had been for almost ninety years. To put it bluntly, the 1965 Voting Rights Bill recognized the culpability of the Democratic Party in thwarting civil rights for Blacks in the past.

By 2013, the United States Supreme Court, in *Shelby County V. Holder*, determined that the singling out "certain jurisdictions" was no longer necessary. The Court—with a liberal Democrat majority—ruled that the old conditions of racial discrimination no longer existed in the targeted states. The most obvious difference was the fact that the racist Democrat old guard in Dixie had been largely replaced by Republican administrations. The decline of institutional racism in Dixie was directly proportionate to the rise of the GOP.

This is an enormously important distinction since it refutes the false claim that the Republican Party had simply gained the votes of the old racist Democrats. But even as the Republicans assumed control at the state level, Democrats retained control of many counties and municipalities where racial prejudices and institutional *de facto* racism flourished.

In many ways, the votes on the civil rights bills in the 1950s and 1960s reflected the weakening of southern segregationist power within the Congress—leaving the remnants of the Democratic Party's historic institutional racism in the big cities of both the North and the South.

Unable now to prevent Blacks from voting in the South by *de jure* Jim Crow laws, Democrats were left with relying on the Party's longstanding urban strategy of institutional *de facto* racism and generational welfare dependency as the means of controlling the Black vote. Johnson's War on Poverty legislation played an important role in advancing that strategy.

Blockbusting in New York

As late as 1963, the New York City Human Rights Commission published a study on the problem in the "East New York section of Brooklyn." The study used the NAACP's definition of blockbusting. The summary of the study included this description:

> In the words of a national official of the NAACP, persons who engage in blockbusting seek "by deception, manipulation and the instilling of fear and anxiety, to induce white people to sell out at the lowest possible price in order to exploit the desperate need of colored people for a place to live and charge them exorbitant prices."

Diverting any responsibility on the part of the Democrat administration of Mayor Robert Wagner and his predecessors, the summary laid the blame on unnamed real estate operators. The report later exonerated licensed real estate agents, suggesting that the problem was not an industry issue, but merely a few unscrupulous individuals.

The summary went on:

> The crux of the complaints registered by these families was that over a span of two years, their previously stable, integrated community had become a target of intense speculation by real estate operators whose practices and procedures were not only disrespectful and exploitive, but also induced tension and disorder.

> The Testimony presented at the hearing revealed a clear-cut pattern of sales practices and procedures designed to panic white homeowners into selling their properties and then to resell these homes exclusively to negro and Puerto Rican families.

Among the practices specified in the report included:

> [A] barrage of telephone calls by day and night warning that Negroes were moving into the area, and that property values would soon collapse. Aggressively insistent home calls were made to busy housewives. At least one such caller warned a housewife that her daughters might no longer be safe on the street.

And another technique was the "deliberate parading of groups of Negroes, presumably prospective buyers, up and down the block to look at homes."

Though the report was a city document, it inadvertently demonstrated the Democrats historic disinterest in solving racial problems. It said:

> It should be noted, however, that while the cooperative effort utilizing the [Human Rights] Commission's services and professional assistance did have a marked effect, it was not until the entire situation was exposed to public view and public criticism that the speculative activity in the area [the East New York section of Brooklyn] appeared to end.

While the investigation focused on East Brooklyn, the report made it clear that it was "only one of several areas of New York City where the changing racial patterns of residency hold attractive potentiality for unscrupulous profiteers."

The report also addressed the racist practices of the banking industry in the city:

> The image of the entire [banking] industry, which has the obligation to serve the whole market in compliance with the law, is affected by the malpractice of a substantial portion of it which declines to make available adequate mortgage financing to Negro and Puerto Rican families.

Studying a problem under pressure, but taking virtually no corrective actions, is the standard operating procedure for the racist Democrat urban machines. This report was no different. The city's Human Rights Commission was simply used to give an appearance of concern without producing any result-based reforms.

The Special Price of Black Ownership

Despite the blockbusting and crony slumlord ownership, some Blacks achieved home ownership. Ironically, blockbusting was often the avenue for a Black person to purchase a home in a "nicer" neighborhood since real estate covenants and red lining prevented Blacks from moving into racially protected White neighborhoods. That nicer neighborhood, however, would quickly decline as city services were withdrawn, allowing the streets, sidewalks, parks, and other infrastructures to deteriorate. A pervasive failure to enforce building codes created tenements and stereotypical slum housing conditions.

Corrupt real estate agents would occasionally provide Blacks with funding to purchase a home with an unsustainable large mortgage payment at high interest rates. They would then reclaim the home when the owners were unable to keep up the payments.

Gene Demby, writing for National Public Radio described the process this way:

The men who peddled contracts in [Chicago's] North Lawndale would sell homes at inflated prices and then evict families who could not pay—taking their down payment and their monthly installments as profit. Then they'd bring in another Black family … and repeat.

The *Chicago Daily News* quoted an "office secretary" to slumlord speculator Lou Fushanis, who explained how her boss would load "them up with payments they can't meet. Then he takes the property away from them. He's sold some of the buildings three or four times."

Arnold Hirsch, an American historian who taught at the University of New Orleans, wrote:

> Working virtually, if not covertly, in tandem, 'respectable' real-estate agents flocked to do business in transitional areas once they had been broken by the maverick blockbusters. The net result was a gold-rush effect that destabilized residential communities as it maximized racial tensions and fears.

The End of Blockbusting

Blockbusting ebbed when Democrats in Washington and in the major cities devised other ways to keep the growing Black community segregated to a defined PLACE.

By the end of the 1960s, blockbusting became too controversial, too illegal, and too unpopular to survive. It was an outrage to both the White and Black communities. The policy was losing in the courts. The NAACP and other civil rights groups revolted against the practice. A series of laws created serious liabilities for real estate agents who engaged in blockbusting.

The end of blockbusting, however, was not the end of segregation in the major cities. The laws allegedly designed to end blockbusting may have had the opposite effect. While this was an unanticipated outcome by many of the proponents of these laws, it seems that the laws were designed by the city hall Democrats to maintain the racial status quo. As Dmitri Mehlhorn, a regular contributor to Medium.com, explained in a 2015 article called "A Requiem for Blockbusting":

> If any [black] clients alleged that their contractual terms were not identical to the terms a white family might have obtained, they would have an automatic cause of action in federal court to challenge the contracts. If a client asked about changing racial demographics, the agent would either have to decline to answer, or could be subjected to substantial civil and criminal penalties. Given the realities of the racially segregated markets of the time, *the only safe way to avoid these lawsuits was to adhere to the prior professional code of racial steering: buy and sell homes only within a single race.* (emphasis added)

Mehlhorn further notes that the laws purported to end racial segregation were intentionally designed to maintain it. He wrote:

> Anti-blockbusting provisions, such as anti-solicitation ordinances, were explicitly designed to stop market forces and preserve the status quo. For example, many segregationist whites during this period voluntarily refused to put up "For Sale" signs for fear of attracting black buyers. This racist norm became law in many cities and states, which banned "For Sale" signs as one of the blockbusters' techniques for inspiring white fear. *Thus, the same racist actions that were explicitly designed to exclude blacks from the white housing market were codified into law by the anti-blockbusting regime.* (emphasis added)

Business in the Ghetto

One of the causes of conflicts in the major segregated cities of America of the 1960s was ownership of local businesses. Ownership, and therefore access to income and opportunity, had been historically denied to local Black residents.

The ghettoes had primarily two types of businesses: small industrial factories and retail operations. The former provided some local employment, but they were mostly low-skilled jobs in small grimy factories—a blight that White neighborhoods resisted.

These began to disappear as Democrat policies of high taxes and increasingly unsafe neighborhoods drove out the industrial sector. The Democrat leaders did little to promote or encourage new businesses or minority-owned business in the ghettoes. It would take Republicans, like Congressman Jack Kemp, to introduce "enterprise zone" legislation in an attempt to bring enterprise and employment to impoverished minority communities.

The 1965 Los Angeles Watts Riots

Los Angeles, with the influence of Hollywood, is often viewed as the epitome of progressive diversity and racial tolerance. In many ways, it is a false image created in later years by the communication power of Hollywood. In the early part of the twentieth century, Hollywood was an entertainment industry devoted to promoting racism and racial stereotyping. Virtually every top Hollywood star preformed in blackface. Black characters in movies were routinely depicted as lazy and simpleminded. When performing on the stage in the 1936 version of *Showboat*, the leading lady was introduced on an advertising billboard as a "coon shouter"—a White person singing music in a Negro style.

Los Angeles has a long history of racism against at the Chinese, Japanese, Mexicans, and Black Americans. The unconstitutional internment of Japanese Americans by Franklin Roosevelt heavily impacted California, with little to no opposition from Democrats at the state and local levels—and no complaints from Hollywood.

Like most American cities, the Black citizens of Los Angeles have been largely segregated since their arrival. Tourist maps, as late as the 1940s, highlighted Black neighborhoods more as a warning than an invitation to visit. In fact, these areas were often designated on the maps as "foreign colonies." Los Angeles, in the 1920s, was the first city to establish an official policy of restrictive covenants to keep Negroes out of White neighborhoods—or more correctly, keep Negroes in their own PLACE.

Even though Los Angeles was founded largely as a Mexican Hispanic community, these original indigenist inhabitants, along with Asians and Blacks, were designated as inhabitants of the "foreign colonies." The movement toward a White takeover of the city was referred to as the Americanization of Los Angeles.

For the better part of the twentieth century, Blacks in Los Angeles were treated like unwelcomed foreigners. They were ridiculed in newspaper cartoons. The LA ghettoes had all the same deprivations of Democrat-controlled inner cities throughout America. Blacks were only allowed to swim in public natatoriums on a given day—after which the pools were drained and sanitized.

World War II brought a migration of Blacks to LA for wartime employment and military duty. It was called the Second Great Migration. Black population of LA in 1940 was approximately 63,000. By 1965, the Black numbers swelled to more than 350,000. Central Avenue was unofficially designated as the area for Negroes. As the Black community spread out, they were greeted by White gangs that would harass or attack them physically. According to SouthCentralHistory.com "The largest of these gangs were the Spook Hunters. "Spook" is a derogatory term used toward Black people. During the 1940s, the Ku Klux Klan also emerged in LA." In response, the 1960s saw the rise of Black street gangs such as the Black Panthers and the Brown Berets. By 1965, Los Angeles had devolved into a fully segregated city.

Mayor Sam Yorty

Democrat Mayor Sam Yorty, who would preside over both the 1965 and 1968 race riots in Los Angeles, was a flamboyant political character. Many attributed the unrest in LA to Yorty's general neglect and disregard for the Black community. He opposed many federal welfare programs because he thought they gave inner city Blacks false hope.

In 1969, he had run a successful racist campaign against Black city councilman Tom Bradley. A 1998 *Los Angeles Times* obituary alluded to Yorty's racism, describing him as a "peripatetic old-style politician who played on the racial anxieties of the city's mostly White electorate to initially defeat Tom Bradley."

With the loss of Black support, and the likelihood of a loss to Bradley in the later 1973 Democrat primary, Yorty attempted to beat Bradley by taking the Republican nomination. After losing to Bradley, Yorty returned to the Democratic Party and made a run for president in 1972.

The *Los Angeles Times* obituary went on to say:

> During the 1965 Watts riots, Yorty brushed aside minority community complaints about police brutality and, riding over the area in his official helicopter a few days later, seemed to delight in the array of troops below.

> It must make those policemen feel pretty good to have those troops behind them,' he said. "'That's the kind of force we've got to have."

On the eve of the Watts riots, Yorty saw the burgeoning Black community as a threat to White domination. He was also picking up on the false communist allegations against Martin Luther King being leaked by the FBI at the behest of the Kennedy and Johnson administrations. According to the *LA Times* "By the summer of 1964, [Yorty] was complaining that 'civil rights extremists' were picking on the big city mayors." Yorty suggested that "all this agitation is by communists, but it's certain that the communists are involved."

In complaining that Black activists were picking on the big city mayors, Yorty was unintentionally pointing the finger for Black frustration directly at the those in charge of the major big cities, Democrats.

Los Angeles Erupts

On August 11, 1965, the suppressed anger and frustration boiled over when a Black man was arrested for driving under the influence. The argument escalated into a brawl. It kicked off a community wide rampage that became known as the Watts Riot.

The violence continued for six days. To quell the rioting, Yorty called on Democrat governor Pat Brown to send in four thousand members of the national guard. By the time relative peace was restored, there were hundreds of injuries and thirty-four dead. An estimated more than $40 million of property was destroyed or damaged—mostly in the Black community.

Later reports placed the blame for the riots on two underlying factors: the high rate of unemployment in the Black community and systemic police racism. Along with general poverty, these causes would be at the root of urban unrest in Democrat-controlled cities for the next half century.

The Civil Rights Movement Travels North

By 1966, the *de jure* racism that had held firm in Dixie was coming to an end. Martin Luther King understood that the victories over Jim Crow in the south did not address the more subtle *de facto* segregation and racism. He said: "In the South, we always had segregationists to help make issues clear. … This ghetto Negro [in the major cities] has been invisible so long and has now become visible through violence."

It was logical that he would take his crusade to the city that best exemplified *de facto* racism—Chicago. King said he came to Chicago because "the moral force of SCLC's nonviolent movement philosophy was needed to help eradicate a vicious *system* which seeks to further colonize thousands of Negroes within a slum environment."

The word *system* has been highlighted to draw attention to the fact that King very clearly saw racism in Chicago in institutional terms, the product of the Democrat leadership and not just some natural social phenomenon.

According to the Stanford's Martin Luther King, Jr. Research and Education Institute:

> Chicago politics made the city a good choice for a northern campaign. Mayor Richard Daley had a high degree of personal power and was in a position to directly mandate changes to a variety of racist practices.

King may have recognized the racism in Chicago and even the autocratic power of Mayor Daley, but he misjudged how the mayor would exercise that power vis-a-vis the Negro community. Daley was the personification and the willful administrator of urban racist policies.

Police Harass Blacks in White Neighborhoods

Racial segregation was designed to prevent social and civic interaction —to keep Blacks in the PLACE. Blacks appearing in White neighborhoods "without good reason" were often intimidated (or worse) by White thugs and harassed by police. Shopping was segregated. In the 1950s and early 1960s, it was rare for Blacks to shop in The Loop—Chicago's central shopping district. Although not as blatant, it was essentially the same policy seen in the Democrat southland where public signs warned: "No niggers allowed after sundown."

Segregation was important to the Democrat machine. Daley saw it as a means of making White citizens feeling safe from the criminality and low standards of Blacks – as portrayed by racist fearmongering by Democrat precinct operatives. This policy was, in large measure, to prevent Whites from fleeing to the suburbs—which would further empower Black voters. It was also a means of keeping the Black community in their defined PLACE—especially in order to control that all-important Black vote.

The Coordinating Council of Community Organizations

The Chicago Freedom Movement was first organized by local Black activists to fight the horrific slum conditions in city's ghettoes on the south and west sides. The movement grew out of the work of the Coordinating Council of Community Organizations (CCCO), which focused on improving education and housing for inner city residents.

The CCCO was formed in the early 1960s. It organized a series of peaceful sit-ins to draw attention to school segregation and classroom overcrowding in minority schools. The organization became more visible when local activist Albert Raby took over as convener in 1964. He brought together a coalition of Black groups, including the Congress of Racial Equality (CORE), one of the more militant groups. The local movement took off after Raby invited King and the SCLC to come to Chicago. It was the most ambitious civil rights campaign ever conducted in the North and for the first time drew national attention to the racist policies of the Democratic Party in Chicago as well as other northern cities.

With education being a centerpiece of the civil rights movement, the initial protest was against the Chicago Public School System and specifically against school superintendent Benjamin Willis. They called for his resignation. While the movement initially focused on education and housing, King expanded the target issues to hiring practices and police brutality.

Mayor Daley initially reacted with great hostility to the movement and King personally. He condemned King and blamed the unrest on outside agitators—an excuse originating in the South since the days of slavery and heard as late as the 2015 Freddie Gray riots in Baltimore.

At almost every public event, King was greeted by angry counter protesters organized or encouraged by local Democrat ward bosses spewing racial epitaphs and waving Confederate battle flags. In one incident, King was hit in the head by a rock and knocked to the ground.

When asked about his reception in the Democrat stronghold of Chicago, King said, "I've been in many demonstrations all across the South, but I can say that I have never seen—even in Mississippi and Alabama—mobs as hostile and as hate filled as I've seen here in Chicago. . . . I think the people from Mississippi ought to come to Chicago to learn how to hate."

The violent hatred that King experienced had been ginned up by decades of Democrat racist governance. The awesome power of the Democrat machine depended on the maintenance of a simmering hostility between the largely well-off White community and the impoverished segregated Black community.

The 1966 West Side Riot

In July of 1966, racial tensions in Chicago erupted in the Black community in what became known as the West Side Riot. Without the benefit of widespread residential air conditioning, especially in the Black tenements, there was little relief from the blistering heat. The violence erupted when a Black man was arrested for opening a fire hydrant to allow the children and others to cool off. While there was extensive damage and some injuries, there were no fatalities. Peace was restored when twelve hundred national guardsmen were dispatched to the scene. Ironically, the city later established a policy of opening fire hydrants in ghetto neighborhoods when temperatures soared.

An Agreement Written on the Wind

Eventually, pressure from King and the Chicago Freedom Movement brought Daley and the real estate leaders to the table. The result was a signed agreement with specific steps for improving schools and housing conditions. Daley promised to pass an open housing ordinance and provide scatter site public housing to begin the process of integration.

While King's movement ebbed in 1967, it is credited with the eventual passage of the Chicago Fair Housing law in 1968. King felt his efforts in Chicago had paid off. Daley signed the agreement in bad faith, however, and had no intention of implementing any of the provisions—and he did not.

Despite the pact, and even the passage of the Chicago Fair Housing Law, the Chicago Democrat machine's racist housing policies continued unabated. As they did for almost one hundred years in the South, Chicago Democrats demonstrated an ability to simply ignore the laws and agreements in pursuing racial discrimination, segregation, and oppression.

When confronted with a lack of solutions to the racial situation in Chicago, Daley told an NBC-TV reporter:

> Well, I asked [King and other protesters] for their answer to the solution of many of these questions, and they had no solution. They had the recitation of the problem, but I said, "Well, how do you eliminate the slum and blight overnight? What would you men do that we haven't done in Chicago?"

Daley's statement was an indication that he had no intention of abandoning the Democrats longstanding segregationist policies. His claim that King and others offered no solutions was an outright lie.

In a 2006 article for *Poverty & Race,* University of Illinois Political Science Professor Dick Simpson noted the continuing failure to address racial prejudice in 1966 by the Chicago Democrat machine. He wrote:

> Many at the time saw the agreement as a sham and simply a way for Dr. King to leave town and take the movement other places where there would be more success. Others note today that the gap between poor Blacks and rich Whites in the Chicago Metropolitan region is greater than in Dr. King's time.

King admitted defeat in Chicago at a March 24, 1967, press conference at which he said:

> It appears that for all intents and purposes, the public agencies have [reneged] on the agreement and have, in fact given credence to [those] who proclaim the housing agreement a sham and a batch of false promises.

As Edward McClelland of NBC-TV Chicago wrote in 2012:

> As long as Daley was mayor, Chicago remained the most segregated city in America. In many parts of town, it still is. On his home turf in the South, King defeated Bull Connor, George Wallace, Lester Maddox, the Ku Klux Klan and the White Citizens Councils. But in Chicago, he couldn't outfox Mayor Daley.

Despite King's efforts, Chicago continued to remain arguably the most Democrat, the most segregated, and most institutionally racist city in America.

New York's Ocean Hill-Brownsville

The Ocean Hill-Brownsville neighborhood of New York historically was an enclave of Jewish left-wing radicalism. Voters there consistently sent socialist candidates to the legislature in Albany.

Between 1940 and 1960, the Black population was gradually increasing, and by the mid-1960s the Black and Hispanic population surged. The progressive Jews were not happy with the growing Black population but encouraged it by a mass exodus in the early 1960s. By 1970, Brownsville was almost 80 percent Black, the result of blockbusting, White flight and segregationist policies.

Brownsville was typical of the ghettoization of Blacks. Lawrence University history professor Jerald E. Podair writes in his book *The Strike that Changed New York:*

> Ocean Hill–Brownsville's social ills were a by-product of its boxed-in economic status. A contemporary observer was blunt: "Brownsville has no middle class. There are no resident doctors, no resident lawyers; Negroes own less than 1 percent of the businesses."

Ocean Hill-Brownsville, like so many other communities that shifted from White to Black, suffered from a lack of city services and general investment as a result of *de facto* racist policies and direct edicts from city hall.

The schools posed a unique problem. In 2014, *The Atlantic* published an article by Nikole Hannah-Jones entitled "How Segregation Has Persisted in Little Rock." She reported that "Despite the Supreme Court's 1954 Brown v. Board ruling against segregated schools, *educational segregation in Brooklyn actually increased in the following years, due to segregationist districting and school construction.*" (emphasis added)

School construction was a major racial issue. Rather than expend funds for new schools, minority schools were allowed to become overcrowded, diminishing the quality of education even more. For the students in the Brownsville Junior High School, it meant an education institutionally inferior to the White students who attended high schools in the same school system. It was as separate and unequal as the old Democrat southland.

Local education and civil rights activists became convinced that the Democrat-dominated New York Central School Board, despite *Brown v. Board of Education*, had no desire to push for integrated schools. Yet another example of Democrat governance simply refusing to obey laws intended to address racial inequities.

In *The Color of Law: A Forgotten History of How Our Government Segregated America* author Richard Rothstein wrote:

> Given a choice between angering politically potent white voters or a marginalized black community, the board, predictably, took the path of least resistance. By 1966, the campaign to integrate the city's public school was at a dead end.

This led to a fight for community control of the local schools. The predominantly White school staffs had switched to a new union—The United Federation of Teachers (UFT)—giving the boot to the Teachers' Union that had supported more aggressive integration policies. Such school union complicity in urban educational racism is found in virtually all of the segregated cities in America to this day.

Once in control of the schools, the local de-centralized school district moved to replace the predominantly White staff with Black teachers and administrators for the predominantly Black schools. The move created a secondary conflict because the White staff had been largely Jewish. The predominantly White UFT used that fact to claim the move was simply anti-Semitism. If that was not the original factor in the firing of the White staff, the UFT claims made it an issue and created a schism between the Black and Jewish communities.

Claiming the firing was a violation of the union contract, the Lindsay administration dispatched 300 police to reopen the school with the original White staff. The UFT called for a wildcat strike, but eventually, the school was reopened with the original White staff. Many of the replaced Black teachers were said to be "too militant."

The victory of the White leadership in New York, including the UFT, led to a lingering resentment in the Black community. The relationship between Whites and Blacks deteriorated with a subtext of hostility between Blacks and Jews. These hostilities played a role in the formation of the Jewish Defense League (JDL) under the leadership of radical Rabbi Meir David Kahane. The JDL would later be declared a terrorist organization.

The Ocean Hill-Brownsville conflict was said to be one of the "political plagues" that virtually destroyed Mayor Lindsay's legacy. The lingering subtext of anti-Semitism among Black Democrat leaders was reflected in Jesse Jackson's later derogatory reference to New York City as "hymie town." It again surfaced in 2019 as a national issue with the expressions of anti-Semitism among newly elected congressional Democrats, including congresswomen Ilhan Omar, Rashida Tlaib, and Alexandria Ocasio-Cortez. And then again in response to the Israeli-Hamas war in 2023.

The Hough Riot in Cleveland

Like virtually every other major city in America in the 1960s, Cleveland was controlled by Democrats and was a hotbed of racial conflict. Democrat mayor Ralph S. Locher was no friend of civil rights. He publicly condemned Floyd McKissick, of the Congress of Racial Equality (CORE), and Martin Luther King as extremists. Using the common excuse, Locher blamed outside agitators for any racial unrest. He went so far as to order police to take down out-of-state license numbers at motels in an effort to identify out-of-town agitators.

In July of 1966, race riots broke out in the Hough (pronounced Huff) area of Cleveland. The unrest began when someone placed a sign outside the 79ers Bar on Hough Avenue that read NO WATER FOR NIGGERS. To prevent Blacks from entering the bar, the manager and an employee posted themselves outside with shotguns. When a Black man entered the bar for wine and water, he was denied service. Soon a crowd of approximately fifty people gathered in front of the bar. Police were called to diffuse the situation.

Unfortunately, Cleveland represented a long history of racial prejudice and abuse. Rather than quelling the crowd, the police presence further incited it. As tensions rose, police shot out streetlights and ordered drivers to extinguish their headlights to prevent being targeted with rocks and bottles—and from potential sniper fire. Shots rang out.

Tensions boiled over when a young mother called out from a window begging for safe passage to go home and attend to her three children. She was shot dead.

As violence and arson spread, Mayor Locher ordered all bars to be closed at 6:00 p.m. The move failed to stop the violence and arson. A second Black citizen was shot to death as he went to help a friend protect his business. Later that evening, a woman and her two children were wounded by gun shots.

The next day a fifty-four-year-old Black man was gunned down as he traveled to a bus stop. A twenty-nine-year-old unarmed Black man, Benoris Toney, was shot dead while sitting in his car. The killer, a White man named Warren LaRiche, was charged with the murder. At his trial, he claimed the shooting was in self-defense and was acquitted by an all-White jury.

Rumors had more impact than fact. Black residents blamed many of the shootings on the police. Police blamed White hot heads. White residents blamed Black snipers. In one instance, two young White men accidentally wounded themselves with a shotgun. The incident was reported in the newspaper as ""two white boys shot by Negroes".

After six nights of rioting four Black citizens were dead, and thirty were seriously or critically injured. Approximately 275 people were arrested, and hundreds of buildings were set on fire.

The damage to Cleveland lasted much longer than the six days of violence. People and businesses left Cleveland. Jobs were lost and unemployment soared. The community descended into abject poverty. The disinvestment lasted more than thirty years. Businesses leaving dangerous segregated communities has been a trend for more than fifty years and counting.

Edward Brooke (R-MA)

Despite the racial turbulence in many American cities, a new racial milestone was reached in America. Not since Reconstruction had a Black served in the United States Senate, but that long streak was broken by Republican Edward (Ted) Brooke of Massachusetts in 1967. He had previously been the first Black attorney general of any state in the nation. At the time, Brooke was only the third Black to serve in the Senate—and the first in the twentieth century. His Republican predecessors served in the Senate during Reconstruction in the 1860s. It would take twenty-six more years after Brooke's election for the Democratic Party to elect its first Black senator in 1993.

In this historic event, partisan considerations naturally trumped the advancement of a Black officeholder. President Johnson supported Brooke's Democrat opponent, Endicott Peabody, in 1966 and Democrat presidential candidate George McGovern supported Democrat John J. Droney against Brooke in the latter's successful 1972 reelection bid.

The Democrats were successful in defeating Brooke in 1978 with Congressman Paul Tsongas largely due to an investigation into Brooke's personal finances by John Kerry, the local Democrat prosecutor who would go on to be the Democrats 2004 presidential candidate and later Secretary of State in the President Obama administration. It was considered to be a sleazy political tactic, and Brooke was ultimately found to have committed no wrongdoing. The plan worked, however, because the bad publicity created by Kerry's dirty trick ginned up a politically damaging investigation.

Brooke's election was significant because the state of Massachusetts had a very small Black population at the time—approximately three percent (and even fewer in the Republican Party). This was in keeping with the long tradition of White Republican voters supporting Black candidates. In those days, Democrats only elected Black candidates from predominantly Black districts—and these were often gerrymandered to consolidate and limit Black representation.

Brooke's Record in the Senate

As the first Negro in the United States Senate since the Democrats drove out the Black congressional Republicans after the Civil War, Brooke focused on civil rights. He coauthored the 1968 Fair Housing Act, which created the Department of Housing and Urban Development's first Office of Fair Housing and Equal Opportunity. This gave Blacks legal and enforceable access to housing by ending race-based discrimination in renting, buying, and financing.

Brooke led the fight in 1974 for the expansion of the 1965 Voting Rights Act. In doing so, Brooke had to face down Mississippi's racist Democrat senator John Stennis.

In his autobiography, *Bridging the Divide: My Life*, Brooke wrote that he believed "sooner rather than later, the United States Senate will more closely reflect the rich diversity of this great country."

George E. Curry, editor of *Emerge* magazine wrote:

> While doing his job, Brooke showed that—as did several Black Republicans who would later follow him in public service, including Assistant Secretary of Labor Arthur Fletcher in the Nixon administration and William T. Coleman, Jr., Secretary of Transportation under Gerald Ford—he could be a Black Republican without selling out his principles or abandoning the fight for civil rights.

In 2004, Brooke was the recipient of the Presidential Medal of Freedom, awarded by President George W. Bush, and the Jeremy Nicholson Negro Achievement Award for his many contributions to civil rights and Negro advancement.

Segregation and Unrest

Segregation is, and always has been, an economic separation. In 1967, urbanologist Pierre de Vise wrote in *The Widening Color Gap* that there was an economic "color gap" between Blacks and Whites that continued growing even after the civil rights acts of the 1950s and 1960s and President Johnson's War on Poverty. Broad-based Black empowerment was still being thwarted by the Democrats in city hall—even Black Democrats in city hall. This widening gap was also noted by University of Chicago sociologist William Julius Wilson, who saw the trend as establishing a permanent underclass.

In terms of segregation-related unrest, 1967 was not much different than 1966. The one distinction, however, was the number of racial outbreaks— officially set at 160 disruptions (riots). The following are among the more significant riots.

The Newark Riots

In 1967, the mayor of Newark, New Jersey, was Democrat Hugh Addonizio. He had previously served in Congress from 1948 to 1966. Addonizio was a typical Democrat machine mayor. He followed the Democrat narrative of talking in favor of civil rights, but his policies did nothing to address the plight of Blacks in Newark's segregated communities.

While he appointed Blacks to public sector patronage jobs and supported them for lower-level public office, Addonizio would follow the more traditional path originally laid out by White plantation owners, Tammany Hall, and Mafia operatives in Harlem. He would employ Black cronies to represent the false narrative of Democrat beneficence and the civil rights of welfare dependency in the community. They were beholden to the White power structure, however.

In his book, *How Newark Became Newark: The Rise, Fall and Rebirth of an American City*, author Brad R. Tuttle addressed this issue in Newark:

> Newark's best known black politician, Councilman Irvine Turner,
> was an Addonizio protégé and one of the mayor's strongest allies.
> To the NAACP and other civil rights groups, Turner was a flashy,

unprincipled demagogue, motivated mainly by his desires to stay in office and keep his powerful friends in City Hall happy.

Tuttle's book included a quote from Black writer and poet Amiri Baraka, who wrote that Addonizio ran the city with "a crew of niggers and Negroes crawling around him that would make any honest person's hair stand on end."

As is so often the case, the relations between police and the Black community in Newark were strained over years of accusations and experiences of police racial brutality. On July 12, 1967, John Smith, a Black cab driver for the Safety Cab Company, was arrested and charged with tailgating and driving the wrong direction on a one-way street—an unlikely combination of charges. Witnesses said that Smith had driven around a police car and then double parked.

Witnesses contacted local civil right leaders and organizations, including the Congress of Racial Equality (CORE). When they visited Smith at the police station, he had incurred significant injuries at the hands of the police. The local civil rights leaders successfully demanded that he be transferred to a hospital.

Angered by yet another example of what appeared to be capricious police brutality against a Black citizen, crowds began to gather in front of the Fourth Precinct Police Station. Several civil rights leaders addressed the crowd and called for peaceful demonstrations, but an angry resident grabbed the bullhorn and riled the crowd to more aggressive action. Bricks, bottles, and other makeshift missiles, including Molotov cocktails, were hurled at the police station.

In what would become characteristic of many racial protests turned violent, many young protestors engaged in looting and arson. Despite the violence, Mayor Addonizio refused to characterize the unrest as a riot. His effort would be proven wrong when a second night of violence spread throughout Newark's Black ghetto. It lasted for several days.

According to BlackPast.org, a website supported by the National Endowment for the Humanities and the State of Washington and devoted to African American history:

> As the riot approached its final hours, 26 people, mostly African Americans, were reported killed, another 750 were injured and over

> 1,000 were jailed.   Property damage exceeded $10 million. The riot, the worst civil disorder in New Jersey history, ended on July 17, 1967.

The Twelfth Street Riot in Detroit

When first elected in 1962, Democrat mayor James Cavanagh produced a documentary entitled *Detroit: City on the Move.* In it, he predicted a bright future for the Motor City. It was not to be. Driven by Democrat economic and racial policies based on welfare dependency, Detroit lost half its population to White flight, most of its tax base, and virtually all its major public services. It became the first major American city to officially go bankrupt.

In July of 1967, Detroit police raided a private party at a "blind pig"—a Depression-era term used to describe an illegal liquor establishment. They arrested eighty-two patrons. While processing the arrestees on site, local residents began to gather, and rumors of police brutality swept through the crowd. A bottle was thrown through the rear window of a police car. Bottles, bricks, and other hand-tossed missiles filled the air.

Black Democrat congressman John Conyers arrived to address the crowd. Standing on a car and using a bullhorn, he implored the crowd to disseminate. "We're with you!" he called out. "But, please! This is not the way to do things! Please go back to your homes!"

The response was a fusillade of rocks and bottles, and Conyers had to be rushed from the scene. One of the riot's more memorable moments came when Detroit Tiger left fielder Willie Horton arrived on the scene to calm the crowd. He was still wearing his baseball uniform.

Firefighters were ordered to stand down as a raging fire, fanned by twenty-five-mile-per-hour winds, burned a one-hundred-square-block area. Allowing rioters to run amok and destroy their own neighborhood was, to some extent, standard operating procedure in dealing with urban riots well into the twenty-first century. As long as the mayhem and destruction were confined to Black neighborhoods, police and firefighters would be ordered to back off. This procedure would be seen in later in the 2020s in such cities as Philadelphia, Ferguson, Missouri, Minneapolis, and Baltimore.

Being a political foe of Republican governor George Romney, Cavanagh refused to seek the intervention of the Michigan National Guard until leaders in both the White and Black communities pleaded with him to do so. The situation on the streets was out of control, and people were being killed. Finally, Cavanagh relented. In addition to the national guard, Congressman Conyers reluctantly asked Lyndon Johnson to send in federal troops. The president used the Insurrection Act of 1807 as the authority for him to respond.

The riots changed nothing. Detroit's Tenth Precinct headquarters remained infamous for its abuse of Blacks. Police mug shots of arrestees proved that many physical injuries were sustained after booking. Black women were made to disrobe in front of male officers and often were fondled.

One of the worst examples of police brutality occurred at the Algiers Motel, approximately a mile from the center of the riot. The Algiers was more of a rooming house and was often used by prostitutes. Detroit police, Michigan state police and national guardsmen responded to a report that shots had been fired. Upon arriving at the scene, police and guardsmen found several Black men and two White male students from Ohio on the premises. There were also a number of White and Black women. None appeared to have been involved in any violence.

Upon entering the building, police shot and killed a young unarmed Black man who they claimed was mistakenly assumed to be a rioter. Two White females and seven Black men on the scene were brutally beaten, and two other Black men were taken to separate rooms where they were summarily executed by police. Several officers responsible for the killing at the Algiers Motel were put on trial. Despite a confession by one of the officers, no one was convicted.

In 2006, with Detroit in desperate condition after almost fifty years of Democrat governance, Democrat governor Jennifer Granholm echoed Cavanagh's misplaced optimism by predicting yet another "renaissance" for the Motor City. "In five years, you will be blown away," she chimed. Those five years have come and gone, and Detroit remains a place with a segregated majority Black population that still suffers the plight of poverty, lack of quality education, high unemployment, high crime rates, and periodic civil unrest. As governor, Granholm did virtually nothing to change the downward trajectory of Detroit, and on July 18, 2013, the impoverished and ravaged city filed for bankruptcy with an estimated debt of $18 to $20 billion—the largest municipal bankruptcy in American history.

Milwaukee, Wisconsin

Police brutality and housing discrimination were simmering issues in Milwaukee despite the beer city's reputation as an example of radical progressive governance—and a succession of socialist mayors. It had not had a Republican mayor since 1908. At the time of the riot, mayor Henry Maier had been in office for seven years—having succeeded Democrat socialist mayor Frank Zeidler.

Tensions were high between the police and the Black community. It did not take much to ignite the riot on a hot summer day. It started on July 29, 1967, with a fight between two teenage girls, which brought the police. No sooner did they arrive than the street fight expanded to a confrontation between police and citizens. Rocks were thrown at police. The evening ended without further incident.

On July 30, a crowd assembled on Third Street. Rumors began to spread. The most serious was that police had badly beaten a young boy. It was not true but based on rumor alone the riot started with looting, arson, and violent exchanges between police and rioters.

By the time order was restored, four people were dead, hundreds were injured and more than seventeen hundred were arrested. The conflict continued over the next few weeks. Some of the most violent incidents were when a local priest, Father James Groppi, led Black marches into all White neighborhoods.

In addressing an organizing meeting at his church, Groppi gave this ominous warning: "If there is any man or woman here who is afraid of going to jail for his freedom, is afraid of getting tear gassed, or is afraid of dying, you should not have come to this meeting tonight."

Groppi's marches went on for two hundred days and resulted in violent clashes between the Black marchers and the White residents. They brought national attention to the institutional *de facto* racism of the Democrat leadership of Milwaukee.

The National Advisory Commission on Civil Disorders

In response to the unrest that was rolling through American cities in 1967, President Johnson created the National Advisory Commission on Civil Disorders to address racial unrest, which was largely composed of establishment Democrats. Johnson appointed the Democrat governor of Illinois, Otto Kerner, as chairman of the commission. Kerner was a hardcore Chicago-machine politician with a vested interest in protecting the status quo and the false Democrat narrative that generational welfare was an existential civil right.

The commission's final report, known as the Kerner Report, clearly outlined the reasons for Black grievance and the frustration that led to protests and riots. The survey of Blacks clearly showed that their most critical concerns or "deficiencies," as the Report termed it, were equal justice, jobs, housing, and education—basically issues of fundamental civil rights.

These are all issues most influenced by municipal government policies. What was near the bottom of Black concerns was welfare—the Democrat's faux civil right. Underscoring that reality was the commission's finding that Blacks were "highly distrustful of the political system." There can be no mistaking who was in charge of the "political system" in the riot-torn cities.

Rather than address the issue of specific accountability or systemic racist policies, the commission laid the blame on generic "White racism." According to the Kerner Report:

> White racism is essentially responsible for the explosive mixture which has been accumulating in our cities since the end of World War II. At the base of this mixture are three of the most bitter fruits of white racial attitudes.

> The report saw "Pervasive discrimination and segregation" as the most important factor in Black unrest.

> The first is surely the continuing exclusion of great numbers of Negroes from the benefits of economic progress through discrimination in employment and education and their enforced confinement in segregated housing and schools. The corrosive and degrading

> effects of this condition and the attitudes that underlie it are the source of the deepest bitterness and lie at the center of the problem of racial disorder.

> The report gave a bleak picture of Black inner-city communities.

> ... segregation and poverty have intersected to destroy opportunity and hope and to enforce failure. The ghettos too often mean men and women without jobs, families without men, and schools where children are processed instead of educated, until they return to the street—to crime, to narcotics, to dependency on welfare, and to bitterness and resentment against society in general and white society in particular.

The commission was very accurate in identifying the issues contributing to Black frustration but totally avoided addressing the question of responsibility. In fact, the common causes of urban unrest, as outlined in the Kerner Report, have been, and are, the political policies and practices of the Democrat machines that have ruled over cities most afflicted with iconic racial unrest. The reason that the Democrat-dominated Kerner Commission did not come to that obvious conclusion is, in itself, obvious.

Fear of Black Power

The report reflected a growing concern among Democrats, that the growth of the Negro population would make it more difficult, if not impossible, to maintain political control of the largely segregated population. They are afraid of "Black power." It was an early manifestation of replacement theory.

In addressing "Negro settlement patterns," the Report stated that there was "little doubt that the trend toward Negro majorities will continue." Not only was the growth in the Negro population a matter of geography, but Democrats feared that when the Black vote reached majority levels, it would no longer be possible to control it for the benefit of the incumbent White Democrat political machines.

With that in mind, the various Democrat political machines employed two strategies—diluting Black voting power as long as possible through creative *de facto* racist policies and recruiting Black leaders into the racist political machine model. The report correctly predicted that several major cities would have Negro majorities in the next twenty years. This did not automatically translate to Black leadership in every case. And where it did, it did not result in reforms that ended segregation and racial oppression.

Detroit became a majority Black city in the mid-1970s. Under Black Democratic rule, the suffering of the Black community actually worsened—largely because the new Black leaders were advocates of the Democratic Party's false narrative—focusing on subjugation through welfare over ending institutional *de facto* racism. Like Black slave owners in the south, many Black Democrat urban leaders gamed the system for their own benefit. They used the same oppressive policies and generational welfare dependency to control the oppressed Black vote for their own power, profit, and prestige.

The Impact of the Kerner Report

With the southern segregationist still holding tremendous power in Congress and in the Democratic Party, it is not clear if President Johnson was looking for the commission to provide implementable recommendations or simply wanted a symbolic public relations exercise, as has been the standard operating procedure in the past. Whatever the case, Johnson basically ignored the findings and recommendations of the report.

In 1970, the Institute of Government and Public Affairs at the University of Illinois convened an assembly to review the work of the commission. It published its findings in a document called "The Kerner Report revisited; final report and background papers," in which the organizer stated their purpose:

> As with many study commission reports, there is a tendency to file
> the report and to virtually ignore its recommendations. To see if
> this was the case, and to review the recommendations, the Institute
> of Government and Public Affairs devoted its twelfth public affairs
> assembly to the topic of the Kerner Report.

The prospect of implementing the Report was grim. Referring to the report in a 2015 article in *The Atlantic*, author Julian E. Zelizer noted that:

> Johnson knew the Kerner Report would embarrass him, and so he tried to ignore it as long as possible. He refused to formally receive the publication from the commissioners, and he didn't talk about the report with the media for weeks.

Johnson elected not to run for reelection in 1968, and his would-be Democrat successor, Minnesota senator Hubert H. Humphrey, showed little enthusiasm for making the Kerner Report a campaign issue. It was Republican president Richard Nixon who would use the report to address the status of those trapped in the ghettoes of the Democrat-run cities.

King Assassinated in Memphis

On March 31, 1968, with the presidential campaigns in full swing, Martin Luther King addressed a mostly White crowd of more than four thousand at Washington's National Cathedral, with many of the overflow crowd listening from the lawn of the unfinished Gothic structure. Even before King's speech, America was in chaos. Anti-war activism and violence were at fever pitch. The feminist movement was on the rise. Gays were coming out of the closet. After decades of racist rule by the Democratic Party in the major cities, the Black ghettoes of the nation were cauldrons of pent-up anger and frustration.

Against this backdrop, King predicted "if nothing is done between now and June to raise ghetto hope, I feel this summer will not only be as bad, but worse than last year."

King's words could not have been more prophetic. In less than thirty days, Martin Luther King would be dead, and an unprecedented wave of racial unrest and rioting would again spread across America.

King's dark premonition of looming violence came to pass on April 4, 1968, when he was assassinated in Memphis, Tennessee. King was getting a breath of fresh air on the balcony of the Lorraine Motel. A shot rang out and King fell to the cement. The civil rights movement's most prominent leader was dead.

In many ways, he was the last real civil rights leader. His dream was of a post-racial America in which Negroes would escape the oppression of segregation and ghettoization and assimilate into the greater American economic, political and social culture. He fought for the inalienable constitutional civil rights of Black Americans.

The loss of King created a vacuum in the civil rights movement. New personalities would rise in the wake of his death, most notably Jesse Jackson and Al Sharpton. They would be more partisan and more devoted to the pseudo civil rights of welfare dependency. They would serve to maintain the Democrats urban political plantations and promote the policies of generational welfare dependency launched in the 1930s. For the foreseeable future, Black Americans would remain confined to a PLACE of impoverishment and oppression under a false rubric of civil rights. In the meantime, leaders like Jackson and Sharpton would gain fame and wealth by serving the Democratic Party establishment over the interests of millions of Blacks trapped in the Party's urban strongholds. They would become part of the political structure of the oppressors.

Following the assassination, President Johnson addressed the nation, pleading for peaceful demonstrations in memory of King's nonviolence. He called on, "every citizen to reject the blind violence that has struck Dr. King, who lived by nonviolence." His words went unheeded in many of the cities where the long history of Democrat racist governance exploded in violence. Major riots broke out in Chicago; Washington, DC; Baltimore; Boston; Newark; and several other major cities. Altogether more than fifteen thousand national guardsmen were deployed in dozens of cities across the country.

Washington, DC

At the time, Washington, DC, had a Black population in excess of 500,000—approximately two and one-half times the White population. They were mostly poor and segregated in areas outside the central government and business core. It was among the most segregated cities in America. It was said that Washington had a "southern mentality" when it came to Blacks and civil rights.

Upon hearing the news of King's assassination, crowds assembled initially in peaceful protest. The Student Nonviolent Coordinating Committee

(SNCC), led by civil rights activist Stokely Carmichael, marched through the Black neighborhood requesting businesses to close out of respect to the fallen civil rights leader. As darkness fell, however, looting and vandalism commenced.

Hoping that the rioting could be contained to a one-day event, mayor Walter Washington ordered a quick clean-up of the debris. Carmichael held a rally to warn against further destruction and violence. Not all those who attended the rally were in a peaceful mood, however. Mayor Washington ordered police to maintain order by whatever means necessary. This led to violent confrontations between police and demonstrators.

When crowds swelled to more than twenty thousand, President Johnson ordered more than thirteen thousand US soldiers into the District. He also took federal control of the DC National Guard. By the time order had been restored, twelve individuals were dead and more than a thousand were injured. More than twelve hundred buildings were destroyed, which included nine hundred local businesses serving the Black community.

Baltimore

With so much emphasis in Baltimore on the conduct of police vis-à-vis the Black community, it is a noteworthy footnote that the first Black police officers hired in Baltimore were the result of proposals by Harry W. Nice, a Republican member of the city council who went on to become governor of Maryland from 1935 to 1939.

In many ways, modern-day Baltimore is yet another example of Black oppression by Democrat-led government regimes. At the time of the 1968 riots, the Black ghettoes in Baltimore bore the typical traits of oppression. Black wages were less than half the national average while unemployment was double the national average. Those employed were paid less than White workers and generally had the least desirable jobs. Education was lacking, housing was substandard, crime was rampant, and infant mortality rates were high.

The mayor at the time of the 1968 riots was Democrat Thomas L. J. D'Alesandro III, the son of racist mayor Thomas L. J. D'Alesandro, Jr., who governed over the highly segregated city from 1947 to 1959.

The D'Alesandro administration proved incapable of dealing with the riots and Republican governor Spiro Agnew sent in the Maryland National Guard to protect the community.

By the time order was restored, six people were dead and more than seven hundred were injured. Almost six thousand people were arrested, mostly for curfew violations. More than sixteen hundred were arrested for looting and burglary. More than one hundred buildings were destroyed or damaged.

Many of the scars of the 1968 Baltimore riot remained to be seen well into the twenty-first century. Despite a trillion dollars in federal aid provided to Baltimore, there is little evidence of its benefit. Most of the money went for the enrichment of Baltimore's elite Democrat leadership, their families, and their cronies. Over the next five decades of Democratic Party governance, there had been little improvement in the conditions of Baltimore's urban Blacks.

Chicago Explodes ... Again

By 1968, the Black community in Chicago had outlived the hopes generated by the Chicago Freedom Movement. The Coordinating Council of Community Organizations had collapsed. Leaders like Al Raby lost their prominence. The Daley-King Pact was tossed into the dustbin of history. And now, Martin Luther King was dead.

Between 1965 and the 1968 riots, Chicago's Black ghettoes were allowed to further deteriorate. When peaceful protest marches were planned for White communities, Daley filed for court injunctions to limit such marches to Black areas—a clear violation of constitutional rights. As was true throughout American history, Democrat policies isolated Black Chicagoans to a PLACE of inferior status and conditions. Poverty, crime, protests, riots, arson, and murder were tolerated as the byproducts of *de facto* racism as long as they did not disrupt the White communities.

The major rioting was along a three-mile stretch of Madison Street, the official dividing line between the south and north sides of Chicago. The Black neighborhoods on the south side were largely spared for two reasons. The southside Black community tended to be more affluent. More of their children could attend parochial or private schools. The housing stock was in better condition. Chicago's more successful Blacks reside in South Chicago. That included Chicago's first two Black mayors, Harold Washington and Eugene Sawyer. Success, however, was no ticket to integration. Most of the middle class and wealthy Blacks still lived in segregated neighborhoods.

The other reason the southside was spared was the relationship between such violent gangs as the Blackstone Rangers and the East Side Disciples, and the Democrat machine. Rather than participating in the chaos, the gangs were used by the Daley machine for intimidation.

As rioting and arson enveloped Chicago's westside, the pugnacious Mayor Daley issued the now infamous "shoot to kill" order. In fact, it was more than just shoot to kill. When asked at a press conference to reiterate his directive to police superintendent James Conlisk, Daley seemed to reflect on his Hamburg Social Club days as a street thug when he said:

> I said to him very emphatically and very definitely that an order be issued by him immediately to shoot to kill any arsonist or anyone with a Molotov cocktail in his hand, because they're potential murderers, and to shoot to maim or cripple anyone looting.

No other modern mayor had ever issued such an order. While he said his "kill order" applied to arsonists and anyone holding a Molotov cocktail, his "maim or cripple" edict gave the police wide latitude in shooting Black citizens—and at the time the police department was infamous for its brutality of Blacks.

The "shoot to kill" order also led to an example of Daley's penchant for the grand lie. Shortly after the riots were contained, Daley told the city council that it was "the established policy of the police department—fully supported by this administration—that only the minimum force necessary be used by policemen in carrying out their duties."

Not long after, Daley denied his own public statements altogether. "There wasn't any 'shoot to kill' order. That was a fabrication," he falsely claimed.

Chicago officials refused to report the number of dead or injured, but it is believed that at least eleven people died as the direct result of rioting. The number killed by police is unknown, but it was reported that forty-eight people were shot by police gunfire. More than 350 were arrested.

Fire destroyed more than two hundred structures, including homes, businesses, and apartment buildings. Thousands were left homeless. Immediately after the rioting, Daley sent in bulldozers to remove burnt out buildings. Many of those spaces remained weed- and debris-filled lots for decades.

More than ten thousand police were on riot duty, in addition to some seven thousand national guardsmen. Lyndon Johnson dispatched five thousand federal soldiers to Chicago to help quell the riot and maintain peace.

Following the riots, Daley put together a blue-ribbon panel of Democrat cronies, friends, and business allies to investigate the riots. They concluded that they were largely spontaneous because of the King assassination. Beyond the obvious conclusion, the report failed to launch any remedies or reforms to address the underlying causes and frustrations. For the Blacks in the inner city, it was business as usual.

The Chicago riots were particularly noteworthy because they came on the eve of the city hosting the Democratic National Convention little more than four months later. The riots outside the convention hall are now an indelible part of American political history.

Riots in Detroit and Beyond

Still reeling from the 1967 riot, Detroit again exploded in the wake of the King assassination. Compared to other cities, the outburst was relatively mild. Rioters torched some thirty-six structures and threw rocks and other missiles at passing cars. Injuries were relatively modest, and there was only one reported death. Democrat mayor James Cavanagh failed to move swiftly to protect the Black community and was again reluctant to ask Republican governor George Romney to send in the national guard to restore peace. Regardless, Romney eventually deployed the guard.

Mayor Cavanagh, who had won election in 1962—with strong support of the Black community—saw his popularity plunge due to his handling of the riots.

Unlike the 1967 riot in the Big Apple, the New York riot of 1968 was mild compared to places like Chicago. Still dozens of buildings were burned down and three people were killed. Republican mayor John Lindsay was given credit for quelling the rioting by going into the Black community to express his condolences and sorrow for the death of King.

Following King's assassination, the Hill District of Pittsburgh erupted in arson and violence. Fires raged for days. More than one hundred businesses were destroyed by fire or vandalism. By the time of the riots, Democrat mayor Joseph Barr had been in office for nine years—and the unbroken string of Democrat mayors went back to 1934.

Republican governor Raymond Shafer deployed more than thirty-six hundred national guardsmen to quell the rioting and protect the Black community. Relative calm was restored after six days. There was one reported death and more than forty injuries.

Initially, Cincinnati remained calm after the assassination. More than fifteen hundred, mostly Blacks, attended a memorial service for King. Nearby a Black man was attempting to thwart the robbery of a jewelry store when he accidentally shot and killed his wife. Rumor spread that she had been shot by White police. In the ensuing riot, more than seventy buildings were set afire. Scores were injured and two were dead.

In the aftermath of the King assassination, Kansas City Democrat mayor Ilus Davis was confronted by a group of Black students at the door of city hall. Police fired tear gas into the crowd which set off the rioting in which five people died.

In Trenton, New Jersey, more than two hundred businesses were destroyed—many by arsonists. Numerous injuries were incurred by police and firefighters, who were bombarded by rocks and other objects. Approximately three hundred people were arrested. There were no fatalities.

Wilmington, Delaware, and Governor Terry

The unrest in Wilmington, Delaware, did not compare to the other Democrat-controlled cities in the magnitude of the violence, but it was notable because of the actions of Democrat governor Charles L. Terry.

Jennifer Alice Delton, professor of history at Skidmore College, wrote in her 2009 book *Racial Integration in Corporate America, 1940–1990* that "Democratic Governor Charles L. Terry (a southern-style Democrat) sent in the entire state National Guard and refused to remove them after the rioting was brought under control."

The reference to Terry as "a southern-style Democrat" had only one meaning. It reflected his segregationist and racist views. His policies were designed to keep the city's Blacks in their PLACE—by military force, if necessary.

In the year before King's assassination, Wilmington had a relatively minor outbreak of racial violence. Terry responded by posting fifteen hundred national guardsmen at the airport, had the legislature pass a bill giving him authority to impose martial law, banned the sale of liquor, and organized a "riot commission."

A year later, when King was assassinated, Black protesters began to assemble in the downtown business district. In response, Terry dispatched twenty-eight hundred guardsmen to Wilmington's downtown, Rehoboth Beach, and the predominantly Black Delaware State College in Dover.

The unrest was considered quite small, with no fatalities, very few injuries, and minimal property damage. After civil order had been restored, Wilmington mayor John Babiarz called on Terry to remove the national guard. Terry refused. National coverage of the "occupation of Wilmington" led business leaders to implore the governor to withdraw the guard. Terry again refused, claiming that he was aware of plans by the Black community to engage in more violence.

In a report in the *New York Times*, Wilmington's city supervisor Francis Biondi was quoted as saying that "The National Guard here has become a symbol of white suppression of the black community." The Biracial Coordinating Committee charged that the military patrols "create an aura of police state repression which is drastically reducing the effectiveness of long-time programs aimed at correcting the urban conditions that cause riots."

Regardless, the national guard stayed in Wilmington for the nine months remaining in Terry's term in office. They were removed only after Terry was defeated by Republican governor Russell W. Peterson. Terry's actions represented an unconstitutional occupation of an American city—and the longest such occupation since the Civil War.

The Aftermath of the Riots

By the time the violence subsided, approximately fifty people had been killed and thousands injured. Tens of thousands were left homeless as the ghettoes burned.

The most obvious common thread in the post-assassination riots—and those that preceded them—was the pent-up frustration from generations of oppression, injustice, and racial violence that characterized the Democrat-run cities. It was racist *de facto* policies that set the stage for riots born out of the misery and frustration.

If the 1967 and 1968 riots had common causes that ignited the unrest, they also had common outcomes. They wreaked economic hardship on neighborhoods, leaving physical scars that would remain as visible reminders for generations to come. They resulted in the loss of business, jobs and tax income as businesses and individuals fled the cities.

What did not change was the plight of the Black residents trapped in that PLACE consigned to them by Democratic urban bosses. While there was a triggering event—such as King's assassination—it was the underlying institutional racism that provided the fuel.

The Fair Housing Act

Next to school desegregation, fair housing was the most vehemently opposed legislation by the powerful southern Democrats. It was the most filibustered legislation, and the inclusion of a housing provision had brought down a 1966 civil rights bill. The reason for the opposition was obvious. The housing legislation would make it more difficult, if not impossible, to maintain segregation and to keep Blacks in that PLACE of subjugation. But pressure was mounting. the Chicago Open Housing law, unenforced by the Daley machine as it was, and the Rumford Fair Housing Act in California gave the issue some initial gravitas.

With the Black community in nationwide unrest, action was needed to quell the frustration and the Fair Housing Act was the most immediate and most obvious opportunity.

In the few days between King's Washington Cathedral speech and his assassination, the Senate narrowly passed the long-awaited Fair Housing Act. Credit for overcoming Democrat opposition to the proposal was given to two Republican senators, Edward Brooke of Massachusetts and Senate Minority Leader Everett Dirksen of Illinois. Also playing a lead role in lobbying for passage was Republican civil rights leader Roy Innis, head of the Congress of Racial Equality (CORE) and a Republican Black activist. Brooke gave an impassioned speech, relating the inability of his family to obtain a home mortgage in Boston upon his return from military duty in World War II despite his obvious qualifications.

Facing the prospect of a very close vote, the Housing Bill's narrow victory was made possible only because the Dirksen-led Republicans were able to again defeat a Democrat filibuster—as they had done in 1964. Thanks to overwhelming Republican support, the Fair Housing Act passed the Senate by the slimmest of margins.

The House Acts

Prior to the assassination, the future of the bill in the House did not look good. Under pressure from his Democrat colleagues, Johnson had initially favored delaying a House vote indefinitely—essentially permanently. The plan was to bury the bill in a committee headed by one of the segregationist southern Democrats—a tactic frequently employed by Democrats to avoid having to go on record with a vote.

That strategy changed dramatically only four days after Senate passage when Martin Luther King was assassinated. The King murder cowered Johnson and congressional Democrats and the bill passed the House with minimal debate less than one week after King's death. The once formidable opposition of the southern Democrat bloc was eviscerated. On April 11, just one week after the assassination, and while rioters were still in the streets, the Fair Housing Act became law.

Urban Segregation Continues

Despite the passage of the Fair Housing Act, *de facto* segregation continued to be the policy and practice of the urban Democrat machines. Like their southern colleagues, big city Democrat administrations found more subtle means to keep Blacks in their PLACE—segregated, impoverished, uneducated and dependent. It is the reason that millions of Blacks in Democrat-run cities are segregated to this day.

Robert Mark Silverman and Kelly L. Patterson, in their 2011 article "The Four Horseman of the Fair Housing Apocalypse: A Critique of Fair Housing Policy in the USA," stated that due to underfunding and lack of adequate implementation by federal, state, and local authorities less than one percent of past discrimination complaints had been addressed. They further found that those responsible for enforcing the law at the local level tended to downplay race in their implementation strategies. In other words, they ignored racial motivations in denying housing.

In his 2004 essay, "The New Geography of Inequality in Urban America," Princeton sociologist Douglas Massey reported that racial demographics were the basis of housing discrimination designed to maintain the *status quo* of urban segregation.

There is an interesting historic footnote attesting to the Democratic Party's ability to thwart civil rights laws. The Republican Civil Rights Act of 1866 made housing discrimination illegal—just as the Thirteenth, Fourteenth, and Fifteenth Amendments and the Enforcement Acts of the mid-1800s provided Negroes with the full rights of citizenship. All these laws were either disobeyed or unenforced by Democrat-run governments in the south, in the segregated cities of the North and even at the national level for more than one hundred years.

Jesse Jackson on the National Stage

When King departed from Chicago, he left behind an unknown but ambitious activist to oversee Operation Breadbasket in the Windy City. His name was Jesse Jackson.

Jackson was born in Greenville, South Carolina, to a sixteen-year-old girl. She later married Charles Jackson, a prominent member of the Black community. Young Jackson's name was changed when he was formally adopted. Unlike many southern Blacks, Jackson was brought up in a comfortable upper middle-class environment, though he would later burnish his civil rights image by claiming an impoverished background.

Jackson had come to Chicago from his home in South Carolina to attend divinity school. Though extremely ambitious, Jackson would remain largely a local personality until the assassination of King.

One of the outcomes of the assassination of Martin Luther King was the rise of Jesse Jackson as a dominant leader of the new civil rights movement. In many ways, he was not the natural successor to King. That would have been Ralph Abernathy, King's immediate associate. However, Jackson was by far the most ambitious and clever. Unappreciated to this day is that Jackson's rise shifted the focus of the civil rights movement away from King's belief in the basic constitutional civil rights through a nonpartisan movement—and his dream of a color-blind society where Blacks and Whites would live in harmony and equality.

Jackson's movement was more the creature of his personal partisan ambitions within the Democratic Party—ambitions made evident by his own candidacy for president in 1984, his endorsement of Democrat candidates, and his family's own roles as public officials within the Democratic Party.

Where King worked for common values and unity, Jackson pursued the Democrat's false narrative of welfare as the new civil rights—creating a cultural schism. While King spoke to unity and assimilation, Jackson promoted racial division. While White America would prosper in the promise of America's opportunity society, masses of segregated and impoverished Black Americans would continue to suffer as part of a government-dependent quasi-socialistic subculture.

After more than fifty years of activism by Jackson—and later Al Sharpton—the plight of those trapped in the segregated communities showed no significant improvement. The only measurable change is that the Black ghettoes became more violent and deadly for the residents.

The Bloody Shirt

In one of the most dramatic moments in civil rights history, the assassination of Martin Luther King, Jackson shamelessly promoted himself as a more involved participant in the tragic moment than he was. While he was among the many Black leaders accompanying King in his visit to Memphis, Jackson was not an actual witness to the shooting.

Following the assassination, Jackson returned to his hometown of Chicago. As he met with the local press, he wore a bloodied shirt—claiming the blood got on the shirt as he held King in his arms in the seconds after the shooting. In fact, Jackson was not on the balcony at that time. He arrived later and, according to civil rights leader Andrew Young in a 1995 PBS interview, "Jesse put his hands in the blood and wiped it on the front of his shirt."

Jackson's shameless self-promotion and his macabre actions at the time of the assassination created animosity between the Chicago activist and the King Family and friends, including Ralph Abernathy who took over the SCLC leadership.

Years later, Jackson's self-promotion was condemned by rapper Game in his "Letter to the King." His lyrics mocked Jackson's claim of being on the balcony when King was shot. Game explained his lyrics.

> On the day King got shot, he wasn't there. When I say, 'How come you couldn't catch your man's body when it dropped?' It's because you couldn't if you wanted to. You was somewhere else. You claimed to be his man. Where were you that day?

The relationship between Jackson and the SCLC became strained. Abernathy and the SCLC leadership believed Jackson had become more focused on his personal and political ambitions than the cause of civil rights.

Jackson Perfects the Civil Rights Shakedown

To finance his ambitions, Jackson became a scam artist of sorts. This author witnessed Jackson's *modus operandi* in person while serving as director of public affairs for Motorola, Inc. in 1968, when Jackson organized a demonstration outside the corporate headquarters, complaining about the company's employment practices. His complaints were not without justification. The company's vice president of personnel, Kenneth Piper, was not inclined to hire Black workers. In fact, the few that were employed worked on the night shift in the factory—not even the daytime janitorial crew was integrated.

Piper argued that Black workers were not inclined to travel from the inner city to Motorola's suburban Schiller Park location. He ignored the fact that the headquarters and factory were not far from the mostly Black suburb of Maywood.

Jackson was quick to settle the issue and withdraw the demonstrators. He wanted a face-saving token increase in Black employment, a deal Piper was more than happy to sign since it did not represent a significant change in Black hiring. More importantly, Jackson wanted a significant financial contribution to his Operation Breadbasket, in the neighborhood of $100,000. Jackson's priority was money not jobs. This scam worked at Motorola, and with other companies. Jackson gained a reputation as a shakedown artist.

Jackson Raids the Corporate Coffers

Jackson's demands to such companies as Toyota, eBay, Google, and Anheuser-Busch have generally resulted in commitments to modest improvements in minority hiring as well as financial contributions to Jackson's personal organization, the Rainbow/PUSH Coalition—a combination of his Rainbow Coalition and People United to Save Humanity.

His demands were not always for money. He would negotiate lucrative business deals for friends and family. Jackson is said to have refrained from attacking Coca-Cola for its business in South Africa during apartheid in return for a syrup distributorship for his half-brother, Noah Robinson. A similar distributorship went to PUSH financial backer Cecil Troy. Robinson also benefited from a KFC franchise negotiated by Jackson.

Jackson went after Anheuser-Busch for its lack of Black-owned distributorships. The problem was resolved with A-B handing over the lucrative Chicago distributorship to Jackson's sons, Yusef and Jonathan.

Jackson opposed the merger between SBC and Ameritech until the latter sold a portion of the cellular phone business to Chester Davenport, a close friend and supporter of Jackson.

Perhaps his most audacious deal was with the Chicago Democratic machine. It is widely believed that Jackson's son's slating for Congress and his daughter-in-law's slating for a city council seat were in return for Jackson not "causing trouble" in Chicago.

In fact, Jackson has never been a major civil rights activist in his hometown despite the overt and obvious racism of the Chicago Democrat machine. His PUSH headquarters on Chicago's South Side has been the site of rallies, celebrations, and some charity work, but it has not played an important role in pressing for civil rights in the Windy City. And even when he does appear at an occasional protest, he almost never points his finger at the Democrat machine in city hall. He has never organized a march on city hall.

One of the reasons often stated for Jackson's absence from Chicago is his own political and financial ambitions. Jackson was more than willing to make himself a major voice in promoting the Democrat Party's faux civil rights of generational welfare dependency. The racist Chicago machine is a powerful force in the national Democratic Party—just as the racist southern bloc was an example of "the tail wagging the dog." The Chicago machine put Barack Obama in the White House, and like Jackson, Obama never confronted the rampant racism in his hometown during his eight years in office. Even as he talks frequently about gun control, he paid little attention to the almost eight hundred murders in 2016 in a city run by his former chief of staff, Mayor Rahm Emmanuel.

Nixon's Southern Strategy—Truth v. Fiction

To explain Nixon's and the GOP's growing popularity in the South in the late 1960s, and to reverse a renewed trend of southern Blacks returning to the Republicans, the Democratic Party advanced another bogus political narrative. It proffered the argument that the Republican Party had gained in the South by becoming the preferred party of all-White racist voters. They claimed that southern racists had simply switched to the Republican Party to support Nixon.

There may have been a "southern strategy" to benefit Nixon, but it was not to win over the hardline racist vote. Many Whites in the South were increasingly offended by the re-emergence of violent racism of the Democrat regimes in the 1950s and early 1960s over school desegregation—which played out on the relatively new medium of television.

In addition, the demographics of the south were changing. There was a steady post-World War II migration of northerners to the sunny coastal environments of places like Florida, Georgia, Texas, and the Carolinas thanks to air conditioning. Metropolitan communities, such as Atlanta, Miami, and New Orleans, were becoming diverse centers of business and commerce. In short, the Democrat institutional racism of the past was losing its popular appeal. The culture was changing, and the GOP was the beneficiary of the new non-racist vote. The Republicans southern strategy was to offer the alternative to the Democrat racist policies. The winning issue for the GOP was not racism but rather traditional constitutional conservatism, personal freedom, and patriotism.

The racist vote still belonged to the old Democratic Party. It was a shrinking vote but enough to keep Democrat racists, such as John Stennis, Robert Byrd, and others in office for many years beyond the Nixon presidency. The old racist Democrats held most governorships, Senate seats, House delegations, and legislatures—in addition to many county and municipal offices—long after Nixon left office. It was not until 1994 that the GOP captured most of the congressional seats in the southern states—more than twenty years after Nixon left office.

If the racist element in the public had switched parties *en masse*, it would be reasonable to expect that a significant number of Democrat elected officials would have done the same. That was not the case. Of the tens of thousands of racist Democrat governors, members of Congress, and state and municipal officials, virtually none joined the Republican Party. They continued to hold the shrinking southern racist voters, which resulted in their eventually losing out to Republican candidates.

Pockets of Democrat racism endured in many local communities into the twenty-first century. Though they were losing influence, the hardcore racist voters understood that the Democratic Party and the Democrat candidates were still the best vehicles for keeping Negroes in their PLACE.

Further evidence that repudiates the Democrats' version of a Nixon racist southern strategy, is found in the statistics. If you look at the number in the three Nixon presidential elections, it would be difficult to find evidence of a racist southern strategy. In 1960, Nixon lost the entire Deep South, except Florida, to the Democrats, and in 1968, he again lost the entire South to Democrats George Wallace and Hubert Humphrey. In 1972, Nixon carried the South as the incumbent president, but he also swept forty-nine of the fifty states against a universally unpopular Democrat candidate, George McGovern—and civil rights was not the seminal issue. Southern voters, including Democrats, disliked the radial left policies of McGovern as much as the rest of the nation. At the time of Nixon's 1968 election, the racist Democrat leaders and voters in the South were in the midst of their Massive Resistance movement against school desegregation.

In his book titled *The South and the Politics of Slavery, 1828–1856*, author William J. Cooper Jr. notes that even at the time of Nixon's 1972 reelection, Democrats were retaining power over the last vestiges of institutional racism:

> "The South was still overwhelmingly Democratic at the state level, with majorities in all state legislatures, and most U.S. Representatives as well.

> Over the next 30 years, this gradually changed. Veteran Democrat officeholders retired or died, and older voters who were still rigidly Democrat also died off. There were also increasing numbers of migrants from other areas, especially in Florida, Texas, and North Carolina."

Additional evidence that there was no racist southern strategy was the fact that Nixon had a strong civil rights reputation and record, which did not endear him to southern racists. As noted previously, Nixon worked very closely with Martin Luther King in securing the passage of the 1956 and 1960 civil rights acts—both of which were intensely opposed by the southern Democrat leadership and their voters. His 1968 and 1972 campaigns further enhanced Nixon's civil rights reputation—as did his affirmative action program. Nixon was never an appealing candidate to southern racist voters, and he never tried to be.

Perhaps nothing more effectively refutes the contention that the GOP simply took over the old racist Democrat voters and policies than the dramatic change in the living conditions for the Black community as Republicans assumed power. Gone were the lynchings, the bombings, the cross burnings, the institutional segregation, the Jim Crow laws, and the denial of voting rights. Those Confederate battle flags placed in positions of official honor by the racist Democrat governors and legislatures as part of the Massive Resistance movement were removed by Republican administrations.

This was also evident in the declining influence of the Ku Klux Klan. There can be no argument that the Klan was an integral part of the Democratic Party's governance and its oppression of Negroes. In fact, Democrat leaders used the Klan as their means to drive Republicans out of the South—and to discourage voters to cast ballots for Republicans. With racist Woodrow Wilson virtually endorsing the Ku Klux Klan from the Oval Office, it grew to hundreds of thousands of active members in the early 1900s—virtually all in the Democrat-controlled southern states.

According to the Southern Poverty Law Center (SPLC), Klan membership in the Democrat southland was still at approximately forty thousand in the early 1960s. The Klan's votes and loyalty remained with the Democratic Party. As the Republican Party gained in southern states, the size and the influence of the Klan subsided significantly. The SPLC estimates the KKK membership at the end of the first decade of the twenty-first century, when Republicans attained considerable power in the old Confederacy, had fallen to fewer than eight hundred members.

Not since Republican Reconstruction following the Civil War has the Black citizens of the South been as free and as safe as they are since Republican ascendency that began in the 1970s.

Racist Southern Democrats Surrender—Again

Recognizing that they were losing the grassroots voters in the South many of the most strident racist governors and senators declined to run for reelection. Some were then defeated, such as Al Gore Sr. of Tennessee. But others held on to their racist Democrat constituencies, such as uber-racist James Eastland, who remained in the Senate as an icon of the Old South until 1978—thirteen years after the Voting Rights Act of 1965. Herman Tallmadge of Georgia remained until 1981, and Russell Long of Louisiana held his Senate seat until 1987. Others who survived had to reinvent themselves as friends of civil rights—or at least the civil rights of welfare dependency. The most successful was Strom Thurmond, one of rare southern Democrats to switch parties. He retired from the Senate in 2003 at the age of 100 and died shortly thereafter. Another was former Ku Klux Klan leader Senator Robert Byrd, who served in the Senate's Democrat leadership until his death in 2010 at the age of 92. He never fully repudiated his role as a Klan organizer and leader and praised of the Klan until the day he died.

Johnson's Legacy

As Lyndon Johnson approached what he had hoped would be his reelection campaign in 1968, he found that his public support had all but collapsed. The economy was beginning to flounder under his "guns and butter" spending policies. The Vietnam War was going very badly with an increasing body count being reported daily. There was deadly civil unrest over many issues— protests about the War, civil rights, women's rights, and early gay rights. His signature War on Poverty was highly controversial. He was becoming one of the most reviled incumbent presidents in American history. His Gallup approval rating had dropped to 35 percent. On March 31, 1968, Johnson surprised the nation by announcing that he would not stand for reelection.

Johnson's reputation and his legacy are quite different. His support of the Civil Rights Act of 1964 dominates the memory of him for most Americans, but his legacy is not quite so positive. His escalation of the war in Vietnam was a key element in his popularity plunge. His War on Poverty was a cynical means, as he is reported to have told southern Democrat senators, "to keep niggers voting Democrat for two hundred years." It expanded the Democrats' hold on the Black vote by expanding generational welfare dependency.

The 1960s is often thought of as the decade of great progress in the advancement of civil rights for Black Americans. It was a blow to the Democrats *de jure* racism in the South but did little to end the *de facto* institutional racism in the major cities. That was why there has been decades of frequent urban demonstrations, protests, and race riots in the Democrat-run cities.

War on Poverty Fails Blacks

In the sixty years following Johnson's War on Poverty legislation, the federal government has spent more than 22 trillion dollars on programs allegedly to fight poverty and joblessness. The only thing accomplished by those expenditures was to keep Blacks in their PLACE and voting overwhelmingly for Democrat candidates. In terms of its social and economic goals, the War on Poverty has been an enormous failure. Throughout the years since Johnson declared his War on Poverty the plight of Black America continued to suffer poverty, violence, high unemployment, second-class citizenship, and inferior education.

The War on Poverty imposed an additional hardship on ghetto-ized Blacks: the breakdown of the family. Government policies encouraged single mother households and thus fatherless families. Over the years, crime and incarceration soared to unprecedented levels. In no small irony, the only upward statistics among inner city Blacks has been the percentage voting for the Democratic Party and the number of Blacks being murdered on the streets of Democrat-controlled cities.

The War on Poverty has been an abysmal social and economic failure. In the preface to the article "The War on Poverty after 50 Years," policy analysts Robert Rector and Rachel Sheffield wrote:

> In his January 1964 State of the Union address, President Lyndon Johnson proclaimed, "This administration today, here and now, declares unconditional war on poverty in America. In the 50 years since that time, U.S. taxpayers have spent over $22 trillion on anti-poverty programs. Adjusted for inflation, this spending (which does not include Social Security or Medicare) is three times the cost of all U.S. military wars since the American Revolution. Yet progress against poverty, as measured by the U.S. Census Bureau, has been minimal, and in terms of President Johnson's main goal of reducing the 'causes' rather than the mere 'consequences' of poverty, *the War on Poverty has failed completely. In fact, a significant portion of the population is now less capable of self-sufficiency than it was when the War on Poverty began."* (emphasis added)

A great percentage of the money was directed at minority urban poverty—money that was ineffective at best or callously misused at worst. Rather than provide Blacks with personal freedom, good education, upward mobility, and all the other blessings of liberty, the Democrats created a new paradigm by which they could keep the mass of Black Americans enslaved in generational dependency and apart from the American Dream so hopefully articulated by Martin Luther King.

In retrospect, the War on Poverty was arguably as damaging as southern *de jure* segregation to the segregated Black communities. It relegated Black Americans more firmly into that PLACE of second-class citizenship with many of the same historic deprivations as Jim Crow laws and slavery. The urban ghettoes had become known as political plantations.

The Election of 1968

The election of 1968 was among the more turbulent since Lincoln's election in 1860. Three social movements coincided to create a perfect storm of civil unrest and violence. The searing issues were civil rights, women's equality, and the anti-Vietnam War movements. In just over four years America had suffered the assassination of President Jack Kennedy, Senator Bobby Kennedy, and the nation's premier civil rights leader, Martin Luther King.

Republicans

Most people, including Richard Nixon, thought his political career was over after losing the race for president in 1960 and then for California governor in 1962. After his second loss, Nixon famously said to the national press, "You won't have Nixon to kick around anymore, because, gentlemen, this is my last press conference." Six years after that farewell statement, Nixon was the Republican nominee for president—making one of the most remarkable comebacks since Democrat Grover Cleveland won a second non-consecutive presidential term in 1892.

Civil Rights and Spiro Agnew

For his running mate, Nixon selected a relatively unknown Spiro Agnew, who had just been elected the Republican governor of Maryland. In Agnew's gubernatorial race, the Maryland Democrats had nominated a racist contractor, George Mahoney. Mahoney's primary campaign issue was opposition to integration. Agnew's pro-civil rights positions were popular with the Republican voters in Maryland and a significant number of Democrats—including an astounding 70 percent of the Black voters.

As governor, Agnew enacted Maryland's first open-housing law. He also fought for the repeal of the old segregationist law against intermarriage, co-habitation, or sexual relations between Whites and Blacks. Nixon considered Agnew's ability to win in a southern state on a pro-civil rights platform as an important asset to the national ticket. Agnew was further evidence that Nixon was not courting the racist Democrat vote in Dixie. Unfortunately, Agnew had ethical issues and was forced to resign as vice president shortly before Nixon resigned as president.

Democrats

The Democrats nominated Minnesota senator Hubert Humphrey, whose efforts to get a strong civil rights plank in the Democrat platform in 1948 had precipitated the breakaway Dixiecrat candidacy of senator Strom Thurmond. In selecting Humphrey, the Democratic Party, for the first time in its history, had chosen a standard bearer with a pro-civil rights record. The convention selected another civil rights advocate, Maine senator Edmund Muskie, for the vice-presidential spot.

The Humphrey-Muskie nominations marked the beginning of a new era for Democrats, although it has rarely been recognized as such by historians. It marked the first time in American history that the national Democrats nominated civil rights advocates for both president and vice president. It interrupted the tradition of giving southern Democrats a place on the national ticket—a tradition that would quickly resume with Jimmy Carter and Bill Clinton.

Thanks to the 1964 Civil Rights Act and the 1965 Voting Rights Act, the general election of 1968 was arguably the first officially legal and constitutional election held in the solid Democrat southland since the Compromise of 1877—although there still remained prejudicial application of the voting laws and procedures by local Democrat leaders and election officials in southern states.

Non-racist national leaders of the Democratic Party continued their tradition of riding on the power of the urban political machines, while ignoring their racist policies. Virtually every Democrat candidate for president would visit Chicago to seek the blessing of arguably the most racist mayor in America at the time, Richard J. Daley.

Democratic Convention

With racial tensions running high throughout America, Democrats ironically selected Chicago for their national convention. That decision reflected the power of Mayor Daley and his political machine. Daley saw it as an opportunity to show off his city and eradicate some of the violent and racist imagery that spread across the nation in the aftermath of the Martin Luther King assassination. That hope was dashed as the entire world watched the image of the Daley political machine get tarnished by brutal infighting inside the convention hall and violent rioting on the streets outside.

At one point, the decorum of the proceedings in the convention hall was disrupted when Connecticut senator Abraham Ribicoff rose to nominate an alternative contender to Humphrey, South Dakota senator George McGovern. Ribicoff had previously offended the pugnacious Daley by trying to adjourn the convention so that it could be moved to another safer city. In his nominating speech, Ribicoff declared that "with George McGovern as President of the United States, we wouldn't have to have Gestapo tactics in the streets of Chicago. And with George McGovern as president, we wouldn't have to have a national guard."

With that, delegates began to react with a mixture of boos and cheers. A red-faced Mayor Daley stood and screamed at Ribicoff. As the cameras trained on Daley, the world could see his lips venting rage and his prejudicial attitude slip out.

Professional lip readers and witnesses within earshot and most of the viewing public understood Daley to yell out, "Fuck you, you Jew son of a bitch." Daley's claim of having said "faker" was never credible—and he never provided an explanation of the "Jew son of a bitch" reference.

Despite Ribicoff's efforts, McGovern lost the nomination to Humphrey and the drama inside the convention hall was eclipsed by the action outside.

Rioting in the Streets

On the night of Humphrey's nomination, millions of viewers across America were transfixed by the television cameras alternating between the now orderly process of nominating a presidential candidate and the increasingly violent confrontation between the Chicago police and the Illinois National Guard and a disorganized mob of violent demonstrators on the other side of the television screen. The juxtaposition of the street violence and the seemingly unaware smiling Humphrey accepting his nomination was said to have doomed his candidacy.

A federal commission later referred to the violence in Chicago as a "police riot." Rebutting the federal report led to one of Daley's famous misstatements: "The policeman is not here to create disorder. The policeman is here to preserve disorder."

Daley's humiliation on the national stage would not end in 1968.

The American Independent Pary in 1968

With no home in the Republican Party, and unhappy with the Humphrey/Muskie ticket, southern Democrats were forced into a third-party bid under the leadership of Alabama's Democrat segregationist governor George Wallace. He entered the presidential race as the candidate of the American Independent Party—representing the powerful racist faction of the Democratic Party.

Though a segregationist, George Wallace was initially viewed as moderate by southern standards. In his bid for governor in 1958, he spoke out against the KKK and even won the support of the NAACP. His Democrat opponent, John Patterson, publicly accepted the support of the KKK and ran a provocatively racist campaign. Patterson won.

Still ambitious, Wallace took on a more racially divisive tone. After losing to Patterson, he told an aide, "I was out-niggered by John Patterson. And I'll tell you here and now, I will never be out-niggered again." From that time on, Wallace was a hardline segregationist.

Wallace had problems getting a running mate. For a time, the staunchly racist governor Marvin Griffin of Georgia stepped in as a placeholder. Eventually, Air Force general Curtis LeMay took the spot. LeMay was tarnished with Wallace's racist reputation even though his personal view ran to the contrary. In fact, LeMay was an early supporter of integrating the armed services.

Wallace did not expect to win the presidency, but he was hoping that his campaign would prevent either Nixon or Humphrey from gaining a majority in the Electoral College and that he would use his electors to win concessions and pick the winner. He almost succeeded, picking up 46 electoral votes from five southern states. However, Nixon picked up a winning 301 electoral votes to Humphrey's 191.

Party Platforms

Under a section entitled "Domestic Policy," the GOP platform again recognized the need for positive programs addressed at the plight of the poor and specifically minorities in the major urban centers. It read:

> Our inner cities teem with poor, crowded in slums. Minorities among us—particularly the black community, the Mexican American, the American Indian—suffer disproportionately.

In a section entitled "The Poor," the Republican platform specifically addressed the needs of the ghettoized Black community: "This nation must not blink the harsh fact—or the special demands it places upon us—that the incidence of poverty is consistently greater among Negroes."

Despite a ticket composed of two civil rights advocates, the Democrat platform was still weak on a full-throated commitment to civil rights. While the Democratic Party platform of 1968 correctly credited President Lyndon

Johnson for his support of civil rights legislation, the platform misrepresented the actions of Democrats in Congress when it said: "Democrats in the Presidency and *in the Congress* have led the fight to erase the stain of racial discrimination that tarnished America's proudly announced proposition that all men are created equal." (emphasis added)

This grand lie of having led the civil rights fight in Congress is a persistent component of the Democrat Party's ongoing false narrative.

In a section entitled "The Inner City," the Democratic platform ironically drew attention to their own party's failure in managing the great cities of America. It reads:

> In the decaying slums of our larger cities, where so many of our poor are concentrated, the attack on poverty must embrace many interrelated aspects of development—economic development, the rehabilitation or replacement of dilapidated and unsafe housing, job training and placement, and the improvement of education, health, recreation, crime control, welfare, and other public services.

This plank recognizes the problem but failed to recognize the fact that it was the Democratic Party's *de facto* racist policies that had long been in charge of those cities and responsible for those conditions. It was the Democratic Party that put Blacks in their PLACE.

American Independent (Wallace)

The platform of the breakaway American Independent Party made yet another attempt at keeping the federal government out of the southern schools. The platform stated that an "enlightened and advancing educational program assisted but not controlled by the federal government."

The Wallace Platform also drew attention to the poor conditions in the cities, again without any reference to the role of the Democratic Party. It stated:

> Its cities are in decay and turmoil; its local schools and other institutions stand stripped of their rightful authority; law enforcement agencies and officers are hampered by arbitrary and unreasonable

restrictions imposed by a beguiled judiciary; crime runs rampant through the nation.

The Wallace Platform continued to wage the old battle, claiming the Tenth Amendment of the Constitution barred the federal government from interference in education and voting. The platform stated:

> The Federal Government, in derogation and flagrant violation of this Article [Tenth Amendment] of the Bill of Rights, has in the past three decades seized and usurped many powers not delegated to it, such as, among others: the operation and control of the public school system of the several states; the power to prescribe the eligibility and qualifications of those who would vote in our state and local elections.

> [T]he Federal Government has adopted so-called 'Civil Rights Acts,' particularly the one adopted in 1964, which have set race against race and class against class, all of which we condemn.

Even as late as 1968, a powerful faction of the Democratic Party was openly pursuing segregationist and racist policies.

Election Results—1968

Why the Democrat ticket with pro-civil rights candidates did not fare better is explained by the unique circumstances of the times. The more liberal Democratic ticket of Humphrey and Muskie seemed too sympathetic to the perpetrators of anti-American violence in the streets. Conversely, Nixon's record on patriotism was unassailable.

As was the case in 1948, the breakaway racist Democrats returned to their home in the Democratic Party and continued to elect racist Democrats in southern states for years to come.

Richard Milhous Nixon (1969–1974)

Nixon came into office with a strong civil rights record that was largely ignored or distorted by Democrats and an adversarial media—as was his close working relationship with Martin Luther King. They myopically focused on Barry Goldwater's vote against the 1964 Civil Rights Act to tar all Republicans as anti-civil rights. The propaganda campaign worked.

Nixon had been a key player in lobbying for civil rights as vice president. His role was deeply appreciated by King and other civil rights leaders. He proposed and signed affirmative action legislation designed to overcome the racial barriers that prevented Blacks from gaining access to colleges and jobs. He used the Department of Commerce and the Small Business Administration to provide unprecedented funding to minority businesses.

George Romney at HUD

Republican Michigan Governor George Romney made a bid for the presidential nomination in 1968. He was unsuccessful, but Nixon later appointed him as Secretary of Housing and Urban Development.

As governor, Romney was an outspoken advocate of civil rights. In 1963, Romney worked closely with Martin Luther King. Unlike Chicago, where King was treated as an enemy of the people, criticized by Mayor Daley and pelted with rocks during his protests, Romney welcomed King to Detroit, officially declaring the occasion as "Freedom Day in Michigan." He sent official representatives to march alongside King and would have appeared himself had the march not been a Sunday. Romney's devotion to the Mormon Church precluded non-religious activities on Sunday.

Following the Civil Rights Act of 1964, he proposed state initiatives to improve the conditions in the inner city of Detroit. At the time, Detroit still had a majority White population and a relatively healthy economy.

A 2012 article in *The Atlantic* by Edward Blum and Paul Harvey stated that "During his term as Secretary of Housing and Urban Development during Richard Nixon's first term from 1969 to 1972, Romney pursued policies of affordable housing and suburban desegregation with zeal ..."

Benign Neglect

Early in the Nixon administration, Democrat Daniel Patrick Moynihan served as an "urban advisor" to the president. He would go on to become a Democrat United States senator from New York. He created a racial controversy when he sent Nixon a memo proposing a policy of "benign neglect" in dealing with civil rights. He wrote:

> The time may have come when the issue of race could benefit from a period of benign neglect. The subject has been too much talked about. The forum has been too much taken over to hysterics, paranoids, and boodlers on all sides. We need a period in which Negro progress continues and racial rhetoric fades.

While Moynihan was among the more progressive members of the Democratic Party, this and other statements suggested that Moynihan was not eager to address the racial realities of the city ghettoes. He was not willing to confront the powerful racist Democrat machine bosses in New York, who he would need in his future election.

His proposal to ignore the problems even went so far as ignoring frequent arson. In their book, *A Plague on Your Houses: How New York Was Burned Down and National Public Health Crumbled,* authors Deborah Wallace and Rodrick Wallace claimed that the use of arson was a social pathology in the ghettoes that would increase due to Moynihan's concept of benign neglect. They were correct.

Whatever his intention, Moynihan's approach to civil rights was very much in keeping with the practices of the various Democrat administrations in the cities. They had been maintaining the segregated slums for generations—and showed no signs of change in their racist policies. They have been ignoring zoning laws, failing to provide public safety, and refusing to devote resources to infrastructure in the Black neighborhoods. Considering the outcome of benign neglect, the more apt term might have been "malignant neglect."

Nixon v. Brewer

The series of civil rights acts from 1957 through 1968 still did not gain compliance from the Democratic administrations in the large cities or the Old South—including Alabama.

One of the racist devices to prevent Blacks from gaining public office was the so-called at-large elections. Black populations would be incorporated into overwhelmingly majority White districts from which several representatives would be elected, making it impossible for a Black to gain a single seat in the Alabama state legislature despite their population numbers.

While Richard Nixon was president, Alabama was still tightly controlled by old guard racist Democrats. The governor was Albert Brewer. He served less than three years after ascending to the office upon the death of Lurleen Wallace, the wife of George Wallace. Lurleen had succeeded her husband as governor and George would again take the office by defeating Brewer in 1971.

In 1970, Black civil rights activist with the coincidental name of Nixon led a group of Black voters in filing a suit against Governor Brewer and other Democrat state officials claiming that the Alabama apportionment system was racially prejudiced. E. D. Nixon had previously worked with Martin Luther King and Rosa Parks on the Montgomery bus case. *Nixon v. Brewer* was one of the earlier cases supported by the Southern Poverty Law Center (SPLC).

The federal courts ruled in favor of Nixon and his fellow plaintiffs. With a President Nixon led Justice Department, Alabama had no options other than to reapportion the state with single member districts. As a result of the two Nixons, the 1974 election saw seventeen Black candidates elected to the state legislature—a Republican accomplishment of enormous significance.

Roy Innis v. Al Sharpton

Roy Innis, a young Republican civil rights activist who took over the Congress of Racial Equality (CORE) in 1968 and who supported Richard Nixon for president in both 1968 and 1972, would spend the next forty years pushing back against the false civil rights of welfare dependency promoted by the Democratic Party. As head of CORE, Innis drafted and presented to Congress the Community Self-Determination Act. It was the first time in history that legislation drafted by a Black civil rights leader was introduced in Congress.

Because of his more conservative Republican leanings, Innis was vilified by those in the partisan Democrat civil rights movement who were promoting and benefiting from the false welfare narrative. Congressional Democrats even claimed that it was members of the Senate staff who had authored the act when, in fact, the staff merely reviewed and edited Innis' draft legislation to bring it in line with legislative language.

As a critic of what he considered Black plantation-style civil rights leaders, Innes would naturally confront another local activist—Al Sharpton.

Innis took up an investigation of the Tawana Brawley case, in which Brawley claimed to have been brutally raped and beaten. Her case was promoted and sensationalized by Black activist Al Sharpton. Innis was among those who challenged the story. This led to a physical confrontation between Innis and Sharpton on the Morton Downey, Jr. television show where guests were provoked into heated confrontations. This one spilled over with Innes knocking Sharpton to the floor.

Sharpton was publicly humiliated when it was revealed that Brawley had fabricated the story. Regardless, Sharpton would go on to supplant Jesse Jackson as the nation's most visible and controversial Black leader in the Democratic Party—largely thanks to President Obama anointing him as the unofficial spokesperson for Black America and a television program given to Sharpton by the left-leaning MSNBC cable news network. From street activist, Sharpton went on to become a multimillionaire Democrat celebrity.

Although a Republican, Innis ran in the 1993 Democrat primary for mayor of New York. In explaining his decision to run as a Democrat, Innis touched on another characteristic of the Democratic Party's approach to governance—one party rule—when he said:

> The Democratic Party is the only game in town. It's unfortunate that we have a corrupt one-party, one ideology system in New York City, and I'd like to change that. But being a Democrat doesn't mean you have to be a fool.

Innis was defeated in the primary election and returned to his Republican roots and civil rights activism. His son, Niger Innis, followed in his father's tradition of Republican civil rights activism.

Black Panther Deaths

The controversy over police using deadly force was an issue in December of 1969 when Chicago police raided the apartment of twenty-one-year-old Black Panther Party leader Fred Hampton and fellow gang member Mark Clark—killing them both. Hampton was a self-styled socialist revolutionary in the mode of Saul Alinsky. Four other Panther members were wounded in the gun fire and others were beaten and then arrested.

The police reports stated that the shooting of Hampton and Clark was in self-defense. Cook County's Democrat states' attorney Ed Hanrahan, who ordered the raid, stated:

> The immediate, violent, criminal reaction of the occupants in shooting at announced police officers emphasizes the extreme viciousness of the Black Panther Party. So does their refusal to cease firing at the police officers when urged to do so several times.

Police claims of being fired upon proved to be untrue. Various investigations determined that police had fired between eighty and ninety bullets. One shot may have come from one of the Panthers. Photos presented by the police showing Black dots they claimed to be bullet holes from shots directed at them turned out to be nail heads.

Claims that the real purpose of the raid was to kill Hampton gained credibility. According to Hampton's girlfriend, who was in bed with the Panther leader at the time—and was eight months pregnant—said police appeared at the door and started firing. After taking her out of the room and determining that Hampton was still alive, they re-entered the bedroom and shot him to death.

Hanrahan was subsequently indicted on charges of obstructing justice and conspiracy to create false evidence. The trial was typical of the racist Democrat political machine. Though it was a jury trial in the District Court,

Democrat Judge Philip J. Romiti gave a directed verdict of acquittal without even hearing witnesses. A civil case was later filed in the federal courts and the families of Hampton and Clark, and the survivors of the raid, were awarded $1.8 million in restitution.

Hanrahan ran for reelection in 1972, but in a rare rebellion against a Democrat candidate, a significant number of Black votes helped elect Republican Bernard Carey as the new states' attorney. He served until 1980, when the Chicago Democrats took back the office with future mayor and political boss Richard M. Daley, whose father had been "Da Boss" in Chicago. Once again, the chief prosecutorial office in Cook County was under the control of the racist political machine.

The All-White YMCA Camp

As late as 1969, racist southern Democrats were still in control of Alabama and were still resisting one hundred years of civil rights amendments, laws, and court decisions in their fight to preserve the last vestiges of segregation and Jim Crow rule. As noted in an article on the website of the liberal-oriented Southern Poverty Law Center (SPLC):

> Despite the sweeping legislative victories of the civil rights movement, the change the new laws promised was slow in coming to the South as community leaders clung fiercely to the last vestiges of segregation.

As is often the case, SPLC article provides a vague reference to community leaders as the culprits—an indication of its Democrat bias. A more specific and accurate description would have been "Democrat community leaders."

At the time the YMCA was a staunchly segregated institution in Montgomery. The Y's racial prejudice was so deep that any White children who swam at the designated Negro swimming pool were automatically disqualified from participating in any city-wide swim meets.

When seven-year-old Black cousins Vincent and Edward Smith attempted to register for the YMCA's all-White summer camp in Montgomery, they were rejected. While the incident may have seemed minor in the totality of

Democrat southern racism, it had an unanticipated major impact of civil rights justice.

The Montgomery Y played a significant and almost unique role in sports and recreation for the citizens—especially the younger generation. This was because the Democrat political leaders had ordered all the public swimming pools closed, filling many with dirt rather than allow Blacks and Whites to swim together as ordered by the federal government. Local officials argued, however, that the Y, as a private pool, could maintain segregation.

Morris Dees, a prominent and controversial civil rights attorney, filed a class action lawsuit against the Y, bringing down the wrath of the city's racist leadership. According to Dees:

> From the moment this case was filed, it struck a raw nerve in Montgomery. Almost every important civic leader in Montgomery was on the YMCA's board of directors. It didn't sit well with a lot of people at the time, but this case changed Montgomery for the better.

Against what many considered long odds, Dees won the case. The victory won Dees the title of "the second most hated man in Alabama." The title of "most hated" was conferred on Republican federal district court judge Frank Johnson, who rendered the decision in the case. Johnson was a Republican appointed by President Eisenhower.

This case formed the basis for the 1971 establishment of the SPLC, which has been a major force in fighting against institutional racism in those days. But now, the SPLC often operates in accordance with the false narrative that protects the Democratic Party from responsibility and consistently condemns Republicans. They are part of the left-wing establishment that condemns racism but never the Democratic Party that is producing it.

Southern Democrats thwart desegregation laws

Well into the early 1970s, Democrat-controlled cities and towns developed schemes to maintain segregated schools, thwarting federal law. These cases resulted in a flurry of lawsuits.

The general approach was to create school districts in which the student population was predominantly, if not exclusively, White or Black. This was not a difficult challenge since Blacks were geographically segregated and already attending segregated schools.

To avoid court mandated integration within a school system, many communities withdrew from the larger city or county systems to form their own. To counter these racist strategies, the courts took up the issue of busing. The landmark case *Swann v. Charlotte-Mecklenburg Board of Education* established busing as an appropriate means of integrating schools. This case created an emotional reaction that rippled not only through the Democrat southland but in many northern Democrat-controlled cities. Prominent Black attorney Julius L. Chambers, who represented the six-year-old plaintiff James Swann, had his home, office, and car bombed.

In *Wright v. City of Emporia*, the Supreme Court ruled that school districts that were created to maintain segregation based on geographical districting could be "paired" to implement the requirement to integrate through busing. They said that when a new school district is created to circumvent bussing, it can be "paired' with a Black school.

Philadelphia Under John Rizzo

In January of 1972, Democrat John Rizzo was inaugurated as mayor of Philadelphia. It was the culmination of an already controversial career as the city's police commissioner. He was credited with increasing the number of Black officers on the force but was still viewed as being a racist in terms of police enforcement policies. His relationship with the Black community was described as volatile.

As police commissioner, Rizzo was involved in a series of high-profile confrontations with the Black community. Under his direction, the police became much more militant. He created special units armed with shotguns to raid those he deemed as enemies of public peace.

According to former Student Nonviolent Coordinating Committee (SNCC) member Hakim Anderson, "Rizzo was responsible for a lot of police frame-ups. About every other week I was being picked up for something. They were frame-ups, never any convictions for any of the charges."

Anderson had been arrested seventeen times in less than three months as a means of intimidation and harassment. More than thirty years later, the Chicago Democrat machine would use an unconstitutional "gang loitering" law to harass and arrest minorities. Like the Philadelphia cases, most arrests were thrown out of court for lack of evidence.

Commissioner Rizzo Unleashes His Police

Shortly after becoming police commissioner, Rizzo led a raid on a bunch of students demanding a Black history curriculum. As they arrived on the scene, Rizzo is reported to have ordered his men to "get their Black asses." What ensued was a police riot in which officers were beating students. The school's public relations director reported that, "A cop chased two Black girls right outside the window of the administration building where we were looking out and just proceeded to beat the crap out of them with a nightstick."

His police force was notorious for planting evidence. In 1966, these early tactical units raided an apartment housing member of the SNCC, a group devoted to Martin Luther King's philosophy of peaceful protest. Police were said to have seized two sticks of dynamite, which the group claimed were planted.

Raid on the Black Panthers

In one of his more controversial moves, Rizzo raided the offices of the Black Panther Party after the murder of a police officer. Police officers strip-searched and arrested Black Panther members in full view of cameras. Photos of the arrests circulated throughout the media. Within days of the arrests, all charges were dropped, and individuals not associated with the Panthers were arrested and convicted in the murder.

MOVE was a militant communal Black liberation organization founded by Vincent Leaphart, known as John Africa. The group had a history of protesting against police brutality, housing discrimination and racism in general.

In 1978, MOVE lived communally in what was described as squalid conditions. Then mayor Rizzo ordered their eviction. In the confrontation, a police officer was shot and killed. Several members of MOVE were arrested. One of them, Delbert Africa, was brutally beaten by police, dragged by his hair and kicked in the face and groin. Nine MOVE members were sent to prison for life. The episode was captured on camera and further damaged Rizzo's reputation in the Black community.

Election of 1972

Despite the Watergate scandal, the four years of Nixon policies and accomplishments were very popular. Conversely, the Democrats were sharply divided along the left-right ideological fault line.

President Nixon and Vice President Agnew were easily nominated for reelection. Nixon's ending the war in Vietnam, his détente with China, his support for an amendment to lower the voting age to eighteen, and his program of civil rights and affirmative action were considered major achievements.

Because of changes in the party rules, the left wing of the Democratic Party increased its influence over the nomination process. Initially, the most likely nominee was Senator Ted Kennedy of Massachusetts. He withdrew from consideration when he could not distance himself from his recent involvement in the death of a campaign volunteer, Mary Jo Kopechne.

George Wallace, the segregationist Democrat governor of Alabama, made a credible run—again proving the power of the racist faction of the Democratic Party. He was taken out of the race by an assassination attempt that left him paralyzed for life. Before being shot, he had won Democratic primaries in Florida, Alabama, Virginia, and Tennessee. Even after the assassination attempt, and before officially withdrawing, Wallace won Democrat primaries in Michigan and Maryland.

Wallace's victories in the five southern states in 1972 tend to further repudiate the claim by Democrats that the southern racist voters had converted to the GOP. His popularity in the North also showed that Democratic Party grassroots racism was not limited to the South.

In the final analysis, Senator George McGovern won the nomination. However, he was not a popular choice even among Democrats. He was considered too far to the left of the American electorate. McGovern was tagged as the candidate of "amnesty, abortion, and acid."

Despite the shadow of the Watergate scandal looming over his presidency, Nixon won the election in a landslide—sweeping forty-nine of the fifty states, including McGovern's home state of South Dakota. McGovern carried only Massachusetts and the District of Columbia.

Equal Employment Opportunity Act of 1972

In the early 1970s there was a discernible political bias shift in major news media. Journalists started to engage in "advocacy journalism" with a left-wing bias. It resulted in the magnification the civil rights actions of the Democratic Party and minimization, or ignoring, the civil rights accomplishment of the Republican Party. This contrast became starker as years went by. Nixon's Equal Employment Opportunity Act of 1972 is a glaring example.

While the 1964 Civil Rights Act is widely celebrated as a breakthrough, there were still critical weaknesses in the legislation—most notably in terms of enforcement. One of the most important provisions of the Nixon bill was to correct some of those watered-down provisions.

In signing the bill, Nixon addressed this need.

> The most significant aspect of this legislation is a new authority consistently advocated by this Administration since 1969--a provision arming the Equal Employment Opportunity Commission with power to bring lawsuits in the Federal district courts to enforce the rights guaranteed by title VII of the Civil Rights Act of 1964. Such actions are to be expedited by the courts whenever possible.

> Everyone familiar with the operation of title VII over the past 7 years has realized that the promise of that historic legislation would remain unfulfilled until some additional, broad-based enforcement machinery was created. This bill provides that enforcement capability.

A Second major correction was in the scope of coverage of the 1964 Act. On that issue, Nixon said:

> Additionally, the legislation extends the protections of title VII to millions of American citizens previously excluded from its coverage. The experiences of both the Justice Department and the EEOC under title VII have demonstrated that considerable discrimination problems have existed in State and local governments, with small employers, and in some educational institutions. Individuals employed in these areas have not heretofore been protected by title VII. This bill corrects that defect.

Nixon's Meeting with Black Appointees

Nixon appointed more Black officials than any previous president. On November 29, 1972, shortly after his landslide reelection victory, Nixon convened a meeting with thirty-nine of his top Black appointees to lay out a bold civil rights agenda for the second term. It was an impressive list. The attendees as listed in the president's official daily log included:

1. Robert J. Brown, Special Assistant to the President
2. Art Reid, OEO Director, Office of Intergovernmental Relations
3. John Calhoun, ACTION Special Assistant to the Director, Public Affairs
4. Frank Kent, OEO Associate Director of Human Rights
5. Connie Mack Higgins, Small Business Administration Director of Equal Opportunity
6. George Haley, Department of Transportation Chief Counsel, Urban Mass Transportation Administration
7. Colston Lewis, Commissioner Equal Employment Opportunity Commission

8. Alfred Sweeney, Department of Transportation Assistant to the Director for News

9. T. M. Alexander, HUD Assistant Commissioner, Federal Housing Authority

10. Gloria Toote, ACTION Assistant Director, Office of Volunteer Action Liaison

11. Norman Houston, HEW Deputy Assistant Secretary for Administration

12. Samuel Jackson, HUD General Assistant Secretary

13. John Jenkins, Department of Commerce Director, Office of Minority Business Enterprise

14. Stanley Scott (White House staff), Assistant to the Director of Communications for the Executive Branch

15. Norris Sydnor, White House Assistant to Robert J. Brown

16. Lois Hobson, AID Special Assistant to the Assistant Administrator

17. Samuel Singletary, ACTION Director of Minority Affairs

18. Daniel James, Jr., DoD Deputy Assistant Secretary for Public Affairs

19. James E. Johnson, DoD Assistant Secretary of the Navy

20. William Parker, Veterans Administration Director of Equal Opportunity

21. Stanley Thomas, HEW Deputy Assistant Secretary for Youth and Student Affairs

22. Samuel C. Adams, AID/STATE Assistant Administrator for Africa

23. Elizabeth Koontz, Labor Director, Women's Bureau

24. Jerome Shuman, Agriculture Director, Office of Equal Opportunity

25. Donald L. Miller, DoD Deputy Assistant Secretary of Defense (Equal Opportunity)

26. Joseph Daniels, GSA Executive Director, Office of Equal Employment Opportunity

27. Sallyanne Payton, White House Staff Assistant to the President
28. Edward E. Mitchell, GSA Director of Civil Rights
29. Reuben R. Jones, Agriculture Director, Livestock and Dairy Division
30. Alfred Edwards, Agriculture Deputy Assistant Secretary for Rural Development and Conservation
31. Barbara Watson, State Administrator, Bureau of Security and Consular Affairs
32. Jewel LaFontant, Public Member, US Delegation to the United Nations
33. Theodore Britton Jr., HUD Deputy Assistant Secretary for Research and Technology
34. John Blake, Labor Director, Job Corps
35. Thad Ware, Department of Transportation Member, Contract Appeals Board
36. Ted Brown, State Special Assistant to the Assistant Administrator (Technical Assistance Bureau)
37. Arthur McCaw, Agriculture Deputy Administrator, Food and Nutrition Service
38. Ben Holman, Justice Director, Community Relations Service
39. William Brown, Chairman Equal Employment Opportunity Commission

Benjamin L. Hooks

Though not among those in attendance at this meeting, Republican civil rights activist and media personality Benjamin L. Hooks was appointed by Nixon as the first Black man to serve on the Federal Communications Commission. Four years later, the board of directors of the NAACP would make Hooks the organization's executive director. He was awarded America's highest civilian honor, the Presidential Medal of Freedom, by President George W. Bush.

Connie Mack Higgins

Part of Nixon's policy was to reach out to the Black community in an effort to break the hold the Democrats had on the Black vote. Connie Mack Higgins was typical of the new breed of Black Republicans who were brought into power and prominence by Nixon. Though their numbers were few at the time, they started a movement that would see the development of a large cadre of Black GOP and conservative voices and office holders.

In August of 1968, Higgins and Black businessman Lamar Hoke were invited to meet with both Nixon and the Republican vice-presidential nominee Spiro Agnew in California.

In a *Chicago Tribune* report on the meeting both Hoke and Higgins spoke out against the destructive welfare dependency culture they saw in the Black ghettoes of Chicago. Hoke is quoted by the newspaper as saying "It's a clear-cut case of economics. The City of Chicago practices a plantation type politics. They talk of bigger welfare programs which just make recipients more dependent on the system."

As a potential presidential appointee, Higgins was introduced to Senator Strom Thurmond, who had recently converted to the Republican Party. Thurmond took an instant liking to Higgins and became his political champion. Higgins and Thurmond developed a lifelong personal and professional friendship. Whatever the Senator's past may have been, Higgins many times attested to his belief that the Thurmond he knew was no racist. Partially based on Thurmond's recommendation, Nixon appointed Higgins as head of the SBA's minority loans office with authority over hundreds of millions of dollars in minority enterprise loans.

Nixon laid out two administration objectives. He wanted to increase the number of government-guaranteed loans to minority businesses and start-up enterprises, and he wanted to reverse the high default rate that had become associated with minority loans in the past. Many viewed the default rate not only as a waste of money but an indication that the past loans were based more on politics than economic reality. Through Higgins, Nixon provided more loans to minority-owned businesses than any previous president.

Executive Order 11458

Nixon's devotion to providing Blacks with jobs with futures, as opposed to the never-ending impoverishment, was seen very early in his administration. In addition to greater employment, Nixon was determined to increase minority entrepreneurship. In 1969, within months of his inauguration, Nixon issued Executive Order 11458 to promote minority owned businesses. When issuing the order, Nixon said:

> I have often made the point that to foster the economic status and the pride of members of our minority groups we must seek to involve them more fully in our private enterprise system. Blacks, Mexican Americans, Puerto Ricans, Indians, and others must increasingly be encouraged to enter the field of business, both in the areas where they now live and in the larger commercial community—*and not only as workers, but also as managers and owners.* (emphasis added)

The last phrase is highlighted to draw attention to Nixon's effort to produce jobs with futures. He recognized that Democrat policies focused on welfare impoverishment or low-level, dead-end jobs as unskilled workers. Nixon further stated:

> We must also provide an expanded opportunity to participate in the free enterprise system at all levels—not only to share the economic benefits of the free enterprise system more broadly, but also to encourage pride, dignity, and a sense of independence. In order to do this, we need to remove commercial obstacles which have too often stood in the way of minority group members--obstacles such as the unavailability of credit, insurance, and technical assistance.

At the time Nixon took office more than twenty-one government departments and agencies were operating approximately 116 uncoordinated and duplicative programs designed to promote Black enterprise. Characteristically, the growth in successful minority business ownership lagged far behind the growth in the government bureaucracies ostensibly designed to support the expansion of Black ownership.

To coordinate government programs, Nixon's executive order established the Office of Minority Business Enterprise within the Department of Commerce "to assist the establishment of new minority enterprises and expansion of existing ones." In empowering the new office, Nixon said:

> This new office will be the focal point of the administration's efforts It will seek to concentrate Government resources, and also to involve the business community and others in order to enlist the full range of the Nation's resources.

In the closing of his executive order, Nixon wrote:

> What we are doing is recognizing that in addition to the basic problems of poverty itself, there is an additional need to stimulate those enterprises that can give members of minority groups confidence that avenues of opportunity are neither closed nor limited; enterprises that will demonstrate that blacks, Mexican-Americans, and others can participate in a growing economy on the basis of equal opportunity at the top of the ladder as well as on its lower rungs.

Affirmative Action

Nixon was also dedicated to ending the curse of Black impoverishment based on generational dependency, so he launched an era of quotas in the name of affirmative action to provide Blacks access to employment opportunities hitherto denied them most notably by Democrat policies in the major cities.

Nixon's affirmative action policy went beyond the "equal opportunity" approaches of Kennedy and Johnson. The equal opportunity approach left the burden on the Black applicant to prove that their failure to be accepted was due to racial prejudice. The Nixon approach put the onus on the employer or school to accept Black workers or students as a percentage of the work force or student body. In other words, it established quotas.

Quotas have become increasingly controversial largely because the need has diminished over time. Affirmative action did not sit well with pure constitutionalists, who saw both discrimination and special treatment (reverse discrimination) as violations of the equal protection provision of the Fourteenth Amendment, but it was well received in the Black community and provided opportunities for millions of Blacks.

One of the earliest attempts at creating an affirmative action program began in Philadelphia.

According to the website BlackPast.org:

> The Philadelphia Plan was a federal affirmative action program established in 1967 to racially integrate the building construction trade unions through mandatory goals for nonwhite hiring on federal construction contracts.

That plan was declared illegal by Elmer Staats, comptroller general of the United States. President Johnson, not wanting to take on the unions, chose not to defend the plan. Whether he agreed with Staats' decision is unknown, but he did embrace it.

Nixon moved swiftly to overturn the Staats' decision. In his inaugural address to Congress, he took up the Philadelphia Plan. In so doing, he took on the unions in a way no Democrat would or could have.

BlackPast.org wrote:

> Declared illegal in 1968, a revised version [of the Philadelphia Plan] was successfully defended by the Nixon Administration and its allies in Congress against those who saw it as an illegal quota program.

After reversing the Staats' decision, Nixon expanded the program to other cities. He also ordered similar affirmative action hiring policies within the federal government.

On the online website Quora, Collin Anthony Spears wrote:

> In the spring of 1969, Nixon expanded affirmative action mandates from government procurement contracts and applied them to any institution that received any federal funds of any kind, which

brought universities, research institutions—basically everyone—into the fold.

While affirmative action programs would become increasingly controversial, and come under challenge from the courts, it is clear that Nixon was not buying into the "welfare as civil rights" policy of the Democratic Party. He saw employment and upward mobility in the private sector as a better option for lifting Blacks out of their PLACE of second-rate citizenship.

Black Genocide

On January 22, 1973, the United States Supreme Court handed down the *Roe v. Wade* decision that legalized abortion of an unborn human fetus up to the point of viability, which was determined to mean when the infant could live outside the mother even if it required medical support. This was generally believed to be around the twenty-fourth week. Over time, that evolved into abortion-on-demand at any time prior to birth—even when partially born.

Planned Parenthood, Inc. became both the lobbying force and the medical practitioners for the progressive's abortions-on-demand program—just as the organization was once a staunch supporter of eugenic-based genocidal sterilization of Negroes, voluntarily or by force.

Like the eugenics movement of the early 1900s, the modern pro-abortion movement was embraced by the White Democrat progressive community. But the "service" was directed initially at Black women.

Whatever the motivation, by the start of the twenty-first century more than 80 percent of the Planned Parenthood abortion clinics were situated in Black or minority neighborhoods. And while Blacks composed 13 percent of the American population, they received more than 37 percent of the abortions. Many Black ministers and civil rights leaders saw abortion and its emphasis on Black births as a subtle form of eugenic-based genocide.

Abortion Unites Republicans and Civil Rights Leaders

Following *Roe v. Wade*, the conservative Republican pro-life community and the civil rights community found common cause in their opposition to abortion. In addition to the common religious view held by both Black and White clergy, civil rights leaders saw the practice of abortion as a continuation of Margaret Sanger's earlier racist and genocidal policies.

At the time of *Roe v. Wade*, it was believed by many that abortions would be relatively rare, limited by cultural factors and medical considerations. By the twenty-first century, the number of annual abortions would exceed three-quarters of a million, with 270,000 being Black babies—by far the highest percentage of any ethnic group, including the much larger White community.

A study conducted by Kenneth C. W. Kammeyer of the University of Maryland, Norman R. Yetman of the University of Kansas, and McKee J. McClendon of the University of Akron concluded that the number one factor in determining the need for abortion services was not poverty or other social issues, as commonly claimed, but that the "percentage Black" was the most common correlation. They made this determination using information from Planned Parenthood's own records. According to the study "This fact gives apparent substance to charges that such programs are designed not to simply assist the poor, but to control the growth of the black population."

Frederick Osborn, founder of the American Eugenics Society, clearly tied the progressive eugenics movement to the abortion movements. He said, "Birth control and abortion are turning out to be the great eugenic advances of our time."

Even though he was a Roman Catholic, longtime Louisiana Democrat political boss and strident racist, Leander Perez expressed his support for Black abortions in this way: "The best way to hate a nigger is to hate him before he's born."

Following legalization, abortion became the number one cause of death among the Black population. *Maafa* is a Swahili word meaning "a terrible tragedy" and was used to define the time of the middle passage during the slave trade. *Maafa 21* (for twenty-first century) is the title of the documentary film on eugenics and genocide. The documentary explains that "legal abortion has killed more African Americans than AIDS, cancer, diabetes, heart disease and violent crime combined."

According to the Rev. Dr. Clenard Childress, Northeast Director of Life Education and Resources Network and civil rights activist "Abortions kills more blacks in four days than the [Ku Klux] Klan killed in 150 years."

In 1982, more than seventeen thousand fetuses were found in a trash dumpster outside a Los Angeles medical facility. Up to fifteen thousand were determined to be from Black mothers and many past the stage of viability outside the womb.

What was once promoted as a social benefit or service soon became a very big business, with Planned Parenthood selling fetal tissue and body parts for medical experimentation. The claim that the fees were only to cover costs did not seem credible on the surface. Whether there was a profit involved in the transaction or not, they were exchanging human organs and limbs for cash. Despite these disclosures, continued financing Planned Parenthood with federal money was a major policy position of the national Democratic Party.

Alveda King, a niece of Martin Luther King, alluded to this partisan change in the interview for *Maafa 21* when she said:

> All across America, you can stand outside of the abortion clinics and see a steady stream of black women coming in and out. But somewhere along the way we got the idea that this is a white issue, or a conservative issue, or a Republican issue and, therefore, it's not an issue that we [Black Americans] have to be concerned about. This attitude has allowed Planned Parenthood and members of the abortion industry to carry out this genocide right under our very noses. Right now in America about half of our babies are being killed in the womb. And in certain parts of America more of our babies are being aborted than are being born.

Black Leaders Speak Out Against Abortion

Following the Supreme Court's *Wade v. Roe* decision legalizing abortion, and the obvious targeting of Black births, much of the civil rights community strongly opposed both abortion as a matter of moral principal and the targeting of Blacks by such organizations as Planned Parenthood as a social genocide. The opposition was so strong that such radical Black groups as the Black Panthers and the Nation of Islam led protests.

Among the most vociferous opponents of abortions and contraception in predominantly minority neighborhoods was Jesse Jackson. He said that "contraception will become a form of drug welfare against the helpless in this nation. . . . Those whom we could not get rid of in the rice paddies of Viet-Nam, we now propose to exterminate, if necessary, eliminate if possible, in the OB wards and gynecology clinics of our urban hospitals."

In 1977, Jackson wrote an article in the National Right to Life newsletter in which he wrote that "as a matter of conscience I must oppose the use of federal funds for a policy of killing infants."

That same year, Jackson spoke at a March for Life and posed these questions.

> What happens in the mind of a person, and the moral fabric of a nation that accepts the aborting of the life of a baby without a pang of conscience? What kind of a person, and what kind of a society will we have 20 years hence if life can be taken so casually? . . .

> It is strange that they choose to start talking about population control at the same time that Black people in America and people of color around the world are demanding their rightful place as human citizens and their rightful share of the material wealth in the world.

In many ways, Jackson was one of the more important personalities in melding together the pro-life Republican view on abortion with a faction of the political left associated with the civil rights movement. He felt so strongly that Jackson was one of the earliest proponents of a constitutional amendment to ban abortion.

Other Voices of the Times

The radical Black Muslim newspaper *Mohammad Speaks* concurred with Jackson, but in a more strident manner:

Black people are the target of birth control not because the ruling politicians like them and care about their economic equality, but because they hate them and can no longer use them in plantations and other cheap-labor conditions.

In an interview in the Black oriented *Jet* magazine, Father George Clements, pastor of Chicago's Holy Angels Church, was quoted as saying: "I believe the entire question of abortions is just one more in a continuous serious of events to eliminate the Black population."

The Detroit chapter of the revolutionary Black Panther Party expressed the opinion of the group in its publication, *The Black Panther:*

A true revolutionary cares about the people … he cares to the point that he is willing to put his life on the line to help the masses of poor and oppressed people. He would never think of killing his unborn child.

Migrant farm worker leader Cesar Chavez responded to the promotion of birth control and abortions among minorities by asking, "Who the hell is getting the pill—the Mexican and the Negro. Do you want to wipe us out?"

Black activist William Bouie Haden wrote that "Into the black community stepped Planned Parenthood; only when they come into the black community, they've become Planned Black-Genocide."

Black physician and NAACP activist Dr. Charles Greenlee initially was a supporter of Planned Parenthood. After observing that the organization was devoting most of its resources and messages to Black neighborhoods, he became a vociferous opponent. He expressed outrage that promotional material distributed in Black communities suggested that pregnant mothers would lose welfare benefits if they gave birth to the child. He summed it up in a newspaper report: "If we keep producing, they're either going to have to kill us or grant us full citizenship."

Black leaders across the nation joined the opposition to the new progressive eugenics' movement, including H. Rap Brown, Stokley Carmichael, California professor Angela Davis, singer Julius Lester, comedian and activist Dick Gregory, among others. Virtually every civil rights organization pointed to the imposition of Black contraception and abortion as a renewed genocide. Black opposition to contraception and abortion as means of genocide resulted in the burning down of a Cleveland, Ohio, birth control clinic by radical Black activists.

Despite both Black Republican and some Democrat opposition to abortion in practice, Democrat political leaders—thanks to the support of the White progressive community and the mainstream news media—overwhelmed arguments of morality and genocide with secular issues of economics and lifestyle. Over time, it became virtually impossible to have a future in the Democratic Party and be opposed to abortion.

The Jesse Jackson Flip Flop

Among the most notable flip flops was that of Jesse Jackson. The once ardent opponent of abortion, as both morally wrong and genocidal in application, switched his position.

In 1988, Colman McCarthy, writing in the *Washington Post,* reported on Jackson's conversion. McCarthy wrote:

> Two Jacksons are on view. In the 1970s, accounts of his mother and his birth were used to support the Baptist minister's arguments opposing abortion. Today, as a Democrat running for president, Jackson has reversed himself. His tales of mother delete allusions to abortion. He supports federal funding of abortion and says moral positions shouldn't be imposed on public policy. Freedom of choice must prevail. He echoes the arguments that make Democrats the party of abortion.

In attempting to explain Jackson's dramatic shift, Rev. Clenard H. Childress Jr. of the Life Education and Resource Network said that "as soon as he [Jackson] found out that, indeed, he could get funding and money to run for president, he flipped-flopped in his position."

Stephen Broden, pastor of Fair Park Bible Fellowship in Dallas, Texas, has pointed out that Jackson had told *Jet* magazine that abortion was genocide. In a video interview, Broden stated:

> Jesse Jackson, on the other hand, wanted to become president.
> And the Democratic Party at that time had sold out completely to

Planned Parenthood and the eugenics crowd—and Jesse Jackson went along to get along.

Broden seemed to be echoing Booker T. Washington and Malcolm X when he said, "There has never been a shortage of black leaders who are willing to sell us down the river if there's enough money and political power in it for them."

Ironically, abortions gained greater acceptance in later years even as the procedure expanded to include the unborn at any stage of gestation—and the number of abortions reached millions each year.

The Court Reverses *Roe v. Wade*

Over several decades, abortion won wider acceptance with the public, including with Black civil rights leaders. In a 2022 politically explosive decision, the Supreme Court reversed *Roe v. Wade* on the basis that the 1964 decision was wrongfully made. That did not ban abortions but left the issue up to the several states for determination. The political polarities on abortion had shifted so dramatically that opposition to abortion in 2022 was deemed racist by the pro-abortion advocates.

End of the Tuskegee Syphilis Experiments

Terminating Black babies and forced sterilization were not the only progressive Democrat assaults on the Black race—and they did not end in the previous progressive era of early twentieth century.

The Tuskegee Study of Untreated Syphilis in the Negro Male, as it was officially known, began in 1932 in Alabama. From the onset, it was both racist and highly unethical. Despite those facts, the study was never challenged until 1966 when whistleblower Peter Buxtun, a government venereal disease inspector, sent a letter to officials questioning the morality and ethics of the study as well as its necessity. The Center for Disease Control, which was conducting the study, pushed back by pressuring the local chapters of both the White American Medical Association and the Black National Medical Association to endorse the program.

The study was again challenged in 1968 when William Carter Jenkins, a Black official of the Department of Health, Education and Welfare, made a formal request of the outgoing Johnson administration to end the practice. His recommendation was ignored. It is not at all clear if the president himself knew of the request, but it is beyond refutation that Johnson, as a southern congressman and senator, was aware of the longstanding program.

The study was first brought to Nixon's attention in 1970 when Buxton took the information to the *Washington Star* and subsequently the front page of the *New York Times*. The following day, Senator Edward Kennedy called for congressional hearings, at which Buxton and HEW officials testified.

Nixon authorized the Center for Disease Control and the Public Health Service to establish a commission to make a recommendation. The panel determined that the study was improper and unjustified. The Nixon administration ordered it to be shut down immediately. A class action lawsuit by the NAACP awarded survivors of the study more than $10 million and free medical service for the remainder of their lives. The last Tuskegee Study patient died in 2004.

As a footnote to the Tuskegee Study, Republican President Ford would sign the National Research Act to ethically regulate medical studies involving human test subjects and require informed consent.

Nixon's Legacy

Despite his landslide victory in 1972, the Watergate scandal was increasing the pressure on Nixon. With Agnew under investigation and possibly facing an indictment, there was no way Nixon would resign. It was necessary to have Agnew resign first and allow Nixon to use the relatively new Twenty-Fifth Amendment to name a replacement. Agnew resigned on October 10, 1973, and Nixon nominated the popular Republican House minority leader Gerald Ford of Michigan. With the possibility of impeachment hanging over his head, Nixon resigned the presidency on August 9, 1974.

Unlike the Democrats policy of focusing on minority welfare, Nixon's thrust was to move minorities in the directions of the competitive private sector—giving them pathways to independence and prosperity. He had a three-prong approach: education, jobs, and entrepreneurship.

Nixon doubled federal financial aid to Black colleges and universities. He moved against the remnants of southern school segregation being retained in the Democrat southland. He forced unions to open their ranks to minorities.

Nixon increased Small Business Administration loans to minorities by 1,000 percent through the SBA office of Equal Employment Opportunity and Compliance and increased federal deposits in Black-owned banks by 4,000 percent. He increased federal government purchases from minority owned businesses from $9 million to more than $135 million.

Nixon appointed more Blacks to government jobs than any previous president, including Kennedy and Johnson—and to higher positions in many cases.

In an article in *Black Enterprise* in January of 1974 White House special assistant Stanley Scott noted that: "President Nixon has appointed the first black assistant secretary of the Navy, the first black general counsel of the Treasury and the first black member of the Federal Communications Commission."

Scott went on to say:

> Well over half a million federal civilian employees are black, Spanish-surnamed, American Indian or oriental. That's a full 20 per cent of all federal employees. Minority employment has gone up while total government employment has gone down. In just one year, from November 1972 to November 1973 minority employment in the super grades [high government positions] went up a whopping 54 jobs.

Despite all those accomplishments, the combination of scurrilous Democrat and media narratives cast Nixon as an adversary of civil rights—just as Democrats and the increasingly biased left-wing media distorted the record of the GOP on the mid-twentieth century civil rights legislation.

1973 Election of Detroit Mayor Coleman Young

In 1973, the voters of Detroit were electing the city's first Black mayor, Democrat Coleman Young. Instead of a new era of economic and social improvement for the Black community, it turned out to be an example of how the rise of Black leaders is not a guarantee for a change in the institutional racist system. His policies and devotion to the party's false civil rights narrative of generational dependency destroyed the economic foundation of the Motor City and turned Detroit into a segregated ghetto. He imposed a social welfare policy that had to be paid off by ever-increasing taxes drawing from an ever-decreasing tax base.

Young was another example of a Black politician who traded away the constitutional civil rights promoted by Martin Luther King for his own power on the political plantation. Young kept the Black population of Detroit in a segregated PLACE of oppression and impoverishment. Though Young did not live long enough to see Detroit fall into bankruptcy, he brought the city to the point of no return.

During Young's tenure, Detroit would be referred to as the Crime Capital, the Murder Capital or the Arson Capital of America. In the spirit of dark humor, one of the more popular tourist T-shirts featured the iconic yellow smiley face with a bullet hole in the forehead. It read, "Welcome to Detroit."

Harvard University political science Professor James Q. Wilson summarized Young's legacy:

> In Detroit, Mayor Coleman Young rejected the integrationist goal
> in favor of a flamboyant, black-power style that won him loyal fol-
> lowers, but he left the city a fiscal and social wreck.

Under Black Democrat leadership, the Black population of Detroit would soar from 30 to 90 percent. Once vibrant neighborhoods would be pockmarked with decaying buildings. Residential areas would become vast open spaces of weeds and rubbles—creating a new phenomenon of "urban prairies."

Despite his failure as a mayor and the plight of the mostly Black residents of Detroit, the national Democratic leadership showcased Young as an example of the party's civil rights accomplishments. He was chosen to lead the United States Conference of Mayors by the Democrat majority membership and the National Conference of Democratic Mayors on several occasions. He chaired the 1980 Platform Committee for the Democratic National Convention, and for four years, served as the Vice Chairman of the Democratic National Committee.

The honors bestowed on Young were part of a pattern of promoting Black advocates of the Democrats' welfare-for-votes strategy that launched in the 1930s by Chicago Democrat Congressman William Dawson.

Keyes v. School District No. 1, Denver

By 1963, Democrats had governed over Denver, Colorado, for ten years with William H. McNichols Jr. as mayor. It was also the year that a group of Black and Hispanic parents filed a lawsuit against the segregated and unequal school system. It would reach the Supreme Court ten years later in 1973. The parents charged that minority students were the victims of unfair and discriminatory education because of *de facto* racism.

The Court found for the plaintiffs—the parents—stating that the Democrat-run school system was in violation of the Equal Protection Clause of the United States Constitution. It was an important case because it gave legal definition to *de facto* segregation and racism. At the time, the Court was headed by Republican Chief Justice Warren Burger.

In writing the opinion for the majority, Justice William Brennan said that the Denver School Board, "through its actions over a period of years, intentionally created and maintained the segregated character of the core city schools."

Gerald R. Ford (1974–1977)

Upon the resignation of President Nixon, Gerald R. Ford ascended to the presidency. He was the first person in United States history to serve as president and vice president without ever being elected to either office. He had never even campaigned for office outside his congressional district in Grand Rapids, Michigan.

Upon assuming the presidency, Ford had this to say about civil rights:

> The United States government, under the Constitution and the law, is committed to the guarantee of the fundamental rights of every American. My administration will preserve these rights and work toward the elimination of all forms of discrimination against individuals on the basis of their race, color, religion, national origin or sex.

When Ford assumed the presidency, he developed an open-door policy for civil rights leaders. Following Nixon's example, Ford made several high-level Black appointments. Notable appointments include Arthur Fletcher as deputy assistant to the president for Urban Affairs, Daniel "Chappie" James as the first four-star general, and James Coleman as special assistant to the president, who went on to be the first Black secretary of transportation over the strong objections of southern Democrats, who still maintained considerable congressional power.

Ford extended the Voting Rights Act for an additional five years and supported and signed the Equal Credit Opportunity Act, which prohibited discrimination in all credit transactions. This was particularly significant in addressing redlining and mortgage discrimination prevalent in the Democrat run cities.

In his brief three years in office, Ford increased federal expenditures for civil rights from $2.9 billion to $3.9 billion, with a 25 percent increase in outlays for civil rights enforcement. He increased the budget of the Equal Employment Opportunity Commission (EEOC) from $56 million to $68 million. Ford followed the Republican Party's century-long tradition of funding Negro colleges and universities.

Ford had been a proponent of civil rights for Blacks all his life. His standing up for his Black college roommate and teammate detailed previously was an early example of Ford's racial attitude. Like Nixon's, Ford's positive civil rights record is obscured by the false Democrat narrative. In fact, Ford was a staunch proponent of civil rights and had a distinguished record to prove it.

One of the best summaries of Ford's history of civil rights advocacy in Congress is a report in the US Government archives. It states:

During his first fifteen years in Congress, Rep. Gerald R. Ford consistently supported Congressional civil rights efforts. He voted in favor of guaranteeing the voting rights of minorities by twice opposing the poll tax (1949, 1962), opposing literacy tests for those with a sixth-grade education (1963), supporting court-appointed referees to guarantee voting rights (1960) and favoring additional enforcement powers against those trying to deprive others of their voting rights (1956,1957, 1963, 1964). He repeatedly supported efforts to provide federal assistance to aid in school desegregation efforts (1956, 1963, 1964) and consistently favored the establishment, continuance and broadening of the Commission on Civil Rights (1956, 1957,1963, 1964). He supported the 1963 Republican civil rights initiative aimed at securing voting rights, banning literacy tests, ensuring employment rights and school desegregation. Later he voted for the 1964 Civil Rights Act which covered voting rights, discrimination in public accommodations and facilities and school desegregation. During this period he also supported equal employment rights and opportunities in the form of a voluntary Fair Employment Practices Commission (1950, 1963) and equal pay for equal work by women (1963).

Ford was a congressional leader in promoting legislation to eliminate racial discrimination in hiring practices. According to the Report:

Rep. Gerald Ford has a solid record of favoring legislation to prevent job and hiring discrimination. Repeatedly voting for the establishment, broadening and strengthening of Commissions for this purpose, he has preferred court action to giving administrative agencies final power to enforce the protections against job discrimination. In 1950, Ford voted for the Fair Employment Practice Commission, in the form in which it was ultimately enacted, which was set up to formulate comprehensive plans for the elimination of job discrimination and to initiate and investigate complaints of discrimination. In 1964, he voted for the Civil Rights Act, Title VII of which outlawed many unfair employment practices based on race, Color, religion, sex or national origin and created the Equal Employment Opportunity commission (EEOC). When the 89th Congress attempted to broaden Title VII's coverage and strengthen it by the addition of cease and desist orders and other powers, Congressman Ford voted for passage of the legislation. In 1969, Ford argued vigorously on the floor of the House against a Senate amendment which threatened the so-called "Philadelphia Plan" preventing discrimination against blacks in the construction industry. Two years later, in 1971 when renewed efforts were underway to broaden and strengthen the EEOC, Rep. Ford again voted to expand the Commission's powers; he supported the Erlenborn substitute as the best way to do this, arguing that giving EEOC cease and desist powers would deny both plaintiffs and defendants the protections they would receive in a court of law.

When the Voting Rights Act of 1965 came before the Congress, Ford was a leading proponent:

Building on his earlier record of solid support for full voting rights for minorities', Rep. Gerald Ford took an active part in the passage of the Voting Rights Act of 1965. As Minority Leader, Ford led Republicans in pushing for a bill that would send federal examiners to voting districts anywhere in the country where 25 or more persons complained they had been denied the right to register or vote because of race or color, provided for a court challenge of the constitutionality of the poll tax, banned literacy tests for those with a sixth grade education and prevented future vote fraud in Federal elections.

In terms of open housing, Ford was again a staunch proponent and fought against efforts to weaken the bill. He voted against an amendment to weaken the bill by allowing real estate agents to discriminate on behalf of property owners.

Ford had hoped to strengthen the bill by having it considered by the House. He "supported sending the bill to conference to give the House an opportunity to contribute to the legislation, but when this move failed, he reiterated his earlier support of open housing legislation by voting for final passage."

The Report also included Ford's position on the all-important school desegregation:

> As early as 1956, Ford voted for an amendment to a school construction bill prohibiting allotment of funds to states failing to comply with the 1954 Supreme Court decisions on school desegregation. In 1960, he voted for the Civil Rights Act which included a provision making obstruction of court orders for school desegregation a crime. The 1963 Republican civil rights initiative, supported by Ford, proposed authorizing federal aid to State and local educational agencies which request funds to desegregate public schools, and the next year the 1964 Civil Rights Act was passed with his support and included not only the Republican recommendations but, in addition, authorized the Attorney General to file suit for the desegregation of public schools and colleges. In 1970 he voted four times for a bill which provided $1.5 billion to school districts with the problems of desegregation or overcoming racial imbalance, and when this legislation was renewed, he voted again in 1972 for a second bill with a similar purpose.

Under Ford, the Voting Rights Act was extended for seven years and expanded to cover non-English speaking citizens. Ford's legacy in terms of implementing and protecting civil rights was one of the strongest of any president in American history.

Louise Day Hicks

Being one of the most progressive Democrat cities in America did not spare Boston from a backlash against school desegregation. Twenty years after *Brown v. Board of Education*, and forty-four years since a Republican served as mayor, Boston gained national attention for its school segregation and violent protests against integration.

Louise Day Hicks first came into public view in 1961 when she was elected to the Boston School Committee, and in 1963 became the Committee chairperson. In that same year, the NAACP demanded that the school authorities and city officials address the *de facto* segregation in the city's schools—thirteen of which were at least 90 percent Black. Boston's schools were segregated based on ethnicity. Schools serving the Chinatown area were 100 percent Asian. North End schools were 100 percent Italian and the South End schools predominantly Irish. These four ethnic groups constituted the majority of Boston citizens.

Hicks pushed back aggressively against the NAACP demand and almost instantly became one of the best known and most controversial figures in Boston. She was said "to personify the discord that existed between some working-class Irish Americans and the African Americans."

Hicks Rises in Democratic Party

Her notoriety as an active opponent of school busing won her a seat on the Boston City Council as a Democrat, where she would eventually become the first female council president under the administration of Democrat Mayor Kevin White. She served one term in Congress.

During her political career, Hicks took up many of the themes of the southern Democrat racists, referring to Blacks as "radical agitators." She stoked White anxiety by raising the Democrats most popular fear mongering subject, a woman's safety. She claimed that "justice [had come] to mean special privileges for the Black man and the criminal" and that "White women can no longer walk the streets in safety."

While Hicks conceded that "a large part of my vote probably does come from bigoted people … I know I am not a bigot." In many ways, she represented the urban Democrats' more sophisticated *de facto* racism and the displacement of civil rights with generational welfare dependency. Still, she alleged that a politician from a progressive northern city cannot be a racist or support racists. Despite her disclaimer, Hicks was very much like those southern racist Democrats she disavowed.

Hear Them ROAR in '74

When Federal Judge W. Arthur Garrity, Jr. ordered Boston to increase busing to bring about greater racial balance, Hicks founded Restore Our Alienated Rights (ROAR)—a community activist group designed to mount physical resistance to school desegregation. Mimicking the civil rights movement itself, ROAR marched in the streets, assembled for public prayers against integration, organized sit-ins, heckled speakers, disrupted meetings, and picketed politicians supporting desegregation.

ROAR's protests outside of integrated schools resulted in outbreaks of violence inside. A fistfight inside Boston's Hyde Park High School resulted in a melee in which thirteen hundred students were fighting inside the school building. Fighting then spread to the neighborhood. Fifteen students were arrested—thirteen of whom were Black.

ROAR members and others demonstrated outside South Boston High School day after day. They were so disruptive that Judge Garrity issued a court order preventing more than three demonstrators to gather at one time. Fighting and rioting would break out periodically. In the more violent confrontations, people were injured, with two dying from their injuries. Relative peace was restored when Republican Massachusetts governor Francis Sargent sent in the national guard to enforce school desegregation.

Election of 1976

As mentioned already, having been appointed to the vice presidency upon the resignation of Vice President Spiro Agnew and rising to the presidency upon the resignation of President Nixon, Ford had never run in a national election. The nation was still ravaged by high inflation rates and the public bitterness over the Watergate scandal and the unrelated corrupt activities of the vice president. The nation wanted closure.

The political *coup de grace* for Ford was his pardon of Nixon. He believed that the emotional and constitutional agony of the possible indictment and conviction of a United States president would not serve the nation well.

The Republicans gave the nomination to incumbent President Gerald Ford but not before a formidable challenge from former California governor Ronald Reagan. For his vice president, Ford again chose the man he had originally named to the post in accordance with the Twenty-Fifth Amendment, Nelson Rockefeller.

Both Ford and Rockefeller were strong advocates of civil rights. According to the "Public Papers of Nelson A. Rockefeller, Fifty-third Governor of the State of New York," Rockefeller was one of the most pro civil rights governors in America. The report specifically stated:

> Rockefeller achieved virtual total prohibition of discrimination in housing and places of public accommodation. He ... increased by nearly 50% the number of African Americans and Hispanics holding state jobs ... He outlawed 'blockbusting' as a means of artificially depressing housing values and banned discrimination in the sale of all forms of insurance.

When the little-known Georgia governor Jimmy Carter entered the race for president, the general response was "Jimmy Who?" At the onset, he was given little chance to win the nomination against such Democrat powerhouses as senator Henry "Scoop" Jackson, congressman Mo Udall, and California governor Jerry Brown. Even segregationist George Wallace was again in contention for the Democrat nomination.

Jimmy Carter was viewed as a southern progressive and an advocate of civil rights, but his upbringing was very much the old South, and his civil rights beliefs were convoluted. In his book, *An Hour Before Daylight,* Carter wrote:

> It seemed natural for white folks to cherish our Southern heritage and cling to our way of life. We were bound together by blood kinship as well as by lingering resentment against those who had defeated us. A frequent subject of discussion around my grandparents' homes was the damage the "damn Yankees" had done to the South during Reconstruction years.

In that same book, Carter took a unique southern interpretation of history. Speaking of his families' lingering bitterness of the defeat of the south, he wrote: "Folks never considered that the real tragedy of Reconstruction was its failure to establish social justice for the former slaves."

Republican Reconstructions did establish "social justice for the former slaves." It was only when the federal troops were removed in 1877 that the terrorist era of Democrat control brutally ended social justice for all southern Black people.

Throughout his early career, Carter allied himself to the staunchest segregationists, such as Lester Maddox, James Eastland and John Stennis. Despite his image as a racially tolerant political figure, Carter had not completely given up his belief in segregation.

Carter's political career commenced when he won a state Senate seat against a staunch racist—making Carter appear to be more of a moderate by southern standards. The comparison was a matter of degree since Carter was also a believer in the segregationist canard that it was "natural" for Whites and Blacks to want to live among themselves.

Carter's public image cast him as a gentle speaking humble Christian. Those who have run afoul of Carter tell quite a different story. Privately, he was very vindictive and ruthless. Writing for *Time* magazine, columnist Hugh Sidey said: "The wrath that escapes Carter's lips about racism and hatred when he prays and poses as the epitome of Christian charity leads even his supporters to protest his meanness."

Carter talked in favor of civil rights as he embraced some of the Democratic Party's most infamous racists to achieve political success. After losing the 1966 Democratic gubernatorial primary to a one-time ally and hardcore racist Lester Maddox, Carter had the opportunity to support moderate Democrat Ellis Arnall or even Republican Bo Calloway. Instead, Carter supported Maddox as a matter of political pragmatism. Four years later, Carter made another run for governor. This time he minimized campaigning in front of Black audiences and sought the endorsements of leading segregationist personalities. It worked and he became governor.

In his successful run for governor in 1970, Carter played the race card by widely distributing photographs of his opponent, Carl Sanders, posing with Black members of the Atlanta Hawks basketball team.

Carter's running mate was Minnesota Senator Walter Mondale. By all public measures, Mondale was a staunch supporter of civil rights. He considered equality as God-given. The University of Minnesota website quotes Mondale:

> For 10 years as attorney general of my State and as a US Senator, I have regarded it as a religious responsibility to treat every man as an equal. And I am offended by racial segregation, wherever it exists.

Even as he said those words, the racial segregation he verbally opposed was being carried out almost exclusively by his own Democratic Party, including in Minnesota. Despite the rhetoric, he never challenged those urban racist policies of the powerful big city Democrat machines.

While Mondale's devotion to civil rights appears to have been sincere, he was among those who wittingly or unwittingly embraced the Democratic Party's false narrative which blamed the plight of Black Americans on vague cultural issues. Like most moderate Democrats, Mondale talked about the "seeds of poverty" without ever identifying or pushing back against those who planted and nurtured them.

American Independent Party

The man who beat Carter in the 1966 Georgia Democrat gubernatorial primary, Lester Maddox, took the nomination for president from the American Independent Party that had been the vehicle of George Wallace's presidential campaign in 1968. Maddox had called Carter "the most dishonest man" he had ever met—a stark contrast to Carter's holier-than-thou public image.

Party Platforms

The Republican platform continued the party's more than one-hundred-year history of support for equal rights. The Democrat platform also expressed support for civil rights and promised a range of programs to address the problem. Despite winning the presidency and controlling the Congress, the promises of the Democrat platform went unfulfilled during Carter's four years in office, except for the commitment to provide more funding for welfare dependency. Conditions in the inner cities did not improve.

Ironically the Democrat platform recognized the problem without addressing the political party most responsible for creating them when it stated:

> Minority unemployment has historically been at least *double the aggregate unemployment rate, with incomes at two-thirds the national average.* Special emphasis must be placed on closing this gap. (emphasis added)

Under the heading of "Welfare Reform," the Democrat platform also recognized the failure of their own advocated welfare programs—but without taking responsibility for their long advocacy of generational welfare.

The Democrat platform conceded the failure of their welfare policies:

> The current complexity of the welfare structure requires armies of bureaucrats at all levels of government. Food Stamps, Aid to Families with Dependent Children, and Medicaid are burdened by unbelievably complex regulations, statutes and court orders. *Both the recipients of these benefits, and the citizen who pays for them, suffer* as a result. (emphasis added)

These noble words were written even as the Massive Resistance Movement against school integration was still being carried out in the Democrat-controlled southern states. The 1976 platform was arguably the most hypocritical political document offered by the Democratic Party up to that time.

Though race was not a primary issue, Carter's background as a southern Democrat helped him win the south and the big cities, where racism still influenced voting. To keep such support, Carter took a compromised position on integration. During the campaign, Carter used traditional racist language and coding to proffer that "ethnic enclaves" (read that as Black and Hispanic ghettoes) result from a natural desire of people preferring to live among their own kind." He pledged:

> I am not going to use the Federal Government's authority deliberately to circumvent the natural inclination of people to live in ethnically homogeneous neighborhoods. I think it is good to

maintain the homogeneity of neighborhoods if they've been established that way.

Carter could not have been more clear. This campaign pledge was an assurance to powerful Democrat segregationist leaders in the South and the powerful Democrat machine bosses in the major cities that he had no intention of addressing issues of *de facto* racism based on segregation. Under his administration there would be no effort to end institutional *de facto* racism. No effort to end segregation. Black Americans would be kept in their PLACE. And they were.

Jimmy Carter and the Baptist Church

Carter and his family were long-time members of Plains Baptist Church in Plains, Georgia. During his entire lifetime membership, the church maintained a Whites-only policy. Carter's lifelong membership in a Whites-only church was never made an issue in his campaign for the presidency until the Sunday before the general election.

Clennon Washington King Jr.

Clennon King was pastor of the Divine Mission Church in nearby Albany, Georgia. King had developed a reputation for taking on one-man efforts to advance integration. He would also gain attention for his causes by running for public offices he had little chance of winning. His exploits earned him the moniker of the "Black Don Quixote." He considered running for president in 1960 as the standard bearer of the Independent Afro-American Party.

In October of 1976, King announced his intention to integrate presidential candidate Carter's Plains Baptist Church by attending services on Sunday, October 31—just two days before Carter would become president-elect of the United States. The church had a longstanding policy to bar "all Negroes and civil rights agitators."

The pastor of the Plains Church, Reverend Bruce Edwards, recommended that King be allowed to attend rather than embarrass presidential candidate Carter on the eve of the election. He was overruled by the church deacons, who voted to uphold the ban and temporarily close the church to services. They also recommended that Edwards be removed from his position as pastor.

In responding to the rejection of Blacks into membership, Carter often claimed that he and his family had quit the Plains Baptist Church. That was never true.

Following his election, Carter was asked by Terence Cardinal Cooke of the New York Roman Catholic diocese where he would be attending church in view of the controversy. Carter responded, "I haven't decided." He told the Catholic prelate that his wife's family was "having a reunion" at the Plains Methodist Church.

In fact, Carter continued as a member of the Plains Baptist Church, even teaching Sunday school. He promised to work to have the discriminatory policy changed. He would eventually leave the Plains Baptist Church in 2000 because of the church's stance against women in clergy, not because of racial issues.

In leaving the Baptist church, Carter may have unintentionally rebutted his own claim to having left the Plains Church in 1976 over the racial policy. In announcing his departure in 2000, he said:

> My grandfather, my father and I have always been Southern Baptists, and *for 21 years, since the first political division took place in the Southern Baptist Convention, I have maintained that relationship.* (emphasis added)

To make Carter appear more moderate on racial issues, his campaign spread the false narrative that he and his family had quit the church. Of course, the election was over before that claim could be proven or disproven. In fact, neither he nor his family left the church.

In another racially charged deception, Carter ran campaign advertisements in Black newspapers falsely stating that independent Republican candidate John Anderson had voted against the 1964 Civil Rights Act. It was an outright lie.

With the burden of the Nixon pardon and a nation eager to turn the page on the aftermath of the Watergate scandal, Jimmy Carter eked out a narrow victory with 50.1 percent of the vote. While President Ford carried more states, Carter bested him in the Electoral College, 297 to 240.

Jimmy Carter (1977–1981)

Carter's civil rights record was limited to symbolic actions to reinforce his civil rights advocacy image. As governor of Georgia, he had declared Martin Luther King Day in that state. He appointed Blacks to key positions in his campaign. He won the endorsements of prominent Black leaders, including Martin Luther King, Sr. and young civil rights activist, Andrew Young, a fellow Georgian.

As president, Carter walked a fine line between the more liberal wing of the Democratic Party and the old guard. He did not propose any civil rights legislation. He issued no significant executive orders on civil rights. At best, he took up the "benign neglect" recommended to President Nixon by Democrat New York senator Daniel Moynihan a decade earlier.

Chicago Mayor Daley Dies

Not long after the 1976 general election, the sudden death of Chicago mayor Richard J. Daley created political chaos in the Windy City with strong racial implications. The politics of succession had never been seriously considered. The city clerk technically took over the duties until the city council acted in choosing a new mayor.

Initially, the council's Black president pro tempore, Alderman Wilson Frost proclaimed himself as "acting mayor." Though a loyal machine alderman, Frost's proclamation was hotly disputed by the White Democrat majority in the city council for basically one reason. Wilson was Black. Being a loyal Black crony of the Democrat machine for years was far more acceptable than being "da boss".

After several days of secret negotiations behind closed doors, the city council named White southwest side Alderman Michael Bilandic—a fifty-three-year-old milquetoast bachelor who lived with his mother—to fill out a six-month term until a special election could be conducted.

Bilandic was to be an interim mayor, keeping the seat warm until Daley's son, Richard M., would be slated in the Special Election. Bilandic reneged on his promise to only serve until the Special Election.

As mayor, Bilandic basically maintained the racist policies that kept Chicago constantly on the brink of racial unrest. In June of 1977, the Puerto Rican community exploded in a three-day riot on his brief watch.

In 1979, he would run for election to a full four-year term.

Chicago's Lady Mayor

In 1979, Chicago mayor Michael Bilandic was expected to win easy reelection as the Democrat machine candidate. He would first have to face Jane Byrne, the former Chicago consumer advocate, in the Democratic primary. She was rumored to be a one-time girlfriend, who he dumped. She was a woman scorned but not considered much of a threat to the machine backed Bilandic. Then it snowed.

As the city hunkered down in a major blast of winter weather, the snow piled up. In the face of the blizzard, Chicago's culture of racism was evident. With snow removal crews overburdened, the White neighborhoods were given priority. This was normal operating procedure, but Byrne capitalized on the snow and made it a campaign issue.

As if the discriminatory snow removal operations were not enough, the Bilandic administration shut down a number of stops along the rapid transit "L" lines to facilitate the flow of commuters. The unannounced shutdowns were mostly in Black neighborhoods—leaving thousands of inner-city workers stranded in the blistering cold as el cars filled with White workers passed through the canceled stops.

In an upset election, Byrne defeated Bilandic. Though she challenged the Democrat machine's endorsed candidate, Byrne was no reformer. She took her place on the fifth floor of city hall as the new boss. Like her predecessors, she placed more emphasis on symbolic civil rights activities than any policies that would significantly change the *de facto* racist system of the Windy City.

Byrne Moves into Public Housing

One of Byrne's most publicized symbolic actions was moving into the Cabrini-Green public housing complex—a ramshackle, gang and drug infested Housing and Urban Development agency disaster. The *Cabrini-Green.com* website describes Byrne's new home: "The Cabrini-Green Housing Projects in Chicago, Illinois were some of the most infamous in the country. Decades of poverty and violence rendered them near uninhabitable."

The fact that Cabrini-Green, and public housing projects like it in major cities throughout the nation, had descended into unsafe slum tenements is the result of a racist management policies by city hall Democrats.

While Byrne's move was largely symbolic, it did make the neighborhood a bit safer—at least for the three weeks she lived there. Her presence, along with a platoon of police protection assigned to the area curtailed local violence for a short time. As added protection, the rear door to her building was welded shut. Inadvertently, the safety measure would later prove beneficial in creating a fortification for gangs, and several of them employed a similar "safety measure" in other buildings in the complex by sealing rear doors.

If moving in was designed to give an image of optimism, her rather quick departure tended to reinforce the negative and dangerous image of public housing. That "image" of public housing was often made real by the endless violence and tragedies.

Laketa Crosby

Laketa Crosby was one of the all-too-common tragedies of ghetto life. Referring to the murder of nine-year-old Crosby, *Chicago Tribune* columnist Mike Royko wrote about the lack of enduring improvement in the wake of Byrne's residency:

And now Laketa Crosby, age 9, is dead because she happened to be in the line of fire when rival savages started shooting. Her uncle, a member of the same gang as the murder suspect and a witness to the shooting, is barely alive after being beaten by fellow gang members who believed he fingered the suspect. And members of the dead girl's family are hiding because they're afraid that they'll soon be dead too. In other words, life is again normal in Cabrini-Green.

What was once shocking—the death of an innocent child—would soon become an iconic event in Chicago and major segregated cities run by racist Democrat regimes.

Byrne Leans White

Having abandoned her Cabrini-Green residence, Byrne enkindled Black outrage with a number of her appointments. She triggered protests when she nominated three White political cronies to the Chicago Housing Authority (CHA), which oversees the predominantly Black public housing. One of the Black members of the CHA resigned in protest.

This was the latest in a series of appointments that offended the Black community. According to *New York Times* writer Nathaniel Sheppard:

> Black unhappiness with the mayor has been growing for the past two years. In 1980, in naming an acting superintendent for the largely black public school system here, Mayor Byrne bypassed over Manford Byrd, a respected deputy superintendent of schools who is black, and named Angeline Caruso, a white who was Mr. Byrd's subordinate.
>
> The mayor raised black ire again when she appointed two whites opposed to the school board's desegregation efforts, replacing two black members.

Byrne had also run afoul of a Black alderman she had appointed to the Democrat dominated city council. After Alderman Allan Streeter had refused to vote to confirm Byrne's appointments to the school board, she publicly opposed his election to a full term. He won his reelection after what was called a "bitter campaign."

Racism Takes Toll on ChicagoFest

How institutional racism can infect every aspect of political and social life is seen in one of Byrne's hallmark special events—ChicagoFest. She conceived of it as a public celebration of Chicago's restaurants. It was the predecessor of what would become Taste of Chicago.

Unfortunately, ChicagoFest also showcased the noted racism of the city and its Democrat administration. In a special *New York Times* article, Sheppard wrote:

> But now the highlight of the mayor's calendar of summer extravaganzas, the $6 million, 12-day ChicagoFest, scheduled to begin Wednesday, may be disrupted by a boycott threatened by Blacks unhappy with some of her appointments and political decisions.

A major casualty in the entertainment sector was the cancellation of renowned Black singer Stevie Wonder. Black exhibitors, such as Leon's Barbeque, owned by prominent Black businessman and civil rights leader Leon Finney, pulled out of the ChicagoFest even though Jesse Jackson, a boycott organizer, had assured them that vendors would not be subjected to harm, harassment, or destruction of property.

ChicagoFest was plagued with complaints from Black vendors who were either denied access to the event or were in the least popular locations. There was also grumbling that those Black businesses allowed in were owned by cronies of the mayor and the political machine. Some vendors were unhappy with Jesse Jackson for his boycott of the event rather than supporting Black entrepreneurs wanting access to the large crowd of visitors or better placement.

Dayton Board of Education v. Brinkman

By 1979, Dayton, Ohio, had been governed by Democratic mayor James McGee for nine years when the Supreme Court upheld an appellate court decision that found the city's Democrat-controlled Board of Education had been "intentionally" operating a dual segregated school system in violation of the Constitution's Equal Rights Clause—twenty-five years after *Brown v. Board of Education.*

The original suit was filed by a group of Black parents alleging that Dayton used gerrymandering, school district boundaries, student transfers and opening and closing schools to maintain segregated schools.

The case reached the United States Supreme Court twice, in 1977 and 1979. In both cases, the high court ruled in favor of the plaintiffs and required a plan for integration. It would be another seventeen years before a federal judge declared that Dayton had finally complied with the plan.

Dayton was not an outlier. It is an example. The resistance to school integration was found in virtually every Democrat-run major city in America at the time.

The Greensboro Massacre

In 1979, the Communist Workers Party (CWP) and civil rights leaders converged on Greensboro, North Carolina to organize the predominantly Black textile workers. At the time, Greensboro was a Democrat racist stronghold. There had been frequent racial incidents since the passage of the 1964 Civil Rights Act.

In July, union activists confronted the Klan at a showing of "Birth of a Nation," the 1915 silent film glorifying the KKK. This led to a general atmosphere of hostility between the groups. The CWP also took the occasion to confront the local Ku Klux Klan and neo-Nazis groups with a protest billed as a "Death to the Klan" march.

Klan members drove up to the starting point to confront and harass the marchers from their vehicles. Members of the Klan exited their vehicles with an assortment of weapons and started shooting. Six union marchers were killed, including Dr. Michael Nathan, a prominent pediatrician who was only there to support his wife. Though there was warning of the potential violence by the Klan, the Greensboro police were not on the scene.

Police arrested sixteen individuals, mostly Klansmen and Nazis, and a few union marchers. Based on evidence gathered by the FBI, six members of the Klan were put on trial for murder. With the judicial system still in the hands of the Democrat old guard, an all-White jury acquitted the men.

Having failed to win a conviction in the criminal trial, later Republican president Ronald Reagan would authorize his attorney general William French Smith to proceed with a civil rights case. In all, nine men were indicted for violating the civil rights of the victims in 1983. Unfortunately, the trial had to take place in a southern federal court before an all-White jury. The accused were again acquitted.

Survivors filed a civil suit with better luck. In addition to the Klan and Nazi Party, they named local police and federal law enforcement officials in the lawsuit. In a courtroom in Winston-Salem, the jury found eight people guilty of the wrongful death of Dr. Michael Nathan. In addition, the jury awarded two of the plaintiffs a $350,000.

Miami Riot of 1980

While Miami's Democrat mayor Maurice Ferré was considered a civil rights advocate, he had come to office in a city with a long history of institutional racism. In May of 1980, pent-up frustrations in the Black community would erupt over the evergreen issue of law enforcement.

Four White police officers were pursuing Arthur McDuffie in a high-speed chase when McDuffie lost control of his motorcycle and fell to the ground. He then attempted to escape on foot. Police gave chase and captured the suspect. He was restrained. McDuffie died from injuries.

Police claim that McDuffie had resisted arrest and that his injuries were sustained when the police vehicle collided with the motorcycle. In the subsequent investigation, it was determined that McDuffie's injuries were sustained by repeated blows to the head with blunt weapons and his skull was "cracked like an egg." The evidence of a collision between the police vehicle and the motorcycle was determined to have been created when one of the officers intentionally drove over the motorcycle after McDuffie had been rendered helpless and mortally wounded.

Despite charges of manslaughter and tampering with evidence, the officers were either granted immunity from prosecution or acquitted by an all-White jury—a practice that was supposed to have ended years earlier.

Upon learning of the verdict, more than five thousand citizens gathered for an afternoon protest in front of the Miami Metro Justice Building. Within hours, the protest turned violent. The violence spread into the predominantly Black sections of the city with arson, looting and personal assaults occurring over a three-day period. As is often the case, the police were ordered to stand down and let the riot take its course—leading to extensive unnecessary damage and injury in the Black community.

By the end of the rioting, 18 men and women had been killed and more than 350 injured. Some 600 were arrested. The cost of destruction and damage was estimated to exceed $100 million. Upon the demand of the Fraternal Order of Police, those involved in the death of McDuffie were reinstated to the police department.

Election of 1980

The Republicans had a large field of candidates in the race. The two most prominent were former California governor Ronald Reagan and Texas congressman George H. W. Bush. Bush was expected to win. Reagan was considered by critics to be too conservative and, at sixty-nine, too old. Regardless, Reagan won the GOP nomination.

Democrats responded with the traditional accusation against any Republican candidate for virtually any office, calling them racists. Reagan biographer Craig Shirley, writing for *Free Republic* online wrote:

> It was a curious and more importantly nasty and unfounded attack,
> as Reagan had a long history of fighting racism and anti-Semitism.
> When Reagan was a young man playing football for Eureka College,
> several African American members were barred from staying at a

"whites only" hotel. While their coach tried to make some other accommodations, Reagan took his teammates to his home, where his parents kindly took them in.

In the 1940s, Reagan quit a country club in Los Angeles in protest when he discovered it had a policy of barring Jewish members. As governor of California, Reagan appointed more blacks to positions in his administration, hundreds more than his so-called progressive predecessors, including Earl Warren and Pat Brown.

Though his popularity was declining, the Democrats re-nominated Jimmy Carter and his incumbent vice president, Walter Mondale. By Carter's own description, the nation was suffering a "malaise."

In a nod to the racist wing of the party, Carter's first campaign appearance was in the small town of Tuscumbia. It was not a community known to the general voting public, but a special place for hardcore southern racists. It was the national headquarters of the Ku Klux Klan at the time. While appealing to the White supremacist faction of the Democratic Party, Carter was hypocritically accusing Reagan of racism.

Party Platforms

The Republican platform undertook a direct attack on the Democratic Party's false civil rights narrative of generational welfare dependency— charging the Democrats with "deliberately" (highlighted) maintaining dependent impoverishment as a means of political control:

> For two generations, especially since the mid-1960s, the Democrats have *deliberately* perpetuated a status of federally subsidized poverty and manipulated dependency for millions of Americans. This is especially so for black and Hispanics, many of whom remain pawns of the bureaucracy, *trapped outside the social and economic mainstream of American life.*

In other words, Democrats were keeping Blacks in that PLACE of inferior citizenship. The 1980 Republican platform predicted a future that would be fulfilled well into the twenty-first century. In part it said: "*This is the 'poverty trap' which will continue to hold millions of Americans* as long as they continue to be punished for working" (emphasis added).

The efforts of urban Democrats to maintain segregated ghettoized schools were seen in other policies advanced by the GOP:

> We are dismayed that the *Carter Administration cruelly reneged on promises made during the 1976 campaign.* Wielding the threat of his veto, Mr. Carter led the fight against Republican attempts to make tuition tax credits a reality." (emphasis added)

These tax credits would have given Black segregated students the resources to attend better schools, as would the later push for school choice—another program strongly opposed by Democrats and their school union allies.

Under the chairmanship of Detroit's failed Black mayor Coleman Young, the Democrats produced an enormously long platform. In general, it was a pledge to fund just about any demand any citizen could make.

Once again, The Democrat platform offered the same old promises of economic opportunities in the Black community. In doing so, however, the platform once again inadvertently admitted to the failures of their own Democrat administrations in the major cities in terms of both job creation and education:

> A major effort must be undertaken to address youth employment. Half the unemployed are under twenty-five. *Teenage inner-city unemployment is at disastrous levels of 50 percent or higher.* The problem is one of both employment and employability—a lack of jobs and a lack of skills." (emphasis added)

It was the intentionally segregated inner-city schools that deprived inner city Black students the "skills" necessary for college admission and career level employment.

What is also noteworthy is that this horrifically high unemployment in the Black ghettoes has been a reality since the Great Depression. From 1932 to the time of the 1980 platform, Democrats-controlled Congress for all but two years, the presidency for thirty-two out of forty-eight years and the cities with the high Black unemployment virtually all the time. The Democrats failure to provide education and jobs to the impoverished Black community was obviously not an unintended consequence.

Again under the guise of welfare reform, the Democrat platform ignored its decades of urban governance and simply points to the failure of the programs. It is a plank that might have been expected to be in the Republican platform rather than the platform of a party urging the reelection of its president.

> The nation's welfare system continues to be inequitable and archaic. The existing organization of our delivery system is chaotic. The roles of the federal, state, and local governments, and of the courts are scrambled, with each vying for power and control over delivery. This confusion lends credence to public outrage.

In terms of solution, the Democrat platform myopically proposed one solution. More funding.

> The fiscal crisis of welfare recipients has also deepened, since states and localities are *unable or unwilling to adjust benefits* to prevent inflation from robbing them of their worth (emphasis added).

Democrats literally conceded that their welfare as the new civil rights scheme is what keeps Blacks impoverished and subjected to generational welfare dependency.

> Incentives continue to cause families to break apart and fathers to leave home so that children may survive. Disincentives continue for welfare families to seek work on their own; no regular method links welfare recipients to the work force."

Even as the platform recognized their own failure to improve conditions for minorities trapped in segregated communities, they failed to live up to the fact that it was their Democratic Party that implemented those policies for generations. Their solution was more money for welfare. More money to keep Blacks in that PLACE of generational welfare dependency..

In the Democrat's civil right plank, they again recognized that racial segregation, discrimination and oppression were most prevalent in the cities they ruled over.

> Ethnic, racial and other minorities continue to be victims of police abuse, persistent harassment and excessive use of force. In 1979, the Community Relations Service of the Department of Justice noted that "alleged use of deadly force by police and the reaction of minorities was a major force of racial unrest in the nation in 1978."

Despite their rhetoric, and their ability to rectify the problem by virtue of their one-party rule over the affected cities, the issue of police abuse would continue unabated into the twenty-first century, as covered more extensively later in this book.

Out of political desperation, Carter played the race card. In response to Reagan's call for shifting programs back to the states, Carter claimed that "states' rights" was code language and accused Reagan of "hate and racism."

Reagan Wins

Though initially considered a weak contender by the establishment media, Reagan swept to a landslide victory over Carter. He took 51 percent of the popular vote to Carter's 41 percent—with the independent candidacy of Republican John Anderson getting approximately 7 percent. In the Electoral College it was a route, with Reagan garnering 489 votes to Carter's 49—and zero for Anderson.

Ronald Reagan (1981–1989)

The racial legacy of Ronald Reagan is hotly debated, with Democrats accusing him of being opposed to civil rights. They may be correct only to the extent that Reagan, like Nixon, did not believe in the Democrat policy of welfare as civil rights. He viewed the years of welfare's failure to bring impoverished Blacks out of the misery of the Democrat urban ghettoes as sufficient evidence of abject social failure, with the need to refocus on real civil rights in the constitutional sense. Reagan believed that Black Americans should be enabled to participate in the fullness of America's opportunity society rather than be trapped in generational welfare.

The King National Holiday

A national holiday for Martin Luther King was originally pushed by the Congressional Black Caucus. Even when the Democratic Party controlled the White House and both chambers of Congress, the proposal lacked sufficient support. Southern Democrats, who still had enormous power in Congress, were outspoken in their opposition to the bill. Some argued that it was not appropriate since the FBI, at the behest of Presidents Kennedy and Johnson, accused King of being a communist, an opponent to the Vietnam war, and an adulterer. Others covered their racial bias by arguing that another holiday was simply too costly because of the loss of productivity.

Republican senator Robert Dole of Kansas responded firmly to that economic issue. He said:

> I suggest they hurry back to their pocket calculators and estimate the cost of 300 years of slavery followed by a century or more of economic, political, and social exclusion and discrimination.

It was Republican House Speaker Newt Gingrich who persuaded members of his conference to get behind the measure. Among those with a change of heart was football star Congressman Jack Kemp. On August 2, 1983, he took to the floor of the House and said:

> I have changed my position on this vote because I really think that the American Revolution will not be complete until we commemorate the civil rights revolution and guarantee those basic declarations of human rights for all Americans and remove those barriers that stand in the way of people being what they were meant to be.

In his extemporaneous remarks, Kemp added:

> If we lose sight of the fact that the Republican Party was founded by Mr. Lincoln as a party of civil rights, freedom, and hope, and opportunity, and dreams, and a PLACE where all people could be

free—if we turn our backs, we are not going to the be the party of human dignity we want, as Republicans, to be known for.

Despite the opposition of southern Democrats, the bill passed Congress by wide margins with the full support of President Reagan and the Republican leadership in Congress. Reagan marked the occasion with a Rose Garden celebration in which he said:

> Now our nation has decided to honor Dr. Martin Luther King, Jr., by setting aside a day each year to remember him and the just cause he stood for. We've made historic strides since Rosa Parks refused to go to the back of the bus. As a democratic people, we can take pride in the knowledge that we Americans recognized a grave injustice and took action to correct it. And we should remember that in far too many countries, people like Dr. King never have the opportunity to speak out at all.
>
> Traces of bigotry still mar America. So, each year on Martin Luther King Day, let us not only recall Dr. King, but rededicate ourselves to the commandments he believed in and sought to live every day. Thou shalt love thy God with all thy heart. And thy shall love thy neighbor as thyself. And I just have to believe that all of us, if all of us, young and old, Republicans and Democrats, do all we can to live up to those commandments, then we will see the day when Dr. King's dream comes true.

The president then quoted King:

> Their [White people's] destiny is tied up with our destiny, and their freedom is inextricably bound to our freedom. We cannot walk alone.

The bill creating the holiday also created the Martin Luther King, Jr. Federal Holiday Commission to coordinate activities associated with the annual celebration. Republican president George H. W. Bush later appointed King's widow, Coretta Scott King, as a "member for life."

Combining Holidays

In several southern states, the creation of the Martin Luther King holiday revealed the devotion to historic racism. In an example of political irony, several states shared King's holiday to that of Confederate leaders. The problem was that in several former Confederates states the birthday of General Robert E. Lee (January 19) was already celebrated as a state holiday.

The solution in three states was to combine the celebration of both men. To honor Lee in equal celebration and on the same day as King was seen for what it was—an insult to the great civil rights leader. All three states had Democrat governors and legislatures at the time Reagan signed the King Holiday legislation. They were Arkansas with Bill Clinton, Alabama with George Wallace, and Mississippi with William Winter.

Regarding Arkansas, Blogger David Badash wrote:

> Lawmakers in Arkansas found a passive-aggressive way to 'honor' and 'celebrate' Martin Luther King, Jr.'s message of freedom and equality … even though they stood for diametrically opposed beliefs.

In Virginia, where General Lee was born, they had combined a holiday honoring Lee and his fellow Confederate general "Stonewall" Jackson. With the creation of the King Holiday, the state combined all three into one celebration. The governor at the time was Democrat Chuck Robb, the son-in-law of President Lyndon Johnson. The tripartite celebration was discontinued, giving King his own day, in 2000 by Republican governor James Gilmore.

End of the Chicago Machine

In 1983, Chicago Mayor Jayne Byrne was up for reelection. In an attempt to regain power and take the old political machine out of storage, the so-called mechanics tapped Richard M. Daley, the son of Richard J., to face Byrne in the primary.

Also in the race was a first term Black congressman, Harold Washington. This was not unusual in that a Black candidate was usually put up by the machine in the spirit of tokenism and to give the appearance of Black empowerment. The token Black candidate was there to siphon off some of the anti-machine Black voters in the inner city and the anti-machine progressive votes in the northern lakeshore wards. In fact, Washington, himself, had been that token candidate on two previous occasions. But this time was different.

Washington was not in this race for the convenience of the Democrat leadership. He was not in it to lose—although most pundits gave him little chance of winning. Hypothetically, it was possible for Washington to win if Byrne and Daley evenly split the White vote. Washington needed 80 percent of the Black vote based on an 80 percent Black turnout—something never seen in Chicago.

Overconfidence on the part of the White Democrat political establishment led to disaster for the Democrat machine. Byrne and Daley evenly divided the vote 33 and 30 percent respectively. Washington eked out the Democrat primary victory with 37 percent. Approximately 80 percent of the Black vote showed up at the polls, and Washington got 80 percent of their vote.

The Republican nomination went to a rather non-descript state legislator, Bernie Epton. No one of any stature wanted the useless GOP nomination. It had been fifty-six years since the people of Chicago elected a Republican mayor. The entire election changed when Washington got the Democrat nomination—and longstanding institutional racism was the driving factor.

Democrats Can't Tolerate a Black Mayor

In Chicago, victory in the Democrat primary generally meant an automatic victory in the general election, but this was not a regular election. Black political leaders were to be subordinate lackeys to the White Irish leadership—and definitely not the boss. Powerful White members of the Democrat machine began to conspire to find ways to sidetrack Washington. Chicago's Mafia leaders pledged millions of dollars to the effort.

One plan was to have Epton replaced by the defeated Mayor Byrne. This author was involved in communications between Byrne and the Republican National Committee. I had advised that mayor against the plan and told her that President Reagan would never approve it. At Byrnes request, I agreed to communicate the offer to the White House through Frank J. Fahrenkopf, the chairman of the Republican National Committee. President Reagan's response was swift and certain. According to reports, the president emphatically ordered that, "Neither the White House nor the Republican Party will be drawn into a scheme to deny a Black candidate access to public office by shenanigan." With the Republican option off the table, Byrne suggested a write-in campaign, but she could not get the Daley faction on board with that plan for obvious reasons.

With few other choices, Chicago's most powerful White Democrat leaders, including County Assessor Tom Hynes, Alderman Ed "Fast Eddie" Vrdolyak, Alderman and Council Finance Chairman Eddie Burke, congressional Ways and Means chairman Dan Rostenkowski, Congressman Bill Lipinski, and virtually every White public official, threw their support, overtly and covertly, to Epton, the Republican candidate.

The racial tension was palpable. The White Democrat precinct captains fought for the White vote with only one issue—keeping the "nigger" out of the mayor's office, as Democrat precinct workers openly said it. When Daly visited a Roman Catholic Church, the main door was vandalized with the words "Nigger die." There were death threats all around. Epton ceased most public campaigning in the final days for fear of physical harm—including from the White community that wanted him out of the race in favor of a stronger replacement to oppose Washington. There was even concern that if the mob could not buy Epton out, they may take him out by more traditional Mafia means.

Washington Wins

None of the desperate Democrat plans worked, and Washington was elected Chicago's first Black mayor. The impact of racism was evident in the results. In a city where the Republican candidates for mayor are lucky to reach double digits, Epton got 48 percent of the vote against 52 percent for Washington. Had Epton been a stronger candidate and a more skilled campaigner, the outcome could easily have been reversed.

Daley's challenge to Byrne impacted negatively on his political career for a short time. It was even conjectured whether he would never again be a leader in Chicago. Much of the White anger at the prospect of a Black mayor spilled over onto Daley. Had he not challenged incumbent Byrne, everything would have gone along traditional lines. So heated was the reaction that Daley was attacked in public—verbally and otherwise.

This incident was recalled in a 2010 article in *The New Yorker* by Evan Osnos:

> Daley was in a toy store with his son when a man accused him of splitting the white vote, and thus clearing the way for the election of a black mayor. They fought. "He is rolling around on the floor getting punched out by some guy," [brother] Bill Daley says, "and the guy's punching him, and his son Patrick's there screaming, 'Hit him, Dad!' A couple of old women were hitting the thug with their purses. So that was kind of a low point post-election."

Chicago Council Wars

Washington's election victory did not end the racial divide between him and the White-controlled city council. Chicago has a strong council/weak Mayor system that the machine bosses had been able to turn upside down. With Washington in the mayor's office, the council began to flex its muscle. The opposition to Washington, including virtually everyone associated with the Democrat machine, created a time of constant racial turbulence in the Windy City.

The majority White machine alderman formed an opposition bloc under the leadership of Alderman Vrdolyak, resulting in what became popularly known as Council Wars. Washington's opposition were known as the "Vrydolyak 29" representing twenty-nine of the most loyal machine aldermen in the fifty-member city council. For the next four years, virtually every policy decision was made against a backdrop of race and antagonism against the Windy City's first Black mayor.

Election of 1984

For the Democrats, the election of 1984 was not so much about who could defeat Reagan but if *anyone* could defeat Reagan. Two of the major issues that brought Carter down, the hostages in Iran and runaway inflation, had both been resolved during Reagan's first term. Where Carter had shown weakness and indecision in foreign affairs, Reagan projected strength and certainty. Race relations were still an issue, but America had gone for four years without serious racial unrest. With President Reagan and Vice President George H. W. Bush riding an enormous wave of popularity, the National Republican Convention was more of a coronation.

The Democrats nominated former Minnesota senator Walter Mondale, who had been vice president in the Carter administration. Facing the popular Republican team, Mondale decided that his only chance was to create an unprecedented dynamic by selecting a running mate who was not the traditional White male southerner. Texas senator Lloyd Bentsen was the choice of the powerful southern wing of the Democratic Party. It was not to be.

In an effort to break with tradition, Mondale considered the Hispanic mayor of San Antonio, Texas Henry Cisneros, the Black mayor of Los Angeles Tom Bradley and the Jewish female San Francisco mayor Dianne Feinstein. He finally settled on New York congresswoman Geraldine Ferraro.

Ferraro spent most of her legislative efforts on women's issues. She was not among the strongest supporters of civil rights and voted in favor of a constitutional amendment that would have abolished school busing to achieve racial balance.

Jesse Jackson

Civil rights activist Jesse Jackson entered the race. He posed no threat to Mondale's nomination and came in a distant third in the balloting at the Democratic National Convention. He did gain a great deal of attention as the first Black to make what was said to be the "first serious presidential candidacy by an African American"—although other Blacks had officially entered Democrat primaries in the past.

Jackson had risen to national prominence initially on his bold misrepresentation of his relationship to Martin Luther King and his controversial "bloody shirt" press conference following King's assassination. His propensity to show up at every civil rights event garnered him a favorable following with the American press corps. But to be a player in the Democratic Party, Jackson had to take up the false civil rights narratives of the Democratic Party. And he did so with enthusiasm.

With large Black populations in Virginia, South Carolina, Louisiana, and Mississippi, and a number of White candidates dividing up the vote, Jackson won Democrat primaries in those states. Across the nation, Jackson won an impressive 21 percent of the Democrat vote, but garnered only eight percent of the delegates at the National Convention—a fact that suggested the Democrat's nominating system was rigged against minority candidates. His showing, however, led the Democratic Party to embrace Jackson as the Party's unofficial representative to Black America—a position he held until Barack Obama literally gave that role to the even more controversial Black activist, Al Sharpton.

The Platforms

The Republican platform directly addressed the issue of Democrat policies that maintain the status quo in the Black inner cities:

> For far too long, the poor have been *trapped by the policies of the Democratic Party* which treat those in the ghetto as if their interests were somehow different from our own. That is unfair to us all and an insult to the needy. Their goals are ours; their aspirations we share. (emphasis added)

Realizing that any hope of success depended on undermining Reagan's popularity, the Democratic platform was an unusual ad hominem attack on Reagan personally. One heading, "The Future if Reagan is Reelected" used anecdotal testimony from Democrat platform hearings to castigate the president. The next major section was entitled "The New Economic Reality: Five Reagan Myths," followed by "Reagan's Recession and a Recovery Built on Debt."

The Democratic Party platform continued its traditional empty lip service dedication to civil rights even as institutional *de facto* segregation and oppression prevailed under Democrat administrations in most of America's major cities.

The Mohammad Ali Endorsement

Boxing legend Mohammad Ali had supported Jesse Jackson in the primaries. Ali said he would have endorsed a Black candidate had there been one in the general election. Instead, he shocked the political and the sports worlds when he endorsed Ronald Reagan. He was not the first Black athlete to line up behind Reagan. Fellow boxers Floyd Patterson and Joe Frazier endorsed Reagan. Given his activist background and high visibility, Ali's endorsement got the most attention.

In fact, Ali was subjected to vicious attacks and innuendoes. Because he had been diagnosed with Parkinson Disease just prior to the endorsement, Democrats and civil rights leaders blamed Ali's mental condition though there was no evidence of any diminished capacity at the time. It was a cruel and ruthless political tactic by former friends and political allies.

In a 2016 obituary feature, Leah Wright Rigueur of *The Washington Post* wrote of this shameless criticism of Ali over the Reagan endorsement:

> The New York Amsterdam News reported that in Los Angeles, people were beginning to conclude that the "former heavyweight champ is losing his mental marbles," while syndicated columnist Carl Rowan asked, 'Is this evidence enough that brain-brutal boxing must be banned.' Jesse Jackson argued that Parkinson's was to blame. "He's not thinking very fast these days. He's a little punch drunk."

Upon Ali's death more than thirty years later, and debilitated by the Parkinson, Jackson and others would eulogize the former boxing champion for his contributions to society, praising how his physical debility had not affected his fine mind, contrary to what they said in 1984.

The popularity of the Reagan-Bush team was unchallengeable. The GOP went on to the most lopsided victory in American history. Mondale only won his home state of Minnesota and the District of Columbia. Ferraro not only did not win her home state of New York, but she failed to win the expected support of the majority of women voters. Mondale was further hurt by less than enthusiastic support from Black leaders.

Philadelphia Bombs Itself

Philadelphia, a city that had not had a Republican mayor in more than sixty years, was the scene of one of America's most bizarre and tragic racial incidents. In 1985, Democrat machine Mayor Wilson Goode was serving as the first Black mayor of Philadelphia.

By 1985, members of the militant Black liberation organization MOVE had taken up occupancy in a row house in West Philadelphia. Neighbors complained that members of the group would use a bullhorn to broadcast messages to the community—although the bullhorn had been broken for three weeks prior to the incident.

On May 13, Mothers' Day, Goode ordered police to evict the group, which he had declared to be a terrorist organization. When the residents resisted, Police Commissioner Gregore J. Sambor ordered that the house be bombed. Using a Pennsylvania state police helicopter, Philadelphia police officers dropped two firebombs on the roof of the building.

As the fire began to burn, city firefighters already on the scene were told to stand down. The fire soon raged out of control. Before it was put out, the fire had consumed approximately sixty-five homes, killed eleven people (including John Africa and five children) and left more than 250 people homeless.

A subsequent civil suit resulted in the city paying $1.5 million to the sole MOVE survivor of the fire and to heirs of some of the victims. The jury determined that Mayor Goode's Democrat administration and the police department had used excessive force and violated the US Constitution's protection against "unreasonable search and seizure."

Sambor resigned over the incident, but no one faced criminal charges or government discipline. Mayor Goode would go on to win the nomination of the Democratic Party and was subsequently reelected. For a time, Philadelphia became known as the "city that bombed itself."

Black Democrat Backs Republican

Alphonso Michael "Mike" Espy, a Democrat, was the first Black to be sent to Congress from Mississippi since Reconstruction. He had served as the state's attorney general before being elected to Congress. He would later serve as secretary of agriculture under President Clinton.

Espy was a champion of civil rights as was his father. The senior Espy was founder of the Afro-American Sons and Daughters that operated a hospital for Blacks for fifty years, starting in the 1920s.

Giving further evidence that the rise of the GOP in the south was not the result of pandering to racist elements, Espy joined a number of prominent Democrats in supporting Republican Haley Barbour for governor. In making his endorsement, Espy said:

> We have to do what's best for Mississippi. In this case it has to be the person above the party, so I'm stepping outside partisan boundaries, and I'm telling you I really intend to vote for Haley Barbour for governor.

Barbour would go on to be only the second Republican governor of Mississippi since 1876.

Chicago's Council Wars End

After four years of race-based "Council Wars" between Chicago's first Black mayor and the White-controlled city council, mayor Harold Washington was up for reelection—and the Democrat machine's White old guard saw yet another opportunity to wrest back control.

There were two attempts. Former mayor Jane Byrne entered the Democratic primary in opposition to Washington. Alderman "Fast Eddie"

Vrdolyak, who had been the point man of the White opposition in the city council, grabbed the banner of the inactive Solidarity Party. The Republican nomination went to Northwestern University Professor Donald Haider.

Washington beat Byrne 54 to 46 percent in the primary, and he went on to beat Vrdolyak 55 to 42 percent in the general election. For Haider, the value of the Republican nomination returned to its traditional level. He garnered less than 4 percent of the vote.

Although the White Democrat leadership remained solid in their determination to return to power, and the voters again cleaved largely on racial lines, Washington had gained some support from White voters—both Republican and Democrat. He also gained some respectability with the business leaders.

Having won a second term, much of the steam came out of the movement to fight against Washington. It appears that even the Council Wars were coming to an end. In just a few short months, however, an ailing heart accomplished what all the political scheming of the past four years could not. In November of 1987, Washington suffered a massive fatal heart attack while conducting business at his desk. His death triggered yet another series of racially motivated maneuvers by the machine operatives to restore White control of the mayor's office.

Upon the death of Washington, city clerk David Orr, temporarily became the acting mayor, but he was never intended to be permanent. Instead, the majority of the city council, being White, wanted to select the mayor from among their group. The Black aldermen protested vigorously and threatened city-wide protests if Washington was not replaced by a Black. Rather than face serious unrest in the city, the majority selected an easy-going Black machine loyalist, Eugene Sawyer, to fill out the remainder of Washington's term. It was not intended for Sawyer to run for reelection, again paving the way for the return of a White mayor

The soft-spoken Sawyer turned out to be a popular mayor across party and racial lines. But he was no match for the determination to restore a White mayor as the "boss" of the historic Chicago political machine. The candidate-in-waiting was Richard M. Daley, son of Richard J., "Da Boss."

Reverend Harold Bailey

Harold Bailey was a Chicago Black minister who had founded and was president of Probation Challenge, an organization that worked to lower recidivism rates among predominantly minority ex-convicts. His success in reducing recidivism won him wide acclaim from many admirers and supporters—and the enmity of the Chicago Democrat machine in City Hall. Bailey won innumerable awards and recognitions, including the prestigious Nelson Mandela Award.

Bailey's Probation Challenge relied on education and jobs as a core service in preventing a return to prison. In an editorial about what he has dubbed a racist "criminal 'just us' system," Bailey said:

> Enough is enough and too much stinks! The suffering taxpayer has a right to know that behind the deviate smiles of particular politicians, rest a diabolical scheme to allow some Chicago Public schools to close so that youth could accommodate the many jails and prisons. According to the unspoken plan which is really simple. With an absence of dollars to educate, students will dropout, then they drop into the criminal "just-us" system. Chicago public school students at the suggestion of some sitting on the Chicago 5th Floor [the mayor's office], are haggling that funds not be found and that some students become candidates for the criminal "just-us" system. Chicago residents ought to be apprised that political hypocrites in Chicago and Springfield, know about schemes to hurt and deprive citizens 10 to 20-years ahead of target dates. However, there is secrecy and honor among some considered thieves.

While Bailey does not make a specific reference to the political affiliation of those he considers culpable, his reference to the mayor's office leaves no doubt. The Democratic Party racist policies are responsible for both the failing education system and the excessive incarceration of minorities trapped in the segregated communities.

In his long association with all aspects of the criminal justice system, Bailey alluded to the reality that under long time Democrat leadership, there have been no reforms—no changes. He said:

I also learned that the public should watch politicians … for most promised everything but guaranteed to give absolutely nothing after an election! And starting with the Cook County Department of Corrections, administrators often promised change—but I never saw it! It became evident that the criminal justice system was never to be a plus for African Americans nor Hispanics.

Like Booker T. Washington and Malcolm X before him, Bailey recognized the reality of Black leaders serving the interest of the racist political machines for their own benefit. In his editorial, Bailey spoke out to "encourage youth to know that the enemy is not always White—but also Black field Negros, both male and females."

Because of Bailey's success, it received support from key civic leaders. The influential City Club of Chicago took up the cause. Ralph Conner, the Black Republican Mayor of Maywood became an active supporter, saying:

> The African American community has been deluded into thinking that it's only important to be a Democrat because compassion has been defined by support for social programs that the Democrats generally support.

In referring to "social programs" supported by Democrats, Conner was talking about generational welfare.

With the support of prominent community leaders Bailey's Probation Challenge was becoming more successful—mostly because he was producing unprecedented drops in the recidivism rate from ex-felons going through his program.

Bailey rose to be chairman of the Cook County Board of Corrections. Probation Challenge was provided space and resources in the Chicago City Colleges—specifically at the Malcolm X campus. Bailey's organization was made an integral part of the corrections system by the Probation Challenge Act passed by the Illinois State Legislature and signed by Republican Governor James Thompson. The good times were not to last, however.

The Democrat Machine Moves Against Bailey

One of Bailey's most important supporters was Judge Eugene Pincham, a powerful and controversial Black justice willing to push back against the racist Democrat judicial system. In anticipation of Pincham's imminent death, City Colleges chancellor Wayne Watson, a Black appointee of Democrat Mayor Daley, illegally evicted Probation Challenge from the college campus. Bailey lamented that "This illegal eviction took place under the very eyes of the Illinois State Black Democrat Legislators with no pushback or reprisal."

Bailey sees the political action taken against him and Probation Challenge as a loss to the Black community in terms of education and criminal justice. He wrote that if the Black community] "learned, they would become aware that they were being used. Political Pay-Off for Education."

According to Bailey, denial of education and high incarceration rates in the inner city are policies maintained by the city's Democrat leadership for their political benefit. He stated:

> This trade-off between education and incarceration is particularly acute at the community level. In many urban neighborhoods where millions of dollars are spent to lock up residents, the education infrastructure is crippled. As the prison population skyrocketed in the past three decades, researchers began to notice that high concentrations of inmates were coming from a few select neighborhoods—primarily poor communities of color—in major cities. These were dubbed "million-dollar blocks" to reflect that spending on incarceration was the predominant public sector investment in these neighborhoods. NAACP research shows that matching zip codes to high rates of incarceration also reveals low-performing schools, as measured by math proficiency, tend to cluster.

This data is noteworthy because it establishes that a very high percentage of Black and Hispanic incarcerations across America are coming from urban centers exclusively controlled by the Democratic Party.

Like so many civil rights leaders before him, Bailey was subjected to threats and intimidations. According to Bailey:

Fighting injustice and speaking hard-core-educational-truth has caused me to have threats made against my life! My house was under police protection for a period of time and my automobile tampered with that could have caused an accident on the expressway as I was traveling to a planned corrections meeting.

Bailey is an example of how Democrat *de facto* racist policies impact on both the general population and those who fight for justice.

Forsyth County

Forsyth County and the city of Cumming, Georgia, came into national attention as yet another one of the infamous Democratic Party's strong-holds of virulent racial prejudice long after the civil rights legislation of the 1960s. Forsyth County might have been just another forgotten story of the tenacity and brutality of Democratic Party governance in the Old South had it not been for the events in 1987—and a remarkable episode of the *Oprah Winfrey Show*.

Following the Civil War, Forsyth County was just another horrific example of the Democratic Party's "redemption" of the old Confederacy. It took on new meaning in 1912 when Black men were accused of a series of rapes on White women. As a result, White "night riders" undertook a series of brutal attacks on innocent Black citizens. One of the accused was wounded by a gunshot and then dragged from the local jail and lynched from a telephone pole on the town square.

Allegedly to restore peace, Democrat Governor Joseph M. Brown declared martial law and sent in four companies of the state militia. The Black residents were forcibly and illegally evicted from their homes, leaving Cumming and Forsyth County an all-White community.

Brown was born in Cumming and has been closely tied to its infamous racist history. His father, Joseph E. Brown, had been the Confederate Democrat governor of Georgia during the Civil War.

Brown's devotion to "southern justice"—as well as his anti-Semitism—was revealed when he was one of the leaders of the Knights of Mary Phagan, named after a teenage girl who was raped and murdered. The killer was alleged to be a Jewish co-worker named Leo Frank. After Frank's execution was commuted to life in prison, Brown was quoted in the *Augusta Chronicle* rhetorically suggesting that "anybody except a Jew can be punished for a crime." Under Brown's leadership, the Knights took Frank from the local jail and lynched him from a tree branch facing Phagan's house. Though the lynch mob was composed of some well recognized prominent citizens, including Brown, no one was ever arrested or prosecuted.

For more than forty years after the Black residents of Cumming were forcefully evicted, the County remained relatively peaceful and all-White. That changed in the early 1950s when the Chattahoochee River was damned, creating Lake Lanier. The new recreational area soon attracted Blacks from Atlanta.

The Democrat leaders responded with all measures of warning and intimidation. Handbills and flyers advised wealthy White families to "leave the [colored] maid behind." Signs were posted that read: "Niggers, don't let the sun set on you in Forsyth County."

The intimidation was successful and under continuing Democrat rule, Forsyth County, including Cumming, remained a virtually all-White community for the next thirty-five years.

Cumming, Georgia (1987)

In 1987, Cumming, Georgia, was still all-White and all-Democrat— and deeply racist. This was nineteen years after Democrats claimed that the GOP had taken over the south with the support of the old racist vote as the result of a racist Nixon "southern strategy." The racist voters had not switched to the Republican Party. There was still a strong undercurrent of the old solid Democrat Dixie in many local communities in the former Confederate states.

Democrat Joe Frank Harris was elected Governor of Georgia in 1983. He would serve until 1991. His successors would also be Democrats until 2003 when Republican George E. "Sonny" Perdue was elected—thirty-five years after the promulgation of the southern strategy myth.

The Brotherhood March

In 1987, in an effort to bring integration to White Democrat Forsyth County, civil rights leaders from Atlanta organized the Brotherhood March. It was led by Reverend Hosea Williams and included comedian Dick Gregory.

The White crowd that gathered in opposition to the march were charged up by speeches from local Democrat officials and Klansmen, such as J. B. Stoner, who had been recently released from federal prison for bombing a Black church in 1958. He had served only three and a half years of a ten-year sentence. Stoner told the cheering crowd that "niggers bring crime and AIDS and we don't need crime and AIDS in Forsyth County."

The marchers' signs begging "Give Brotherhood a Chance" were met with signs reading "Sickle-Cell Anemia—the Great White Hope," alluding to a predominantly Black disease. According to one of the marchers, Robert Thompson, "They was throwing rocks before we even got off the bus. First they broke the windows, then they broke our heads."

The *New York Times* reported:

> When the marchers, most of them black, arrived on a bus from Atlanta, white onlookers began chanting, "Go home, niggers," and some pelted the marchers with stones, bottles and mud. Seventy-five officers from several agencies tried unsuccessfully to herd the whites away from the marchers.

Initially, the state militia formed a blockade between the three to four hundred segregationist residents and the biracial marchers. Racial insults continued to fly. Without resistance from the local militia, the White mob flowed through the ranks and descended on the marchers in a violent rampage.

After routing the marchers, Ku Klux Klan Grand Dragon David Holland said, "The Klan drove out Hosea Williams and his busload of race traitors" with only three or four broken windows as a result.

The Georgia Bureau of Investigation said that local law enforcement authorities had "lost control." County Sheriff Wesley C. Walraven blamed the violence on not being prepared for such a large crowd. Police arrested fifty-five rioters, including White supremacist David Duke.

David Duke Unwelcomed in Both Parties

Duke started his political career in Louisiana as a Klan Democrat. He would opportunistically switch parties in a number of campaigns for state and national office. In a three-way race, Duke would later get elected to one term in the Louisiana state senate as a Republican despite the endorsement of his opponent by President Reagan and Vice President Bush.

After several attempts for public office as a Democrat, Republican and third-party candidate, Duke made one last effort for a Louisiana Republican congressional seat. Representing the almost universal opinion of the Republican Party leadership, GOP National Chairman Jim Nicholas stated: "There's no room in the party of Lincoln for a Klansman like David Duke." Claiming he had always opposed Klan violence, Duke quit the group in 1980, saying he could not stop them from doing "stupid and violent things." In a real sense, it was Duke, not Nixon, who had a strategy to appeal to racist Democrat voters as a Republican. He was completely rejected by the Republican Party, however.

Duke's long ties to the segregationist leadership of Forsyth County was seen as early as 1975 when he ran for the Louisiana state senate as a Democrat. He was criticized for using the name and mailing list of the Georgia Forsyth County Defense League (FCDL) to raise money. The FCDL was one of the racist ancillaries to the local Democratic Party.

Democrat talking points have always pointed to David Duke as an example of Republican racism, even though he spent most of his political career as a Democrat. Democrats and the media hyped Duke's brief and unwelcomed participation in the Republican Party as a counterpoint to the literally thousands of racist Democrat officeholders and activists deploy institutional racism and racial violence against Black Americans in the south and the major American cities for decades after the mid-twentieth century civil rights acts.

The Second Brotherhood March

The segregationists' victory in Forsyth County was short lived. A national outrage prompted a second and larger march. This time between fifteen thousand and twenty thousand protestors assembled in Cumming. Several nationally prominent individuals participated, including comedian Dick Gregory, Jesse Jackson, Atlanta mayor Andrew Young, and Martin Luther King's widow Coretta Scott King. Curtis Sliwa and a group of his Guardian Angels volunteered to serve as a protection force. Fearing another outbreak of violence that would only draw further negative attention to Forsyth County, the various law enforcement agencies were in place to protect the marchers from the threatened violence of the Klan and other Democrat segregationist groups.

This time, the marchers succeeded in reaching the steps of the county courthouse where a number of speakers called for the removal of Forsyth County's and Cumming City's institutional racism.

The racist events in Forsyth County were not just the result of the local Democrat leadership. It was the result of benign neglect by Democrat state and national party officials.

Winfrey Arrives in Cumming

All the coverage Cumming, Georgia, received in the national media attracted the attention of television talk show hostess Oprah Winfrey. She traveled to Cumming to interview the White residents and hear their feelings about race.

Her decision to put White residents on the show offended Black civil rights advocates. Hosea Williams and six others were arrested for protesting Oprah's decision to feature only the White residents. Another unexpected outcome was the number of White residents who were more than willing to accept Black neighbors. Some of the most heated on-air confrontations were between the more tolerant residents and the White supremacist Klan faction of the community. That debate suggested that official Democrat leadership was more the cause of segregation and racism in Forsyth County than the people.

Howard Rosenberg, writing for the *Los Angeles Times* on February 16, 1987, said of Winfrey's broadcast that "It was an amazing show, a hellraising in the sun." He wrote:

Her stated purpose was to provide a forum for Forsyth Countians who felt unjustly maligned by the media. Yes, the show was self-serving, just as the news media always exploit the problems of others for a good story. Yes, Winfrey knew that showing her black celebrity face against a sea of Forsyth County whites promised blockbuster ratings. But that didn't invalidate the premise of the show.

The show had everything: spontaneity, drama, conflict, tension, peril, anger and honesty. Emotions were high and raw. Forsyth County's record of barring black residents is no fantasy. Yet the vast majority in the room preached racial harmony, and only a minority--only a handful of Klan, Nazis and other white supremacists present--spewed hatred.

Just picture Winfrey standing eye to eye with racists and not flinching: A bearded white bozo defines the status quo--accepting Negroes as 'blacks' and those who come there "causing trouble" as "niggers." Another white man, who can barely put two sentences together, tells Winfrey blacks lower the level of education.

She keeps her composure.

Then moderate whites attack the extremist whites. One white woman says that bigots are the real "niggers."

It would have been nice if someone had noted that good thoughts were not enough that any of these so-called moderates not fighting racism in their community were a party to racism.

As the Democrat South, Georgia and Forsyth County, lost its absolute power to a Republican resurgence, the cultures changed. In 2003, George "Sonny" Perdue became the first Republican governor of Georgia in 121 years. While Democrats claim that the Republican Party had inherited the racist vote, events prove otherwise. The change in the south under Republican governance was dramatic. Lynching ended. The Ku Klux Klan was decimated. Blacks registered and voted in record numbers. One might ask if the Republicans had, in fact, taken the racists votes from the Democrats, why didn't the horrific racial violence and racist policies remain under GOP governance?

Today, Forsyth County has joined the Twenty-First Century. In a 2011 article on the website of Atlanta's NBC affiliate WXIA-TV, reporter Keith Whitney wrote of Forsyth County:

> Once notorious for its Jim Crow heritage and complete absence of African American residents, the county has recreated its image and redirected its future, emerging as one of the wealthiest in the nation, and becoming more diverse along the way.

Arguably another example of the racial justice characterized by the rise of Republican leadership in Dixie.

Racism in the Big Apple

Like every other major Democrat city, New York has had longstanding systemic *de facto* racism. This was the subject of a major feature story in the *New York Times* on March 29, 1987, by staff writer Samuel G. Freedman. In his lead, he wrote:

> Despite some significant progress in race relations, most New Yorkers say important divisions between blacks and whites are now as wide as they were a decade ago, or wider.

> And there is a widespread perception that racial tension in the New York area has increased markedly in the last several months, according to interviews with dozens of residents and experts in the field and the findings of a poll by *The New York Times*.

As one example of the rise in racial tension, Freedman cited the December 1986 attack at Howard Beach in Queens in which a mob of Whites attacked and beat three Black men who were seeking help with a broken-down car. Michael Griffith of Trinidad was hit and killed by a car as he tried to escape. This was the third time a Black man had been killed by angry White mobs at Howard Beach in the 1980s. The first was Willie Turks in 1982 and then Yusuf Hawkins later in 1989. These White attacks on Black men in Howard Beach would continue into the twenty-first century.

Who Put Blacks in that PLACE?

While Freedman reported some unspecific improvement in education and workplace integration, he said those same interviewees found "that any real movement toward achieving equality has stalled and that in some critical ways the overall racial climate has worsened."

Freedman quoted Black professor Charlotte M. McPherson of the College of Staten Island as saying:

> In a city where you should see a melting pot, I definitely see polarization. The kinds of things that were being dealt with covertly are being dealt with overtly and, unfortunately, with violence. And I don't see anyone coming up with a rational solution. *They* are fixing a very deep surgical problem with Band-Aids. (emphasis added)

It is reasonable to assume that the "they" to which McPherson referred was the Democrat leadership of New York City.

As part of the investigation, the *Times* conducted a poll that found that that 64 percent of the respondents believed that that there has been no progress in race relations, or they are worse, than they were ten years previous.

Freedman reported that housing in New York was as segregated as it was in 1970. Similar analysis in the early 2000s suggests that segregation in the Big Apple is even worse than in the past.

The *Times* poll revealed the fact that Black crime was more likely to have a Black victim. In an issue on race and crime, the *Crime & Social Justice* journal documented the obvious—that both the perpetrators and the victims of Black crime come from the "super exploited sectors" of the community, which were described as the poor and unemployed. In other words, from the Black segregated ghettoes.

While the *Times* article went into depth about the problems and opinions of racism in New York City, it, like most media reports on racism, made no effort to identify the source of the problem. The policies and practices that have maintained institutional racism in America's largest city for generations were left unidentified. Rather than point the finger at the Democrat leadership, the common practice has been to blame the unrest, the violence and the crimes on the nature of Black citizens or something that just naturally happens.

What's in a Name?

To understand race and racism in America, it is important to understand who composes Black America. That question reached a milestone in 1988 when Jesse Jackson sought to resolve the issue of what Negroes should be called or call themselves, and what defines the American Negro. The official term of Negro had given way to "colored people." That term had been the acceptable designation for generations, and most notably enshrined as the name of the leading civil rights organization, the National Association for the Advancement of Colored People (NAACP).

Jackson was a leading advocate of changing the designation to "African American" as a means of creating a nationalistic identity for people who had lost their association with Africa over the course of hundreds of years. It was not a designation based on biology, ethnicity, or genetics. It was purely a cynical political designation to create an artificial distinction within the American public. It was divisive rather than unifying.

After hundreds of years since their ancestors were brought to the New World as slaves, most Blacks had lost even knowing their nation of origin—and they have most assuredly lost experience in the cultural issues of food, dance, religion and customs of Africa. Many who had Caribbean ancestry going back hundreds of years were suddenly African American in the United States.

In advancing his mostly inappropriate designation, Jackson also fostered the creation of a faux culture. As the movement progressed, Blacks donned dashikis, wore African beads, and let their hair go "natural." To further cement the new ethnic solidarity, the new holiday of Kwanzaa was created with nominal ties to Swahili East Africa even though the vast majority of Blacks descending from slaves have their roots in West Africa. There even evolved a "Black national anthem." But again, it was about politics not ethnicity or nationality.

This was not an unanticipated outcome. In making his declaration at a press conference, Jackson said, "It puts us in our proper historical context. . . . Every ethnic group in this country has a reference to some land base, some historical cultural base. African Americans have hit that level of cultural maturity."

In claiming to give geographical identity, Jackson was actually proposing an arbitrary political identity. The African American designation lacked logic and defied ancestry. If you come from the Middle East as an Arab, you are not an African American in America. Nor are you such if you are a White Afrikaner from South Africa. It also did not matter if you were half Caucasian, as is former President Obama, or even mostly Caucasian. African Americanism is defined by how one looks and consequently how one is socialized into the culture in the United States as a competitive demographic interest group. It was a means of keeping Blacks separated and in their PLACE. The designation thwarted America's most iconic feature, assimilation. It reversed that process and set up a new Black/White division to be used by politicians rising to power on the basis of competitive divisiveness.

People of Color

In the 1980s and 1990s, the African American designation would begin to evolve into an even more political and divisive designation, "people of color." The designation was to incorporate an imprecise array of nationalities and ethnicities whose only common bond is that they are not White Europeans. Theoretically, "people of color" includes sub-Saharan Africans, Arabs, Hispanics, Asians and almost anyone with darker skin than Snow White.

Within the people-of-color designation, there is no common culture. It arbitrarily declared cultures to be colored that are not. While all Hispanics are people of color in leftwing ideology, most Hispanics declare themselves to be White. The confusion has caused the United States Census Bureau to create a new designation of "White Latin."

The impact of the name changes cannot be overestimated. It widened the schism between Blacks, Hispanics, Asian, Native Americans, Arabs, and Whites that had been narrowing. It further reversed the process of assimilation—e pluribus unum. It led to the identity politics and political correctness that thrust America into political and interest group tribalism. It enabled the politics of victimization and complicated racial harmony well into the twenty-first century.

People of color have no common language. No common religion. No common food. No common music. No common traditional attire. Nothing that shows ancestry or nationality.

Jackson's purpose was to create a political based juxtaposed to White people. In doing so, he was one of the fathers of the tribalism that came to characterize political discourse in the twenty-first century. I may have been one of the least appreciated and yet most damaging political strategies to the cultural unity of the American people.

Election of 1988

In many ways, the election of 1988 was a referendum on the Reagan presidency. Reagan left office as one of the more popular presidents in American history. The economy was in good shape and America was a respected leader in international affairs.

Vice President George H. W. Bush was the logical choice to continue the so-called Reagan revolution. He was the unanimous choice of the convention delegates. For his running mate, Bush selected the young senator from Indiana, Dan Quayle.

To challenge Bush, the Democrats selected a little-known governor of Massachusetts, Michael Dukakis. He was credited with the state's economic recovery, labeled as the Massachusetts Miracle. Much of the recovery was based on Dukakis penchant for high taxes, earning his state the nickname Taxachusetts.

For vice president, the Democrats again reached into the south and selected Texas senator Lloyd Bentsen. Though generally viewed as a progressive legislator, Bentsen did not begin his career in Texas as a civil rights advocate. He initially was elected to the House in 1948 and quickly became a protégé of the powerful Speaker of the United States House of Representatives, Texas Democrat congressman Sam Rayburn—a staunch segregationist.

The Bush-Quayle team won an easy victory, carrying forty states and winning more than 53.4 percent of the popular vote. Bush was also the first incumbent vice president to win the presidency since Martin Van Buren in 1836.

George Herbert Walker Bush was very supportive of civil rights but is given mixed reviews because of his opposition to quotas. He believed that the goals were to bring about equal opportunity and not special privilege to cover up past Democratic Party racial injustices.

He was a civil rights advocate from his youngest days. While attending Yale, he headed up a project raising money for the United Negro College Fund. In writing his autobiography, Bush noted that "As county G.O.P. chairman, I'd place our party funds in a black-owned bank and opened a party office with a full-time staff near Texas Southern, one of the state's major black colleges."

In voting for the Fair Housing Act in 1968, he defended his action against Democrat critics by saying that "Somehow it seems fundamental that a man should not have a door slammed in his face because he is a Negro." As vice president, he was able to negotiate a deal with Congress which led to the passage of a stronger Fair Housing Bill.

According to a *New York Times*/CBS News poll at the onset of his reelection campaign, Bush's approval rating among Black voters reached as high as 70 percent.

Rise of Republican Colin Powell

Colin Powell was born in New York City's Harlem in 1934—a time in which its residents suffered from the strident racism of Tammany Hall and the growing involvement of the Mafia. His decision to join the City College of New York Reserve Officer Training Corps (ROTC) opened the pathway to his future success. He spent thirty-five years in the military rising to the rank of four-star general.

His ties to the Republican Party began in 1972 when he received a coveted White House Fellowship in the Nixon administration. During the Reagan administration, Powell was appointed as senior military advisory to secretary of defense Casper Weinberger. President Reagan later named Powell as his national security advisor. In 1989, the newly inaugurated George H. W. Bush elevated Powell to Chairman of the Joint Chiefs of Staff—a position that placed him over all branches of the armed services and reporting directly to the secretary of defense. Powell was the first Black to serve in all those positions.

Bush also promoted Powell to the rank of four-star general, making him only one of three men to achieve that rank since World War II—the other two being Dwight Eisenhower and Alexander Haig—and the only Black.

Powell carried over as chairman of the Joint Chiefs of Staff in the administration of President Bill Clinton, but he soon clashed over policy with the United States UN ambassador Madeleine Albright. There was an effort to award Powell a fifth star, making him general of the army, but the idea was rejected by the Clinton administration.

He would eventually be appointed as the first Black secretary of state by President George W. Bush

Support for Historically Black Colleges and Universities

Bush was a strong proponent of education, and especially Black education, in the tradition of several Republican Presidents described earlier. He understood the importance of quality education in enabling inner city students to escape poverty and welfare dependence by an education that can lead to career level jobs. Bush has been a lifelong contributor to the United Negro College Fund and the predominantly Black Morehouse College. Mrs. Bush has served on the Morehouse board of trustees.

Within three months of his inauguration, Bush issued Executive Order 12677. According to the Department of Education Office of Civil Rights the Order was issued to:

> … strengthen the capacity of HBCUs [Historically Black Colleges and Universities] to provide quality education and to increase their participation in federally sponsored programs. It mandates the taking of positive measures, by federal agencies, to increase the participation of HBCUs, their faculty and students, in federally sponsored programs. It also encourages the private sector to assist HBCUs.

New York's Racist Robert Moses

To his fans, Robert Moses, of New York, was one of the leading urban planners of his time. He was a favorite of the Democrat Tammany Hall organization that controlled the city. Moses held as many as twelve titles in organizations dealing with urban planning and development, including New York City Parks commissioner and chairman of the Long Island State Park Commission. At the height of the Great Depression, Moses was provided with funds from Roosevelt's New Deal Work Progress Administration and the Civilian Conservation Corps. With his control of millions of dollars without accountability to the taxpayers, Moses was essentially a czar over the growth of the Big Apple. His obsession was keeping Blacks in their PLACE.

Even during the Great Depression, Moses was a man who enjoyed the trappings of wealth. In addition to his own financial resources, he was occasionally criticized for his use of public money. He had neither an automobile nor a driver's license, preferring to travel daily by government provided chauffeur driven limousines.

For all his accomplishments and financial controversies, Moses was above all a racist—a fact that did not repulse New York City's Democrat leaders. His low regard for Blacks influenced many of his public works projects.

Journalist Daniel Kolitz wrote an article posted at the website *Hopes & Fears* called "The lingering effects of NYC's racist city planner." In it Kolitz wrote:

> New York City was famously shaped by the powerful urban planner Robert Moses who, along with being a visionary, was demonstrably racist. . . .
>
> The fair housing laws passed in the last half-century have forced racists to devise whole new methods of discrimination, subtler but serving the same purpose: to keep people of color out of "white" spaces. The villains in these cases—landlords, brokers and neighbors—are often tough to identify, but once exposed, are easy to loathe. It's harder to find fault with a sidewalk or a highway; when some feature of the city has seemingly always been there, you can lose sight of the fact that it was once new, conceived and constructed by people with

their own inbuilt prejudices. But a city's landscape can exclude as effectively as any policy or person, in subtle but sinister ways.

In his biography of Moses, *The Power Broker*, author Robert Caro wrote that "Moses had always displayed contempt for people he felt were considerably beneath him [and] considered African Americans inherently 'dirty'."

Lowering the Barrier

As an example, Caro described how Moses had kept the overpasses on the Long Island Parkway as low as seven feet so that buses could not travel the route. This essentially prevented Blacks, who largely relied on public transportation, to reach the *de facto* all-White beaches Moses developed. Moses planning kept Blacks in their PLACE.

Writing about Moses for the *Yale Law Journal*, University of Maine Law Professor Sarah Schindler wrote that "Moses was interested in maintaining these Long Island beaches as pristine places for the people he wanted to be there."

Of course, that meant White people. In addition to keeping Blacks segregated by urban planning, Moses' racism resulted in scores of needless accidents.

Moses placed the Robert F. Kennedy Bridge exit ramp in Harlem, clogging the already crowded Black community with heavy car traffic, rather than locating it in the more sensible wealthy and White Upper East Side.

According to Kolitz, Moses public works projects were kept distant from Black access. "Jacob Riis Park, Alley Pond and Riverside Park," wrote Kolitz, "as well as 255 of the 256 playgrounds he built in the 1930s were placed out of reach of the poor."

For the only pool that could serve Blacks, Moses ordered the water temperature to be kept "deliberately icy" because he believed that coming from warm ancestral nations Blacks would not swim in chilled water.

In an article on the online BoingBoing blog site, Cory Doctorow saw Moses and his policies as an example of the trend in American cities, that: "resemble a machine for stripping Black people of prosperity, dignity, and comfort, and reallocating their share of all three to whites, especially rich ones."

Doctorow did not -- but could have -- accurately reported that those cities to which he referred were long governed by racist Democrat political machines with pervasive policies based on systemic racism to keep Blacks in their PLACE.

Racism in Transportation

Brooklyn architect Daniel D'Oca has studied *de facto* racism and racial segregation in city planning. His blog, *The Arsenal of exclusion and Inclusion,* offers examples of how public projects are designed to directly and indirectly maintain a separation of Whites and Blacks in the urban environments. D'Oca poses the questions: "When we talk about public space, we ask questions like: Who gets to be where in a city? And what are the different tools that are used to exclude people from public space?"

D'Oca notes that in New York's affluent Rockaway neighborhood of Queens, which abuts on public beaches, street parking is very limited to discourage people from the predominantly Black east end from traveling to the beach. According to Jeanne DuPont, executive director of the Rockaway Waterfront Alliance (RWA), parking bans are one of several means of keeping racially undesirable east side residents away.

Another means of discouraging "visitors" is a lack of public amenities. The beaches of Rockaway lack public toilets and food concessions—which is not a problem for local residents. According to DuPont:

> There is no reason for someone to come to that beach and hang out—there's no bathroom there, there's no amenities, there's no food, there's nothing. But the people who live there are quite content with that.

Public transportation is also used to limit access to upscale White communities. The city's A train serving the area terminates at the edge of the upscale west end. The line only goes as far as 116th Street even though the west side neighborhood stretches all the way to 169th Street. Since many Blacks from the east side do not own cars, they have to find local transportation to get to the beaches.

It should be remembered that these subtle, but effective, means of maintaining *de facto* segregation are not exclusive to New York City. Nor do these examples represent the greater reality. They are, however, the historic and current means by which racist Democrat administrations in America's major cities operate.

Chicago's Racist Legacy Continued

The same year that Moses died in New York, Richard M. Daley, son of "Da Boss" Daley, finally succeeded in acquiring the Chicago mayor's office. He would continue the tradition of using urban planning to continue the Windy City's long tradition of confining the Black community to a PLACE where education and justice were unequal, housing was segregated, jobs were unavailable, and violence was iconic.

Following the death of Harold Washington, Chicago's first Black mayor, the city council was under pressure to select a Black successor. They picked Alderman Eugene Sawyer as a placeholder to fill out a little more than a year before a special election. The preferred candidate to eventually assume the office was the younger Daley. Sawyer decided to run for reelection and Daley challenged him in the Democrat primary.

As a longtime Democrat machine alderman, Sawyer failed to anticipate how much the White Democrat leadership, even longtime friends, would turn on him. The old machine still controlled the White precincts. Tens of thousands of Sawyer's brochures were distributed to the precinct captains only to be dumped in the trash—even after party workers were paid "walking around money." The literature was also dumped by a number of machine-loyal Black precinct captains.

To lock in the White vote, the Daley forces carried out one of the most overtly racist campaigns in the city's history—even by Chicago standards. Democrat precinct workers spread throughout the White neighborhoods with only one message—Chicago needed a White mayor. In a controversial recording that hit the news, Daley is allegedly to have specifically said that Chicago needed "a White mayor."

Daley won the Democrat primary and faced Democrat-turned-Republican mayoral candidate, Alderman Eddie Vrdolyak and Black Alderman Timothy Evans under the Harold Washington Party label.

Again, the Daley machine resorted to the most extreme racist tactics. Throughout the White precincts the message was "a vote for Vrdolyak is a for the nigger." They spread fear of Blacks moving into all-White neighborhoods. They claimed Blacks would spend all the taxpayers' money on welfare. Blacks cannot be trusted. They breed crime. They pointed to Detroit as an example of what will happen to Chicago under prolonged Black leadership. Of course, none of those things happened while Chicago had a Black mayor.

Daley's racist strategy worked. "Fast Eddie" Vrdolyak, received a humiliating 3.5 percent of the vote. Daley bested Evans 55 to 41 percent—almost perfectly cleaved on Chicago's racial fault line.

The old racist Chicago Democrat machine was back stronger than ever, and for decades the major Black population in Chicago would remain in its PLACE, segregated, impoverished, dependent on sustenance level generational welfare and subservient to the perceived benevolence of the Democratic Party. The only change for the Black community would be the inner city's increasingly dangerous and violent atmosphere.

Daley's Bold Plan—Segregation Walls

Though not as renowned, Chicago had city planners like New York's racist Robert Moses. Throughout the twenty-one-year reign of the senior Daley, the lines between Black and White neighborhoods were intangible but specific. Red-lined streets and avenues were the equivalent of walls. In later years, the walls became more physical. The city closed off streets, barricaded viaducts, and created cul-de-sacs as racial bulwarks to confine the Negro masses to their PLACE.

As late as 1993, under the son of Da Boss, the practice of walling off Black neighborhoods was still a matter of government policy. With crime rates reaching record highs, Daley claimed the closing off neighborhoods was a matter of crime control. Despite higher crime rates in Chicago's Little Italy Taylor Street neighborhood, no such barriers were ever proposed.

In an interview with the *Chicago Tribune,* Daley said:

On some streets you can go for 14 or 20 or 30 blocks. We have to change that. When you have those types of streets, there's where you have drive-by shootings, there's where you have the rapists. So, we're going to cul-de-sac the city—all the wards.

It is noteworthy that Daley would justify his policy of shutting down travel between Black and White neighborhoods on the old southern Democrat canard of rape.

Daley's plan was more ambitious than the occasional street barriers imposed in other cities, or even his father's barricades. Richard M. proposed the citywide creation of permanent cul-de-sacs that would isolate what he called high crime areas—which everyone understood to mean Black neighborhoods. In fact, the plan would add bricks and mortar to Chicago's long-standing policy of racial segregation.

Urbanologists claimed that it was the first time an urban administration proposed that an entire city be subdivided in this manner. While crime was the pretext in almost every case, the walls of segregation erected by Democrat regimes were clearly built to divide White and Black communities for several reasons, including the maintenance of school segregation, preventing social interchange, and to control political messaging. Public opposition prevented Daley from fully implementing his plan, however.

Seeing through the mayor's thin veneer in justifying his barriers, leaders in the Black community protested. Not surprisingly, they called it a throwback to the formal segregation in the old Democrat southland. Black community activist and radio talk show host Lutrelle "Lu" Palmer called the plan "frightening." He said, "The city will have control of people's movements from one area to another. It is oppressive and extremely dangerous. The whole rhythm of the neighborhoods, of the city, will be destroyed."

While people in White areas accepted it as a means to keep Black criminals out of their neighborhoods. Black leaders argued that the plan would only trap impoverished Black resident in conclaves of high crime—victimized by gangs and drug dealers—and where racially deployed police protection would be inadequate. Of course, that was the plan.

Black activist Nate Clay compared Daley's plan to the apartheid in South Africa, where areas were set aside for Blacks. He said, "It's nothing but Bantustans. It's a Chicago version of black homelands." And he added that

"Every neighborhood becomes a fortified bunker. It's an act of desperation. Daley is beginning to look like a failed version of his father."

As is often the case, Black politicians beholden to the Democrat machine supported the mayor. Alderman Ed Smith, who represented one of the Black wards, said, "I don't see it as drastic. I don't see this as an impetuous move. I see it as a move indicating that the administration is thinking."

This type of Black crony support for racist policies was similarly found in the eras of slavery and southern Jim Crow *de jure* segregation.

Black Crony Tokenism and the Silent Six

Blacks in positions of power in Chicago were put there by Daley and the Democrat machine. They served more like street bosses for the Party than partners in power. The technique was disturbingly like how the Mafia controlled Harlem. The practice of putting a few Blacks in positions of limited power was so widespread throughout the Democrat-controlled cities that it earned its own moniker, "tokenism."

Black leaders were in Daley's pocket. Since the 1930s, Black men like William Dawson maintained power as long as they kept their fellow Blacks confined to the ghetto and dependent on welfare—and voting Democrat.

So controlled were these so-called Black leaders that a group of Black Chicago alderman, known as the Silent Six, voted with Daley and against every open housing bill introduced in the city council. They were William Campbell, Robert Miller, William Harvey, Benjamin Lewis, Ralph Metcalf, and Claude Holman. For his subservience to the Democrat Machine, Metcalf would eventually become a congressman for the ghetto—as was William Dawson before him.

In Chicago you could be a Black leader if you followed orders from the White "boss" in city hall. To a large degree, this custom applied to Barack Obama. He saw himself as a "community organizer" but has no record of accomplishment for the Black community he organized. The same was true as a state senator and a United States senator. Many, including civil rights leaders, argue that his support of civil rights as president was mostly talk and symbolism without progress in alleviating the plight of impoverished and welfare dependent Blacks trapped in their historic PLACE of social, economic, political, and civic inferiority. Arguably, Obama can be viewed as the Democratic Party's Black crony system's greatest success.

Racism Beyond New York and Chicago

The concept of maintaining racial segregation by constructing physical barriers was not reserved to New York and Chicago. In fact, the practice went back to the slave era in the South. In more modern times such Democrat cities as Los Angeles, St. Louis, Baltimore, and Miami were among those sealing off minority neighborhoods in the name of crime prevention.

Democrat mayor Vincent C. Schoemehl of St. Louis began to block off Black neighborhoods in 1981 and by 1993 had cut off approximately 260 thoroughfares. The large cement sewer sections he used as barriers became known as Schoemehl Pots.

Early in the 1990s, White neighborhoods in Los Angeles were cut off from adjoining Black areas to create what residents ironically called "Isles of Peace" and "Islands of Tranquility."

The euphemistic Liberty City Wall in Miami was first constructed in 1930 to separate a new Black neighborhood from an existing White area.

The conjunction with the article about New York's Robert Moses, Daniel Kolitz' website *Hopes & Fears* offered a few examples of racist urban planning in other cities:

Palo Alto, California

Crossing Highway 101 to reach the wealthy West Palo Alto from low-income East Palo Alto is dangerous due to the presence of median barriers and the need to pass through numerous busy intersections; the area has one of the highest rates of car-pedestrian collisions. The lack of secure pedestrian infrastructure makes areas more difficult to access in a safe and easy manner.

Detroit, Michigan

In Detroit in 1940, a private developer constructed a six-foot-high wall—known as Eight Mile Wall—to separate an existing black neighborhood from a soon-to-be constructed white one. At the time, the Federal Housing Administration (FHA) provided financing for a new development project only if the neighborhood was sufficiently residential and racially segregated. In the case of the Eight Mile Wall, the FHA required its construction. The wall still exists today—and Detroit is the most racially segregated metropolitan area in the U.S.

Buffalo, New York

Sometimes transit will allow a person to get close to a given area, but not all the way there, leaving the rider in a dangerous situation. Cynthia Wiggins, a seventeen-year-old woman in Buffalo, was hit and killed by a dump truck while she was attempting to cross a seven-lane highway to get to the mall where she worked. The mall's owners had actively resisted requests to allow the bus that Wiggins rode from the inner city to stop on its property; rather, the bus stopped outside the mall on the other side of the large highway. Documents produced during a subsequent trial revealed that this transit citing decision was motivated at least in part by race or class bias; a local transport official wrote in an internal document that "[mall decision-makers] feel it will not bring in the type of people they want to come to the mall.

Baltimore, Maryland

An eight-foot tall, spiked fence was installed in 1998 around a public housing project in Hollander Ridge in Baltimore. Constructed by the local housing authority with funding from the Department of Housing and Urban Development (HUD), this fence blocked access to and through Rosedale, a mostly white neighborhood. Rosedale residents wanted the fence to keep out crime and keep their property values up, and "there was a not insubstantial vocal segment of Rosedale whose racist views were made readily apparent."

Atlanta, Georgia

Wealthy, mostly white residents of the northern Atlanta suburbs have vocally opposed efforts to expand the Metropolitan Atlanta Regional Transit Authority subway system into their neighborhoods for the reason that doing so would give people of color easy access to suburban communities. The lack of public-transit connections to areas north of the city makes it difficult for those who rely on transit—primarily the poor and people of color—to access job opportunities located in those suburbs.

These efforts to maintain segregation were all in cities under Democratic Party leadership for generations.

Black Diaspora

In addition to segregation, many cities have used major urban highway construction to totally displace minorities. Using the power of eminent domain to remove so-called blight has been a common practice since the creation of the interstate highway system.

While highway construction in rural and suburban areas was designed to minimize the impact on local residents and businesses, the political leadership in the largest cities intentionally planned construction to disproportionately impact on minority communities. Between 475,000 and 1 million households, with millions of family members, were displaced by federal highway projects, according to the United States Department of Transportation.

According to a 2021 article in the *Los Angeles Times*:

> The U.S. Interstate Highway System — built from the 1950s to the early 1990s — is one of the country's greatest public works achievements, but it came at an enormous social cost. More than 1 million people were forced from their homes, with many Black neighborhoods bulldozed and replaced with ribbons of asphalt and concrete.

Farrell Evans, in a September 21, 2023 (updated from 2021) article for the History Channel titled "How Interstate Highways Gutted Communities—and Reinforced Segregation" reported:

> The neighborhoods destroyed and families uprooted by highway projects were largely Black and poor, wrote New York University law professor Deborah N. Archer in her article "White Men's Roads Through Black Men's Homes: Advancing Racial Equity Through Highway Reconstruction." And that was by design, she noted. Policymakers and planners saw highway construction as a convenient way to raze neighborhoods considered undesirable or blighted. And they deployed the massive infrastructure elements—multi-lane roadbeds, concrete walls, ramps and overpasses—as tools of segregation, physical buffers to isolate communities of color.

Just as with the construction of physical barriers to isolate Black ghettoes, the racist Democrat machines that controlled the major cities used the planning and location both local and federal highway construction to maintain urban segregation.

More Riots

Los Angeles Erupts … Again

On March 3, 1991, nearly a quarter of a century after the Los Angeles race riots of 1965, 1967 and 1968 during the administration of Democrat Mayor Sam Yorty, racism and racial tension remained problem. The mayor at the time of the 1991 riot was Democrat Tom Bradley.

Rodney King was intoxicated when he led police on a high-speed chase. After being stopped, King continued to resist arrest. Three officers continued to pummel King, kicking him as he lay helpless on the ground as their superior officer stood by and observed. He later filed what was determined to be a false police report.

In one of the first cases of the new video age, the beating was captured by an amateur cameraman. All four officers were indicted and put on trial. Despite the evidence and testimony, an all-White jury acquitted the three officers and their supervisor.

The verdict enraged much of America, and especially the Black community in Los Angeles. Riots broke out. In less than twenty-four hours, hundreds of fires had been set, scores of people were injured, and twelve were dead. At the end of five days, the death toll had risen to fifty-five with more than two thousand injured. More than four thousand buildings had been destroyed by fire, and seven thousand people had been arrested. It was the worst civil unrest of the twentieth century up to that point. The rioting finally ended when Republican president George H. W. Bush sent in federal troops.

Following the Rodney King video and riots, an independent commission was convened to investigate the event and underlying causes. In a special to the *New York Times* headlined "Violence and Racism Are Routine in Los Angeles Police, Study Says," author Robert Reinhold reported that "the independent commission today issued a harsh indictment of the Los Angeles Police Department as an agency that has tolerated excessive force and overt racism among its officers."

Among the findings of the report were repetitive use of excessive force, persistent ignoring of written guidelines, falsified police reports, and on-air racist transmissions, like "sounds like monkey-slapping time." Even fellow Black police employees were subjected to racist insults and were "concentrated in the lower ranks of the police force." The report called the citizen control program "illusionary." At the time the report was issued, Democrats had ruled over Los Angeles—and its police department—for more than thirty years.

Washington Heights Riot

In July of 1992, New York police officer Michael O'Keefe shot and killed Jose Garcia. Rioting broke out as rumors spread that the officer had beaten and then shot an innocent Black man as he lay on the ground. That was far from the case. Garcia was a known gang member, drug dealer, and gun carrier. Still the rumor ignited racial tension that was constantly simmering close to the boiling point because of historic Black oppression.

According to reports in the *New York Times*, "bands of 50 to 100 people ran through a 40 square block area, overturning garbage cans, lighting fires and shouting 'Killer Cop' and 'Justice.'" Only one death was recorded. It involved a man being pursued over rooftops after being observed throwing bottles down on the crowd. He slipped and fell five stories to his death.

Office O'Keefe was never indicted as the rioters demanded. The Washington Heights riot was a test for Democrat David Dinkins, New York City's first Black mayor. According to the *Times:*

> The eruption represented the most serious outbreak of neighborhood violence to confront the Dinkins administration, which received high marks for keeping the calm in the wake of the recent riots in Los Angeles. Mayor David N. Dinkins paid a personal visit to the Washington Heights neighborhood around 5 P.M. yesterday in an attempt to ease tension, but less than three hours later trouble erupted.

The praise bestowed on Dinkins would not last.

Crown Heights Riots

According to a *New York Daily News* retrospective article in 2016 by Rich Schapiro, tensions between Jews and Blacks in New York City were rather intense at the time over "housing, city resources, political access to local community boards and alleged preferential treatment from police." It reached a flash point on August 19, 1991, when a car that was part of a motorcade for Rabbi Menachem Schneerson, Grand Rebbe of the Lubavitch Hasidic community, struck two Black children—killing seven-year-old Gavin Cato and injuring his cousin Angela Cato, also seven years old.

The three-car motorcade was led by 71st Precinct police vehicle—a courtesy afforded Schneerson on many of his travels. This alone created resentment among many in the Black community. It represented only one of many White privileges that characterized *de facto* racism in the Democrat city.

Outraged residents descended on the driver of the car and two other occupants and began to beat them. When police arrived, Black residents were working on the injured children. Soon after, a Hatzalah medical vehicle arrived. They are first responders that operate in large Jewish populations.

Police aided getting the driver into the ambulance and ordered the driver to the hospital. When the ambulance left without attending to the children the gathering crowd exploded into violence—throwing bottles, bricks, and any other available missile at the police.

Thirteen-year-old Joslin Glover was watching the scene when the rioting broke out. He later described the beginning of the rioting:

> They rushed this guy [the driver] off the scene. They were only focused on him. They did not care about the kids that were hit. That's what set the whole thing off. Everyone was angry. They started looting, breaking windows. It was chaos for days.

Rioting spread throughout the area, with gangs of Blacks and Jews preying on each other. Innocent individuals also were attacked. When Mayor Dinkins and Police Commissioner Lee Brown arrived on the scene, they were greeted with jeers and flying objects. Dinkins made a visit to the family home of the Cato children and was again jeered and pelted with bottles.

It was only on the third day of rioting that more than 1,800 police were dispatched and relative calm was restored. Dinkins had run for mayor as the one candidate who could heal the racial divide that had characterized the city for generations. In his one term, however, Dinkins did little to change the *de facto* racist culture that was deeply ingrained in the New York political and governmental structure. The Crown Heights riots was evidence of that.

And after a quarter of a century, the underpinnings of racial tension remained. According to Schapiro's 2016 *Daily News* article, racial tensions had subsided, but not disappeared, after a quarter of a century. He wrote:

> While the Hasidim and African American and Caribbean residents now share their space more comfortably, many of the old-time community leaders who helped broker the peace 25 years ago are still in the neighborhood doing the same work.

Riot of a Different Color

Two months after the Washington Heights riot and one month after the Crown Heights riot, New York City was the scene of yet another major outbreak of race-based violence. Writing for the Cato Institute in 2016, Nat and Nick Hentoff described the outbreak of violence:

> It was one of the biggest riots in New York City history. As many as 10,000 demonstrators blocked traffic in downtown Manhattan on Sept. 16, 1992. Reporters and innocent bystanders were violently assaulted by the mob as thousands of dollars in private property was destroyed in multiple acts of vandalism. The protesters stormed up the steps of City Hall, occupying the building. They then streamed onto the Brooklyn Bridge, where they blocked traffic in both directions, jumping on the cars of trapped, terrified motorists. Many of the protestors were carrying guns and openly drinking alcohol.

Despite the violence the uniformed police did little to stop the rioters. That was because they were nearly all White, off-duty NYPD officers.

The rioting began when the Patrolmen's Benevolent Association (PBA) called for a public demonstration against Mayor Dinkins for a number of grievances based on criticism of police misconduct. The *New York Times* specifically named the Washington Heights and Crown Heights riots as a reason more than ten thousand protestors took to the streets:

> The harsh emotional pitch reflected widespread anger among rank-and-file officers toward the Mayor for his handling of riots against the police in Washington Heights last July, his refusal to give them semiautomatic weapons and his appointment of an outside panel to investigate corruption.

Dinkins attempted to deflect responsibility from himself and from his acquiescence to the historic racism of the New York Democrat machine by saying the PBA's action was "bordering on hooliganism."

Gang Loitering in Chicago

Getting tough on crime in the early 1990s would lead Democrats to enact laws with enormous implications for Black and other minorities. In 1992, Chicago passed a so-called gang loitering law. Simply put, the law allowed police to disperse any two or more individuals standing on a street corner doing nothing more than talking if, in the opinion of the officer, one of the individuals was a criminal or discussing potentially criminal activities. The police could also arrest the individuals, exposing them to up to six months in jail and a $500 fine.

The law had two very serious problems. Opponents charged that the law was unconstitutional and violated a citizen's right of assembly. Given the racist culture of the Chicago Democrat machine, it was feared that the law would be applied only to minorities—Black, Hispanic, and Asian. In fact, that was the case.

Very quickly, the law became a model for other cities, but three years after its enactment, the law was declared unconstitutional by the United States Supreme Court. Because of the tenuous quality of the charges, a very high percentage of the cases were dismissed by judges. In the meantime, however, more than 89,000 dispersal orders were rendered and more than

42,000 people were arrested in Chicago alone—many being left with permanent felony arrest records.

While many minority individuals were repeatedly arrested, the law was rarely enforced with White citizens. Though the law was declared unconstitutional, the police and court records remained—leaving those improperly and unconstitutionally arrested with damaged reputations.

Election of 1992

Going into the election, the Republicans clearly had the advantage. George H. W. Bush was completing his first term as a popular president. The country was still enjoying the Reagan recovery. Internationally, the United States was respected worldwide. China had evolved into an economic partner and the Soviet Union was on the verge of crumbling. The re-nomination of both Bush and his vice president Dan Quayle was without opposition.

As was the case in 1976, the Democrats reached into the South to select a hitherto obscure governor—this time William Clinton of Arkansas. In many ways he was a stark contrast to Carter. The latter was a soft-spoken pious man while Clinton was brash and outspoken, and most definitely not pious. The campaign would be undermined by sex scandals and corruption.

Even more than Carter, Clinton was one of the new breed pro-civil rights Democrats. He was not necessarily a devotee of the party's false narrative of welfare as the new civil rights, however. One of Clinton's major moves was to work with Speaker Newt Gingrich and the Republican majority in the House of Representatives to reform the welfare system to get people back to work.

In a high-risk gamble, Clinton chose another southerner for his running mate—Tennessee senator Al Gore. Gore was another of the new breed southern officeholders but very much unlike Clinton in terms of his background. He came from wealth and privilege as the son of Democrat United States senator Albert Gore, Sr., a wealthy tobacco plantation owner and traditional southern racist.

The Democratic Party, and specifically Al Gore Jr., blatantly lied about the senior Al Gore as part of the party's ongoing effort to promote its false civil rights narrative. For most of his career in Congress, Gore Sr. was a staunch segregationist and aligned with the Democrat segregationist southern bloc. He was a signer of the Southern Manifesto, a participant in the Massive Resistance movement against school integration. He voted against the 1964 Civil Rights Act.

It was not just a matter of his vote. Gore Sr. was one of the most active anti-civil rights senators. He proposed an amendment that would have essentially nullified the 1964 Civil Rights Act. His amendment provided that federal funds could not be withheld for any school district even if they were in defiance of a court order to desegregate. Gore, Sr. also participated in the seventy-four-day filibuster in hopes of defeating the bill in the Senate.

The younger Al Gore would often say how his father was pleased that he attended regular schools with Black kids. It was a lie. In truth, Gore, Jr. attended exclusive private schools in Tennessee that rarely, if ever, had Black students.

In addressing the NAACP, the younger Gore made the preposterous claim that his father had lost his seat because of his support of civil rights. That was another outright lie. It is these types of historic distortions that reinforce the Democrat's greater false narrative of civil rights advocacy. Gore Sr. lost the election to Republican congressman Bill Brock because southern voters were moving away from the racist Democrats.

1992 Election Results

Clinton ran as what might be called a moderately progressive candidate. Though he was considered as a staunch supporter of civil rights, he did not entirely abandon his Dixie heritage. Much of the Clinton-Gore campaign material in the South featured the Confederate battle flag—occasionally emblazoned with the "Clinton-Gore" names.

Businessman Ross Perot, running as an independent, received 20 percent of the vote, pulling off one of the most successful independent presidential campaigns in American history. Many believe that Perot cost Bush the election since his vote came mostly from the incumbent president. However, a state-by-state analysis shows that the Perot vote would not likely have given Bush enough Electoral College votes to win the presidency.

William Jefferson Clinton (1993–2001)

Clinton was born William Jefferson Blythe. His father was William Jefferson Blythe Jr. who died in a car accident before Clinton was born. His mother, Virginia Dell Cassidy, then married Roger Clinton. Clinton described his stepfather as an alcoholic and violent abuser of the family. After the senior Clinton deserted the family, the future president was raised by his mother. Because of his impoverished upbringing and other elements of his youth, Clinton was described as America's first Black president by Toni Morrison, novelist and Princeton University professor.

With the inauguration of Clinton, and his campaign promise to create an administration that "looked like America," Black leaders had high hopes for a strong policy of civil rights advocacy from the White House.

Welfare Reform

Clinton came to office perceived as arguably the strongest pro-civil rights Democrat president in American history. He was not, however, a strong proponent of his party's false civil rights narrative of generational welfare dependency. He disappointed the progressive wing of the Democratic Party by joining with Republicans in reforming a welfare system that had failed to lift impoverished Blacks out of poverty for generations.

Clinton's approach to civil rights was more aligned with Nixon's affirmative action approach in that both wanted to put emphasis on job opportunities and upward mobility rather than welfare dependency. Working with Republican House Speaker Newt Gingrich, Clinton signed welfare reform legislation. The Personal Responsibility and Work Opportunity Reconciliation Act was designed to enable those trapped in poverty to gainful employment.

Those devoted to the Democrat strategy of ever-expanding generational welfare claimed it would cut the economic lifeline for millions of Americans. Statistics show that the legislation had the desired effect in reducing the welfare rolls. However, studies also showed that implementation of the program in the Democrat cities tended to be biased against Blacks who were disproportionately moved off welfare rolls while being denied access to jobs.

Clinton Crime Bills

With crime rates soaring across the country, Clinton and Congress were under pressure to act. Crime was particularly high in the urban segregated Black communities. By viewing the problem as some sort of natural condition of the Black community, the Democrat machines feed the racist narrative that Black people were just more inclined to be criminals. They had no incentive to point to the systemic racism and oppression as a contributing cause.

The Violent Crime Control and Law Enforcement Act of 1994 was the longest and most comprehensive crime bill in American history. It contained a federal assault weapons ban, expanded the federal death penalty, added new categories of crimes, established mandatory sentencing, provided for 100,000 federally funded policemen, and allotted billions for new prison construction. It also included a "three strikes" provision that mandated incarceration.

Statistics suggest that the bill did result in an overall reduction in crime. Ironically, the reduction may not have been as obvious in Black communities where Black offenders were arrested and incarcerated at record numbers. Some have argued that selective racist enforcement in the Democrat run cities put a disproportionate number of Black offenders behind bars—and with longer sentences than White counterparts. The bill became more controversial as the prisons became overcrowded, especially with minority offenders serving time for relatively minor crimes.

Prison studies showed that the vast majority of individuals incarcerated in overcrowded prisons were not only Black, but they were overwhelmingly arrested, tried and sentenced from Democrat-controlled cities in which systemic racism was a historic problem. The new PLACE for young Black men was prison.

Growing Problem of Mass Arrests

There were several reasons for the disproportionate imprisonment of inner-city Blacks. Statistics clearly show that there is a higher crime rate in impoverished and oppressed communities—one of the byproducts of racism. This, in and of itself, draws greater police involvement.

Comparative statistics, however, do reveal a significant racist underpinning. In terms of minor infractions, Blacks were more likely to be arrested while Whites are "given a pass" by police. Big city prosecutors were more likely to bring more charges or more serious charges against Blacks than similar offenses committed by Whites. Blacks were more likely to receive longer sentences. Blacks are far more likely to be mistreated during arrests and while in detention.

The problem with Clinton's crime bills was how they were handed in cities where long-term institutional racism was at play. The crime bills provided racists urban political machines with a new tool to oppress Blacks and other minorities. The Clinton crime bills greatly exacerbated the situation. Clinton would later express his regret for his signature legislation.

A key proponent in the passage of the crime bills was then-chairman of the Senate Judiciary Committee, Joe Biden. As a presidential candidate in 2020, Biden would downplay his key role in the passage of the Clinton crime bills that wrought such havoc on segregated Black citizens.

Black Opposition

Black Chicago congressman Gus Savage was an outspoken opponent of the federal legislation. In a November 1, 2015, online obituary to Savage, journalist Chinta Strausberg quoted the congressman's longtime chief of staff Louanne Peters recollection of the crime bills: "We knew then it was only designed to lock up people at the street level. It was written that way. The entire bill was designed to lock you up and to create a prison population."

Noting the effect of the bills, Peters said they "ended up sending hundreds of thousands of young men to prison." Most of those young men were Black and overwhelmingly arrested and sentenced by law enforcement agencies and courts controlled by urban Democrats. Some twenty years later, President Barack Obama would order the release of thousands of what he called "non-violent" prisoners—creating yet another controversy surrounding American law enforcement.

Legislation that Haunted Hillary Clinton

The crime bills her husband supported and she strongly endorsed in the 1990s became an issue in the 2016 presidential campaign when the Black activist group Black Lives Matter (BLM) confronted Hillary Clinton, the frontrunner at the time for the Democrat presidential nomination. They were especially offended not only by Mrs. Clinton's early support for the legislation but also of her description of young Black men as "the kinds of kids that are called super-predators." It was a term that had been applied to young Black men who were into drug dealing and extreme violence. She underscored her remark by saying, "No conscience, no empathy. We can talk about why they ended up that way, but first we have to bring them to heel."

In suggesting that "we can talk about why they ended up that way" at some indefinite later time, Clinton was revealing the long-standing Democrat strategy of deferring serious discussions about the causes of high crime rates in the Black ghettoes. In fact, the entire Democrat false narrative of racial advocacy is hinged on never discussing the root causes of the most obvious racism. It would become apparent that the Democratic Party continued to be the primary cause of the institutional *de facto* racism that was still keeping Blacks in their PLACE.

When confronted in the 2016 campaign by representatives of BLM, former President Bill Clinton defended his wife's initial remarks and the crime bill in general. He angrily retorted:

> You are defending the people who killed the lives you say matter. You are defending the people who caused young people to go out and take guns and kill other black people, including a 13-year-old girl.

In creating an allusion to the most heinous criminals, Clinton sidestepped the reality that tens of thousands of less serious Black offenders were doing major time—and that the disparity between Black and White sentencing for similar crimes was profound.

Judicial Appointments

One of the major demands from the civil rights community during the Clinton years was the appointment of more minority federal judges and judges who would be more activist in terms of civil rights. Instead, Clinton, not wanting to engage in controversy or offend his southern base, tended to appoint Democrat judges with little commitment to civil rights.

In the book *Judicial Nominations and Confirmations During the First Half of the Second Clinton Administration,* authors Elliot Mincberg and Tracy Hahn-Burkett wrote that Clinton's failure to provide strong support of the more activist judges caused an "erosion of the principle of judicial independence and the consequent degradation of the quality of justice delivered to the citizens of America." While the opinion of the authors must be judged by their philosophic viewpoint, it is fair to say that the Clinton appointments, along with his crime legislation, were factors in the subsequent judicial bias against Black defendants.

Apology for Slavery and Reparations

One of the issues that gained some momentum during the Clinton administration was the question of a national apology to Black Americans for the years of slavery. The issue of an apology naturally drifted into demands for reparations. It was another example of creating a symbolic issue, the value of which was giving the appearance of empathy while not confronting the basic problem of existing institutional racism. It was mostly advanced by Democrats as a means of continuing the false narrative of civil rights advocacy and pandering for the Black vote.

Many believed that a national apology and reparations were inappropriate since most White Americans were descendants of immigrants who arrived in America after slavery. Many Blacks in America were not the descendants of slaves. So, as the opposition argument went, why should those whose ancestors had nothing to do with slavery be part of an apology or payment to a great number of people who had no slave ancestors.

If Clinton wanted to make a symbolic apology, it would have been better to apologize on behalf of the Democratic Party as the primary defender of slavery, segregation, and the continued oppression of Black Americans. There were no slave owners to apologize to at the time of Clinton's proposal and no living slaves to whom to apologize. There were, however, many living racist Democrat officials to apologize to the many Blacks who suffered oppression and terror in the major segregated cities.

In a 1998 trip to Africa, Clinton did offer something of a personal apology on behalf of America for its role in the slave trade. It was not an official apology on behalf of the nation; however, it was as much criticized as it was applauded. In 2009, Congress passed a resolution apologizing for slavery but prevented the resolution from being a basis for reparations. Over the years, nine states passed apologetic resolutions—the latest being Delaware in 2016. It is not coincidental that Delaware resident Joe Biden was running for president at the time.

The Johnson Chesnut Whittaker Case

Over sixty years after Cadet Johnson Chesnut Whittaker was brutally assaulted at West Point and summarily court marshaled, and when it was claimed that he had faked his life-threatening wounds, Clinton exonerated him and posthumously commissioned him as a second lieutenant in the United States Army. While it was a positive action in terms of correcting an injustice in the historic record, it represented Clinton's and the Democratic Party's tendency toward symbolism over substance in terms of civil rights.

Black Loyalty to the Clintons

In many ways, Black loyalty to the Clintons is as imponderable as Black loyalty to the Democratic Party in general. Both are based on widely held misconceptions.

In looking back at the Clinton election, Black social activist and writer Michelle Alexander wrote in 2016 that Blacks were largely "trapped in racially segregated, jobless ghettos." She well recognized the plight of Blacks in urban ghettoes—although she, like so many others, failed to note which political party had long overseen those cities.

In analyzing Clinton's specific contributions to the impoverished Black community, Alexander posed and answered several questions challenging Black loyalty:

> What have the Clintons done to earn such devotion? Did they take extreme political risks to defend the rights of African Americans? Did they courageously stand up to right-wing demagoguery about black communities? Did they help usher in a new era of hope and prosperity for neighborhoods devastated by deindustrialization, globalization, and the disappearance of work? No. Quite the opposite.

Even in view of Alexander's palpable dislike of President Reagan, she accused Clinton of "ultimately doing more harm to black communities than Reagan ever did."

Alexander summarized Clinton's eight years in the Oval Office by saying that "the American economy rebounded. Democrats cheered. The Democratic Party had been saved. The Clintons won. Guess who lost?" The answer to Alexander's rhetorical question was obviously the Black community, especially those trapped in the urban Democrat political plantations.

By the time Clinton left office in 2001, the United States already had the highest percentage of incarceration of any nation in the world—superseding such oppressive rogue nations as China, Russia, North Korea, and Iran. In many states, Blacks represented up to 90 percent of prisoners, mostly incarcerated on drug-related charges.

While the disproportionate incarceration of Blacks has been an ongoing reality since the days of slavery, it spiked significantly under Clinton and since. Bryan Stevenson, founder of the Equal Justice Initiative, said "President Clinton's tenure was the worst."

It's Not Just Crime

Clinton developed and maintained a reputation for singularly producing a vibrant economy—so much so that in Hillary Clinton's campaign of 2016 she suggested putting her husband in charge of the economy. His reputation for economic growth was not without some justification, but it tends to disregard the fact that he inherited a basically sound growth economy from the

Reagan-Bush years, and many of the economic policies for which he is given credit originated in the Republican House of Representatives under Speaker Newt Gingrich.

In fact, from the perspective of the Black community, the unemployment statistics were subject to debate. While there was a claimed reduction in overall Black unemployment under Clinton, it was partially due to the mass incarceration. Prisoners are not officially unemployed. Among the younger generation, the picture was grimmer. Other than incarcerating more Blacks, Clinton did virtually nothing to challenge the segregation and *de facto* institutional racism of the big city powerful Democrat political machines.

In her writing, Alexander did what few political analysts do. She pointed the finger of culpability at the Democratic Party:

> As unemployment rates sank to historically low levels for white Americans in the 1990s, the jobless rate among black men in their 20s who didn't have a college degree rose to its highest level ever. . . .

> It's about whether the Democratic Party can finally reckon with what its policies have done to African American communities, and whether it can redeem itself and rightly earn the loyalty of black voters.

Ignoring Court Orders

Since the end of the Civil War, Democrat leaders had a pattern of ignoring civil rights laws and court rulings. On December 15, 1994, the Clinton administration was hit with a civil rights court order issued by California federal Judge David Kenyon. In *Fairchild v. Secretary of Labor Reich*, Kenyon ordered that 100 west coast shipping companies develop a plan to end discrimination against Blacks, Hispanics, women, and the disabled. Blacks were relegated to some of the lowest paying jobs—a category commonly known in the region as "nigger jobs." Clinton and his Labor secretary basically ignored the order and consequently no affirmative action plan was every produced by the shipping companies.

J. C. Watts

In 1995, a young Black Republican from Eufaula, Oklahoma entered the United States House of Representatives. He had first gained political attention when he was elected to the Oklahoma Corporation Commission—the first Black to win a statewide election in the western state so closely associated with the Confederacy. Four years later, the House Republicans elevated him to the chairmanship of the House Republican Conference—one of the key leadership positions. This represented the first time a Black American had served in one of the major leadership positions in Congress. Once again, it was the Republican Party breaking through the racial ceiling in Congress, not the Democrats.

Chicago's 1995 Mayoral Election

In 1995, Mayor Richard M. Daley was running for reelection. The Black former Illinois attorney general Roland Burris was running as an independent Democrat candidate in the general election. This author was running for the Republican nomination. Everything about the 1995 mayoral election had to do with racism—and making sure no Black candidate would win in the future.

Despite the general belief that Daley was unbeatable, polling numbers and voting analyses suggested the possibility of a repeat of the 1983 election in which the two White candidates divided the White vote, giving Harold Washington the winning plurality in the primary election. The Democrat machine faced the same possibility in the 1989 but used overt racism to keep the White vote from dividing.

It was calculated by political strategists that to keep Burris from becoming Chicago's third Black mayor, Daley had to keep the Republican candidate under 15 percent of the vote in the general election. According to Daley's internal polls, I would take up to 20 percent of the White vote. That would give Burris an odds-on chance to win a plurality in the general election. However, I lost the primary to a perennial candidate and a clown (literally), Ray Wardingley a.k.a. Spanky the Clown. But the result was not a natural outcome. Forty-two percent of the votes for mayor in the GOP primary never got counted. They simply dropped out of the system.

In true Chicago style, corruption can be openly discussed among "friends." Daley's top aide, Tom Clancey, told me the obvious. The mayor did not want to take any chances. The aide said:

> There was just no way that the mayor could allow you to be the Republican candidate. He did not want to debate you. We needed someone who could not possibly get past 10 percent in the general election. I know you understand.

Wardingley got an abysmal 2.8 percent of the vote in the General Election and Daley sailed to victory over his only serious opponent, Roland Burris. In yet another election cycle, the racist Chicago political machine maintained its White "boss."

After coasting to an easy reelection in 1995, Daley and his people traveled to the state capital to have the legislature change Chicago's election laws to a "nonpartisan" run-off system—meaning that there would be a run-off election between the candidates with the two highest vote count if no candidate received 50 percent or more of the vote total.

The change in the law was based on a belief that only White Democrat machine candidates would be elected mayor for the foreseeable future. There would be no more three-way races.

In a report in the *Chicago Sun-Times*, political writer Mark Brown referenced the real racist purpose for the change in the election law:

> It was a change the city's white Democratic political establishment had wanted since Harold Washington had taken advantage of a split-white vote in the 1983 primary to become Chicago's first African American mayor. Washington beat back the effort when he was alive, but after he died and his coalition splintered, a switch was just a matter of time.

As noted on the online *Encyclopedia of Chicago*:

> In 1995, the state legislated a major change, providing for election of Chicago's three citywide offices in a manner similar to the election of aldermen—a nonpartisan election with a run-off between

> the top two vote getters if no candidate wins a majority. *This system was suggested in the mid-1980s by local white politicians in reaction to the election by plurality of the city's first African American mayor, Harold Washington.* (emphasis added)

Chicago Tribune political reporter Tom Hardy and others in the press provided cover for Daley by repeatedly reporting that the mayor was "ambivalent" regarding the change in the law. In reporting Daley's "ambivalence," Hardy apparently forgot that he had previously reported Daley as among those "eager" to impose the nonpartisan election in the past for a very specific reason. According to Hardy's earlier report "In 1986, Daley endorsed a nonpartisan plan *advanced by white ethnic Democratic committeemen* eager to oust Harold Washington, Chicago's first black mayor" (emphasis added).

At the time of his alleged "ambivalence," Daley's campaign consultant (and future advisor to President Obama) David Axelrod was promoting the nonpartisan plan as "a good idea."

Axelrod, in defending the racist plan, advanced the preposterous contention that "in a situation where you have two candidates, and only two, you can't play factions politics." In fact, the plan was to ensure factional politics in which the much larger White voter population would ensure the defeat of any Black candidate.

No one understood the racial implications more than the Black community, and in his article, Hardy conceded that "some African American political activists have strongly criticized it"—an understatement to say the least. The Harold Washington Party spokesman, Bruce Crosby, called the law a "conspiracy to thwart African American mayoral aspirations."

Impact of Poor-Quality Education

Of all the elements of institutional *de facto* racism, none is more damaging and immoral than the unwillingness to provide millions of young Black students with a quality education that can lead to college and career level employment.

Lack of proper education leads to unemployment and poverty, which leads to substandard housing and crime. It restricts social and economic upward mobility. It imposes the reliance on generational welfare dependence. It keeps Blacks in that PLACE.

The racism becomes obvious when you compare schools in the segregated communities to the education provided in the predominantly White schools in the same school systems. No difference in union representation. No difference in curriculum. Both schools are governed by the same school board and the same municipal administrations. And yet funding and outcomes are remarkably different.

Martin Luther King drew attention to the race-based difference when he wrote:

> Statistical evidenced revealed that in 1964 Chicago spend an average
> of $366 a year per pupil in predominantly white schools … but the
> Negro neighborhoods received only $266 per year per pupil.

In 2019, more than fifty years later, a report by Reardon, Weathers, Fahle, Jang, and Kalogrides noted that "White students score an average of 1.5 to 2 grade levels higher than black students in the average district."

The use of racist funding had its antecedents in the Democrat Old South where *de jure* racism was in play. In 1920, the NAACP reviewed the allocation of money between White and Black segregated schools. Black schools were receiving $4.59 per pupil while White schools were receiving $36.29 per pupil.

In later years, there was a shift in favor of minority schools. In 2018 in New York City, the average spending in Black schools was $28,808 per pupil and $24,173 for White pupils. In Chicago, it was $16,226 for Black students and $14,771 for White students.

This did not change educational outcomes, however. Regardless of funding increases, the achievement levels in the Black segregated schools remained significantly lower than White schools in the same school system. That points directly to institutional racism as the primary reason—not money.

Per-pupil funding is not a complete picture. It often applies only to students in class each day. A more serious problem with education in segregated schools is the drop-out rate. There are two ways to ascertain it. Most school boards prefer to publish the drop-out rate per year. A more meaningful analysis is the drop-out rate for students who never complete school.

At the time this author served as a consultant to the Chicago and Detroit boards of education, the official annual dropout rate among Black students was said to be approximal 8 percent per year. In reality, more than 50 percent of Black students who started in the segregated public schools did not achieve a high school diploma. They dropped out along the way.

Another evidence of racial prejudice as a systemic problem was a 2011 study by Reardon, Weathers, Fahle, Jang, and Kalogrides. It analyzed the performance of White students in predominantly Black schools. Their achievement level was as poor as the Black students. That means it was an institutional problem, not a difference between White and Black intellectual abilities, as the folks in city halls often contend.

In the mid-1990s, a new term entered the lexicon to re-label the academic experience of inner-city Black students. "Warehousing" basically is the act of storing student bodies in a school building in which there is poor quality education.

Without basic education, Black students are so ill-prepared for anything but unskilled labor that major corporations have had to undertake intensified remedial training just to find sufficient workers. Ronald J. Gidwitz, the former chief executive officer for the Helene Curtis cosmetics company, said that his company had to set up a high school level training program to enhance the job skills of Black public high school graduates before they could enter into his company's work force.

In an October 8, 2014, editorial, the *Los Angeles Times* succinctly defined the problem: "Too often, students spend weeks pleading for access to classes they need to graduate or apply to college. Many are assigned to multiple periods of empty class time every day."

According to the editorial, the situation was sufficiently serious to warrant legal action:

> The American Civil Liberties Union, Public Counsel and others are suing California on behalf of students, claiming that the state must do whatever it takes to stop *warehousing them in non-instructional, content-free classes.* The lawsuit cited as examples seven schools in four districts, including two in Los Angeles Unified." (emphasis added)

New York City's PS 106

Referring to New York City's PS 106 as the "school of no," a 2014 *New York Post* feature by Susan Edelman gave an intimate look at a school that is not atypical of Black education in many inner cities. It stated that: "five months into the school year, PS 106 classes still don't have the books or teacher's guides." Edelman went on to note that:

- The 234 kids get no gym or art classes.
- The school nurse has no office equipped with a sink, refrigerator or cot.
- The library is a mess: "Nothing's in order," said a source. "It's a junk room."
- No substitutes are hired when a teacher is absent — students are divvied up among other classes.
- A classroom that includes learning-disabled kids doesn't have the required special-ed co-teacher.
- About 40 kindergartners have no room in the three-story brick building. They sit all day in dilapidated trailers that reek of "animal urine," a parent said; rats and squirrels noisily scamper in the walls and ceiling.
- With no phys-ed or art classes, students are left to watch movies, including "Alvin and the Chipmunks" and "Fat Albert."

The *Post* article also brought up the question of funding at the macro level. Where have all those trillions of dollars spent by Washington in its never-ending war on poverty? In the case of PS 106, Edelman wrote:

PS 106 is allocated $2.9 million to serve a low-income population with 98 percent of its students eligible for free lunches. As a Title 1 school, it gets extra federal funds, but community members say they've never seen a budget tracking the income and spending.

Since warehousing students is a phenomenon in segregated urban minority schools, it clearly reflects administrative racism that comes down from the Democrats controlling most of the large urban city halls.

Social Promotion

The concept of "social promotion" had its roots in progressive ideology. In an article titled "Repeating a Grade: Pros and Cons" education writer Amanda Morin defined it as:

> "The practice of promoting a student to the next grade after the current school year, regardless of when or whether they didn't learn the necessary materials or are often absent, in order to keep them with their peers by age, that being the intended social grouping. It is sometimes referred to as promotion based on seat time, or the amount of time the child spent sitting in school.

Under a specious theory that holding students back damages their self-esteem and potential more than providing education, the urban minority school systems merely moved students up and out regardless of educational achievement. Social promotion is a euphemism that attempts to cast a more positive light on the policy of keeping Black kids uneducated.

As inner-city school quality declined, the use of social promotions increased. New York City eliminated social promotions in favor of the more traditional grade repetition system in 1999. It was reinstated, however, when the number of students being held back exceeded 100,000—creating issues of cost, overcrowding and discipline. The unanswered question is why 100,000 mostly Black students did not get a proper education.

The re-imposition of social promotion may have solved a number of administrative issues, but it institutionalized the racism of poor-quality education for the most disadvantaged in society. It harkens back to the Old South's separate but (un)equal education. Urban segregation and systemic racism results in substandard education for Black students.

De Facto Social Promotion

Social promotion is not just a matter of policy. It is often a matter of practice. In 1997, the American Federation of Teachers conducted a study of social promotion. It showed that eighty-five of the large urban school districts do not officially endorse the concept. The study pointed out, however, that even though social promotion is not officially endorsed in these districts, more than half the teachers surveyed indicated that they had promoted unprepared students the previous year. Reasons given for these social promotions were fear that high failure rates would reflect poorly on the school and school personnel, pressure exerted by principals and parents to promote unready students, knowledge that retention is ineffective, and the absence or *insufficiency of effective educational alternatives to social promotion.* (emphasis added)

The most damning admission is that school officials see no "effective educational alternatives." In other words, educating Black students was not a viable option.

Progressive Racism Repackaged

For more than a century, American progressives have advanced proposals ostensibly to help society that actually were based on a belief, stated or implied, in an innate inferiority of Blacks.

Progressive educators introduced concepts alleged to help Black achievement that, in reality, maintained the Black community as an underachieving underclass. As an overarching concept, the programs were all designed to lower the standards of achievement for Blacks—implying that Blacks were incapable of performing intellectually at the same level as Whites. It was nothing less than an updated version of the Democrats long racist claims of Negro laziness, immorality and ignorance. And just as with the old policies, the new concepts essentially served to keep Blacks in a PLACE apart from the White community—physically and socially. They served to maintain two separate cultures in America.

Ebonics

While the affirmative action programs were a double-edged sword, providing special access to upward mobility because of the disadvantages of early life racism under various Democrat regimes, the new concepts tended to imply inferiority without any advantage to those targeted. Among the most obvious was the suggestion that Blacks should be taught "in their own language," which was called *Ebonics*. Many linguists who studied the Negro dialect referred to it as African American Vernacular English (AAVE). Though coined in the 1960s, the term *Ebonics* did not come to the attention of the general public until the mid-1990s.

Proponents of the idea argued that teaching Blacks in essentially street slang was no different than educating foreign students in their native tongue. Rather than no difference, there was no comparison. Improper use of the English language is not a "native tongue." With foreign born youngsters, the goal was to have them fluent in the proper use of both languages. While Ebonics can be normalized and graded within the closed academic community, the improper use of the English language only hindered Blacks operating in the real world. In many ways, it was a mark of inferior education as evident as the physical branding that was applied to mark slaves. Ebonics is actually a means of keeping Blacks segregated, uneducated, and incapable of competing in the job market.

In 1996, in the Democrat city of Oakland, California, the board of education passed a resolution recognizing Ebonics as an official language to be studied as part of the core curriculum. An immediate national controversy ensued. In response to widespread condemnation, the board claimed it would help Black students transition from the dialect to proper English.

A phrase in the Oakland resolution that harkened back to the eugenics controversies was the claim that the dialect was "genetically based"—suggesting that there was some biological inability by Blacks to learn proper English. Throughout most of American history, the reliance on Black dialect in posters, stage plays and movies was a means of suggesting ignorance on the part of Blacks. The use of the Black vernacular in comedy and entertainment was considered mocking.

Critics charged that in legitimizing it as an urban language, it would make it more difficult for Blacks competing for jobs. The proposal to normalize the slang brought together Republicans and prominent Blacks in opposition, including Republican secretary of education William Bennett and Black poet laureate Maya Angelou. Jesse Jackson initially opposed the Oakland resolution but switched sides as his Democrat political ambitions grew—just as he did on abortion and gay marriage.

Though Ebonics did not catch hold in most official curricula, Black slang is still common in casual communications within minority schools. It remains in use even by many school staff, and by inner city students whose Black dialect goes largely uncorrected, leaving the street language as a social stigma.

Election of 1996

Heading into the election of 1996, President Clinton was considered highly vulnerable to a Republican challenge. No Democrat had won a second term after a full first term since Franklin Roosevelt. The Republicans had won the Senate and the House in the 1994 interim elections.

Progressives were unhappy with Clinton's more moderate "third way" approach to governance, specifically his welfare reform that pushed people into jobs, his perceived failure to push harder for national healthcare, his tough crime bill and his declaration that "the era of big government is over."

On the other hand, conservatives were displeased with his failure to keep his promise to cut taxes and address budget deficits—something he would do in his second term. After sweeping the primaries with almost 90 percent of the vote, the Democratic National Convention nominated both Clinton and his incumbent vice president Al Gore for a second term.

The Republican side was very different. Sensing victory in the early polling numbers, several significant GOP candidates threw their hats in the ring, including senators Robert Dole, Phil Gramm, Richard Lugar, and Arlen Specter; governors Lamar Alexander and Pete Wilson; publisher Steve Forbes; conservative activist Pat Buchanan; and ambassador Alan Keyes, a Black activist.

Among the early leading candidates was General Colin Powell, who by then had earned the moniker "the political general." He was the first serious Black contender for the GOP nomination. He was subject to a potentially successful nationwide draft movement, which ended when he definitively declared that he would not run.

By the time of the convention, Dole had virtually locked up the nomination. As his running mate, Dole selected Jack Kemp, former secretary of Housing and Urban Development and one time star quarterback in the American Football League. Both had strong civil rights backgrounds.

Dole on Civil Rights

Dole was among the Republicans who gave near unanimous support in both ending the Democrat filibusters and passing the Civil Rights Act of 1964 and the Voting Rights Act of 1965. He has referred to them as "two of the most important votes" in his Senate career. In 1982, he co-sponsored the Voting Rights Extension Act.

In 1970, Dole was among the earliest supporters of a national holiday honoring Martin Luther King. And in 1983, he co-sponsored Senate Bill 400, which officially designated the holiday. In support of the holiday, Dole said:

> I would make a distinction in the fact that this has happened over my lifetime and I have watched the change taking place because I have been in Congress ever since the first time Dr. King demonstrated his effectiveness in pointing out discrimination and injustice in this country. I did not know Columbus and I did not know Franklin D. Roosevelt. When you have seen the dramatic change that has happened all across this land and other lands because of one man, because of his dream and his vision and his diligence and his commitment; that really, as I see it, is what the debate is all about today.

Kemp on Civil Rights

Next to free market economics, Kemp's most burning issue was civil rights—and even his economic proposals were articulated to end the welfare dependency poverty in the inner cities. He was the leading advocate of "urban enterprise zones" to encourage business and job development in the most distressed Black communities.

Kemp favored granting voting rights to ex-criminal offenders even though that population leans heavily Black and Democratic. He supported creating a fully empowered seat in the House of Representatives for the District of Columbia.

In 1965, Kemp was among the leaders calling for a boycott of the AFL All-Star game because it was being held in New Orleans—a city where Democrats still imposed severe *de facto* segregation.

In 2014, remembering Kemp as a friend and protégé, Black New Jersey Democrat senator Corey Booker said he "watched him interact in poor communities with so clearly a love of people, and a fierce idea of equality."

Kemp's devotion to civil rights gained him the title of bleeding-heart conservative, which was evident in 2009 when President Barack Obama posthumously presented Kemp with America's highest civilian honor, the Presidential Medal of Freedom. Clinton scored a convincing win over Dole by 8 million votes, but it was not enough to win a majority. For the second time Clinton won the presidency with less than 50 percent of the popular vote.

Black Home Ownership

Another key area of urban racism is home ownership. Ownership by Black Americans in White neighborhoods beyond the invisible walls of segregation was a significant challenge well into the twenty-first century. In his book, *Places of Their Own,* author Andrew Wiese writes:

> To defend their neighborhoods, whites created a gauntlet of discriminatory practices that limited African Americans' access to the housing market. As early as the 1910s, white real estate agents had created Realtors organizations and pledged to uphold a code of ethics that prevented them from being party to transactions that permitted blacks to move into white neighborhoods. Similarly, white financial institutions almost uniformly refused to lend money to African Americans hoping to buy property outside 'established Negro areas' -- and they charged premium for credit inside as well.

Wiese is correct, as far as he goes. However, in laying the blame at the foot of "white real estate agents [and] white financial institutions," he unintentionally gives credence to false narratives by failing to specifically recognize the all-important overarching role of the ruling Democratic Party as the primary cause through politically intimidating policies and practices—using the iron fist of government to threaten banks and realtors.

White Only Covenants

While urban *de facto* racism was mostly a matter of unofficial understandings, the Democrats running the urban machines would occasionally take up the more formal unconstitutional practices of housing covenants. These were a mix of laws, regulations and policies that imposed racial homogeneity.

In an online article, Dmitri Mehlhorn, a senior fellow at John Hopkins University Institute for Education Policy, wrote that Roosevelt's New Deal Federal Housing Administration encouraged racist housing covenants because they "provide the surest protection against undesirable encroachment and inharmonious use."

The covenants prevented Black homeowners in previously integrated neighborhoods from selling to a Black family, essentially setting up a system of permanent segregation. According to Mehlhorn this was so effective that "by the 1940s, integrated neighborhoods had ceased to exist in every major city in the United States."

Despite Supreme Court rulings against many of the racist practices, the Democrat administrations in the cities did what their southern colleagues had done. They simply ignored the law. According to Mehlhorn:

> White racists, however, found ways to work around the rulings in order to maintain segregation. For instance, both federal and local agencies encouraged white flight by steering resources to whites seeking segregated suburban houses and schools, while cutting those resources for black families. So-called "urban renewal" laws were used to raze expanding black neighborhoods that threatened white institutions. Federal funds were used to construct massive public housing projects for the displaced Black residents.

Like Weise, Mehlhorn uses the general term "White racists" to source the problem, and only by allusion does he draw attention to the role of the local one-party leadership of the Democratic Party.

Blockbusting

By the 1960s, the growing Black population had limited access to housing while having a need for more housing. To maintain *de facto* segregation with a growing Black population, the Democrat machines fostered a concept known as blockbusting. At the time, the White communities had an abundance of housing. Ironically, this made ghetto real estate more valuable than many of the homes in the White middle-class communities. As the segregated Black ghettos became overpopulated, there was a need to expand the borders. Blockbusting was the modus operandi.

Once a neighborhood was targeted, White fear drove prices down below market levels, providing an opportunity for crony real estate operators to flip the property into more valuable Black tenant homes. In the book *American Apartheid* authors Douglas Massey and Nancy Denton noted that:

> Rapid black migration into a confined residential area created an intense demand for housing within the ghetto, which led to a marked inflation of rents and home prices. The racially segmented market generated real estate values in black areas that far exceeded anything in white neighborhoods, and this simple economic fact created a great potential for profits along the color line, guaranteeing that some real estate agent would specialize in opening up new areas to black settlement.

Very often the blame for blockbusting was placed on unscrupulous real estate agents acting on their own. This was rarely the case. Blockbusting was how city hall could use the real estate professionals to achieve a controlled expansion of the segregated community into new areas. It was not for the purpose of integration but to unofficially annex new turf for the expanding segregated ghetto.

Target neighborhoods, which bordered on the Black inner city, were generally populated by poor to middle class Eastern European Americans.

Blockbusting in Chicago was almost never seen in Mafia-dominated Italian neighborhoods or the Irish neighborhoods in which the leaders of the political machine resided.

How blockbusting worked is described in an article on the online *Encyclopedia of Chicago*. In it, historian Arnold R. Hirsch writes:

> "Blockbusting" refers to the efforts of real-estate agents and real-estate speculators to trigger the turnover of white-owned property and homes to African Americans. Often characterized as "panic peddling," such practices frequently accompanied the expansion of black areas of residence and the entry of African Americans into neighborhoods previously denied to them. In evidence as early as 1900, blockbusting techniques included the repeated—often incessant—urging of white homeowners in areas adjacent to or near black communities to sell before it became "too late" and their property values diminished. Agents frequently hired African American subagents and other individuals to walk or drive through changing areas soliciting business and otherwise behaving in such a manner as to provoke and exaggerate white fears.

Blockbusting often resulted in racial violence against incoming Black families in the hope of driving them out. Author Arnold Hirsch, in his 2021 book, *Making the Second Ghetto*, described this as the "era of hidden violence"—from World War II to the civil rights era of the mid-1960s. Unlike the earlier and later race riots, these neighborhood outbreaks received very little national attention.

According to the online *Encyclopedia of Chicago*:

> The aftermath of World War II saw a revival of white attacks on black mobility, mostly on the city's South and Southwest Sides, but also in the western industrial suburb of Cicero.
>
> Aspiring African American professionals seeking to obtain improved housing beyond the increasingly overcrowded South Side ghetto, whether in private residences or in the new public housing developments constructed by the Chicago Housing Authority, were

frequently greeted by attempted arsons, bombings, and angry white mobs often numbering into the thousands.

Cicero, Illinois

Institutional *de facto* racism was not confined to the largest cities. Segregated Blacks in smaller communities with long Democrat histories experienced similar oppression and deprivations. Cicero, Illinois—noted above in the Encyclopedia of Chicago—is but one of many examples. Cicero was an all-White suburb of Chicago and commonly understood to be a stronghold of the Mafia. It had very close ties to the Chicago Democrat machine. It was no PLACE for Blacks. This made integration a double challenge.

In 1951, Harvey Clark, a Black college graduate war veteran, rented an apartment in Cicero for him and his family. Attempting to move in was a challenge, in itself. Housing expert Charles Abrams wrote in his book *Forbidden Neighbors: A Study of Prejudice in Housing*:

> At 2:30 pm, on June 8, [1951] a moving van containing $2000 worth of Clark's furniture was stopped by the police. The rental agent was ushered out with a drawn revolver at his back. A jeering crowd gathered, and Clark was told by the police to get out or he would be arrested "for protective custody." A detective warned Clark that, "I'll bust your damned head if you don't move." At 6:00 pm, Clark was grabbed by 20 police officers. The chief of police told him, "Get out of here fast. There will be no moving into this building." Clark was hit eight times as he was pushed towards a car which was parked across the street and was shoved inside the car. The police told him, "Get out of Cicero and don't come back in town or you'll get a bullet through you."

Despite the threats, the Clark family moved in, which was further described by Abrams:

> On July 11, 1951, at dusk, a crowd of 4,000 whites attacked the apartment building that housed Clark's family and possessions. Only 60 police officers were assigned to the scene and did little

to control the rioting. Women carried stones from a nearby rock pile to bombard Clark's windows. Another tossed firebrands onto the window and onto the rooftop of the building which 21 family members fled before the rioting. The mob also destroyed a bathtub, woodworks, plaster, doors, windows, and set fires to the place. Most of the whites who joined in the rioting were teenagers. Firemen who rushed to the building were met with showers of bricks and stones from the mob. Sheriffs' deputies asked the firemen to turn their hoses on the rioters, who refused to do so without their lieutenant, who was unavailable.

Rioting ended when the Illinois National Guard was sent in to restore peace. In the Democrat stronghold of Chicago, Cicero and Cook County, no charges were initially brought against any of the rioters or their organizers. However, Clark's attorney, the building owner's rental agent and the owner of the building were all charged with inciting a riot. Prompted by public outrage, the US attorney general stepped in. The previous charges were dropped, and the Cicero chief of police and two police officers were each fined $2,500—a substantial amount at the time.

The Cicero riot might have been typical of the "era of hidden violence" except for the fact that it received national attention as the first race riot to be televised live.

Three Phases of *De Facto* Housing Segregation

Ever since former slaves moved to the major cities in the North and west to find employment and escape the oppression of Democrat regimes in the former southern Confederate states, most Black Americans have lived in segregated urban communities and under institutional *de facto* racism. Urban segregation endured because it adjusted to changing times. There have been essentially three phases of segregation in American cities.

The first phase was to keep Blacks confined to a limited segregated community by institutional *de facto* racism was the establishment of invisible barriers enforced by red lining that prevented Blacks from purchasing homes in White neighborhoods. These borders established by the racist Democrat administrations were enforced by compliant banks and realtors. There was also social pressure on landlords to reject Black tenants. Finally, the so-called social clubs would terrorize, brutalize and occasionally kill Blacks who did not know their PLACE and had the audacity of entering, shopping, dining and especially trying to move into White neighborhoods.

As the Black population continued to grow, it was literally impossible to maintain historic border lines. In the second phase of racist housing policy, the segregated ghetto was allowed to expand through the practice of block-busting. Officials in city hall, relators, and bankers would again cooperate to select low-income White neighbors on the edge of the ghetto for Black expansion. They would move in Black families and use scare tactics to reduce property values and drive out White residents.

This had a downside for the racist bosses of the Democrat political machines. A byproduct was "White flight" to the suburbs. This meant that the growth of the Black voting population would be further empowered by a reduction in the number of White voters. While segregation and redlining created a PLACE of confinement for impoverished Black citizens, it did not stem the growth in the number of Black voters. It did not assuage the fear in city halls of the election of a Black mayor in the future.

The third phase of racist segregation was the construction of public housing. The stated official purpose of public housing was to provide those confined to the slums with a cleaner and safer living environment. While many well-intentioned people believed that, it was never the intention of the racist urban planners. Public housing never provided cleaner and safer living environments. Public housing high rises quickly became dilapidated structures with residents victimized by high crime, gangs, and drugs.

The real purpose for public housing was to thwart geographic expansion of the ghetto by increasing the population density. A parcel of ghetto land with homes housing hundreds of Black residents could be converted to high-rise structures housing thousands of residents. The growing Black population could be contained to its PLACE without expanding the footprint of the segregated ghetto.

But that did not solve the problem of a growing Black population and voters. The only option for the White Democrat political machines to retain power was to reduce the number of Black residents, voters.

Ethnic Cleansing Chicago Style

In the late 1990s, Chicago again proved itself the center of creative *de facto* racism. Since the election in 1989, when the younger Mayor Daley re-established the power of the old White ruling class, the Chicago Democrat machine was obsessed with preventing city hall from again falling into the hands of a Black mayor.

The segregated Black ghetto was composed of neighborhood housing and high-rise public housing. To reduce the Black population and its voting power, the diaspora required two different strategies to move out Black residents. One for the neighborhoods and one for the public housing projects. Many regarded these policies of the Democrat machine to be a form of ethnic cleansing.

Gentrification

In the case of the neighborhoods, the Daley administration worked with crony developers and investors to target Black communities for "revitalization." It was called gentrification. These inner-city areas were unattractive to individual home buyers other than the politically connected slum landlords. The sale of individual homes would not improve the value of the local market and would not drive out the impoverished Black population.

By unofficially designating larger areas for "revitalization," developers and cronies could swoop in and buy up entire blocks to either renovate or replace the older structures. The new and improved housing was marketed at prices well above the ability of the original Black resident to pay. As house prices soared and taxes increased, even the slum lords sold out. What were once primarily Black neighborhoods were gentrified as overwhelmingly upscale White neighborhoods.

The city would further enhance the value of the properties by undertaking an aggressive program of infrastructure improvement, including updating schools, parks, and fire stations and repairing streets. Policing was improved to ensure that the new gentrified areas would be safe. None of these improvements were provided for the original Black residents. With the segregated neighborhoods already overcrowded, the pressure was on displaced residents to move to the predominantly Black suburbs.

To understand the effectiveness of this process, you only need analyze the gentrification of the area surrounding Chicago's North Avenue, Halsted Street, and Clybourn Avenue intersection. In the 1970s, it was a Black ghetto. Crime was rampant, and the local schools were among Chicago's worst. Through gentrification, the area became one of the hottest upscale neighborhoods in Chicago. Halsted Street was transformed into a strip of live theaters and chic eateries. Three-story frame houses that once sold for $20,000 or less have been transformed into, or replaced by, multi-million-dollar townhouses. Wealthy new residents, including such elites as the billionaire family of Illinois governor J.B. Pritzker constructed multi-million-dollar homes in the newly gentrified neighborhood.

This was not a singular phenomenon. The once seedy west Loop area surrounding Chicago's Greek Town is now filled with trendy loft-style condo conversions and is the home of Oprah Winfrey's Harpo television studios. The largely Black area south of Chicago's Loop called Printers' Row, was transformed into an upscale neighborhood drawing wealthy White suburbanites back to the central city. Mayor Daley moved from the family's historic base in the southside Bridgeport neighborhood to Printers' Row.

The Democrat administration often boasted of the improvements in the schools in newly gentrified areas. Improvement in student achievement was not due to school reforms, however. The only thing that changed was the skin color of the students. The improved test scores were achieved by simply replacing the predominantly economically disadvantaged and poorly educated Black students with White children who had already been well educated in the suburbs or from the outlying city neighborhoods. The schools' teaching staffs in gentrified neighborhoods were upgraded. Gentrification would not work if the schools remained inferior.

In many ways, gentrification was like reversed redlining. Instead of the segregated Black ghetto expanding into neighboring poor White neighborhoods, an upscale White population was reclaiming portions of the ghetto and driving out the impoverished Black residents. The banks were providing mortgages and loans to developers that they refused to provide to Blacks.

Racism of Public Housing

The second method of reducing the numbers of Black voters, and influence of the minority community involved public housing. Many of Chicago's public housing "projects," as they were called, were the legacy of the first Mayor Daley. The new 1990s plan, under the younger Mayor Daley, was to demolish several of the larger public housing projects.

The election of Black congressman Harold Washington as mayor of Chicago was a wakeup call for the White Democrat political establishment. Unless the demographics trends were reversed, Chicago could again elect a Black mayor—which it did. Mayor Daley had already changed the election system to prevent a three-way race—virtually eliminating the potential of a Black mayoral candidate winning the election in the foreseeable future. But that would work only if the Black population did not become a majority.

While the primary racist purpose for the construction of public housing was to confine more Blacks into a smaller geographical area, the decision to tear down major portions of the so-called projects was equally and ironically racist. The only way to stop Blacks from gaining a voting majority was to decrease the size of the Black population relative to the size of the White population by government policy—an institutional *de facto* racist policy.

In 1999, Mayor Richard M. Daley advanced the Plan for Transformation to be overseen by the Chicago Public Housing Authority (CHA). The central feature of the Plan was the demolition many of the 1960s public housing "projects."

A prime example of the Daley Plan was the Cabrini-Green public housing complex. Like virtually all such projects, Cabrini-Green became a high-rise slum. In an article titled "Cabrini-Green: How Racism Turned a Promising Neighborhood into a Nightmare" author Elizabeth Edwards wrote that a "history of neglect, racism, and government corruption led the housing projects into disrepair."

The CHA promised that most of those living in Cabrini-Green would be able to return to attractive and affordable housing in the neighborhood or new scattered-site subsidized housing throughout the city. This was never the real plan or the result. As buildings were being torn down, most residents were on their own to find housing—with many fleeing to Black suburbs.

The land upon which Cabrini-Green had rested was turned over to developers, with significant infrastructure improvements provided by the city. Streets, curbs and sidewalks would be repaired or replaced. Crumbling parks would be modernized, and new parks created. Transportation services would be expanded. Schools would be rehabbed, and the teaching staff upgraded. Police would provide safe streets. The zoning department downgraded the public housing areas to single family dwellings. The building department made sure all the new and rehabbed dwellings met the safety and occupancy codes. What resulted was a White upscale gentrified community, with housing prices far beyond the means of the original residents. The Daley Plan's promise of newer housing in the neighborhood and new scattered-site housing throughout for Cabrini-Green residents never materialized.

Though cloaked in bureaucratic language, the failure to provide new housing in the old locations was addressed in a CHA Report. Writing about the Report for *Progress Illinois,* Sally Ho wrote:

> Still, the report failed to discuss the problems the relocated families face, chief among them the slow pace of redevelopment at former public housing sites designated as mixed-income areas. As of late July 2009, just 36 percent—2,656 out of 7,303—of the public housing units the Chicago Housing Authority plans to build at 12 former CHA sites around the city were complete. And then there's the fact unearthed by the Sun-Times that "a disturbing 2,202 families are unaccounted for. Under the plan they had the right to return to CHA, but the agency has now lost track of them and has no idea where they are."

This failure was predicted at the onset by those who believed the CHA Plan had less to do with quality housing for the largely impoverished Black minority than with a cynical effort to alter the voting demographics of Chicago.

A report on Cabrini-Green done by the University of Chicago twelve years after the Daley Plan stated:

> Units in the new mixed-income developments will be limited, with only about 7,700 projected to be available for the more than 16,000

relocated public housing families. These units also tend to be smaller and contain fewer bedrooms than other relocation options, making them less feasible for larger families.

In other words, fewer than half of the displaced residents, at best, would be able to find accommodation in Chicago under the Daley Plan—and then only if they were willing to squeeze their already overcrowded families into smaller units.

In addition, the pre-occupancy screening for the scarce units established criteria that many public housing residents could not meet. The Daley-run Chicago Housing Authority further thwarted the public housing residents from taking advantage of alternative housing in the city by administrative procedures.

According to the U of C report "Relocating residents was a highly complicated process with shifting policies and procedures and numerous actors with overlapping roles."

It appeared to many at the time that the CHA was intentionally evicting public housing tenants before adequate relocation options were in place. Many were promised a "right to return," but there would be nothing to return to. The report went on to say:

> Years of mismanagement and poor service had also resulted in low levels of trust in the information shared and commitments made by the CHA. In many cases, residents had little information on which to base their housing choices, were heavily dependent on relocation counselors, and ended up with very limited time to make high-stakes decisions about where to live.

In the 2016 article "2 Bedrooms In Cabrini-Green's New High Rise Start At $3,200 A Month," published in the *Chicagoist,* Rachel Cromidas wrote:

> Ten years ago, Cabrini-Green was best known for its notoriously struggling public housing project of the same name. Today, it's becoming something of a goldmine for developers who have planned a new, luxury high rise on the Near North Side area not far from where the dilapidated public housing towers once stood.

Cromidas noted that these new buildings with predominantly White residents "sprung up from around Cabrini-Green demolition rubble." She added that living in the new Cabrini-Green neighborhood "sounds divine—if you have the income for it."

Specifically discussing Cabrini-Green, a *Sun-Times*-Better Government Association investigation of the Daley Plan found that "demolition of high-rise projects like Cabrini-Green has cleared the way for rapid gentrification by wealthy whites and businesses."

Ethnic Cleansing Worked

Evidence that the Daley Plan was to force Blacks out of Chicago worked is seen in the statistics. The Daley Plan resulted in 193 out of 245 suburbs seeing significant increases in subsidized renters—with the greatest increases in such predominantly Black suburbs as Markham, Lansing, Calumet City, Maywood, and Robbins.

According to Andrew Greenlee, assistant professor of urban and regional planning at the University of Illinois at Urbana-Champaign, the Daley Plan "in some ways reinforced historical divisions"—displacing families and continuing racial and class segregation.

Census figures show that the plan to reduce the Black voting population of Chicago was very successful. The 2010 census—ten years after the Daley ethnic cleansing plan—the Black population of Chicago had dropped. According to a June 24, 2016, feature article by Marwa Eltagouri in the *Chicago Tribune* "Chicago … lost 181,000 black residents between 2000 and 2010, according to census data."

If White flight had given Blacks increased voting power, the Democrat scheme to tear down public housing without adequate options for the residents to remain in the city, plus the White gentrification of city neighborhoods, resulted in a significant loss in voting power for the Black community.

The Daley Plan was arguably one of the greatest examples of institutional Black voter suppression since the Democrats governed over the segregated southland. Because of the power of the false racial narrative, it was accomplished without an outcry from the hypocritical progressive community. There was almost no reaction from Black city officials and community leaders—many of whom are beholden to the Democrat machine. One notable example was a young Barack Obama who served as a community organizer and machine Democrat state senator during the period of Chicago's ethnic cleansing. His voice was never raised in opposition to the Daley Plan. His future depended on loyalty to the Democratic political machine more than the people of his community.

Gentrification Nationwide

According to a 2020 study of 1000 neighborhoods in 935 cities by the National Community Reinvestment Coalition (NCRC), gentrification was most aggressive in such Democrat-controlled cities as New York, Baltimore, Los Angeles, Chicago, Philadelphia, and San Diego. These cities represented 55 percent of national gentrification.

The Study noted that "large-scale gentrification and displacement" in the major cities displaced Blacks from portions of segregated communities in which they lived for generations. It is noteworthy that the study pointed out that such ethnic displacement is "rare" in other areas even where gentrification takes place. In 230 urban neighborhoods, the rising costs associated with gentrification forced out 135,000 mostly Black residents.

In the nation's capital more than twenty thousand mostly Black residents were displaced by gentrification. New York's one predominantly Black Bedford-Stuyvesant community is now predominantly White.

Moving masses out of the ghetto to make room for upscale predominantly White developments is not an unanticipated result of gentrification in the major Democrat cities. It is the goal.

Black diaspora in the Democrat-controlled northern cities led to a Black migration to the newly Republican dominated southland. The movement was so notable that a Brookings Institution demographer referred to it as the "reverse migration." The Atlanta, Georgia, area, for example, gained more than 190,000 Black residents between 2000 and 2010—almost the same number as left Chicago. This migration south can be seen as yet another indicator that the Republican ascension in the South was not based on a switch of allegiance by the old racist Democrat voters. GOP leadership was creating a more tolerant environment for Black residents and migrants.

Election of 2000

Racial issues were not on the front burner in the 2000 election. The focus was on the economy, the growing problem of Islamic terrorism under the direction of Osama Bin Laden. The sex scandal and impeachment of President Bill Clinton was also part of the national debate.

While there was a large field of Republican contenders, most were no match for Texas governor George W. Bush, the son of George Herbert Walker Bush. For vice president, Bush selected former secretary of defense Dick Cheney.

Once again, the Democrats would look south for their presidential candidate—this time it was Vice President Al Gore. Like Bush, Gore had an easy path to the nomination. He chose Connecticut senator Joe Lieberman for his running mate.

The Election of 2000 was one of the closest and most controversial in American history. When it appeared that Bush had carried the Electoral College vote while Gore edged to a win in the popular vote, Democrats went to court to seek a special recount in Florida. The case ended up in the Supreme Court, which certified the original vote making Bush the winner.

The Confederate Battle Flag in South Carolina

In 2000, South Carolina remained the only former Confederate state to fly the Confederate battle flag atop the dome of the State Capitol Building—although other states had incorporated the controversial image into the state flag or officially honored it by including it in the state seal, affixed it to license plates or had it flown in alternative places on the grounds.

Leading the fight to remove the flag was the NAACP, which called for a boycott of South Carolina if the flag was not removed. While the civil rights group wanted the flag completely removed from any place of honor, Democrat governor Jim Hodges favored a plan to have the banner moved to a place of honor on the grounds. Hodges' plan was successful, and the flag was relocated next to a monument honoring fallen Confederate soldiers and near the statue of uber racist Democrat senator "Pitchfork" Ben Tillman.

The governor's plan was strongly opposed by the twenty-six Black legislators in the general assembly, twenty-two voted against Governor Hodges' relocation plan. The NAACP refused to end the boycott.

In explaining his vote against relocating the flag, Black representative Joseph H. Neal said, "That flag represents the Confederacy that enslaved, exploited, murdered, raped and killed our people for 300 years." For historical accuracy, Neal could have pointed out that since the end of the Civil War—and particularly after the Compromise of 1877—the Democratic Party was uniquely responsible for those atrocities.

The 2000 flag controversy was only a precursor to a broad assault on Confederate flags, statues, and memorials that would rise in the future, which is covered in more detail later in this book.

George W. Bush (2001–2009)

As a Republican, George W. Bush was demonized as weak on civil rights. In reality, he was a strong proponent of racial equality.

Racial profiling is fundamental to institutional racism. It was an iconic feature of general racist governance. It led to the faux crimes of DWB (driving while Black) and WWB (walking while Black). More seriously, it led to the over-prosecution and incarceration of Black citizens—resulting in a racially imbalanced and overcrowded prison system.

Democrats often expressed their revulsion and opposition to racial profiling. The great irony, however, is that the vast majority of troublesome racial profiling was being carried out by police departments ruled over by Democrat administrations and law enforcement agencies in America's major cities.

On this issue, Bush was very clear:

I can't imagine what it would be like to be singled out because of race and harassed. That's just flat wrong. So, we ought to do everything we can to end racial profiling. One of my concerns, though, is I don't want to federalize local police. I believe in local control of governments. Most officers are dedicated citizens who are putting their lives at risk, who aren't bigoted or aren't prejudiced. I do think we need to find out where racial profiling occurs and say to the local folks, get it done and if you can't, there'll be a federal consequence.

Faith-Based Initiatives

Bush recognized that much of the real progress in overcoming racial prejudice throughout American history came through the religious community—in both the Black and the White communities. One of his primary initiatives was to re-energize and re-empower that community.

In one of his earliest acts as president, Bush presented legislation to Congress that would broaden the activities of religious organizations by removing many of the regulations that had stifled action. The legislation separated a church's religious activities from its charitable activities to allow federal support for the latter. He also created the nation's first White House Office of Faith-Based and Community Initiatives.

Despite the anticipated opposition of progressive groups, atheists, pagans and the American Civil Liberties Union (ACLU), the program passed constitutional muster and provided billions of dollars for social services that pushed back against the ills of institutional racism.

PEPFAR

While the president's Emergency Plan for AIDS Relief (PEPFAR) provided for the prevention and treatment of HIV/AIDS worldwide, it has its greatest impact Blacks in the United States and Africa. It was the most effect world health program since the eradication of smallpox in 1977. It is credited with saving the lives of more than 25 million people in 55 countries, including 5.5 million who were born free of HIV.

According to an Associated Press report in 2023:

> The number of children in sub-Saharan African newly orphaned by AIDS reached a peak of 1.6 million in 2004, the year that PEPFAR began its rollout of HIV drugs, researchers wrote in a defense of the program published in The Lancet medical journal. In 2021, the number of new orphans had dropped to 382,000. Deaths of infants and young children from AIDS in the region have dropped by 80%.

Bush's Key Black Appointments

Prior to Bush, there was an unwritten rule that Blacks were only appropriate for specific Cabinet positions—the departments of Housing and Welfare, Labor, and the Post Office. Bush broke that informal barrier with the appointment of Colin Powell as the first Black secretary of state and then Condoleezza Rice as the first Black female secretary of state. He also appointed the first Hispanic attorney general, Alberto Gonzales. For the first time, minorities held the two most important Cabinet positions.

Cincinnati Riot of 2001

The Cincinnati Enquirer labeled 2001 the city's "year of unrest." In a reflective article, reporter Dan Horn wrote:

> Looking back, there were warning signs.

> Citizens complained about police officers, protesters hollered and hauled signs at City Hall, community leaders demanded change.

> But no one fully understood the danger of Cincinnati's deep racial divisions until a white police officer shot and killed an unarmed black man in April.

African Americans were outraged. Within days, the anger and frustration that had been building for years spilled into the streets. Rioters broke windows, looted stores, burned trash bins and threw bricks at passing motorists. A city once known as a good place to live and raise kids was embarrassed and stunned.

What is significant in this article is the recognition that the riot was due to Cincinnati's "deep racial divisions" reflected in those past complaints and protests, the triggering event was a White police officer killing an unarmed Black man—an action that would bring forth protests and riots in American cities into the twenty-first century.

Prior to the riot, tensions in the Over-the-Rhine neighborhood regarding alleged police racism and abuse was spiking. In the six years leading up to the riot, fifteen Black men were killed by Cincinnati police. During the same period, no White suspects were killed. In two cases, the police officer stood trial. One was acquitted and the other ended in a mistrial, but there was no further prosecution.

Within days of the riot, a group of civil rights organizations, led by the American Civil Liberties Union filed a suit against the Democrat administration of Cincinnati and its police department. Among the charges was a prolonged history of racial profiling. In its investigative report the local *CityBeat* newspaper's analysis showed that out of 141,000 traffic citations written by Cincinnati Police in a twenty-two-month period, Black drivers were "twice as likely as whites to be cited for driving without a license, twice as likely to be cited for not wearing a seat belt and four times as likely to be cited for driving without proof of insurance."

On April 7 of 2001, a nineteen-year-old Black man, Timothy Thomas, was shot and killed by police officer Stephen Roach during an arrest attempt in connection with unresolved traffic tickets. Officer Roach said he thought Thomas was reaching for a gun, but he was unarmed. It was believed that Thomas was just trying to pull up his low-slung pants.

Once again, years of oppression in a Democrat-run city and an incident of dubious or unfortunate law enforcement led to rioting. On April 9, the rioting began. It ran for five days, with each day getting more violent. Fortunately, there were no deaths due to the rioting. There was, however, a significant impact on the city. Damage from the rioting in the Over-the-Rhine community was estimated to exceed $3.5 million and another $2 million in costs to the city. The longer-term financial impact was due to a boycott led by the NAACP. Several entertainers, including Whoopi Goldberg and Bill Cosby, cancelled appearances."

Over-the-Rhine community would be the subject of another Democrat urban strategy with racist implications.

Gentrification in Cincinnati

In the early 2000s, the Over-the-Rhine neighborhood was considered to be among the most dangerous communities in America. It is composed of several "districts" including Washington Park, the Brewery, and Liberty Street. Gentrification to decrease the influence of the Black community was used by the Cincinnati's Democrat administration in the Over-the-Rhine neighborhood.

Washington Park was the initial focal point for gentrification. More than one thousand poor Black residents were forced out of the area between 2000 and 2010—turning Washington Park into a predominantly White upscale neighborhood.

The headline over an online article in the *News Record* read: "Gentrification in the Over-the-Rhine: Revitalization efforts intensify class divide downtown." The article covered presentations at the University of Cincinnati's Fall Poverty Lecture Series. According to University of Massachusetts Professor Andrew Leong:

> We are beginning to experience a hyper-gentrification that's focusing on corporate welfare. The city then turns a blind eye on its duty to protect the area's already-existing communities.

Miami University Professor Thomas Dutton added:

> People are failing to understand that this renaissance narrative has masked an empirical account of what Cincinnati has done through legislation to drop kick people out of the city and directly or indirectly create policy that makes people into economic others rather than citizens in a community.

The article in the *News Record* reported on the opinion of Alice Skirtz, who the publication described as "a leading expert on gentrification of Over-The-Rhine." It reported:

> Outraged when local power brokers used what she saw as a campaign of disinformation to justify the removal of longtime residents, Skirtz combined scholarship and passion to produce "Econocide: Elimination of the Urban Poor." The book challenges the stereotypes associated with the historic neighborhood. Dr. Skirtz said it is a prime example of gentrification run amok.

The article alluded to the Democrat's historic racial scare tactics—demonization of Blacks and a form of blockbusting. It stated:

> Skirtz also noted that the powerful public and private forces created a narrative to make OTR appear hopeless, a dangerous gathering point for criminals, drug addicts and the homeless. She said those stereotypes swayed public opinion and decreased property values, allowing speculators to control the renovation process.

Skirtz was quoted as saying, "We just sort of fell into that stereotype. Buildings that were once the homes of families are now the glitzy bars, coffee shops and restaurants." Recognizing the loss of influence of the local community, Skirtz said, "We are eliminating a whole segment of our population by economic means. In the process, all of us are losing the decision-making power to change that."

Twenty-First Century Race Riots

The post-civil rights era of the mid-twentieth century, itself, was a period of intense racial unrest and rioting—mostly in the major cities in which racist Democrat political machines exerted one-party rule and continued *de facto* racist policies for generations.

Even as southern Jim Crow racism was defeated in the courts and strident racism ebbed from the hearts of the American people, institutional racial prejudice retained its hold on America's cities into well into the twenty-first century. The iconic race riots continued largely in those major urban centers that remained segregated under Democrat rule.

As in Cincinnati, the segregation and oppression of Black populations in major cities across the nation continued to erupt in violence and riots throughout the first quarter of the twenty-first century.

Toledo 2005

In response to a neo-Nazi march, counter protest erupted to a riot. Both police and Nazi machers were pelted with bottle, rocks and other missiles. Several people were injured and more than one hundred were arrested.

Oakland, California 2009

On New Year's Day, a White transit officer shot and killed Oscar Grant III, who was unarmed. The ensuing anger resulted in arson, looting and vandalism. In the clash with police, dozens of people were injured, and scores arrested.

Baltimore 2015

A serious of protests occurred over a one-month period in Baltimore, Maryland, after the death of Freddie Gray, who died of a spinal cord injury incurred while in police custody. The rioting involved clashes with both police and National Guard personnel during the arson and looting rampage. More than two hundred people were injured or arrested. The Freddie Gray rioting spread to cities across the nation.

Milwaukee 2016

Rioting erupted after a Black police officer fatal show Sylville Smith, a Black man who was armed with a stolen gun. Rioters threw rocks, bottles and other weapons at police, injuring several officers. The mob looted and burned businesses and cars.

Charlotte, North Carolina 2016

Keith Lamont Scott, a Black man armed with a gun, was fatally shot by a Black police officer during a search. Scott had an outstanding warrant for his arrest. Rioters engaged in arson, looting and vandalism. Police responded with tear gas and rubber bullets. One person died of gunshot wounds.

St. Louis 2017

On September 15, the police officer, Jason Stockley, who had shot Anthony Lamar Smith, a suspected drug dealer, was acquitted. For the next several weeks a series of protests and riots occurred in St. Louis with more than 160 arrests. Businesses were vandalized and looted. The home of newly elected Mayor Lyda Krewson was attacked. Chemical agents were used against police. There were dozens of injuries, including among police. As is often the case, the St. Louis riots spawned disruptions in other cities across America.

Minneapolis/Saint Paul 2020

Worldwide protests broke out in cities across the nation after the suffocation death of George Floyd. He was in the process of being arrested for passing a counterfeit twenty-dollar bill. Cities across America broke out in protests and riots against the reoccurring theme of police violence against Black citizens. Floyd cardiac arrest as a result of his neck being leaned on by the knee of police officer Derek Chauvin as two other officers stood by and watched. The incident was dramatically captured on cell phone video by a bystander.

The death of Floyd spawned a serious of protests across the nation unlike any other event since the assassination of Martin Luther King in 1968, when more than one hundred American cities experienced rioting. Chauvin and two other officers were convicted of murder in 2021.

In what was a departure from tradition, the officers involved were tried and convicted of murder.

Kenosha, Wisconsin 2020

Weeklong violence erupted on August 23 after White police officer Rusten Sheskey shot Jacob Blake, Black man, several times. Blake was not killed but was paralyzed from the waist down. Sheskey was responding to a domestic violence call. The rioting included arson, looting and vandalism and clashes with police and between armed civilians.

Kyle Rittenhouse, a seventeen-year-old vigilante killed two rioters and wounded a third who were about to attack him—one with a gun. He was subsequently acquitted of all charges in a jury trial. Sheskey was not charged. The riots spread to several other cities, mostly controlled by Democrat political machines.

Louisville, Kentucky 2020

A series of protests and riots occurred between May and October of 2020 in Louisville following the killing of Breonna Taylor, a Black correctional officer. She was shot eight times by White officers executing a no-knock raid on her boyfriend's apartment. The riots involved arson, looting, vandalism and clashes with police and National Guard troops, and spread to several other cities.

Philadelphia 2020

Rioting in the City of Brotherly Love continued from October 26 to November 4 after two White police officers shot and killed Walter Wallace, Jr., a Black man who was later said to have bi-polar issues. The officers were responding to calls reporting a man with a knife. The rioting included arson, looting and vandalism and clashes with police. There were no fatalities in the rioting, but dozens were injured or arrested.

The Common Traits of Racial Unrest

These incidents triggered scores of riots in many American cities with large segregated and oppressed Black populations. While the unrest noted above represents the triggering event, the copycat riots were violent and deadly. In addition, there have been hundreds of less violent rioting by smaller groups and with less injury and destruction. These go largely unreported by the national media.

In his memoir *Stride Toward Freedom*, Martin Luther King outlined three responses to oppression. The first was passive acceptance. Here are his words in terms of the second response:

> A second way that oppressed people sometimes deal with oppression
> is to resort to physical violence and corroding hatred. Violence often
> brings about momentary results. But despite temporary victories,
> violence never brings permanent peace. It solves no social problem;
> it merely creates new and more complicated ones.

It is no coincidence that that vast majority of the violence arises in Democrat-controlled cites—and in response to institutionally racist government policies that brutally oppresses the Black population and keep Blacks in their PLACE for generations. Obviously, police enforcement is a hot button issue—inciting the most violent and deadly race riots. The oppression, however, spans the full range of political and social life.

The Election of 2004

At the time of the Election of 2004, the major issues were the aftermath of the 9/11 attack on the World Trade Towers in New York City and the toppling of Iraqi dictator Saddam Hussein—although that was becoming increasingly controversial. With the focus on war and Islamic terrorism, civil rights were never a major issue in the campaign.

The Bush-Cheney ticket was easily re-nominated. Democrats produced a large field of candidates, including two Black leaders—Illinois senator Carol Moseley Braun and civil rights activist Al Sharpton. Neither gained significant traction with the Democrat electorate or leadership.

However, during a 2003 Democratic Primary debate, Sharpton made a rare admission of the Democratic Party's oppression of Black voters. He specifically said that the Democratic Party takes the Black vote for granted and treats Blacks like a mistress. "They [Democrats] will take us to the dance, but they don't want to take us home to meet mama."

Despite this earlier view, Sharpton has since become one of the staunchest defenders of the Democratic Party establishment—having garnered enormous power, prestige, profit, and privilege by promoting racial division and the false civil rights narrative of generational welfare dependency.

Democrats settled on Massachusetts senator John Kerry. Following Democrat tradition, Kerry looked to the south for a running mate. He selected Senator John Edwards of North Carolina.

Bush won a relatively easy victory over the Democrat team.

Voting Rights Act Reauthorization

In 2006, Bush signed the Fannie Lou Hamer, Rosa Parks and Coretta Scott King Voting Rights Act Reauthorization. The press release from the White House read:

> Today, The President Signed into law The Fannie Lou Hamer, Rosa
> Parks, And Coretta Scott King Voting Rights Act Reauthorization
> And Amendments Act Of 2006. The Voting Rights Act of 1965

(VRA) was designed to restore the birthright of every American - the right to choose our leaders. It has been vital to guaranteeing the right to vote for generations of Americans and has helped millions of our citizens enjoy the full promise of freedom.

The Authorization Act extended the Republican drafted and passed 1965 Voting Rights Act for an additional twenty-five years. While the original Act prohibited the use of "tests or devices" to deny voting rights and required, where appropriate, that voting information should be in multiple languages, the Reauthorization Act incorporated amendments that further strengthened the law.

According to the White House statement, the amendments covered:

The use of election examiners and observers;

Voting qualifications or standards intended to diminish or with the effect of diminishing the ability of U.S. citizens on account of race or color to elect preferred candidates; and

Award of attorney fees in enforcement proceedings to include expert fees and other reasonable costs of litigation.

The press release concluded:
The President Has Committed His Administration to Vigorously Enforce the Provisions Of This Law And To Defend It In Court. The President will also continue to work with Congress to ensure that our country lives up to our guiding principle that all men and women are created equal.

The Administration Will Continue To Build On The Legacy Of The Civil Rights Movement To Help Ensure That Every Child Enjoys The Opportunities America Offers.

These opportunities include the right to a decent education in a good school, the chance to own a home or small business, and the hope that comes from knowing you can rise in our society through hard work and using your talents.

2008—Election of the first Black President

With former First Lady and New York senator Hillary Clinton as the favored candidate, and Illinois senator Barack Obama as the chief rival, the Democrat standard bearer in 2008 was certain to be a precedent breaker. Though other Black candidates have run for President of the United States in the past, none were considered to be serious contenders. For Democrats like Shirley Chisholm, Carol Moseley Braun, Jesse Jackson, Al Sharpton, and Republican Alan Keyes, the campaigns were more of a platform to promote themselves and their issues rather than actually win the election.

At the onset of the 2008 presidential campaign, it was assumed that Hillary Clinton would be the Democrat nominee.

Senator Biden's Campaign Gaffe

During the campaign, fellow presidential candidate at the time, Senator Joe Biden, was criticized for a comment he made to distinguish Obama from other Blacks. Biden seemed to be suggesting that Obama's appeal was because he was unlike other Black men generally or unlike previous Black presidential candidates specifically. In describing Obama, Biden said, "I mean, you got the first mainstream African American who is articulate and bright and clean and a nice-looking guy. I mean, that's a storybook, man."

Biden saw bright and clean as being exceptional traits in a Black person. He apologized and Obama said he took no offense, but he did push back to say that other Black presidential candidates were not exceptions to Biden's description.

> I didn't take Sen. Biden's comments personally, but obviously they were historically inaccurate. African American presidential candidates like Jesse Jackson, Shirley Chisholm, Carol Moseley Braun and Al Sharpton gave a voice to many important issues through their campaigns, and no one would call them inarticulate.

Despite the kerfuffle, Obama knew he needed to balance off his outsider status and his lack of experience with an establishment Democrat.

Biden filled that bill and was selected by Obama as his vice-presidential running mate.

Obama went into the general election with a great advantage: he was a gifted campaigner. Conversely, McCain ran one of the worst campaigns in presidential history, and the economy tanked in the weeks leading up to the election.

Race, if not racial issues, played a major role in the campaign. In the greater sense, polls dispelled the contention that America is a racist nation. According to an NBC News-*Wall Street Journal* pre-election poll, more than 90 percent of voters said that race was not a factor in their vote. Ironically, it was the Black community that placed greater importance on race, with 20 percent saying it would be the most important consideration while only eight percent of White voters said the same.

Barack Obama (2009–2017)

Obama made history by becoming the first Black president—at least in terms of contemporary identity politics standards. But he also achieved two other historic firsts—ones that were hardly considered even though they may have been as big an influence on his policies as his ethnicity. Obama was the first president to have personally matured outside the American culture and the first president who was the product of the racist Chicago Democrat machine.

The Community Activist

Obama came to public office as a so-called community organizer. Community activists in Chicago often functioned more like advocates for the Chicago political machine—not unlike the house Negroes in the days of slavery. They would make sure the Black community would see access to generational welfare as the primary civil right—and would vote accordingly. While they would protest racism in general terms and at community meetings, Black community organizers drew their power and profit by being part of the Democrat political machine, not by confronting it. Community organizers worked close with the Democrat ward bosses. They got ahead by going along.

The First Chicago Machine President

The principal handlers in Obama's rise from community organizer to the White House were two key operatives of the Chicago machine—David Axelrod and Valerie Jarrett. While it may be a bit of an oversimplification, Axelrod functioned as the Democrat machine's political consigliere, dealing with image, messaging and overall strategy. Jarrett was more of the ideologue and policy wonk, dealing with issues.

Neither of them grew up in Chicago. Axelrod was born into leftwing political activist parents in New York City. His mother was a writer for the left leaning PM newspaper and his father, a psychologist, was a devotee of radical leftist Saul Alinsky.

Jarrett was born of American parents in Iran. She is of mixed European and African ancestry. Her father was a pathologist/geneticist and her mother an educator. They moved to Chicago when Jarrett was six years old.

In Chicago, both developed deep ties to the racist Daley administration—embracing the lip service false welfare narrative of civil rights advocacy.

According to a 2008 article in *The Economist*:

> Mr. Axelrod has been the leading political consultant in Chicago for more than two decades. He helped run Richard Daley's successful campaign to reclaim his father's job as mayor of Chicago; he also helped Rahm Emanuel, now one of the Democratic Party's most powerful figures, to win his congressional seat.

He was also credited with having a special skill for improving the image of Black candidates with White donors and voters. In Obama, Axelrod had a client willing to follow his consultant's game plan.

Obama was never a typical community organizer. He did not rise from the community. Rather, he came to that job with the resume of a blue blood—a Harvard education and a cadre of influential friends. Among the more controversial was former Weatherman Underground terrorist Bill

Ayers and his wife, terrorist Bernadette Dorn, who spent time in prison as an accessory to the murder of a police officer. Ironically, they became accepted members of the Chicago political establishment. Another early Obama supporter was George Soros, international funder of radical left-wing causes. He hosted a fundraiser for Obama when he ran for the state senate—not an office that usually attracts fat cats at that level. Soros would later invest millions in Obama's US Senate and presidential races.

In his successful run for the Illinois State Senate, Obama had an obstacle. Incumbent Alice Palmer was a popular Black legislator who planned to run for reelection. Now with the backing of the Democrat machine, Obama was gifted with the seat when the party bosses, in an unprecedented move, successfully challenged Palmer's nominating petitions—tossing her off the ballot.

As a state senator, and consistent with both Chicago machine politics, Obama arranged for taxpayer money to be granted to his friends in a process known as "earmarking," over which there were virtually no restrictions. In one case, Capers Funnye, a distant cousin of Mrs. Obama, received $ 75,000 for an organization called Blue Gargoyle. There was never any public accounting for the money.

In his book *The Amateur: Barack Obama in the White House* author Edward Klein wrote:

> Barack Obama reveled in that system. He sent money to friends and family (Michael Pfleger and Jeremiah Wright were two more recipients of his largesse) as an Illinois state senator, and as a US Senator, he sent money to his wife's employer. He was a master of patronage, rewarding loyal supporters with jobs and contracts.

These examples are just a few of the innumerable times funds intended to help the people, especially the poor Blacks kept in that PLACE of generational segregation and poverty, were misdirected to more affluent individuals based solely on political and personal friendship.

With less than two years in the Illinois State Senate, the push was on to give Obama the nomination for the United States Senate seat being vacated by Republican Senator Peter Fitzgerald. Obama would easily beat Black Republican gadfly Alan Keyes who was imported to oppose Obama when the millionaire businessman Jack Ryan dropped out of the race after getting embroiled in a messy divorce and sex scandal. Keyes was an outsider who was selected largely because he was Black.

The influence of the Chicago Democrat machine of Obama can be seen in two personal characteristics. He came to Washington with a sense of boss-ism. The Congress was expected to be more in the rubber stamp tradition of the Chicago city council. This attitude was reinforced by the machine-bred political operatives who joined him in Washington. In addition to Axelrod and Jarrett, there was chief of staff Rahm Emanuel, secretary of education Arne Duncan, economic advisor Austan Goolsbee, secretary of commerce Penny Pritzker and William Daley, brother of the former Chicago mayor. These were all insiders in the corrupt and racist Democrat Machine. Under Obama, the Chicago Democrat machine had more influence in the White House than ever.

As a creature of the Chicago Democrat machine, Obama never was a fighter against the institutional *de facto* racism that oppressed millions of Black Americans living in segregated ghettoes in the major cities controlled by his own party. Despite the horrendous Black murder rates, a growing gang and drug problem, pernicious unemployment and inferior education, Obama largely ignored those issues throughout his eight-year tenure in the Oval Office.

The fact that this outrageous institutional racism can occur in contemporary times in a city where Obama was a community organizer, state senator, US senator, and president demonstrates just how egregiously wrong are the Democrat's false narratives of racial beneficence and civil rights advocacy. Mayors Daley and Emanuel gave nice speeches about civil rights but never took serious action against the most flagrant examples of *de facto* institutional racism that permeated their own political base and had done so for generations.

During the Obama years, Chicago was run by the longest operating and arguably the most powerful political machine in America, and the most racist. With Richard J. Daley and Richard M. Daley serving more than fifty years combined, it was almost a family business. In 2011, when the younger Daley stepped down, the people of Chicago elected Obama's one-time chief of staff Rahm Emanuel as mayor.

Laquan McDonald

In November of 2015, the Chicago police department was ordered to release a video of the shooting of a seventeen-year-old Black man, Laquan McDonald, that had occurred one year earlier.

McDonald was walking down the middle of the street away from several officers in multiple police cars. Seeming without provocation, a White officer, Jayson Van Dyke, opened fire and continued to shoot as McDonald lay on the ground. He fired a total of sixteen times. The release of the video resulted in mass demonstrations in the Black community. Officer Van Dyke was subsequently charged with first degree murder.

The shocking fact is that McDonald was shot in October of 2014, more than a year before the forced release of the tape and the indictment of Van Dyke. The police department refused to release the tape, claiming the event was still under "active investigation"—a fact that would protect the video from Freedom of Information requests. The court finally ordered the release at the request of independent journalist Brandon Smith because of the length of time that had gone by and the fact that there was no evidence of an ongoing investigation.

What was going on was a political cover-up. Apart from the one video, all the police audio recordings suffered "technical difficulties," preventing investigators from hearing what was said by police and the victim. Police secured surveillance tapes from local stores. They were returned erased. Privately, McDonald's family was paid $5 million in compensation. Hush money that required a promise not to release the tapes.

Because of the video, hundreds of Blacks took to the streets in protest. Protesters were guided to the Michigan Avenue Gold Coast business district. They threatened to "shut down the city" during the Thanksgiving shopping holiday as if the merchants and shoppers were to blame for the tragic death of McDonald. Most Black protests take place far from city hall and the officials most responsible for the conduct of police.

Black Pastor Boycott

Under Chicago mayor Rahm Emanuel the historic racism of the machine came under attack from the Black community. In the wake of the McDonald shooting protestors took to the streets. Approximately sixty of the city's leading Black pastors announced their boycott of the mayor's annual Martin Luther King prayer breakfast. Bishop Edgar Mullins of the Grace Family Worship Center said, "Our problems cannot be solved with bacon and eggs."

Bishop James Duke of the Liberation Christian Center was more direct in blaming Emanuel. "We don't think that a kumbaya breakfast at this moment is the time that we should be at the table with our mayor."

Pastor Ira Acree of the Greater St. John Bible Church said, "It would be a shame for us as ministers to provide Mayor Emanuel political cover that he would desire."

Father Michael Pfleger, a White civil rights Catholic priest with a Black congregation at St. Sabina's proclaimed, "King was my mentor and I'm tired of having him pimped."

Emanuel's Black Democrat allies on the city council remained in support of the mayor against the community, as was most often the case.

Unfortunately, such occasional protests by the Black community in Chicago, as well as other Democrat run cities, has not had the Black community reconsidering their electoral support for the people in charge.

Ghetto Law Enforcement

Law enforcement in Democrat run cities has had an undercurrent of racism since the Great Migration of the early twentieth century. This is one of the reasons inner-city Blacks took to the streets in Baltimore, Maryland as late as 2015, with sympathy demonstrations in cities across the nation. All statistics establish that Blacks, mostly from the ghettoes, are detained, arrested and convicted at disproportionate rates—and given harsher sentences—than White counterparts. It is no coincidence that this disparity occurs largely where Democrats control the police, the prosecutors and the courts.

One explanation for this is the amount of crime in Black communities. It naturally requires increased police surveillance and apprehension. Even considering that fact, however, the hammer of justice routinely comes down harder on urban Blacks than on any other ethnic group—and that is particularly true in the segregated urban centers.

While most police officers do not engage in racially abusive policing, there is often a code of silence that protects and thereby tolerates abusive racist tactics. Historically, police commanders and political machine prosecutors have shown little interest in addressing police brutality. Too often they are part of it.

Jon Burge

Jon Burge was a Chicago police commander, a position that can only be attained in Chicago with the approval of the city hall. He became the face of police torture when his excesses caught the attention of investigative reporters, reform-minded law students and honest lawyers.

Burge would torture those in custody and promote torture techniques among lower ranking officers. Between 1971 and 1992, more than 100 detainees—mostly Black—were confirmed to have been tortured with electrical devices, burned against hot radiators, or beaten with night sticks and other weapons according to reports uncovered by investigative journalist John Conroy.

Prisoners were subjected to hours of harassment, threats, and other forms of intimidation. Police torture and brutality was widely known, not only in the minority community but among the general public and political leaders. It could not have been so violent and pervasive without the intentional inattention and acquiescence of the Democrat leaders from the ward organizations to the office of the mayor. It should be kept in mind that the Burge case was not the Democratic Party in Mississippi in the 1940s. It was the Chicago Democrat machine in the twenty-first century.

Ronald Kitchen

The case of Ronald Kitchen is both shocking and typical of abusive police tactics that were employed by the Democrat political machine bosses.

Kitchen was arrested and told the charge was auto theft. Once in custody, the real charge was a sensational murder of two White women and three children. Kitchen was beaten. In one method, the police placed a phone book on his head and beat it with nightsticks to deliver maximum impact without leaving lacerations. Nightsticks were also used against his groin area. Shades of the old Democrat-controlled South; Kitchen was told "we have ways of making niggers talk."

After sixteen hours, Kitchen agreed to sign anything. He was subsequently convicted of murder and sentenced to death. He spent twenty-one years in prison, thirteen on death row, before being released and exonerated of the crime.

Burge Gets a Slap on the Wrist

The Democrat machine was not eager to prosecute Burge. By the time he was to be brought to justice, the local Democrat prosecutor had allowed the statute of limitations to run out on the torture charges. In 2010, he was convicted on a far less serious charge of lying about the torture that took place under his command. He was sentenced to a short term in prison and released. He continued to draw his full taxpayer-paid pension. Racist police enforcement did not end with the removal and conviction of Captain Burge.

America's Capital of False Confessions

Though false confessions by Blacks have been an issue in most cities, Chicago, with more than an eighty-year history of Democratic Party dominance, receives the dubious honor of having the most cases. In 2012, CBS News show *60 minutes* ran a segment on Chicago, highlighting the cases of two groups of Black teenagers who were intimidated into giving false confessions to murder charges. The title of the show declared Chicago as the False Confession Capital of America. In the report, Peter Neufeld of the Innocence Project said "Quite simply, what Cooperstown is to baseball, Chicago is to false confessions. It is the Hall of Fame."

The problem is not unique to Chicago. At that time, the Innocence Project had exonerated more than three hundred men wrongfully convicted across the country by using DNA testing. Mostly Black men sent to prison from Democrat-controlled cities and counties.

Both groups consisted of four Black teenagers who were coerced into making false confessions in rape/murder cases. The youngest was fourteen years old. All were convicted with sentences ranging from fifteen years to life. During their interrogations, they were subjected to constant harassment and abuse by teams of police officers for extended periods of time—as much as twelve hours.

During his interview, Terrill Swift said he wanted to call his mother or a lawyer. The request was denied. He cried during much of the interrogation. Swift was finally told he could go home if he just signed the confession. Emotionally spent, he signed.

Others spoke of the same technique—long interrogation and the promise to go home if they signed. Many young kids in such situations believed that if they signed, they could get home and recant, and the truth would come out. In fact, they were not released as promised. Though they attempted to recant their confessions, they were jailed, prosecuted, and convicted with no physical evidence to prove their guilt except the false confession.

After spending half their lives in prison, they were all eventually exonerated and released. The police who forced the confessions were never brought up on charges. In fact, the Democrat Cook County state's attorney Anita Alvarez defended the police against strong evidence of their guilt. She said in the interview that "We have not uncovered any evidence of any misconduct by the police officers or the state's attorneys … in these cases."

Alavarez further admitted that they found none of the boys' DNA on the scene. No fingerprints. Nothing.

In fact, the authorities had rejected DNA evidence. The Innocence Project arranged to test DNA found in one of the victims. It matched a serial rapist named Johnny Douglas who had since died. Despite that new evidence, Alvarez did not change her mind regarding the convictions of the young men.

In the second case, DNA found in the victim was tested. A match was made to Willie Randolph, a convicted rapist.

With compelling evidence that these two groups young men were innocent, Alvarez' prosecutors posed an absurd theory. That the rapists had come across the dead bodies and engaged in necrophilia—having sex with a dead person. Ignoring the obvious, Alvarez said of the necrophilia theory: "It's possible. We have seen cases like that."

The CBS host pressed the issue incredulously, but Alverez stuck to her preposterous theory that it was possible that the young man "wandered past an open field and had sex with a 14-year-old girl who is dead?"

Alvarez supported that possibility and continued her refusal to consider the DNA evidence as exonerating of the Black men who had now been proven to be falsely convicted. She said: "Well there's all kind of possibilities out there. What I am saying, I don't know what happened. I could not tell you today if they are all guilty or all innocent."

The arrests of Black teenagers, forcing false confessions, and convicting them to long sentences or in some cases death, smack of the same White Democrat methods in the Old South—even to the point of coming up with the most nonsensical explanations.

This kind of conduct would have been expected from Democrat terrorist organizations such as the Ku Klux Klan or the all-White Democrat justice system in such places as Mississippi in the days of Jim Crow justice. These cases, however, were in the twenty-first century in a city in which the Democratic Party had controlled police, prosecutors and the courts since 1931.

For most law-abiding citizens, it is hard to imagine that innocent people would provide a false confession to crimes, especially capital crimes. Part of the reason people cannot understand false confessions is because it is hard to believe that police would employ the brutal tactics necessary to get those confessions through extreme fear, lies and desperation. These are the same war criminal tactics used in World War II, the Korean War and the Vietnam War to secure public confessions from American prisoners of war.

Homan Square, Chicago

The Homan neighborhood tells the story of Chicago's institutional racism from two very important vantage points. The first shows how institutional racism is carried out. It is not theoretical or a one-off anecdotal story. It also shows how such activities had the tacit support by the greater community, including the business leadership.

Homan was one of those all-Black sections of Chicago commonly referred to as "a bad neighborhood"—meaning crime ridden and unsafe. It was also the national headquarters of Sears, Roebuck & Co.

The mostly White employees traveled to work by rail on the Chicago Transit Authority's Eisenhower Line. They would walk the three blocks from the station to the headquarters between two squads of police on each side of the street before entering the fortress-like fenced-in Sears executive offices and warehouse complex.

Because Sears headquarters was essentially a gated community, there was little economic benefit for the residents of the surrounding neighborhood. The overwhelmingly White Sears employees rarely left the security of the compound to visit local restaurants, fill a prescription, or drop off cleaning. It was an economic island of White wealth surrounded by a Black commercial desert.

In Mayor Daley's Chicago, there were no inquiries into Sears' hiring practices. There was no outcry from local civil rights leaders, such as Jesse Jackson, or from the Black politicians representing the citizens of the impoverished and segregated community. Even though Sears was an enormous economic engine for Chicago, there was virtually no economic benefit to the neighborhood surrounding the headquarters other than modest financial support for the local YMCA.

Sears Leaves Homan Avenue

Sears chairman at the time of the Sears Tower construction was Gordon Metcalf, a very close friend of Mayor Daley—as were almost all the major Chicago CEOs.

With growing Black unrest in America, including Chicago, Sears decided to move out of the all-Black west side for a new headquarters office in one of the growing suburbs. That was the plan. Daley wanted Sears to stay in Chicago, preferably by moving to a downtown Loop location. The suburban plan was virtually locked in until Metcalf met with the mayor.

After a meeting with Daley, Metcalf told this author that Daley was very persuasive in insisting that the company move downtown. According to Metcalf, Daley laid down a friendly threat. "Gordon," he said, "you have every right to move out of Chicago, but you will still have a lot of stores in my city, and I have a lot of inspectors who can shut them down." Daley chuckled, but the threat was not toothless since he had recently used inspectors to shut down neighborhood movie theaters for showing X-rated movies.

As Daley demanded, the decision was made to move the Sears corporate headquarters into Chicago's main business district. Daley had another request, however. He wanted Sears to publicly state that the company was considering three options: moving to the suburbs, moving downtown, or rebuilding at the Homan location.

The latter was nothing more than a public relations panacea for the Black community. There was no intention of rebuilding in the Black community on the west side. But the idea was floated to keep Black "agitators" from coming out against the actual plan at the onset. Daley would oppose the suburban option but praise both in-city options—moving to the Loop or a major development in Homan—as acceptable to him, even though he already knew there was only one option. His downtown option.

After Sears departed, a consortium of political insiders took over the Homan area to create an integrated mixed-use development called Homan Square. The group included Sears new chairman Ed Brennan, former Sears vice president Charley Moran and real estate developer Charlie Shaw. Again, the floated plan was merely a public relations gambit. While the promised development never reached its expectations, it did result in an even darker side of the Chicago's institutional racism.

Police Take Over Homan Square

In 2015, Homan Square would become connected with the continuing institutional racism of the Chicago machine. Within the Homan Square development was established a large police detention and interrogation facility. Various reports later alleged that the Homan Square police facility operated like a CIA Black site, where prisoners were secretly held, questioned, and even tortured. It did not remain secret, however.

The headline in an August 5, 2015, article by Spencer Ackerman and Zach Safford in the *Guardian* read "Chicago police detained thousands of Black Americans at interrogation facility." Ackerman and Safford claimed that "At least 3,500 Americans have been detained inside a Chicago police warehouse described by some of its arrestees as a secretive interrogation facility, newly uncovered records reveal."

In a later article, the *Guardian* reported that the real number was more than seven thousand people were detained from August of 2004 to June of 2015, with only sixty-eight being allowed access to attorneys. There was no public notice of their whereabouts as required by law. More than 86 percent of those taken to Homan Square interrogation facility were Black. Most of the remainder were Hispanics.

The article gave examples of how individuals were "abducted by masked officers, shackled, and held on false charges without access to food, water or attorneys based on an authority referred to only as "covert operations." Media reports and a subsequent lawsuit by the *Guardian* have delineated a horrific array of illegal "enhanced interrogation" techniques, including beatings and sleep deprivation.

Of the more than seven thousand "arrests" uncovered by Ackerman and Safford, two-thirds occurred during the mayoralty of Rahm Emanuel, previously President Obama's chief of staff and political confidant. Despite a long list of specific examples of violations of law and constitutional rights, Emanuel insisted that his police department was "following the rules."

While more than 54 percent of arrests by Chicago police occur within 2.5 miles of Homan Square, the facility is more than a neighborhood police station. Arrestees from all over the city were transported to Homan Square for interrogation.

Most involved drug crimes, but also such minor offenses as urinating in public or failure to wear a seatbelt. This would land arrestees in prolonged detention without outside contact. One seventeen-year-old was held for fourteen hours without the required public listing of his whereabouts as his family frantically searched for him—and his was one of the shorter secret detentions.

According to defense attorney David Gaeger, whose client was held there on a marijuana charge:

> Operating a massive, red-brick warehouse between two of the most crime-filled areas in the city of Chicago, equipped with floodlights, cameras, razor-wire—this near-paramilitary wing of the government that we've created, I would say that people who live close to it know what purpose it serves the most. The demographics that surround it speak for themselves.

Gaeger added:

> Try finding a phone number for Homan to see if anyone's there. You can't, ever. If you're laboring under the assumption that your client's at Homan, there really isn't much you can do as a lawyer. You're shut out. It's guarded like a military installation. . .. It's a scary place. There's nothing about it that resembles a police station. It comes from a Bond Movie or something.

While the Chicago example of police racist brutality is extreme, the abuse of Black prisoners in the segregated communities of the major American cities is iconic.

Chicago Civic Committee Report

The Chicago Civic Committee is composed of the top chief executive officers of the largest corporations in the Windy City. It serves as an example of how the business community is cowed into passivity when operating under politically racist governance.

The CEOs were casually referred to as the Cardinals. Below them was a working group of "loaned" mid-management personnel volunteered by the Cardinals. They were called the Monsignors. The author was one of them.

Because police brutality and racism were attracting public attention, the Cardinals launched a study to address the issue, and the monsignors were commissioned to craft and produce it.

The initial draft of the study produced by the Monsignors pointed the finger at city hall. It proposed that the Cardinals meet with Mayor Daley to encourage him to take specific actions since the institutional racism was being carried out with the acquiescence, if not always the direction, of city hall. Only the all-powerful mayor could change the system.

That carried the implication that Mayor Daley and the Democrats were responsible for knowingly presiding over a racist government. He was, but that was not what the Cardinals were prepared to address.

In discussing the report then Sears chairman Arthur Wood, he told me "there was no way in hell that we will carry that message to my good friend Mayor Daley." The report was never approved or published. The old system of city hall sanctioned institutional racism would continue unabated.

Black Protests Against Police

The ubiquitous presence of video recorders, including security cameras, cell phone cameras and police body cams changed the outcome of police violence, giving credence to Black claims of a double standard in policing. Racist policing – real and perceived – has been the point of the spear in terms of violent responses to institutional racism in America's Democrat-run major cities.

I Can't Breathe" in New York City

In 2014, three New York City police officers approached a large Black man, Eric Garner, illegally selling individual cigarettes on the street. The entire incident was captured on video cam.

The suspect appeared to be protesting his arrest when officer Daniel Pantaleo came up from behind, grabbed him around the neck and took him to the ground. He retained his hold until the man could be handcuffed. Even as the suspect repeatedly cried out that he could not breathe the office did not appear to release the choke hold and Garner died as a result. His death triggered demonstrations and riots in New York City resulting in the arrests of eighty-three people. Protest and violent riots broke out in other cities across the country—cities with similar incidents of racist policing and virtually all with Democrat municipal leadership.

It would be hard to find any Democrat mayor who personified the Democrats false civil rights narrative more than then New York Mayor Bill de Blasio. As a far left progressive, de Blasio talked the talk of civil rights, but ruled over a city with a long and sad tradition of Black oppression. He failed to bring resolution to the issue of inner-city crime and racist policing. By all demographic and statistical measures, de Blasio improved nothing for the Blacks trapped in that PLACE.

Pantaleo was never brought to trial, but was removed from the police force by administrative action five years after Garner's death by administrative action.

Baltimore Riot, 2015

On April 12, 2015, several Baltimore police arrested Freddie Gray, a twenty-five-year-old Black man with a rap sheet of largely petty offenses. Why they wanted to take him into custody and why he chose to run was never convincingly explained, one way or the other. Gray had to be forcibly restrained and was placed in a police van to be taken to the police station. In that process, Gray suffered a broken neck and died from his injuries a few days later.

The fury in the Black ghetto of East Baltimore was not to be restrained. As was often the case in such outbursts of public frustration and anger, the peaceful demonstrations quickly led to full scale rioting characterized by the same type of looting and arson that is seen in racial rioting in many cities over many years.

In the aftermath of one night of rioting, some six hundred small businesses and residences, mostly belonging to members of the local Black community, were burned to the ground. Scores of motor vehicles were torched, including police cars. More than four hundred residents were arrested. The negative economic impact was between $20 and $30.5 million dollars, according to various estimates.

The riot in Baltimore was fueled by Black frustration over generations of Democrat racist rule. As far back as 1959, and Urban League report titled "The Negros in Baltimore" cited the problems of racial segregation and injustice in the city. The damning Report covered education, housing, employment and justice. The report was issued following the twelve-year tenure of Democrat Mayor Thomas D'Alesandro.

Chicago Machine Loses Expands

By the time Rahm Emanuel was elected as mayor of Chicago, the number of Black voters had increased despite Chicago's Black diaspora policies of the late 1990s. Emanuel sparked outrage from the Black community due to a serious of incidents that were seen to be racist.

Emanuel's apparent acceptance of the Homan police detention facility, and his defense of police following the media reports, angered back leaders and citizens.

Following the 2014 murder of seventeen-year-old Laquan McDonald by White police officer Jason Van Dyke, the Emanuel administration, in conjunction with the police department, engaged in what appeared to be an effort to cover up the nature of the killing. The incriminating video was withheld from the public for more than a year. Upon release of the video the Van Dyke was convicted of second-degree murder and other charges and sentenced to six years in prison. He was released after serving less than half is terms, which renewed anger among Black citizens.

The Emanuel administration focused community investment money on wealthy White neighborhoods, such as basketball arenas and a recreational river walk. While this was a common racist approach by the Chicago machine, Black tolerance was ebbing. Emanuel ordered the closing of more than 50 public schools impacting mostly on Black and Hispanic students.

In 2018, Emanuel appeared to be endorsing the old racist canard that Blacks are less moral and more prone to criminality than White people when he said Blacks need to develop "a sense of values and character."

Facing growing hostility from the Black community, Emanual chose not to seek reelection in 2019. It set up the dramatic downfall of the historic Chicago political machine.

Chicago Elects a Black Woman Mayor

What the White Chicago Democrat leadership feared more than anything was the return of a Black mayor. That was the reason for the change in Chicago elections to a nonpartisan runoff system in 1995. But that method would only work if the number of Black voters did not reach a critical mass, and only two White candidates would reach the runoff stage. That is not what happened in 2019.

Among a number of White candidates was William Daley, son and brother of the two previous Daleys and who was expected to be the new "boss" of the political machine. Instead of Daley facing one Black candidate in the final round, the White candidates divided the White vote, and two Black candidates were left to face off in the final round. They were Cook County board president Toni Preckwinkle and a one-time Democrat machine bureaucrat Lori Lightfoot, who surprisingly finished first among the field of candidates. Lightfoot went on to win the general election.

In many ways, Lightfoot was reminiscent of Jane Byrne, the Wind City's only previous female mayor. Both were loyal machine bureaucrats who eventually broke with the incumbent mayor. Neither was a reformer. Lightfoot had been head of the police board that was primarily responsible for defending police actions.

Ironically, it would be Chicago's soaring crime rate, and Lightfoot's seeming siding against police and with Black Lives Matter activists that would be among a number of factors resulting in a drop of popularity, which eventually led to her defeat in 2023.

Democrats' Confederate Dilemma

Since the founding of the Republic, prominent people from all walks of life have been honored with statues, memorials and public recognitions of one sort or another. Many of these were related to the Civil War, and understandably they are found in greatest numbers in the old Confederate states.

The Old South was riddled with monuments to Confederate military and political leaders. The Confederate battle flag was enshrined in places of honor in several southern states. The battle banner was imbedded in state flags, depicted on license plates or flown on state government grounds.

Contrary to widely held beliefs, the honoring of the Confederate battle flag in places of prominence was not a holdover from the Civil War. They were enshrined as acts of civil rights defiance carried out by several southern governors and legislatures in the 1950s and 1960s as part of the Democrat's Massive Resistance movement against school desegregation and the federal government's more aggressive support of civil and constitutional rights following from the *Brown v. Board of Education* Supreme Court decision in 1954. In a larger sense, they were symbols of defiance against the Eisenhower civil rights acts of 1957 and 1960, and the Republican-supported civil rights acts of 1964 and 1965.

Demands to remove the names and images of racist political figures from places of public and academic honor created a serious threat to the Democrat false narrative of civil rights advocacy. If it spread, the Democratic Party could be faced with embarrassingly removing thousands of names from millions of places. In fact, the number of honored historic Democrat racists is so huge that there would be a paucity of Democrat leaders to honor.

Though she did not note the overwhelming Democrat political affiliation of those under assault from a civil rights standpoint, Hava Holzhauer, of the American Defense League (ADL) of Florida said:

> There have been debates taking place nationally … about schools, streets, parks and landmarks whose namesakes do not live up to the ideals that we today hold dear. From Confederate flags … to streets named after KKK founders, many of us are oblivious to the historic figures who were once considered heroic icons and today would never make the list.

It these historic personalities were ever "considered heroic icons," it was mostly to a shrinking population of White racists and Civil War romantics. It was not until Republicans took control in the South that these symbols of slavery and Black oppression came under serious assault, with many removed.

Florida Takes Down the Battle Flag

The Confederate battle flag has flown in a place of honor on the capitol grounds in Tallahassee since 1978. It was placed there under the administration of Democrat governor Reubin Askew. It was removed at the order of Republican governor Jeb Bush in 2001.

The Georgia Flag

In 1956, under the administration of racist Democrat governor Marvin Griffin, the Confederate symbol was added to the official Georgia flag. Griffin was a staunch segregationist and proclaimed that Georgia's schools would remain segregated "come hell or high water." Griffin's flag design made the southern battle flag the most dominant feature, taking up almost three-quarters of the state flag area.

In 2003, the offensive Confederate battle flag was removed in a redesign of the Georgia flag under the administration of Republican governor Sonny Perdue.

The South Carolina Flag

In South Carolina, the flag had been placed in the highest position of honor atop the South Carolina statehouse by then-Democrat Governor Ernest Hollings in 1961 as an act of defiance. It was later moved to a location on the grounds of the Capitol.

In response to the Charleston murders in 2015, Republican Governor Nikki Haley requested that the legislature remove the flag from the grounds. Republican State Senator Paul Thurmond, son of the late segregationist United States Senator Strom Thurmond, delivered an impassioned speech in favor of removing the flag. It was completely removed by the overwhelming vote of the Republican-controlled state house and senate.

Flagless Mississippi

Mississippi flew a flag that included the Confederate battle flag since 1894. However, it was discovered that due to an error in filing Mississippi officially had no official flag. That was discovered in 1993 when the NAACP filed a lawsuit to remove the battle flag from the state banner. Democrat governor Ronnie Musgrove pre-empted the lawsuit by issuing an executive order declaring the state flag incorporating the Confederate battle flag to be the official Mississippi flag. The proposal to redesign the flag without the Confederate battle flag was the subject of a 2001 referendum. The issue divided on party lines, with Democrats, including Democrat governor Ronnie Musgrove, favoring the retention of the battle flag and Republicans, such as Mississippi House speaker Philip Gunn and future Republican governor Haley Barbour calling for the battle flag's removal. The proposed change was defeated and despite Republican efforts, the battle flag remains on the official state flag.

The Tennessee Flag and More

Shortly after his election as governor of Tennessee in 2010, Republican Bill Haslam moved to have Confederate symbols and statues removed from places of official honor, and the official displaying of the Confederate battle flag in any manner. He called for an end of the special-order vanity license plate promoted by the Sons of the Confederate Veterans which receives $35 from the taxpayers for each plate. Haslam also called for the removal of the bust of Tennessee Ku Klux Klan founder and slave trader General Nathan Forrest from its PLACE of honor on the grounds of the state capitol.

The installation of a bust Forrest was again not a carryover from the Civil War. It was enshrined in the capitol building, between the house and senate chambers by Democrat governor Ray Blanton in 1978. The initial request for the placement of the statue was made in 1973 in the final days of the Massive Resistance movement by Democrat state senator Douglas Henry of Nashville. In making his announcement, Haslam said: "I think it's appropriate to move the flag to museums and off of Tennessee symbols."

Haslam could legally have all flags and symbols removed since an earlier Democrat-controlled legislature passed a law that specifically prohibited the removal of any monuments honoring the Confederacy from public property. Haslam said he would support any legislation that would accomplish that purpose.

Tennessee's two Republican senators, Lamar Alexander and Robert Corker, both publicly endorsed Haslam's call for the removal of Confederate memorials on state property. The Tennessee Historical Commission finally removed the Forrest bust in 2020.

Confederate Flag Loses its License in Texas

In 2011, Texas Republican governor Rick Perry expressed his opposition to an application from the Sons of Confederate Veterans to have a specialty or vanity plate with the image of the Confederate battle flag. Perry garnered bipartisan support for his position, especially among Black officials. He said, "That's just a part of history that you don't need to scrape that wound again."

After the board of the Texas Department of Motor Vehicles (all nine appointed by Perry) unanimously rejected the application, they were slapped with a lawsuit by the Sons of Confederate Veterans, who claimed it was covered by constitutional free speech, as are the flags on private property. In June of 2015, however, the United States Supreme Court held that the depiction on the license plate was the speech of the state government and therefore could be removed from the plates at the will of the Texas government.

The case for removal of the flag on the license plate was argued by Republican solicitor general Jonathan H. Mitchell, who had recently been appointed by Texas Republican attorney general Greg Abbott. Abbott would go on to be governor of Texas.

In arguing the case, Mitchell said: "Texas is not willing to propagate the Confederate battle flag by etching that image onto state-issued license plates that bear the State's name."

Alabama Removes Battle Flag

The Confederate flag had flown atop the Alabama capitol building along with the American and Alabama state flags. The flags were temporarily removed for renovation in 1993. At the time the flags were to reappear atop the capitol, Republican governor H. Guy Hunt refused to reinstall the Confederate flag citing an 1895 law limiting such display to the national and state banner. The law was upheld in court and the Confederate flag was no longer flying over the capitol building.

In the 1950s, as part of the Southern Resistance Movement against school integration, and to get around the 1895 law, Democrat governor George Wallace add the battle flag as a feature on the official state flag.

Republican governor Robert Bentley of Alabama ordered the battle flag removed as part of the official state flag in June of 2015.

In taking the action, Bentley said: "This is the right thing to do. This had the potential to become a major distraction as we go forward. And it was my decision that the flag needed to come down."

Bentley was subsequently sued by attorney Melvin Hastings, who expressed his opposition to the flag removal as an "aggrieved citizen." In his lawsuit, he requested that the court restrain Bentley from: "unilaterally and unlawfully alter[ing] the historical and heritage significance of objects, buildings, monuments and landmarks from the Confederacy era."

His suit was subsequently dismissed in court.

It Was Not Just the Confederates

What began as an effort to remove honors provided to individuals most associated with slavery, racism and treason against the Union, soon expanded, mostly by leftwing activist, to an assault on the Founders who owned slaves. Rather than the orderly and legal removal of statues and memorials, leftwing mobs indiscriminately defaced, destroyed and toppled statues of George Washington, Thomas Jefferson, and others. Inexplicably, even Abraham Lincoln was not spared. For the radical left, it became a pervasive assault on American culture and values.

Who Put Blacks in that PLACE?

Surprisingly, it was on the campuses of America's great institutions of higher learning that racist iconography retained great prominence. Colleges and universities, especially in the South, have statues, busts, murals, windows, halls, academic chairs and buildings honoring some of the most infamous racist figures in American history. Many of the Democrats most infamous White supremacist icons remained officially celebrated and honored despite an occasional public protest.

The Princeton Story

In 2015, Black students at Princeton University—calling themselves the Black Justice League—demonstrated against honoring of the school's former president Woodrow Wilson for his White supremacist views. They demanded the removal of memorials celebrating Wilson and the renaming of the Woodrow Wilson School of public and international affairs.

The *HuffPost Black Voices* noted that "Student activists at Princeton have taken action against President Woodrow Wilson's legacy of racism by forcing the school administration to consider taking his name off of the school of public policy."

When the University refused to remove the name of the institution's racist president from campus buildings and programs, the Black Justice League put out a statement that said:

> Princeton remains unable to even reckon and wrestle with its white supremacist foundations and its ongoing role in perpetuating racism, instead delivering shallow words and hollow promises. . . .

> Princeton continues to demonstrate its seemingly intractable investment in white supremacy and its vestiges. Princeton's decision today demonstrates unambiguously its commitment to symbols and legacies of anti-Blackness in the name of 'history' and 'tradition' at the expense of the needs of and in direct contravention with the daily experiences of Black students at Princeton.

Interestingly, the student demonstration did not attract the support or attention of the major Democrat civil rights personalities such as Jesse

Jackson and Al Sharpton. It is not unreasonable to assume that their reticence was due to the fact that this particular protest brought too much focus on the Democratic Party and one of the Party's most revered icons. It is no small irony that the major leftwing leaders of the Democratic Party continue to assemble at the Woodrow Wilson Center at One Wilson Plaza in Washington, DC.

Calhoun College

In 2020, a Black dishwasher named Corey Menafee took a broom and broke a stained-glass panel that depicted two slaves picking cotton. The panel was on display at the residential Calhoun College on the campus of Yale University. The College is named after Democrat vice president John C. Calhoun, a slave owner and a staunch advocate of slavery. Menafee said he was tired of looking at the panel every time he came to work.

Menafee's action produced a campus protest demanding the renaming of the college and the removal of allegedly racist artifacts. The school removed from display many items associated with Vice President Calhoun and the era in which he lived but refused to rename the school. In 1957, the Democrat-controlled Congress named Calhoun one of the five greatest United States senators of all time.

Forrest Street

Hollywood, Florida is typical of many southern cities in which innumerable public places were named after prominent Civil War leaders and Democrat racist officeholders during the Jim Crow era. Forrest Street, named after Confederate General Nathan Bedford Forrest, takes residents from the city's western neighborhoods to the ocean. The city has two other streets named after Confederate generals, Robert E. Lee and John Bell Hood. While there had been calls to also rename them, the more intense focus has been on Forrest because of his leadership role in the Ku Klux Klan.

Who Put Blacks in that PLACE?

In 2015, protesters demanded the renaming of the streets. The demands were resisted for three years, but in 2019, the streets were renamed Freedom, Hope, and Liberty.

The Renaming Movement Expands

The movement to remove the names and symbols of Confederate racists first launched by Republican State administrations in the south spread throughout the country as municipal governments renamed streets, parks, schools and public buildings. Many of the streets were renamed after notable Black leaders in the civil rights movement.

Following are a few of the hundreds of examples.

Lee Highway in Fairfax County, Virginia, was renamed Langston Boulevard after John Langston, the first Black Congressman from Virginia and founder of Howard University.

Austin, Texas, renamed Robert E. Lee Road as Azie Taylor Morton Road after the first Black woman to serve as United States Treasurer.

Montgomery, Alabama, renamed Jeff Davis Avenue as Fred D. Gray Avenue after the civil rights attorney who represented Martin Luther King and Rosa Parks.

While many of the actions were ultimately taken by Democrat administrations under public pressure, there was no effort by Democrats to address the pantheon of racist officeholders in their own ranks during the 100 years of institutional *de jure* and *de facto* racism in the south and the major cities.

Obama, The Great Hope

Upon entering office, President Obama promised to improve the plight of Black Americans and lead the nation to an era of post-racism. After four years in office, he accomplished neither.

Obama came to office as a product of the racist Chicago political machine. He exacerbated racial tension by governing as a strident urban Democrat devoted to the false civil rights narrative of generational welfare.

Nowhere was that more evident than in the conduct of his Justice Department under Attorney General Eric Holder and his anointing racial provocateur Al Sharpton as the national spokesperson on matters civil rights for the Obama administration. Sharpton is the type of Black leader presaged by Booker T. Washington when he said:

> There is another class of coloured people who make a business of keeping the troubles, the wrongs and the hardships of the Negro race before the public. Having learned that they are able to make a living out of their troubles, they have grown into the settled habit of advertising their wrongs — partly because they want sympathy and partly because it pays. Some of these people do not want the Negro to lose his grievances, because they do not want to lose their jobs.

As with the White Democrat presidents before him, Obama was given to grand racial gestures and strong rhetoric with little change in policy or outcomes. In response to a question from April Ryan, the White House correspondent for the Urban Radio Network, Obama said, "Like the rest of America, Black America, in the aggregate, is better off now than it was when I came into office."

The facts say otherwise. Black unemployment in 2008 was 9.1 percent, compared to a 5 percent unemployment rate over all demographics. By 2010, overall unemployment rate peaked at 9.7 percent (with the White rate at 8.7 percent). Black unemployment at the time was 16.7 percent. It is fair to say that while the White community was suffering a recession, the Black community was still in a full depression.

In 2015, after almost seven years in office, White unemployment was 4.5 percent, but Black unemployment was 9.5 percent—higher than White unemployment at the peak of the recession. The number of individuals on the Supplemental Nutrition Assistance Program (SNAP), often referred to as food stamps, had risen by 45 percent during Obama's tenure office.

Obama and the Democrats often cite the expansion of SNAP as a civil rights benefit. Rather than promote Black employment, Obama placed emphasis on more welfare that would keep millions of Black Americans in that PLACE of generational poverty. It was the same old welfare for votes scheme that has kept millions of Blacks segregated, uneducated and living below the poverty level.

Under Obama, the Black community was actually losing ground. Real Clear Politics reported that the poverty rate for Blacks was 25.8 when Obama took office, and by 2014 it had risen to 27.2. Almost 50 percent of Black children under the age of six live in poverty compared to 14.5percent White children in that age group.

Having a Black president in the White House has not brought improvement to those trapped in the Democrat's urban ghettoes. There were more racial protests and criminal violence in Democrat controlled cities than at any time since the height of the civil rights movement in the 1960s.

It is no small irony that one of the cities suffering the greatest human carnage in the segregated Black communities was Obama's political base of Chicago. Tavis Smiley, a progressive media personality summed up the Obama years. In an article in the *Huffington Post*, Smiley lamented: "Sadly—and it pains me to say this—over the last decade, black folk, in the era of Obama, have lost ground in every major category."

On January 15, 2015, Black journalist and author Lauren Victoria Burke wrote a column summarizing Obama's first six years in office under the headline: "Is Black America Better Off Under Obama?" In response to the president's contention, Burke answered:

> What planet African Americans are doing "better off" on is unknown. What is known is that President Obama is about to leave office with African Americans in their worst economic situation since Ronald Reagan. A look at every key stat as President Obama starts his sixth year in office illustrates that.

She covered several issues—unemployment:

> The average Black unemployment under President Bush was 10 percent. The average under President Obama after six years is 14 percent. Black unemployment, "has always been double" [that of Whites] but it hasn't always been 14 percent. The administration was silent when Black unemployment hit 16 percent—a 27-year high—in late 2011.

On poverty in general:

The percentage of Blacks in poverty in 2009 was 25 percent; it is now 27 percent. The issue of poverty is rarely mentioned by the president or any members of his cabinet. Currently, more than 45 million people—1 in 7 Americans—live below the poverty line.

On the Black/White wealth gap:

The wealth gap between Blacks and Whites in America is at a 24-year high. A December study by PEW Research Center revealed the average White household is worth $141,900, and the average Black household is worth $11,000. From 2010 to 2013, the median income for Black households plunged 9 percent.

On income inequality:

Between 2009 and 2012 the top one percent of Americans enjoyed 95 percent of all income gains, according to research from U.C. Berkeley. It was the worst since 1928.

In terms of education:

The high school dropout rate has improved during the Obama administration. However, currently 42 percent of Black children attend high poverty schools, compared to only 6 percent of White students.

The reference to "high poverty schools" meant that Blacks are disproportionately attending urban schools where education is substandard if it exists at all.

On minority business, Burke writes:

In March 2014, the Wall Street Journal reported that only 1.7 percent of $23 billion in SBA loans went to Black-owned businesses in 2013, the lowest loan of SBA lending to Black businesses on record. During the Bush presidency, the percentage of SBA loans to Black businesses was 8 percent—more than four times the Obama rate.

In her column, Burke gives credit to Obama for "understanding" the plight of Black America, but not acting on it:

> President Obama said of African Americans that, "They're working hard… They're out there hustling and trying to get an education, trying to send their kids to college. But they're starting behind, oftentimes, in the race." Obama seems to understand the historic adversity Blacks have faced yet that understanding hasn't translated into the hard mechanics of specific policy such as funding for summer jobs, budget increases for community block grants or substantial increases for Pell Grants or programs such as Gear Up.

This inability to translate rhetoric into action is central to the Democrat's false narrative. The lack of action on civil rights has not been a Democratic Party oversight, it has been a matter of intentional policy.

Burke also understood how so-called civil rights leaders like Al Sharpton fit into the scenario. She wrote:

> In 2011, when Al Sharpton told CBS' 60 Minutes that, "Obama already said he won't do anything for Blacks, duh," it signaled that Black civil rights leaders would not push the first Black president hard on Black issues. Sharpton has been in the White House 61 times since 2009, probably more than any member of Congress, including leadership, over that period. With that type of access to power one has to ask: Where are the positive policy results?

Unlike Martin Luther King, who risked his life and fortune in the pursuit of civil rights for Black Americans, Sharpton has pursued civil rights as a lucrative business and has made millions of dollars in the process. Where King dared to look down the barrel of guns, Sharpton faces the lens of news cameras.

Burke concluded that "All segments of Black America seem willing to give President Obama a pass on his failure to deliver for African Americans."

In referring to "all segments of Black America," Burke seems to be exposing such distinguished civil rights organizations as the NAACP and the Urban League as proponents of the pseudo-civil rights of entitlement and dependency. Both these organizations transitioned in the 1940s. They were once politically independent and focused on traditional constitutional civil rights. Now they are part of the Democratic Party coalition and proselytizers of the Party's false narrative of civil rights advocacy.

Obama Declares Welfare Dependency as the Norm

In a White House speech, Obama declared that generational dependency on welfare and entitlements is the new norm, calling them "the realities of how people live now."

Even though the Obama administration policy greatly expanded the scope and cost of federal government programs, the president misrepresented the truth and reality by saying the following:

> And let me be clear, this is not about big government, or expanding some fictional welfare-and-food-stamp state, the 47 percent mooching off the government. *It is accounting for the realities of how people live now, today—the necessities of a 21st century economy.* (emphasis added)

In these remarks, Obama clearly states the Democratic Party's belief in policies to create and maintain an ever-growing underclass in direct opposition to the Republican Party's commitment to reducing welfare entrapment and giving those indentured to the Democrat's political plantation access to the American opportunity society.

The Re-Segregation of America

The federal Government Accounting Office (GAO) analysis of racial demographics showed that between 2001 and 2014—six years into the Obama administration—the number of primarily Black schools had more than doubled.

The *Washington Post* made note of the separate but not equal nature of modern segregated schools in the major cities. They wrote:

> The problem is not just that students are more isolated, according to the GAO, but that minority students who are concentrated in high-poverty schools don't have the same access to opportunities as students in other schools.

The highlighted reflects the multifaceted impact of institutional racism. It keeps Blacks in that PLACE.

The *Post* article further noted that the GAO analysis cited specific problems associated with segregated schools:

> High-poverty, majority-black and Hispanic schools were less likely to offer a full range of math and science courses than other schools, for example, and more likely to use expulsion and suspension as disciplinary tools, according to the GAO.

More results of institutional racism. The GOA study claimed that the situation was an "overwhelming failure to fulfill the promise of *Brown v. Board of Education.*"

Democrat Congressman John Conyers, one of those who called for the GAO study, said that America is reestablishing "educational apartheid." Like so many who advance the false narrative of the Democratic Party, Conyers did not make note of the fact that the overwhelming examples of reestablished segregation and "educational apartheid" has been, and is, overwhelmingly the result of his own party's governance.

The *Post* article, however, addressed the situation as yet another example of President Obama's failure to address *de facto* racism:

> Advocates for desegregation as an essential tool for closing the nation's persistent achievement gap have criticized the Obama administration for giving lip service to the issue without taking meaningful steps to address it.

In responding to the GAO report, the Obama Justice Department became defensive, saying that they already "carefully monitor" cases of illegal segregation. If that were true, it is unlikely that school segregation could be so prevalent and worsening. And it leaves the question, is there such a thing as "legal" segregation?

Democrat Segregation by the Numbers

Though the word "segregation" and the term "separate but equal" have fallen out of the modern lexicon, the urban Democrat policies that have created those situations are still being played out in America's major cities. *De facto* segregation is not only a feature of virtually every urban center but virtually every study and analysis prove beyond a doubt that the metropolitan public-school systems are separate and unequal.

The lead paragraph in University of California Professor Gary Orfield's "Reviving the Goal of an Integrated Society: A 21st Century Challenge" was succinct in its analysis of school desegregation progress:

> Schools in the United States are more segregated today than they have been in more than four decades. Millions of non-white students are locked into "dropout factory" high schools, where huge percentages do not graduate, and few are well prepared for college or a future in the US economy.

Orfield wrote that "For Blacks a significant part of the reversal reflects the ending of desegregation plans in public schools throughout the nation." This "ending of desegregation plans" is a clear reference to the city administrative policies of the governing Democratic Party.

Orfield debunked the perception that school segregation remains an issue in the South based on its history of racial oppression when he wrote that the "Civil Rights Study shows that most severe segregation in public schools is in the Western states, including California—not in the South, as many people believe."

In singling out California, the study offers further evidence that progressive Democrat policies are not synonymous with integration and racial equality.

This was confirmed by presidential candidate Hillary Clinton in a 2015 speech in Ferguson, Missouri when she said, "The truth is equality, opportunity, civil rights in America are still far from where they need to be. Our schools are still segregated, in fact, more segregated than they were in the 1960s."

She knows the facts, but like all Democrats, avoids placing accountability.

In a 2023 appearance on MSNBC, Chicago Mayor Brandon Johnson joined the chorus of Democrat leaders who inadvertently reveal the problem. He said that "we have not totally disrupted or ended decades of systemic racism." He could have said "Democrat systemic racism."

He apparently did not appreciate the irony of confirming the institutional *de facto* racism of Chicago's Democrat political machine for generations. It is the same institutional racism that has plagued most other major American cities for generations.

Racist City Services

Racism was an underpinning of all municipal services. One of the most common racial complaints is that Blacks do not care for their property or the surrounding environment. Any travel though the inner city shows houses in poor condition, streets in need of repairs and parks in shambles. While these conditions are often cited as evidence of Black laziness and slovenliness, they are the result of racist policies emanating from Democrats in city hall.

Once the area was converted from White to Black by blockbusting, official negligence commenced to transform the once pristine White area into a classic slum. City negligence means that curbs would go unrepaired, potholes in the street go unfilled and sidewalks crumble and parks fall into disrepair.

Housing stock deteriorates as buildings are converted into low-rent multi-family tenements—often in violation of housing laws. Slumlords— many of whom are campaign donors, political cronies or relatives of the Democrat leadership—overcrowd housing units and make illegal and unsafe building conversions without fear of city inspection or the necessity of a building permit. This often requires the payment of a political gratuity to the local housing inspector. For the privilege of bleeding the money out of the housing stock, slumlords contribute generously to the Democratic Party. By contrast, housing conditions and occupancy laws—and even graffiti removal—in White neighborhoods are strictly enforced. It is part of the separate and unequal character of racial segregation.

The conditions in the Black neighborhoods ironically provide another opportunity for the Democrat power structure to reinforce the negative image of the Black community, even though the slum conditions were most often the result of official inattention to infrastructure, housing codes, educational quality, and policing.

Obama and the Judiciary

If Obama wanted to make fundamental changes for the millions of ghetto-ized Blacks, he could have started with the judiciary, where he has unique arbitrary powers. Rather, he bent to the will of the Chicago Democrat machine that "brought him to the dance."

Journalist Steven R. Strahler writing in *Crain's Chicago Business, said that* "In his seven years in office, President Barack Obama has filled half of the 22 District Court seats in his hometown without nominating a single black man."

Black author and human rights activist Michelle Alexander summed it up this way:

- There are more African Americans under correctional control today–in prison or jail, on probation or parole–than were enslaved in 1850, a decade before the Civil War began.
- As of 2004, more African American men were disenfranchised (due to felon disenfranchisement laws) than in 1870, the year the Fifteenth Amendment was ratified, prohibiting laws that explicitly deny the right to vote on the basis of race.
- A black child born today is less likely to be raised by both parents than a black child born during slavery. The recent disintegration of the African American family is due in large part to the mass imprisonment of black fathers.
- If you take into account prisoners, a large majority of African American men in some urban areas have been labeled felons for life. (In the Chicago area, the figure is nearly 80 percent.) These men are part of a growing under caste–not class, caste–permanently relegated, by law, to a second-class status. They can be denied the right to vote, automatically excluded from juries, and legally discriminated against in employment, housing, access to education, and public benefits, much as their grandparents and great-grandparents were during the Jim Crow era.

Obama did nothing to stop real police prejudice even in his hometown of Chicago, where the police department maintained a dungeon-like lock up facility during the mayoralty of Rahm Emmanuel, his own chief of staff, and a city in which a record numbers of innocent Blacks were being killed on the streets. More than thirty-nine hundred citizens of Chicago, mostly Blacks, have been murdered during his eight years in office with 762 being killed in 2016 alone, and neither Obama nor his Justice Department under the leadership of Attorney General Eric Holder addressed the issue in any meaningful way.

True to the false narrative of welfare dependency, Obama took pride in expanding the numbers of people trapped in the economic "political plantations" run by powerful Democrat political machines.

As Alexander further noted:

> Recent data shows, though, that much of black progress is a myth. In many respects, African Americans are doing no better than they were when Martin Luther King Jr. was assassinated, and uprisings swept inner cities across America. Nearly a quarter of African Americans live below the poverty line today, approximately the same percentage as in 1968. The black child poverty rate is actually higher now than it was then. Unemployment rates in black communities rival those in Third World countries. And that's with affirmative action!

Black Protesting Against Obama?

Nothing demonstrated Obama's failure as the promised post racial president than the protest march on the president's Justice Department organized by the largely lap dog congressional Black Caucus. Michigan Democrat congressman John Conyers had originally called for a march on the White House. The plan was changed to the Justice Department presumably to not directly confront the first Black president in such an overt fashion.

On September 22, 2016, members of the Black Caucus assembled blocks away from the Department of Justice to commence a symbolic civil rights march to protest the inaction of the Obama administration in addressing police shootings of Black suspects. In leading off the protest, North Carolina congressman G. K. Butterfield, chairman of the Black Caucus said, "Enough is enough." He went on to say:

> The Department of Justice must aggressively pursue investigations, indictments and, yes, prosecutions against any and all law enforcement officers who harm or kill innocent, unarmed African American citizens.

Congresswoman Alma Adams, whose district includes Charlotte, North Carolina, where the most recent shooting took place, said:

I asked the citizens in Charlotte last night what did they want me
to take back to my colleagues here. They said to tell them that we
need the Attorney General to step in and use her power to help make
change that we need.

Had this been a march on a Republican administration, the event might
have received massive and continuing coverage, but since it did not fit
the false narrative, it received very modest media attention. Several outlets
ignored it altogether.

Disappointing Legacy of Barack Obama

Barack Obama made history as the first Black president in American
history. That is not an achievement. That is only a fact. With his election,
Black and White Americans alike expressed hope that he would open the
door to a post-racial color-blind society. For Blacks, he offered hope that the
plight of impoverished Black Americans trapped in segregated cities would
improve—including equal justice under the law, employment opportunities,
better schools, and safer neighbors. He failed to meet those expectations
in every regard. In fact, the plight of Black America measurably worsened
during his eight years in office.

Despite his lip service admiration of Martin Luther King, Obama abandoned the doctrines of the slain civil rights leader to elevate the pandering
racist and highly partisan false narratives preached by Al Sharpton. In many
ways, Obama was more disappointing than any typical White president
might have been because of the enormously heightened anticipation among
Blacks and, indeed, among most Americans.

Like most presidents, Obama left a legacy based on who he is, what
he had achieved, and what he did not. Certainly, his election was a significant indicator that the American public was not the collection of hateful
White supremacists as Democrats and the left constantly proclaim. In
terms of civil rights, his record was a failure. His presidency turned out
to be a lost opportunity. Instead of being the hoped for post-racial president, he arguably deepened the racial divide. The disappointment in him
is profound.

The Tubman Twenty

Slightly more than a century after her death, Republican abolitionist Harriet Tubman became a political issue. Tubman was an escaped slave when she made several trips into the South to guide slaves to freedom. She is the only Negro to have led a detachment of the Union Army into Confederate territory during the Civil War.

A 2015 plan to remove Democrat president Andrew Jackson from the twenty-dollar bill in favor of Black abolitionist Harriet Tubman triggered a racial debate. Democrat leaders lobbied against the removal of Ole Hickory since he is often considered the founder of the modern Democratic Party and the namesake of the Party's annual fundraising dinners. Consequently, President Obama refused to implement the plan.

Despite this onerous background, Democrats have played a leading role in immortalizing Jackson with tens of thousands of monuments, highways and byways, schools, municipalities, public buildings, and the twenty-dollar bill. All across the nation, Democrats celebrated the seventh President of the United States with annual Jackson Day dinners. Jackson, like Presidents Woodrow Wilson and Franklin Roosevelt are revered by Democrats despite their White supremacy views and racist policies.

The Republican Party had every reason to support honoring Tubman on the twenty-dollar bill, and with annual celebrations reflecting her good works and her association with the GOP. While the plan to PLACE her on the American currency was never officially rejected, it was never implemented either.

Election of 2016

The election of 2016 was arguably one of the most significant elections in American history. Businessman Donald J. Trump secured the Republican nomination by way of arguably the most unconventional and bitter primary elections in American history, and the most divisive general election since Abraham Lincoln won the White House in 1860 on the verge of Civil War. As a balance to his own eclectic political philosophy and pugnacious personality, Trump selected the mild-mannered solid intellectual conservative governor of Indiana, Mike Pence.

Democrats gave their nomination to former First Lady, former New York Senator and former secretary of state, Hillary Clinton. For her vice-presidential running mate, she selected Virginia senator Tim Kaine.

With polls and pundits all predicting an easy win for Clinton, Trump's victory represented one of the biggest upsets in presidential election history. The midwestern battleground states that were said to be Clinton's firewall virtually all went to Trump. Clinton eked out a narrow victory in the popular vote, but Trump crushed her with a 302 to 227 vote in the all-important Electoral College.

Democrats and those on the left were so stunned by Clinton's defeat that they immediately launched a resistance movement against Trump. Impeachment was proposed within days of the election, and an impeachment bill was introduced by Democrats on the day of Trump's inauguration. Apart from his statements and behavior, no modern president had been subjected to such rabid opposition from the day of his election. There would be no traditional political honeymoon for Trump.

The Trump Presidency

Trump came to the presidency as a disrupter—to disrupt the Washington establishment, colloquially referred to as "the deep state" or "the swamp."

For all his faults and problems, Trump proved to be among the more beneficial presidents for Blacks, especially those in the impoverished segregated ghettos of the major cities.

Trump signed the First Step Act in 2018 which was designed to address the over incarceration primarily of Black males. It reduced the number of federal prisoners by releasing more than forty-seven hundred inmates serving time for relatively minor charges. While it could only address federal prisoners, it was the first time the federal government had acted against the problem of excessive arrest, sentencing, and incarceration of young Black men. The problem had stemmed from the crime bills passed during the Bill

Clinton administration, ironically with then senator Joe Biden spearheading the legislations as chairman of the Judiciary Committee.

Picking up on a concept first introduced by Republican congressman Jack Kemp during the Reagan administration, Trump created "opportunity zones" in the segregated Black communities. It provided tax breaks and other incentives for economic development. It is credited with creating tens of thousands of inner-city jobs, lifting individuals and families out of poverty.

These and other policies brought the 2019 Black unemployment rate down to a record low of 6.1 percent. That was still higher than the national rate of 3.7 percent at the time, but an enormous accomplishment for those trapped in Democrat maintained segregated cities.

Trump supported and signed a bill that provided $255 million annually for historically Black colleges and universities, exceeding Obama's $235.

Trump's Provocative Rhetoric

Despite his accomplishments for Black Americans, Trump's bellicose language was deemed to be racist by Democrats. It was part of their historic false narrative that the Republican Party itself was racist. His provocative statements enabled Democrats to demonize him and the GOP as racists, unlike any time since 1964 and the presidential campaign of Arizona senator Barry Goldwater.

Trump Undermines the GOP Race Record

In many ways, Trump was his own worst enemy. At the time of his inauguration, there was a distinct line between the Republican efforts to remove the symbols of Black oppression from places of honor and the Democrats reluctance and outright opposition to address the history of such party icons as Woodrow Wilson and Franklin Roosevelt.

Rather than underscore the GOP's efforts to remove the symbols of oppression and racism from places of honor, and clearly juxtapose the Republican position from the Democrats, Trump made a symbolic trip to the home and gravesite of Democrat president Andrew Jackson, arguably the most vicious slave owner and White supremacist to ever hold the presidency.

Trump doubled down on his misguided admiration of Jackson by having the former president's portrait restored to the Oval Office. This led to an embarrassing gaffe when Trump arranged to have a photo-op with a group of Native Americans taken in front of the portrait of Jackson, the man responsible for the deadly "Trail of Tears" and the slaughter of Native Americans in battle—a man with a White supremacist's hatred of Native Americans, Negroes and Asians.

As an icon of the Democratic Party, Trump could have justifiably included Jackson among those who should have had their names and images removed from places of honor. He did not, and handed the race issue to Democrats.

Election of 2020

Not since the 1960s has race played such a prominent part in the campaigns.

Republicans renominated the Trump-Pence team without much controversy—one of the benefits of incumbency. Although off to a slow start in the Democrat primaries, former vice president Joe Biden picked up support and essentially cinched the nomination with a win in South Carolina due to the strong support among Black voters. Among the major racial issues was the Voting Rights Act and his promise to select a woman as his vice-presidential candidate. It was whispered at the grassroots level that it would be a Black woman And it was.

The results of the election were controversial, with a number of accusations of voter fraud. The legitimacy of the vote count remained a political issue for years afterward. However, the official result in the popular vote and in the all-important Electoral College gave the victory Biden.

The Biden Presidency

During the first years of the Biden presidency, there was a lot of talk about the Voting Rights Act. The original Republican-sponsored Voting Right Act of 1965 was originally passed to further empower the Fourteenth and Fifteenth Amendments granting rights to freed slaves, passed over total opposition of the Democratic Party. It was to monitor elections in southern states where Democrat *de jure* racism had prevented Blacks from voting for more than one hundred years after the Civil War.

Whether people believe it was incidental or causal, Blacks were able to register and vote without harassment or intimidation as the Republican Party gained control of southern state government and the administration of elections. By 2020, many authorities saw no need to essentially punish southern states further for racist voting practices.

Still, the Voting Rights Act was still an important issue in the Democrats' racial narrative. It was used as a cudgel to attack Republicans on race, and as a means of diverting away from the issue of the deadly institutional *de facto* racism in urban America.

Democrats accused southern Republican administrations of using power to suppress the Black vote. The specious narrative is disproven by the actual voting history.

When Democrats controlled the south in 1976, ten years after the 1965 Voting Act, Blacks were only 16 percent of the vote in Georgia. Alabama, 18 percent. Louisiana, 17 percent. Mississippi, 20 percent. North Carolina, 22 percent. South Carolina, 21 percent.

In the 2020 presidential election, Blacks represented more than 30 percent of the voters. In Alabama, 29 percent. In Louisiana, 31 percent. Mississippi, 31 percent. North Carolina, 29 percent. South Carolina, 33 percent. That was the pattern all across the southland. Many of these numbers represent record registration and turnout. The growth in voting participation occurred after the GOP had assumed leadership in the south. That is not what you find when there is voter suppression.

Employment is essential for Blacks to rise out of that PLACE of segregation and oppression, and to take advantage of America's opportunity society. Following the Covid pandemic shutdown, people were returning to work. White unemployment dropped to 3.6 percent by 2022, but Black unemployment remained much higher at 6.1 percent—the highest of any ethnic group. Despite his claim to be the most job-producing president in history, Biden policies remained in line with past Democrat polices since Franklin Roosevelt—mostly benefitting White workers.

Mixed Bag on Race Issues

Jessica Washington, writing for *The Root*, said: "It is not a stretch to say that without Black Americans, Joe Biden might not have been sent to the White House." According to David Dixon, political science professor at Howard University, "The soul of the Biden administration is Black, Black and female."

But how does that stand up to Biden's record in race related policies. He selected Senator Kamala Harris for vice president. She is often politically identified as an African America although her mother is Indian and her father Jamaican. Biden put the first African American woman on the Supreme Court, and he appointed twenty-five Black Americans to the lower federal courts.

Biden put Harris in charge of securing passage of a new Voting Rights Act. Even though Democrats controlled the Senate and the House in the first two year of the Biden administration, no new voting rights legislation was passed.

The three major issues affecting those trapped in impoverished segregated communities in the major cities is education, jobs and crime.

Education

Biden and Democrats generally, placed a lot of focus on Diversity, Equity and Inclusions (DEI) programs and the usual demands for more money. DEI had virtually no significance to failing Black schools that are segregated.

According to numerable studies, there has been no improvement in educational outcomes and graduation rates for Black children on the urban public school systems in the first four years of the Biden presidency. The large urban school districts run almost exclusively by Democrat administrations remained as segregated as ever. There also remained the wide gap between White and Black student education outcomes.

Biden and urban Democrat leaders remained vehemently opposed to school choice programs that would enable parents to send their children to better performing schools. They could divert a portion of the per-pupil state money to send their children to private, parochial, or even alternative public schools. Many consider school choice to be the greatest hope for improving the education of inner-city Blacks and Hispanics.

That opinion is shared by a large majority of Black parents. In February 2021, the National Coalition for Public School Options released a survey that found 75 percent of Black parents would like to have the options to choose alternative public schools outside the segregated boundaries. The same survey showed that 84 percent of Black parents favored Educational Savings Accounts (ESV). And 82 percent of Black parents favored grants that would allow them to send their students to private or parochial schools. A January 2022 Morning Consult Poll showed that 72 percent of Black parents wanted school choice as an option for their children's education.

Despite the desires of the Black community, Biden and Democrats have consistently sided with the most powerful education union lobbyists—the American Federation of Teachers (AFT) and the National Education Association (NEA)—in opposition to school choice.

Jobs

Biden placed a lot of emphasis on his proclaimed "jobs programs." He often claimed he created more jobs than any president in history. Most of those additional jobs were workers returning to the workplace after the Covid pandemic shutdown. Jobs created by his controversially named Inflation Reduction Act and his infrastructure legislation had very little benefit for inner-city Blacks.

While overall unemployment levels returned to per-pandemic levels, the unemployment levels among inner-city Blacks remained at depression levels. As the national unemployment levels reached 3.4 percent, inner-city unemployment hovered at 14 percent, according to the US Bureau of Labor Statistics.

Looking at the 2022 unemployment levels of Blacks living in the segregated urban communities, the effects of longtime institutional *de facto* racism become more evident. In New York City's Harlem zip code 10039, the unemployment rate was 15 percent—more than four times the national average. In Chicago's 60608 Black zip code, the unemployment rate hovered around 23 percent—more than six times the national average. In Detroit's 48238 zip code, unemployment was at 20 percent. In Baltimore's 21205, it was 12 percent. St. Louis the unemployment rate was 10 percent—twice the Missouri state rate and three times the national rate.

These numbers clearly show either a failure or an unwillingness of the Biden administration to address the high unemployment among segregated Blacks. One could even argue that Blacks trapped in the segregated PLACEs in American cities have not yet recovered from the Great Depression of the 1930s.

Despite his rhetoric and intentions, it can safely be said that the Biden administration did little to nothing to change the realities of ghetto life for millions of Black Americans.

Crime

Of the three major concerns of inner-city residents, addressing the surging crime rate may have been Biden's major failure. Heading into the 2024 reelection campaign, handing over the crime issue was a major negative in Biden's polling numbers. In October of 2023, a year before the presidential election, only 36 percent of voters were favorable to Biden's handling of the crime issue.

What was a crime crisis in most of America was a catastrophe for those trapped in the segregated big city communities. In Chicago, 81 percent of murder victims were Black. In New York, it was 64 percent, and in Baltimore 95 percent.

In every major city in America Black residents are victimized by crime at much higher rates than other citizens. Nationally, Blacks comprise 14 percent of the population, but account for 54 percent of murder victims. Those numbers are the result of institutional racism.

Defund the Police

One of the most critical issues in terms of institutional racism is law enforcement in ghetto communities. Institutional racism in law enforcement has two elements. Racism in the enforcement and application of the law—from traffic stops to the use of deadly force—and the nature of prosecution of criminals. Racism in law enforcement ran in two directions. First was the more severe application of the law in terms of arrests, prosecution, and sentencing of Black arrestees. At the same time, there was the issue of police abuse based on race. The latter manifested itself in highly visible cases of police killings that led to outbreaks of periodic violence.

As a result, progressive Democrats proffered a misguided argument that reducing police enforcement would be beneficial to Blacks in the segregated communities. In response to a number of Black men being killed by police officers, the progressive wing of the Democratic Party launched a movement to defund the police.

Ironically, institutional racism is at the heart of the high crime rates that has innocent Black Americans dying at disproportionately higher rates—either due to inadequate enforcement or at the hands of police.

President Biden said he did not favor defunding police, but he did support transferring money away from traditional police enforcement activities in favor of social and psychological intervention and diversity training. That essentially reduced money and personnel for basic law enforcement.

The funding of police was not a hypothetical debate. Local Democrat administrations across the nation drew down funding of police:

> **New York City** reduced the police budget by $1 billion dollars by shifting programs to other agencies.

> **Austin, Texas** cut $150 million from the city police budget. That amounts to one-third of the entire police budget. Money was redirected to housing, mental health services and violence prevention programs.

> **Seattle, Washington**, despite spiking crime, reduced police funding by $69 million, a full one-fifth of the total budget. The city

eliminated mounted police and harbor patrol. Money was put into such vague programs as "restorative justice."

Los Angeles, California slashed $150 million from the police budget. Money was shifted to mental health, job programs, youth employment and violence prevention.

Minneapolis, Minnesota cut $8 million from the budget, shifting money to "community initiatives," including youth programs.

Lack of Law Enforcement

Perhaps the most dangerous and yet inexplicable policies advanced by Democrat officials was the reduction in prosecution of crimes committed by younger Blacks. That has been the reality for generations in terms of rioters, arsonists and vandals. It seems to be based on a belief that not charging Black criminals is a perverse civil right that would be viewed favorably by the greater Black community.

At the same time that local law enforcement was arresting, prosecuting and sentencing Blacks more aggressively for minor non-violent crimes, there was a coincidental practice of not prosecuting Black offenders for the more serious crimes, such robbery, looting, arson, rioting.

In city after city, local police, and even the National Guard, had been ordered to stand down as mobs of rioters who looted, burned, vandalized, assaulted, and even killed were not held accountable. Very few of the looters, arsonists, and vandals were arrested, and most of them were released. A bias in favor of Black criminals over Black victims is so endemic within the Democratic Party that Vice President Kamala Harris personally raised money for the release of rioters.

Democrat administrations in the cities with the most frequent and violent riots disregard the suffering and loses to the Black community in terms of damage, loss of businesses and homes, economic devastation and loss of life. Not only were Blacks confined to a PLACE, but it was also a violent PLACE thanks to years of systemic *de facto* racism.

Official Non-Prosecution

As if using prosecutorial discretion used to release rioters and other criminals was not bad enough, progressive Democrat prosecutors in major cities declared that some crimes would no longer be prosecuted. It generally applied to looting, rioting, vandalism, robbery, assault, battery (with minimal injury), shoplifting (of less than $900), and a number of other crimes.

The decision to not prosecute these crimes has a disturbing racist implication. It suggests that minorities are naturally more likely to commit crime as part of their nature, and that the Black community in general is more tolerant of crime. It is a subtext that goes back to the justice system in the old Democrat southland, but with a modern woke twist. Instead of excessive punishment, many contemporary Democrat prosecutors use their power of discretion to declare individual perpetrators essentially innocent of a crime—or at least not subject to the rule of law.

In 2019, in Suffolk County (Boston), Massachusetts, Democrat district attorney Rachel Rollins declared they she would no longer prosecute individuals for what she deemed to be low-level offenses. Her list included shoplifting, hard drug possession, resisting arrest, and a number of other crimes. Police and federal prosecutors were outraged by her personal decision.

Los Angeles district attorney George Gascón issued directives eliminating a number of minor crimes from prosecution. In addition, he ordered prosecutors to no longer pursue death penalties and ended cash bail and sentencing enhancements for gang membership and prior convictions. Gascón promised to review past convictions with a plan for exoneration.

Manhattan prosecutor Alvin Bragg announced they he would no longer prosecute such crimes as drug possession, prostitution, public transit fare evasion, and shop lifting. He also reduced sentencing for burglaries and assault.

In Portland, Oregon, district attorney Mike Schmidt announced that he would no longer prosecute such crimes as disorderly conduct, trespassing, interfering with an officer. He had already made it his practice to use prosecutorial discretion to not prosecute rioters and other crimes, such as shoplifting, vandalism, and unarmed robbery.

Like other progressive prosecutors, Seattle, Washington, district attorney Dan Satterberg used prosecutorial discretion to not prosecute rioters. He also refused to seek jail time for repeat offenders, drug addicts, and those he determined to be mentally ill. Instead, he advanced the policy of using social workers in what has become known as social sentencing.

These are only a few of a rash of local prosecutors who have ended what they consider low-level crimes, despite the impact on the public as victims. The policies have generally been opposed by police unions, federal prosecutors, and the public.

In 2020, the US Department of Justice (DOJ) under President Trump issued a report condemning such arbitrary actions by local prosecutors. The Report specifically pointed the finger at prosecutors in New York City, Portland, Oregon and Seattle, Washington, charging that those jurisdictions allowed "violence and destruction of property" by refusing to "undertake reasonable measures to counter criminal activities." The report proposed specific DOJ "guidance" for local prosecutorial offices designated in the report.

Among the earliest actions of the President Biden DOJ was to issue a memorandum withdrawing the designation and guidance, placing the new Democrat administration on the side of criminals in opposition to the safety and well-being of a largely affected Black and Hispanic communities.

Biden Is Old School

For the most part, the Biden administration, and the Democratic Party under his leadership, maintained their civil rights focus on the promotion of destructive generational welfare dependency, a faux narrative of Black voter suppression by Republicans, and the *de facto* racist policies of segregation and oppression imposed on millions of Black citizens.

The Last Word

This book documents only a fraction of the oppression and violence against Black Americans carried out by institutional *de facto* racism for more than 150 years since the Civil War. Whether it was slavery, the Civil War, the *de jure* racism of Jim Crow, the Massive Resistance movement against school desegregation, terrorist groups like the Ku Klux Klan or *de facto* institutional racism in the major cities, they were all predominantly the manifestations of Democratic Party governance to this day. No institution in America more consistently and more aggressively and more violently oppressed the Black community into a PLACE characterized by generational poverty, high unemployment, inferior housing, unequal application of the law, police harassment, unsafe streets, and crumbling infrastructure.

Institutional *de facto* racism is not only prejudicial to rights and ambitions of millions of Black citizens, but also deadly. In cities like Chicago, 40 percent of the residents are Black, and 81 percent of murder victims are Black.

If no fact or statistic convinces a person of the malignant role of the Democratic Party has played historically in promulgating institutional racism, it is clearly proven in the response of the oppressed people and legitimate civil rights leaders. Virtually all the protests, demonstrations, and riots are borne out of injustice-based frustration, and aimed at the leadership the protesters deem responsible. The long string of protests and riots—and the notable marches, sit-ins organized by such civil rights leaders as Martin Luther King—were overwhelmingly carried out against the Democrat racist policies instituted and maintained by Democrat officials in Democrat-controlled cities.

This book began noting the Democratic National Committee's website history that opens with, "For *more than 200 years, our party has led the fight for civil rights,* health care, Social Security, workers' rights and women's rights." It is appropriate that the book ends as a refutation of that false claim.

Upon that grotesque big lie, the Democratic Party has maintained a mendacious political narrative of civil rights advocacy—ignoring its own horrific culpability in the enslavement, segregation, oppression, impoverishment and killing of Black Americans by the millions for many generations.

To the extent that institutional or systemic racism exists in America today, it is not the fault of the people, but of political leaders who game and maintain the system of oppression for power, profit, and prestige. It is no small irony that the historic segregation and oppression of millions of Black citizens is continued even as Black leaders rise to the top of the urban political machines. It is for the same reasons—power. profit and prestige.

As the world enters the second quarter of the twenty-first century, the Democratic Party continues to rule over the last vestiges of systemic *de facto* racism in America. Generational welfare dependency and racist policies have kept millions of Black Americans impoverished, undereducated, unemployed, unsafe, and segregated to that PLACE of social and economic oppression.

About the Author

Larry Horist has been a life-long civic and political activist with extensive professional and personal experience in segregated urban communities. His consulting firm served as advisors to the Chicago and Detroit boards of education – two of America's largest predominantly Black school systems. His firm has represented a wide range of clients, including the White House, magazine publisher Steve Forbes' presidential campaign, the City Club of Chicago and Nobel Laureate Milton Friedman. He currently writes several political commentaries each week for PunchingBagPost.com. His family includes three biological children, including a Black daughter. He retired from consulting to pursue writing in Boca Raton, Florida.